Men's Work

Men's Work:
Gender, Class, and the
Professionalization of Poetry, 1660-1784

Linda Zionkowski

palgrave

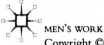

First published 2001 by
PALGRAVE™
175 Fifth Avenue, New York, N.Y. 10010 and
Houndmills, Basingstoke, Hampshire, England RG21 6XS.
Companies and representatives throughout the world.

PALGRAVE™ is the new global publishing imprint of St. Martin's Press LLC Scholarly and Reference Division and Palgrave Publishers Ltd (formerly Macmillan Press Ltd).

Library of Congress Cataloging-in-Publication Data

Zionkowski, Linda.
    Men's work : gender, class, and the professionalization of poetry, 1660-1784 / Linda Zionkowski.
        p. cm.
    Includes bibliographical references and index.
    ISBN 0-312-23758-8
    1. English poetry—18th century—History and criticism. 2. Poetry—Authorship—Economic aspects—Great Britain—History. 3. Poetry—Authorship—Social aspects—Great Britain—History. 4. English poetry—Early modern, 1500-1700—History and criticism. 5. English poetry—Male authors—History and criticism. 6. Johnson, Samuel, 1709-1784. Lives of the poets. 7. Pope, Alexander, 1688-1744—Authorship. 8. Dryden, John, 1631-1700—Authorship. 9. Gray, Thomas, 1716-1771—Authorship. 10. Authorship—Sex differences—History. I. Title.

PR551 .Z56 2001
821'.509—dc21   00-051485

A catalogue record for this book is available from the British Library.

Design by Westchester Book Composition

First edition: January 2001
10 9 8 7 6 5 4 3 2 1

Printed in the United States of America.

To My Mother and the Memory of My Father

Contents

ACKNOWLEDGMENTS

Research for this book began with a fellowship from the National Endowment for the Humanities; funding and research support from the College of Arts and Sciences, the Honors Tutorial College, and the Department of English at Ohio University allowed me to complete the manuscript. Gathering materials for this project would have been much more difficult without the courteous help I received from the staff at the William Andrews Clark Memorial Library, the Huntington Library, the Newberry Library, and especially Alden Library of Ohio University. Research assistants Corey Andrews and Erika Pfleger were remarkable in anticipating my requests as well as executing them.

My interest (and pleasure) in eighteenth-century poetry took root during graduate seminars with Lawrence Lipking and Richard Wendorf; I learned a great deal about scholarship from them, even if I would not admit it at the time. Since then, my most rigorous and generous readers have been J. Paul Hunter, Robert Mayer, Frank Donoghue, Kristina Straub, and Claudia Thomas; they have my deepest thanks for their constant help over the years. Thomas Bonnell, Dustin Griffin, Taylor Corse, and Lance Bertelsen also deserve thanks for their valuable advice and suggestions. A debt of gratitude and affection must be paid to my English Department colleagues Mara Holt, Linda Hunt Beckman, and the late John Hollow—their interest and faith in my work has carried me over many impasses.

The final measure of thanks, of course, belongs to my family: to my spouse, Adam Baker, whose devotion and encouragement are unsurpassed; to my daughter, Gillian Baker, who each day reminds me how delightful reading and rhyming can be; and most of all to my parents, Josephine and

Edward Zionkowski, whose selfless, loving support has been the mainstay of my life. I dedicate this book to them.

Part of chapter three appeared under the title "Not 'The Only Trifler in the Nation': Pope and the Man of Leisure in the *Dunciad*," in *"More Solid Learning": New Perspectives on Alexander Pope's* Dunciad, edited by Catherine Ingrassia and Claudia N. Thomas (Lewisburg, PA: Bucknell University Press, 2000), 129-46. Part of chapter four appeared as Linda Zionkowski, "Bridging the Gulf Between: The Poet and the Audience in the Work of Gray," *English Literary History* 58 (1991): 331-50. Another section of chapter four appeared under the title "Gray, the Marketplace, and the Masculine Poet," in *Criticism* 35 (1993): 589-608.

INTRODUCTION ✒

In the field of consumption, consumer goods should not be seen as
the mere objects of a semiotic democracy, but rather as the objects
through which social struggles are conducted and social relationships
between groups articulated in everyday life.
    Martyn J. Lee, *Consumer Culture Reborn* (1993)

In his *Life of Johnson*, James Boswell illustrates Johnson's concern for the "dignity of literature" by recording an incident in which Oliver Goldsmith found himself slighted by a nobleman:

> Goldsmith, in his diverting simplicity, complained one day in a mixed company, of Lord Camden. "I met him (said he) at Lord Clare's house in the country, and he took no more notice of me than if I had been an ordinary man." The company having laughed heartily, Johnson stood forth in defence of his friend. "Nay, Gentlemen, (said he,) Dr. Goldsmith is in the right. A nobleman ought to have made up to such a man as Goldsmith; and I think it is much against Lord Camden that he neglected him."[1]

Boswell's condescension toward Goldsmith, whom he occasionally portrays as a fool and repeatedly censures as "a scholar aukwardly affecting the easy gentleman" (*Life*, 1:413), here received a check. Although the company laughed at what they considered Goldsmith's pretensions, Johnson validated his friend's feeling of superiority: at the time of this incident (probably sometime in 1771), Goldsmith was known and celebrated as the author of *The Citizen of the World, The Vicar of Wakefield, An History of England,* "The Traveller," *The Good Natured Man,* and "The Deserted Village" (his most popular work, *She Stoops to Conquer,* appeared on stage two years later). Boswell and others found Goldsmith's regard for himself amusing, and viewed his complaint against Lord Camden as a comic and ineffectual protest against established social hierarchies. Yet Johnson believed there was nothing to laugh about in Goldsmith's expectations of esteem. To him, Goldsmith's literary abilities, or what Boswell terms "the higher intellectual qualities," not only made him a fit companion for gentlemen, but should have exacted a kind of homage from the great: Lord Camden showed only his own insufficiency and ignorance in failing to make up to an author, and Johnson subsequently censured him for preferring to consort with the actor David Garrick.

Between the company's laughter at Goldsmith and Johnson's vindication of him lies a major rift in conceptions of masculinity, social class, and writing. This brief anecdote, for instance, reveals that the writers (Goldsmith, Johnson) held new assumptions about authorship, and that these concepts were still alien to the rest of the "mixed"company (including Boswell, a gentleman's son). Whereas Boswell and others assumed that Goldsmith was an "ordinary man"—someone of undistinguished birth and rank—and thus rightfully beneath the notice of a peer, Johnson and Goldsmith maintained that literary talent elevates one above the conventional assessments of social worth. In their view, "such a man as Goldsmith"—a celebrated author by profession—required deference from those above him in the traditional sense; despite their position at the top of gender and class hierarchies, noblemen deservedly lose public esteem by their neglect of these authors. Although obviously complimentary, the phrase "such a man as Goldsmith" suggests the advent of an emergent, and not yet defined, social category: neither ordinary nor noble, but somehow superior to both, the male writer seems to exist in an uncharted cultural space. In fact, Johnson suggests that other categories of distinction have become unstable as well; he implies that far from being fixed standards themselves, Camden's own class and professional status are relative and fluctuate according to the company he keeps: upon hearing of his intimacy with Garrick, Johnson calls him "*a little lawyer*" for "associating so familiarly with a player" (*Life,* 3:311).[2] While Boswell presents the vignette as an instance of Johnson's overly generous support of Goldsmith, the anecdote raises issues that Boswell's narrative framework cannot contain: the company's prejudice against those who engage in the marketplace, the function of rank as the ultimate determinant of social status, and the subordinate position of bourgeois men on hierarchies of gender—all of which would have been fairly undisputed one hundred years earlier—are challenged by the claims of professional writers such as Johnson and Goldsmith. The role of class and gender in defining an occupational identity for such writers becomes apparent during the course of that century.

I

Early studies of the man of letters in eighteenth-century England portray his rise in status—an ascent displayed by his intellectual and, primarily, financial independence—as emerging directly from his economic success. Alexander Beljame, A. S. Collins, and J. W. Saunders celebrate the male author's triumph over material and ideological obstacles to reach a position of autonomy and self-sufficiency, a position that, they argue, the growing market in literature enabled him to attain. For Beljame, Alexander Pope—who made his profession "the sole occupation and passion of his life"—eventually "claimed his own rank" among his aristocratic friends;[3] Collins remarks that since "there was nothing to be gained by . . . mingling with the aristocracy,"[4] writers of the period "had no need to step" beyond the "congenial sphere" of the middle classes who sympathized with their devotion to their work. Praising Johnson as the model for modern authors, Saunders applauds his achievement of "security . . . without loss of independence, high status without the stigma of commercialism, dignity without the slackening of full-time industry and devotion"; significantly, Saunders mentions no women among the "first genuine professionals of letters," noting that women's reliance upon husbands or fathers for support kept them "insulated from the corruptions of trade," corruptions that male authors necessarily had to face and overcome.[5] Narrating the author's transition from the dependence entailed by patronage to the autonomy enabled by the consumer marketplace, Beljame, Collins, and Saunders complete a process of categorization that, as Clifford Siskin points out, began in the eighteenth century: their histories define the work of professional authors against that of "amateurs"—primarily aristocrats and women—whose social identities are not conflated with their occupation, and thus definitively prescribe both the class and the gender of the "man of letters."[6] In these studies, the middle-class male author wrests authority from patrons and gentlemen for the good of literary culture as a whole, and the results of his success (freedom of expression in a democratic marketplace) justify the increasing social power of the bourgeoisie.

More recently, the narratives offered by these initial accounts of authorship have been revised, if not altogether replaced, by studies skeptical of print's inherently democratic qualities and the power of authors to shape the contours of their lives. Investigations of print technology and the book trade have emphasized how material changes in the mode of literary production influenced concepts of authorship,[7] while, following Michel Foucault, studies of the economic and legal determinants of authorship in this period take as their focus the cultural discourse about writing and the social construction of the authorial subject rather than the emerging self-consciousness and autonomy of individual writers.[8] An emphasis on the institutional determinants of writers' literary careers also underlies current accounts of review criticism and patronage, both of which are shown to have a formative influence upon the extent and nature of writers' productivity.[9] Yet as contemporary scholars have dismantled former histories that valorized the man of letters' cultural and economic ascent, they have also downplayed the attention to class antagonisms that these histories had provided. My study attempts to restore, and perhaps complicate, the focus on commercial literary production as a site of struggles between social groups.

II

Besides questioning the ontological freedom that the eighteenth-century man of letters supposedly attained, recent studies have also emphasized the specific prohibitions and constraints that concepts of gender laid upon women writers in a commercial literary culture. In articulating the restrictions that patriarchal structures of meaning and value imposed upon women's literary work, and in delineating the strategies that writers adopted to overcome or circumvent those restrictions, feminist analyses of women in fiction, poetry, and drama of the period repeatedly show the inadequacy of the model of professional autonomy for women writers.[10] For instance, Catherine Gallagher's important account of professional women writers, *Nobody's Story*, acknowledges the effects of commercial literary production on men and women alike, but assumes that it influences the sexual self-representation of women alone: "In comic, pathetic, heroic, and even tragic forms, authors of both sexes called attention to their existence in and through their commodification and their inseparability from it. The rhetoric of female authorship differs, in this regard, from that of authorship in general by exaggerating and sexualizing the common theme."[11] Other studies of the novel, however, have viewed representations of men in the marketplace as equally problematic. Jill Campbell's work on Henry Fielding, for instance, portrays the ways in which Fielding both advocates and critiques the "economic and ideological structure of 'separate spheres'" that underlies capitalist social formations, viewing dominant concepts of male and female identity not as opposed, but as necessarily (and disturbingly) connected.[12] Centering more explicitly on the relation between the development of fiction and capitalist systems of finance, studies by James Thompson and Catherine Ingrassia outline novelists' participation in the discourse (and institutions) of a credit economy, and their articulation of the tensions regarding gender roles that this economy aroused.[13] My book also concerns itself with the relations of gender, class, and writing in the commercial marketplace, but its focus is on male poets by profession, and their cultural role in unsettling the hierarchies of masculine social power. Of course, one might argue that these hierarchies are always in flux: as Michael Roper and John Tosh observe, the "volatile and unstable" quality of masculinity itself "is never fully possessed, but must perpetually be achieved, asserted, and renegotiated"[14] through various rituals, acts, and conflicts; Mark Brietenberg goes a step further to assert that masculine anxiety itself "is a necessary and inevitable condition" in the reproduction of patriarchy.[15] Yet the anxieties of the eighteenth century were also specific and unique, for the period saw the emergence of a new "stereotype of manliness" that took as its reference point the market rather than the court, the bourgeois or economic man rather than the gentleman or aristocrat.[16] With their long cultural tradition as clients and supporters of the nobility being superceded by contractual relations with booksellers and a dependence upon the reading public, male poets of the period helped shape this emergent stereotype in crucial ways. I argue here that whether these poets viewed themselves as professionals engaged in commercial literary culture or vehemently rejected that identification, their verse constituted an important arena for conflicting definitions of masculinity—definitions that, in turn, legitimized particular forms of literary production and certain configurations of literary careers.

III

Of all writers, poets were especially affected by changes to the economies of literature, and their writing from the period after the Restoration to the final decades of the eighteenth century reveals most clearly the class and gender anxieties that such changes generated. Throughout this period, the commercial system of literary production, which entailed the development of the book trade, the legal determination of copyright, and the cultivation of a mass reading audience, offered poets (unlike writers in other literary forms) few advantages. While some poets clearly benefited from the trade's new strategies of financing and marketing texts, the majority remained unaffected; as Brean Hammond observes, the spectacular rewards of subscription publication—itself a recently-introduced hybrid of collective patronage and commercial enterprise—were very limited: "Apart from one or two celebrated cases such as those of Dryden [the translation of Virgil, completed in 1697] and Pope [the translation of Homer, completed in 1725] . . . to which we might add the 4000 guineas earned by Matthew Prior for Tonson's subscription edition of *Poems on Several Occasions* [1718], there was comparatively little to be earned from poetry."[17] Even established and celebrated poets had to bargain with booksellers over their copy money: a letter to Dryden from Jacob Tonson written shortly before the Virgil translation shows the two haggling over the number of lines per guinea for verses that appeared in *Examen Poeticum* (1693).[18] The low profits that booksellers expected from poetry were reflected in the value they placed upon poets' literary property. Compared to the price booksellers offered for the copyrights to prose fiction (200 pounds for Fielding's *Joseph Andrews* [1742], 1,000 pounds for Laurence Sterne's *Sentimental Journey* [1768], 210 pounds for Tobias Smollett's *Humphrey Clinker* [1771], and 500 pounds for Ann Radcliffe's *Mysteries of Udolpho* [1794]), the ten guinea sum that Johnson received for "London" (1738) seems paltry.[19] Yet Johnson earned more than some of his contemporaries: Robert Dodsley offered no advance money for Thomas Warton's *Pleasures of Melancholy* (1747), explaining that "so very few Poems sell, that it is very hazardous purchasing almost any thing," and William Collins, who may not have gained anything from Andrew Millar's printing of his *Odes* (1746), apparently did the bookseller a great favor by buying back the unsold copies.[20] Even the copyrights to poems that booksellers considered lucrative were relatively low: in 1738 Millar received only 105 pounds for rights to James Thomson's *The Seasons* and other works, the pirating of which provided the basis for the 1774 decision that finally determined the extent of copyright. Much later in the century, Goldsmith's rewards for verse suggest little improvement in the poet's relation to the literary marketplace: despite the acclaim for his "Traveller" in 1764, Goldsmith earned a mere 20 guineas for the poem, and the 100 guineas that he received from William Griffin for "The Deserted Village" (1770) he deemed insufficient for the time and labor employed in writing it.[21] Addressing the earl of Lisburne at a Royal Academy dinner, Goldsmith easily justified his decision to drop poetry for history writing: "My Lord, I cannot afford to court the draggle-tail Muses; they will let me starve; but by pursuing plain prose, I can make shift to eat, and drink, and wear good clothes."[22]

Apparently little had changed since 1705, when John Dunton proposed it as a truism that poetry made a nice hobby, but a poor livelihood: "I wou'd not . . . disswade any noble *Genius* to pursue this *Art* as a little pretty Divertisment, but where 'tis made the very *Trade of Life*, I am pretty positive the Man's in the wrong Box."[23] The debasement of poets in the marketplace that Dunton observes ("when I see an Ingenious Man set up for a *meer Poet* . . . I give him up as one *prick'd down by Fate, for misery and misfortune*")[24] became one of the central tropes of Augustan literary and visual satire, with the figure of the "Distressed Poet"—ragged, hungry, pretentious, neglectful of his duties, and delusional about his own abilities—immortalized in verse, on stage, and in printed caricatures.[25] Much of the satire composed early in the century blames poets themselves for their hardships rather than the conditions of authorship at the time, and represents their exploitation by booksellers as just punishment for their presumption and incapacity; as Pope maintains in his "Letter to the Publisher" that prefaces the *Dunciad Variorum* (1729), "It is not charity to encourage them in the way they follow, but to get 'em out of it: For men are not bunglers because they are poor, but they are poor because they are bunglers."[26] Nearly 40 years later, James Scott, in the aptly entitled *The Perils of Poetry* (1766), describes the fate of such a bungler in "Neddy Green," a poet whose "dire misfortunes" include attacks from reviewers, deadlines, and all-night writing sessions:

> Neddy for shame! lay down thy pen and ink,
> 'Tis not for Thee, believe me man, to think;
> It wastes the spirits, wears the vital clue,
> And keeps from Bridget what is Bridget's due![27]

Self-conscious about his own dabbling in verse, Scott (a Fellow of Trinity College at Cambridge) explains that he "wanted better employment, and did not chuse to be altogether idle" (vii); this excuse, which calls attention to Scott's genteel status, was unavailable to writers by trade, who could not claim to be motivated only by self-amusement. Eventually, though, the target of this satire shifts. A more sympathetic critic such as Percival Stockdale grounds his portrayal of the starving poet in a critique of the entire system of literary production and reception, and in doing so reveals a new perspective on the poet's role in the culture of a commercial nation. Stockdale's *The Poet* (1773), for example, attacks both the booksellers and the reading audience for their abuse of poets and their verse:

Condemned to drudge in sickness, and in health,
To starve, and raise thy dull oppressor's wealth,
Who pities thee, who values thee no more
Than Barbary-pirates those who tug the oar;
To sooth, with change, the idle, and the vain,
Who sick of trifles, trifle with thy strain;
Amuse a coxcomb lounging o'er his tea,
Or while the Frenchman forms the smart toupee;
Divert from cent per cent the city-sage,
Tired with the Ledger's more important page.[28]

Treated as a source of profit by booksellers and a source of idle diversion by readers, the "hapless genius" cannot perform to his capacity or exercise the high moral authority that accompanies his talent. Stockdale views poets' depressed state as damaging to the tenor of the nation at large, for he extols them as the repository of heroic values and sentiments that have lost ground in England's increasingly mercantile society: he requests poets to keep their thoughts "liberal," in defiance of aldermen—those representatives of a market mentality and middle-class taste—"Who would not suffer wits, or kings to range/Beyond the frigid maxims of the 'Change" (34).

The resistance to the commercialization of writing that Stockdale's poem displays emerged from a deep ambivalence toward the marketing of culture in general: as John Brewer maintains, the "tension between disinterestedness" (the production of commodities for intellectual appreciation) and the "interests and the passions" (the motives of profit and unrestrained consumption) "was a source of profound unease" in the public sphere of the period.[29] Whether they were novelists, dramatists, poets, or journalists, writers who lived upon the sale of their work faced the charge of debasing their talents, often being stigmatized as hacks or prostitutes who exchanged their abilities for maintenance by a patron, bookseller, political party, or combination of the three.[30] William Dunkin's "The Poet's Prayer" (1734) reveals the kind of distress that these accusations aroused; in verses resembling a litany, the speaker—a poet by profession—begs Apollo's protection from circumstances that would debase his writing. Along with the customary complaints about "patrons unworthy,/Who hear, and receive, but will do nothing for thee,"[31] Dunkin describes new threats to the integrity of poets, particularly the hardships entailed by the book trade ("scribbling for hire, when my credit is sunk" [2:296]), which as an industry caters to the taste of a rich and ignorant female audience ("very fine ladies with very

fine incomes/Which they finely lay out in fine toys, and fine trincums"
[2:295]). The subordination of poets to "the idle, and the vain"—portrayed
by Stockdale and Dunkin as women and men of the middle and upper
classes who purchase verse for amusement—emerges as a constant theme in
poetry, particularly after 1700, when fears about the influence of female
readers escalated sharply.[32]

Writers' concern for the loss of status that commercialization entails
also had its roots in class-based conceptions of masculinity inherited from
the Renaissance. Richard Helgerson observes that for men of lower rank
in the sixteenth and seventeenth centuries, making a career out of poetry
signified taking up the role of a menial paid to provide entertainment; for
men of higher rank, writing verse meant indulging in an adolescent practice, one that courtiers, as they entered into adulthood, were supposed to
reject for a more serious and prestigious pursuit, such as state service.[33]
According to Helgerson, aristocratic hegemony over literary practice
remained strong even after challenges to that authority enabled the emergence of a new category of poet: "So firm was the amateurs' hold on the
name of poet that the laureates [Edmund Spenser, Ben Jonson, John Mil-
ton] could not wholly reject amateur attitudes," even if they could not
wholly accept them.[34] Also threatening to the masculine identity of poets
by profession were residual anxieties about the shift from manuscript circulation to print. As Wendy Wall details, writers of the sixteenth and early
seventeenth centuries articulated and sexualized their concerns over the
widespread public display of their work allowed by the commercial press:
"Worries about unlicensed, unauthorized, textually corrupt or indiscriminately circulated poems coalesce in the emblem of the wanton Muse,
whose possible disrepute and erotic allure act as a vital cultural idiom for
expressing the anxieties generated by the print medium."[35] While it
occurred more frequently before 1700, the image of the wanton muse sur-
faced even as late as 1761 in descriptions of writers' entry into print and
called attention to their feminization through that process; Robert Lloyd,
in his epistle "To George Colman," explicitly links publication to the loss of
virginity and the possible "ruin" that such a loss entails:

> Authors, like maids at fifteen years,
> Are full of wishes, full of fears.
> One might by pleasant thoughts be led
> To lose a trifling maiden-head;
> But 'tis a terrible vexation
> To give it up with reputation.[36]

Lloyd's metaphor of print and circulation, playful as it is, refers to long-established, pervasive tensions about the role that poets assume when they venture into print: by making their works public, they become a vehicle for the reader's pleasure, which undermines their autonomy and integrity as masculine subjects. Yet from the Restoration onward, this conception of the poet's compromised manhood was gradually challenged by the emergence of an alternative rhetoric: one which proposed the commercial market in texts as the arena where manhood and cultural authority are established. Some of the tensions that accompanied this transition—tensions that this book will investigate at length—are apparent in the career of Oliver Goldsmith, whose reputation in his lifetime reflects his era's uncertainty over the poet's position on the hierarchies of class and gender.

IV

Goldsmith stands as a pivotal figure in eighteenth-century constructions of authorship because his conspicuous failure to establish a coherent authorial identity exposes at its peak the conflict over the professionalization of poets' work. Public response to this failure was often scornful: perhaps more than any other writer of his stature, Goldsmith faced a remarkable lack of respect from his contemporaries. Although many critics and readers praised his writing, viewing him as "a figure stamped on the intellectual life of his society,"[37] Goldsmith's abilities seem to have been dismissed by members of the gentry within Johnson's circle, and their assessments of him have been inordinately influential. They almost invariably represent him as the antitype to Johnson: whereas Johnson is self-confident, eloquent, wise, generous, and deservedly prosperous, Goldsmith is socially insecure, inarticulate, foolish, envious, and improvident. While less derogatory than Horace Walpole's assessment of Goldsmith as "an inspired ideot," Boswell's *Life of Johnson,* for instance, constantly portrays him as vain, pretentious, and inescapably Irish in his verbal ineptitude:

> It has been generally circulated and believed than he was a mere fool in conversation; but, in truth, this has been greatly exaggerated. He had, no doubt, a more than common share of that hurry of ideas which we often find in his countrymen, and which sometimes produces a laughable confusion in expressing them. He was very much what the French call *un etourdi,* and from vanity and an eager desire of being conspicuous wherever he was, he frequently talked carelessly without knowledge of the subject, or even without thought. His person was short, his countenance coarse and vulgar, his

deportment that of a scholar aukwardly affecting the easy gentleman. Those who were in any way distinguished, excited envy in him to so ridiculous an excess, that the instances of it are hardly credible. (*Life*, 1:412-13)

In this passage, Boswell most emphatically censures Goldsmith's speech, for he views his inadequacy as a talker as a sign of social overreaching: Boswell asserts that the coarse, vulgar scholar cannot possibly possess the self-confident "deportment" and the ease of self-expression that accompany gentility. Boswell was not alone in his assessment of Goldsmith's shortcomings: David Garrick in verse proclaimed that he "wrote like an angel, and talk'd like poor Poll," and even Johnson, his constant defender, admitted that "No man was more foolish when he had not a pen in his hand, or more wise when he had" (*Life*, 1:412 n.6; 4:29). As Johnson recognized, the pen—the access to print and self-presentation through that medium—was essential to Goldsmith because he could not otherwise acquit himself honorably in polite company. To Goldsmith's contemporaries, the art of conversation was premised on a kind of discipline and self-control that Goldsmith apparently had failed to master; indiscretions of the tongue, or too-fluent speech without the proper share of learning to support it, were viewed as the traits of the disenfranchised—women, the lower classes, foreigners—who encroached upon the privileges of gentlemen. As Michèle Cohen points out, "cultivation of the tongue," which had long been a dominant theme in Renaissance prescriptions for courtiers, became integral to the eighteenth-century discourse of politeness: the proper deployment of this organ was "essential to . . . the construction of the gentleman" since "tongues (languages) and the tongue (of the speaking subject) came to be critical sites for the representation, articulation and production of national and gender identities."[38] Policing the linguistic boundaries of his own class, Boswell frustrates Goldsmith's pretensions to gentility by showing him repeatedly bested in conversation by another professional writer—Johnson—whose eloquence resounded while "Goldsmith rattled away as usual" (*Life*, 2:256). In the exasperated reaction from Goldsmith that Boswell records, Goldsmith questions the purpose of Boswell's excessive praise of Johnson: "One evening, in a circle of wits, he found fault with me for talking of Johnson as entitled to the honour of unquestionable superiority.'Sir, (said he,) you are for making a monarchy of what should be a republic'" (*Life*, 2:257). While Boswell interprets this reaction as an upsurge of jealousy and an indication of Goldsmith's inferior moral character, Goldsmith phrases his response in explicitly political terms: the public sphere of letters "should be a republic" and by endowing

Johnson with absolute authority (or making him a monarch), Boswell dis-
enfranchises all other participants in that sphere.[39]

While Goldsmith drew criticism for his failed attempts to speak and act
like a gentleman, he also came under censure for too closely imitating the
behavior of those at the other end of the social hierarchy. Sir John
Hawkins, for instance, claims that the other members of Johnson's Literary
Club mistakenly viewed Goldsmith as a minor talent because of his participation in the commercial book trade: "As he wrote for the booksellers, we,
at the club, looked on him as a mere literary drudge, equal to the task of
compiling and translating, but little capable of original, and still less of
poetical composition."[40] The "we" in this case might have been gentlemen
like Hawkins and Boswell, who perhaps found Goldsmith's attention to
bookseller-sponsored projects (such as his *Roman History* and *History of the
Earth and Animated Nature*) beneath the dignity of an author. Hawkins also
dismisses Goldsmith as an "idiot in the affairs of the world" for preferring
booksellers over noble patrons for his support—a sentiment that led him to
reject an offer of assistance that Hawkins had helped procure for him from
the earl of Northumberland.[41] This residual attitude against commercial
print, and the relations of production that it fostered, remained popular
throughout the eighteenth century: one reviewer in the *St. James's Chronicle* (July 1770) while praising "The Deserted Village," lamented that Goldsmith should be "obliged to drudge for Booksellers, and write, because he
must write, Lives of Poets much inferior to himself, Roman History, Natural History, or any History, and be forced to curb his Imagination, lest it
should run him into Distresses."[42] Other reviewers and critics read literally
the lines in "The Deserted Village" that hint of the speaker's farewell to the
unprofitable art of poetry ("That found'st me poor at first and keep'st me
so" [414]): John Hawkesworth, writing in the *Monthly Review* (June 1770),
hoped that "for the honour of the Art and the pleasure of the Public, Dr.
Goldsmith will retract his farewel to poetry, and give us other opportunities
of doing justice to his merit"), while the writer in the *St. James's Chronicle*
predicted that Goldsmith's plight would result in a renewal of royal patronage ("From royal George the royal means shall spring,/To give thee
strength to fly and power to sing").[43] Disapproval of the market in literature, and sympathy (or pity) for Goldsmith's position within that market,
was not, however, the prevailing attitude of the time: although some of
Goldsmith's contemporaries characterized him as the dupe or victim of
booksellers and the commercial order they represented, the majority
insisted that his hardships arose from his own negligence. Thomas Davies,
for instance, defends his fellow booksellers and instead criticizes Goldsmith

for his reluctance to adopt the proper work discipline necessary for success in a commercial enterprise: even though "the booksellers understood the value of his name, and did all they could to excite his industry," his own inattention to business set him at odds with them:

> His appetites and passions were craving and violent; he loved variety of plea-
> sures, but could not devote himself to industry long enough to purchase
> them by his writings: upon every emergency half a dozen projects would
> present themselves to his mind; these he communicated to the men who
> were to advance money on the reputation of the author; but the money was
> generally spent long before the new work was half finished, or perhaps
> before it was commenced. This circumstance naturally produced reproach
> from one side, which was often returned with anger and vehemence on the
> other.[44]

Johnson, who steadily defended Goldsmith against detractors, recognized that he, like Richard Savage before him, could not accommodate himself to the expectations and practices generated by the new economics of authorship: Goldsmith, he claimed, "would have been a great man had he known the real value of his own internal resources" (*Life*, 1:213)—that is, if he had recognized his own stock of talent and exploited it fully for his own profit. But to Johnson, Davies, and others, Goldsmith wasted his potential by failing to act like a professional writer: his "violent" appetites (including one for gambling) and the too-profuse "liberality of his disposition" placed him in direct contrast to the commercial ethos that he had to adopt for success in the literary marketplace.[45]

Contemporary representations of Goldsmith, and particularly their assignment of him to the categories of failed gentleman and failed professional, may have been a response to the problem of defining the status of writers, a problem that reached its height during the middle decades of the century. Goldsmith's own confusion over his place appears throughout his work, as he attempted to claim a position of authority for himself within literary culture. He began writing in earnest at the age of 28, when, after unsuccessful attempts at pursuing a career in medicine, he took up employment in 1758 as a reviewer for Ralph Griffiths's *Monthly;* a memorandum dictated by Goldsmith to Thomas Percy in 1773 describes the terms of their employment contract:

> [Goldsmith] was drawn into an agreem[ent] to write in his Review, in con-
> sideration of his board, Lodging, & 100 [pounds] per annum. In this thral-

dom he lived 7 or 8 Months, Griffith & his Wife continually objecting to every thing he wrote & insisting on his implicitly submitting to their Corrections Interpolations &c. During this intercourse the D[octor] thought it incumb[ent] upon him to drudge for them constantly from 9 o'clock till 2.—The above agreem[ent] (which was in writing) was to hold for a twelve-month, but by mutual agree[ment] they dissolved it at the end of 7 or 8 months.[46]

Goldsmith's job was secure and well-paid—one of his biographers calls it "possibly the biggest step forward of his entire career,"[47] and it offered him more leisure and a salary far above the 20 pounds per annum that he seems to have received during his brief tenure as a schoolmaster in Peckham. Moreover, his fellow reviewers at the *Monthly* comprised "a team of highly qualified specialists," including clergymen (the Reverend Dr. William Rose, who cofounded the *Monthly*, and Dr. Benjamin Dawson), poets (James Grainger), and political writers (James Ralph).[48] Despite the job's advantages, Goldsmith's discontent with his work for the *Monthly* seems to have arisen from the supervision of his labor and the corresponding decline in autonomy that he experienced; he suffered the indignity of having not only Griffiths, a tradesman, correct his pieces, but Griffiths's wife Isabella as well. Goldsmith viewed his position as being that of a servant under petticoat government; especially galling to him was the editorial power accorded to Mrs. Griffiths. The demotion of authors to menial laborers supervised by booksellers is a common theme in midcentury satires: Fielding's *The Author's Farce* (1730) features the hacks Dash, Blotpage, Quibble, Index, and Scarecrow, whose work, lodging, and diet ("good milk-porridge, very often twice a day") are managed and provided for them by the bookseller Bookweight.[49] This system of literary production reduces literature to a commodity for sale, often with a solely ornamental function ("books are only bought to furnish libraries, as pictures and glasses, and beds and chairs, are for other rooms" [8:221]), and it demotes authors to laborers whose products possess only exchange value ("a poem is a poem, and a pamphlet a pamphlet with me" [8:221]). Goldsmith's colleague James Ralph, writing in 1758, also viewed the relations of literary production as detrimental to writers, for their supposed subjection to booksellers placed them in the lowest class of laborers. Ralph's *The Case of Authors by Profession or Trade* declares that the economics of commercial literary production work to the disadvantage of writers; since "the Rules of the Trade oblige [booksellers] to buy as cheap and sell as dear as possible" while providing "what Assortments of Wares will best suit the Market," authors dependent upon them for a living lose their autonomy and take on the status of chattel: "There is no Difference between the Writer in his Garret, and the Slave in the Mines; but that the former has his situation in the Air, and the latter in the Bowels of the Earth: Both have their Tasks assigned them alike: Both must drudge *and* starve; and neither can hope for Deliverance."[50] Complaints about the literary system seem to have been so pervasive that Tobias Smollett, who employed writers to contribute to his own *Critical Review,* carefully distanced himself from the practices of the "trade" and blamed the incompetence of British authors on their domination by capital-owning booksellers:

> [The bookseller] furnishes him [the author] with a few books, bargains with him for two or three guineas a sheet; binds him with articles to finish so many volumes in so many months, in a crouded page and evanescent letter, that he may have stuff enough for his money; insists upon having copy within the first week after he begins to peruse his materials; orders the press to be set a going, and expects to cast off a certain number of sheets weekly, warm from the mint, without correction, revisal, or even deliberation. . . . Nay, the miserable author must perform his daily task . . . otherwise he will lose his character and livelihood, like a taylor who disappoints his customers in a birth-day suit.[51]

Smollett's leveling of writers with tailors—both function as mechanics providing nonessential goods—indicates his concern over the trivialization of literary labor. Perhaps more than any of his contemporaries, however, Goldsmith made this issue a prominent theme in much of his writing. Published in April 1759 by Robert and James Dodsley (a slight that Griffiths did not overlook), Goldsmith's *Enquiry into the Present State of Polite Learning in Europe* offers a sustained analysis of the author's status, especially that of poets. Goldsmith finds polite learning in decline, and attributes its demise to the lack of suitable patronage; the increase in "studious triflers," or critics; and, most emphatically, the commercialization of literature. Adopting the persona of a gentleman appealing to other men of taste as literary arbiters, Goldsmith views the expansion of the book trade as opening the floodgates to the corruption of letters by the unlearned and unqualified:

> If tradesmen happen to want skill in conducting their own business, yet they are able to write a book; if mechanics want money, or ladies shame, they write books and solicit subscriptions. . . . Avarice is the passion of inferior

natures; money the pay of the common herd. The author who draws his quill merely to take a purse, no more deserves success than he who presents a pistol. (*Works*, 1:310)

According to Goldsmith, the severing of the link between patronage and learning—a link that he declares was strongest at the end of the seventeenth century—leads to the author's transformation from a talented intellectual and arbiter of social mores ("a merciful substitute to the legislature") into a dehumanized laborer, or "a thing little superior to the fellow who works at the press" (*Works*, 1:315). Entering into commercial relations with booksellers insures this transformation for authors: the booksellers' need for copy prevents the cultivation of genius, an emphasis on productivity replaces the exercise of imagination, and "a long habitude of writing for bread" turns the author's desire for applause into a desire for profit (*Works*, 1:316). Yet if commercial involvement for authors transforms them into mechanics devoid of social authority, Goldsmith's alternative—increased patronage—infantilizes them. Identifying himself as a member of the patron class, Goldsmith exposes the illogical, contradictory treatment of authors by contemporary elites: "Like angry parents, who correct their children till they cry, and then correct them for crying, we reproach him for living by his wit, and yet allow him no other means to live" (*Works*, 1:314). Goldsmith extends the parent/child metaphor to suggest that an author should be treated as "a child of the public" rather than a "rent charge on the community" (*Works*, 1:315). This relationship implies not only the economic dependence of writers (if not supported by patrons, they fall prey to venal booksellers), but their emotional and psychological immaturity as well:

And, indeed, a *child* of the public he is in all respects; for while so well able to direct others, how incapable is he frequently found of guiding himself. His simplicity exposes him to all the insidious approaches of cunning, his sensibility to the slightest invasions of contempt. Though possessed of fortitude to stand unmoved the expected bursts of an earthquake, yet of feelings so exquisitely poignant, as to agonize under the slightest disappointment. (*Works*, 1:315)

In a culture that prized and encouraged the masculine traits of self-management and self-containment—even while it acknowledged the softening influence of sensibility—authors appear immature, indeed childlike: the heightened sensitivity that nourishes their artistic temperament also renders them incapable of engaging in the profit-driven practices of book-sellers and reviewers. Goldsmith's construction of an authorial character whose refinement is incompatible with the values of the commercial world depicts writers as the repositories of feelings threatened by the hegemony of the market, but also categorizes them among children and women, whose naïveté also requires their subjection to masculine guidance and supervision.

Although Goldsmith himself composed the *Enquiry* "in a wretched dirty room, in which there was but one chair" (*Life,* 1:351), he would not admit his affinity with the professional writers whose case he pleads, but chose instead to adopt the persona and perspective of a gentleman amateur writing to an audience of gentlemen.[52] Secured by affluence from the pressures of the commercial book trade, "this happy few, who have leisure to polish what they write, and liberty to chuse their own subjects" (*Works,* 1:317) are in Goldsmith's view the only bulwark against the decline of English learning and genius; in 1759, Goldsmith could not imagine, or believed his audience would not accept, an alternative to the authority of polite writers. Yet as Frank Donoghue observes, in the 1774 edition of the *Enquiry* (published posthumously), Goldsmith "came to abandon the notion that gentlemen writers were numerous enough to constitute a class, or that they would be able to act in unison,"[53] and thus deleted references to their cultural influence and their role as arbiters of literature. Essays written in the interim between the two editions of the *Enquiry* also reveal Goldsmith's growing acceptance and increasing endorsement of commer-cial authorship. In his Chinese letters to the *Public Ledger* (1760-61), col-lected and reprinted as *The Citizen of the World* (1762), he argues that the expansion of the reading public makes writers, particularly poets, both wealthy and independent, for "they have now no other patrons but the public, and the public collectively considered, is a good and generous mas-ter" (*Works,* 2:344). In a later letter, Goldsmith's spokesman Lien Chi Altangi marvels at the undeserved appeal that aristocratic status bestows upon English poets, to the prejudice of untitled professionals: "A man here who should write, and honestly confess that he wrote for bread, might as well send his manuscript to fire the baker's oven; not one creature will read him, all must be court bred poets, or pretend at least to be court bred, who can expect to please" (*Works,* 2:376). In a significant departure from the *Enquiry*'s stance, *Citizen of the World* severs the association between talent and rank, disputing the belief that "title [is] alone equivalent to taste, imag-ination, and genius" in the English republic of letters (*Works,* 2:237). Yet the *Citizen* goes even further in legitimating the very commercial practices that the *Enquiry* disparaged: Goldsmith's speaker elevates the talents of writers for bread over those of genteel writers, arguing that the social division of labor creates specialized abilities that result in specialized products:

> For my own part, were I to buy an hat, I would not have it from a stocking-maker but an hatter; were I to buy shoes, I should not go to the taylor's for that purpose. It is just so with regard to wit; did I for my life desire to be well served, I would apply only to those who made it their trade, and lived by it. . . . [B]e assured, my friend, that wit is in some measure mechanical, and that a man long habituated to catch at even its semblance, will at last be happy enough to possess the substance; by a long habit of writing he acquires a justness of thinking, and a mastery of manner, which holiday writers, even with ten times his genius, may vainly attempt to equal.[54]

In this passage, and throughout the *Citizen,* Goldsmith advocates without irony the competence of mechanics in their trade, and constantly attacks the pretensions of aristocratic dilettantes. Moreover, he implies that a commercial society equates intellectual and manual labor or brings them to the same level: although wit is the product created, the writer's text performs the same economic function as stockings and shoes, circulating as a commodity with a particular exchange value. Yet while Goldsmith legitimizes the commercial motive for writers, he still views this motive as compromising their pretensions to masculine cultural authority, for it ranks them among mechanics rather than gentlemen. Goldsmith's self-presentation as the Indigent Philosopher illustrates the contradictions that writers' ambivalent position created: the first issue examines "The Author's Motives for Writing" (1760), and shows Goldsmith's need to justify himself to the public that, he believes, looks with suspicion upon the commodification of intellectual labor. The Indigent Philosopher, reduced to writing "in a News-Paper *for bread,*" notes that his occupation ill supports "the dignity of a Scholar or a Gentleman" (*Works,* 3:182). Yet despite this perceived decline in status, the Philosopher attempts to retrieve his self-esteem by comparing his genius to the inherited estates of aristocrats: "I must write, or I cannot live. . . . I must be thought an hireling if I receive small retribution for attempting to instruct society; while others escape the censure, though they receive immense fortunes for this purpose, without scarce an effort to instruct themselves. . . . This power, if I have any power, was the only patrimony I received from a poor father! And shall I be ashamed of this! *By Heavens I more glory in it, than if possessed of all the wealth that ever fortune threw on fools*" (*Works,* 3:182-83).

Goldsmith's conception of genius as a form of capital that, converted into commodities, allows for the writer's survival ("I must write, or I cannot live") shows his ambivalence: the detachment from commerce of the scholar or the gentleman remained the standard against which Goldsmith measured his own professional activity. The appeal of such disinterested amateurism continued to be strong for Goldsmith's contemporaries. Even the practical-minded James Ralph found himself caught in the contradiction between residual perceptions of writing as a liberal art and the widespread commodification of goods that accompanied Britain's expanding economy: while Ralph laments the decline of a hierarchy of intrinsic values ("As Things should be, I apprehend the Scale or Climax should be thus: Labour, Money, Ingenuity, Knowledge, Wisdom, Honour, Virtue, Piety, public Spirit or Magnanimity"), he acknowledges the growing importance of exchange value as a measure of worth: "Where nothing is liberal, nothing ought to be liberal: And where all must pay, all ought to be paid."[55] But although he enjoins authors to follow the example of tradesmen and regulate their literary production with regard to the market system of supply and demand, Ralph, like Goldsmith in the *Enquiry,* views authors as constitutionally incapable of adopting commercial practices and mentalities, since their values are fundamentally at odds with them: "Were Authors to consider Times as other Manufacturers do, they would act as reasonably— But then they would not be Authors—Pride and Pleasure in their first Sallies not only serve them instead of Profit, but render them . . . deaf to all other Considerations."[56] The perception of authors as disengaged from the commercial economy retained its hold for several years after Goldsmith and Ralph addressed the issue; as Zeynep Tenger and Paul Trolander maintain, "the antagonism between the discourses of genius and political economy marked a fundamental split between the ideology of the marketplace and that of intellectual and artistic production."[57] Even Adam Smith in the *Wealth of Nations* ignores the industry that grew around the construction, sale, and circulation of printed texts, as well as the increasing fees for authors' copyright, and categorizes men of letters along with other "unproductive labourers" (churchmen, lawyers, physicians, players, buffoons, musicians, opera singers, opera dancers) whose work does not "fix or realize itself in any permanent subject, or vendible commodity."[58]

In the 1750s and 1760s, arguments for the division of labor based upon the discourse of political economy offered a rationale for questioning the connection between social class and literary performance. In writings of the period, John Barrell observes, "no one is not implicated in the process of separation" of callings; even "the position of detachment and leisure"—

the privileged stance of the gentleman—may "be regarded itself as a *determinate* position, a calling in itself"[59] that offered no comprehensive grasp of the whole economic and political order and no mastery over particular areas of expertise. Responses to Goldsmith's social impersonations suggest the transition occurring here: Boswell and Hawkins resent his assumption of gentlemanly status, for they believe it encroaches upon their prerogative, while Johnson observes that Goldsmith needn't seek that status at all (he "would have been a great man had he known the real value of his own internal resources"), for his abilities alone vindicate his literary production. After the *Enquiry,* Goldsmith himself dropped the persona of gentleman writer, yet he found no alternative that gave him the authority his previous stance had granted him. For Goldsmith, the commercial model of masculine professional behavior was also unsuitable for writers, and he portrays them as incompetent economic agents whose disinterested genius repeatedly causes them to act against their own self-interest. Poets are especially prone to failure in the marketplace; as Goldsmith maintains in *The Citizen of the World,* the emotional susceptibility necessary for their craft places them in opposition to capitalist values and practices: "Fond of enjoying the present, careless of the future, his conversation that of a man of sense, his actions those of a fool; of fortitude able to stand unmoved at the bursting of an earthquake, yet of sensibility to be affected by the breaking of a teacup; such is [the poet's] character, which considered in every light is the very opposite of that which leads to riches" (*Works,* 2:341–42). While Goldsmith ends this essay by optimistically declaring that "a writer of real merit now may easily be rich if his heart be set only on fortune" (*Works,* 2:344), he describes the mentality, or the hearts, of poets in such a way as to preclude this single-minded purpose.

Neither gentlemen nor tradesmen, poets by profession occupied the contradictory category of intellectual laborers. This book will investigate how male poets of the Restoration and the eighteenth century employed the discourses of class and gender to determine a stable character for themselves in the culture of commercial print. The first chapter analyzes the different possibilities established for poetic careers by the earl of Rochester and John Oldham at the close of the seventeenth century. Oldham's relationship with Rochester was a blend of attraction and repulsion: although Oldham to a degree admired, even imitated, the libertine style of his patron, he also reacted against the sexualized mode of literary production flaunted by men of Rochester's class, and his antagonism toward that class takes the form of sexual antagonism as well. Oldham levels his challenge by critiquing the erotics of scribal publication, and in doing so also disputes the class prerogatives that underlie this type of writing. Rochester and other court wits perceived the private exchange of manuscripts as creating a kind of exclusive homoerotic tie among aristocratic male poets and their male audiences (most often poets themselves); they viewed their proficiency at composing verse as a validation of their dominant social status and aberrant sexual practices. By contrast, Oldham interprets this textual exchange as dangerously corrupting, even unnatural: he suggests that print (the customary venue for professional writers) rather than surreptitious circulation is the medium appropriate for men of all ranks because printed texts are subject to forms of public scrutiny that enforce normative sexual behavior. How Oldham appropriates and reconfigures the characteristics of masculine authority—particularly the violence of verse-writing—will be the focus of the chapter.

The connection between poets' engagement in the commercial book trade and their assertion of sexual power in their culture appears again in John Dryden's writings. Chapter two examines how Dryden represented in gendered terms his transition from the playhouse to print—from reliance upon stage profits to contracts with booksellers. Throughout the time of his laureateship, Dryden's income was secured by his work as a dramatist, and the prologues and epilogues to his plays reveal the anxiety that he experienced over their public performance. Dryden represents his work for the theater as a kind of prostitution—he assumes this role by his enforced subordination to the demands of theatergoers (particularly women) for pleasure and entertainment, a demand that he describes as an imposition upon his body and an exposure of its insufficiencies and occasional impotence. Yet toward the end of his career, Dryden viewed his involvement with the book trade as a means of securing a different type of audience: male or "masculine" readers who privilege the mind over the body, or the pleasures of understanding above those of the senses, and who prefer the poet's disembodied intellect over both the playhouse performances of his work and the witty conversation of the poet himself. But Dryden's success in cultivating such readers, I argue, is tempered by the public's celebration of his achievement in publishing the Virgil translation: in panegyrics on Dryden, the poet's mental vigor is associated with the vigor of his body, thus undermining the dissociation between physicality and literary talent that commercial print and the commodified text enabled Dryden to propose.

For Alexander Pope, the relation between the poet and his readers—even those with "masculine" sensibilities—was equally vexed. From the time he began writing poetry, Pope faced the problem of achieving an authoritative position in a culture that had begun to classify poets by profession as purveyors of entertainment for leisure hours. His critics charged that circulating and selling his verse to a heterogeneous reading public compromised Pope's independence and self-sufficiency—qualities that were judged essential to manhood—and thus placed him in the category of those women and sexually ambivalent men (such as castrati and actors) whose job was to please. The ambivalence toward pleasure apparent throughout Pope's verse reveals his awareness of this dilemma: the poet must please in order to be read, and yet the poet's very success at pleasing undermines his claims to masculine status. In chapter three I argue that Pope attempts to resolve this contradiction by representing his career as a professional poet in a way that makes it seem a legitimate extension of conventional patriarchal practices rather than a departure from them. In doing so, he expands the boundaries of masculinity to allow for a professional writer's participation in the commercial marketplace, while exposing alternative literary economies (particularly patronage) as grounded in unauthorized, illicit relations among men.

The strength of the emerging association between normative manhood and the commodification of literary work can be seen in the career, or anticareer, of Thomas Gray. Gray's resistance to commercial print (typified in his reluctance to publish and profit from his writing) was unusual enough to become a subject of disapproving commentary in his own lifetime, and his reluctance to produce and circulate poems for a general audience of readers drew criticism for his "effeminacy," or his shrinking from the kind of self-presentation that had become expected of male poets. Yet Gray himself justifies his rejection of the marketplace and validates his attempts to recreate the intimate audience of an exclusive, male coterie as the only means of preserving the masculine character of English verse; he joins other midcentury writers in declaring that poetry was threatened with trivialization by an expanding audience of women and unlearned men. Chapter four analyzes Gray's creation of an alternative to professional authorship—one that enabled poetry to retain its character as an activity by and for a masculine elite.

It was not Gray, however, but Samuel Johnson whose writings helped establish a poetic canon exclusive to men. Johnson's last major project—the *Lives* that prefaced the *Works of the English Poets* (1779-81)—departs from literary biographies that preceded it by omitting female poets entirely. The selection of poets for the *Works* was not anomalous or unusual at the time: a rival collection—John Bell's *The Poets of Great Britain* (1776-82)—also constructs an all-male canon, and the similarity of poets included in both projects shows a similar conception of literary history (and a similar idea of what might appeal to the purchasers of these texts). Yet although the London booksellers who designed and initiated the *Works* were overtly responsible for the omission of women, Johnson's prefaces set forth an aesthetic that justified the booksellers' decision. In chapter five I argue that *Lives*'s ultimate dismissal of aristocratic male poets (and antagonism toward poets with aristocratic pretensions) implies a dismissal of female poets as well: what begins as an attack by a professional writer upon a literary system that privileges rank and birth as determinants of merit ends in a set of prescriptions for poetic work that privileges new, different configurations of class and gender. Johnson's assertions about the kind of labor that poetry entails, the cultural status of poets, and poets' relation to audiences culminate in a professional identity for poets that fundamentally conflicted with the conduct of writers whose rank or gender proscribed engagement in commercial literary culture. In this way, the *Lives* offers an aesthetic complementary to the workings of the marketplace—an aesthetic that devalues other modes of literary production, circulation, and reception by representing them as appropriate only to amateurs—that is, aristocrats and women. Johnson's success at characterizing poetry as an occupation suited to bourgeois men (requiring, for example, rigorous self-discipline and a strong work ethic) explains his importance to early Victorian writers: they viewed him as an example not of literary brilliance or critical acumen but of social and economic triumph, and celebrated his attainment of independence, respectability, and authority—the qualities they equated with manhood—as a victory (and a blueprint) for all (male) writers. How the poet became such a man is the subject of this book.

Chapter One

POETS OF THE TIMES:
ROCHESTER, OLDHAM, AND
RESTORATION LITERARY CULTURE ∽

> *"What's all this? —verses!— By Heaven, Frank, you are a*
> *greater blockhead than I supposed you!" My father, you must rec-*
> *ollect, as a man of business, looked upon the labor of poets with*
> *contempt; and as a religious man, and of the dissenting persuasion,*
> *he considered all such pursuits as equally trivial and profane. Before*
> *you condemn him, you must recall to remembrance how too many*
> *of the poets in the end of the seventeenth century had led their lives*
> *and employed their talents.*
>
> Sir Walter Scott, *Rob Roy* (1817)

Although a poet himself, John Wilmot, earl of Rochester, agreed with Frank Osbaldistone's father about the triviality and profanity of seventeenth-century English verse. Yet for Rochester and other court wits, these characteristics carried no pejorative resonance; rather, the playful, licentious quality of poetry identified it as a pastime suitable for aristocratic males, whose indulgence in this kind of writing displayed their social power (they were above the restraints of decency imposed upon their inferiors) and status (they had leisure for composing poetic "trifles"). "[I] never Rhym'd, but for my *Pintles* sake,"[1] declares one of Rochester's rakish speakers, and although a dissenting merchant like Osbaldistone might abhor the motives that brought forth such rhymes, Rochester viewed them as the only ones appropriate for men of his class. Rochester, too, "looked upon the labour of poets with contempt": for him, a poet's need to work at writing revealed his deficiency in wit and suggested that, whatever his rank, his character was suited to the drudgery engaged in by the lower classes. By contrast, the "easy" poetry of Rochester and his coterie was invoked as evidence of their cultural dominance and sexual prowess alike, and thus was used to support their authority within the period's interconnecting systems of class, gender, and literature.

Yet if poetry helped maintain the complex ideological structure of aristocratic power, it also represented and contributed to the tensions underlying this structure. This chapter will investigate the way in which John Oldham, a poet outside of court circles who tried and failed to earn a living as a professional writer, articulated his opposition to the hegemony of his patron, Rochester. The contradictions that shaped Oldham's career suggest his location at the margins of polite culture: highly educated and impoverished, attracted to and repulsed by the court's libertine ethos, suspicious of commercial print and yet aware of the possibilities it offered him, Oldham used his position as a writer engaged in the book trade to question both Rochester's concept of literary production and the hierarchies of status and gender that it helped maintain. Here I will examine how the oppositions that characterized verse of the period—oppositions between coterie and professional poets, and between manuscript circulation and printed texts—threatened those hierarchies by enabling new constructions of masculine authorship to emerge.

I

In the "Advertisement" for his second volume of verse, entitled *Some New Pieces Never before Publisht* (1681), Oldham describes the unusual genesis of his pastoral on the recent death of Rochester:

> The Translation of that upon *Bion* was begun by another Hand, as far as the first Fifteen Verses, but who was the Author I could never yet learn. I have been told that they were done by the Earl of *Rochester;* but I could not well believe it, both because he seldom meddled with such Subjects, and more especially by reason of an uncorrect line or two to be found amongst them, at their first coming to my hands, which never us'd to flow from his excellent Pen. Conceiving it to be in the Original, a piece of as much Art, Grace, and Tenderness, as perhaps was ever offered to the Ashes of a Poet, I thought fit to dedicate it to the memory of that incomparable Person, of whom nothing can be said or thought so choice and curious, which his Deserts do not surmount.[2]

Oldham's explanation of his printed elegy, which developed from his elaboration on a manuscript fragment by another, unknown poet, reflects many of the characteristics that defined English literary culture of the late seventeenth century—characteristics that also shaped his ambivalent relationship with the man eulogized in his verses. Perhaps the most distinctive element of Oldham's "Advertisement" is the symbiosis that it depicts between printed texts and those in manuscript. The poet received his inspiration from an anonymous set of lines that he probably discovered through the circulation of a scribal collection of verses; he then completed the poem and published it in his own miscellany, one which also may have existed initially as a selection of manuscript pieces. Oldham invokes precedent to justify his act: "Nor is the printing of such Miscellanies altogether so unpresidented, but that it may be seen in the Editions of Dr. *Donne,* and Mr. *Cowley's* Works, whether done by their own appointment, or the sole direction of the Stationers, I am not able to determine" (88-89). Although Oldham's references to Donne and Cowley indicate some hesitancy over the propriety of printing this kind of collection, he judges it better than the alternative; earlier, Oldham had suffered the "misfortune" of seeing manuscript texts "stoln into the Press without [his] leave, or knowledg, and . . . expos'd to the world abominably false and uncorrect" (88). His significant misgivings about the aggressive self-promotion implied by the printing of this volume cannot overcome the even stronger fear of appearing at a disadvantage to his audience. Here Oldham acknowledges the traditional format of manuscript circulation, but ultimately finds the accuracy of the press more useful for his purposes.

Another feature of Oldham's "Advertisement"—the initial attribution of "Bion's" source to Rochester—reveals a contemporary outlook on authorship very different from that of Oldham himself. The attribution of stray lines and verses to Rochester occurred frequently throughout his life (particularly when those verses were pornographic), and even while he lay dying he received credit for a verse lampoon circulating at court.[3] Rochester's deliberately noncommercial perspective on his work in part created this confusion, yet his reluctance to sign, collect, and organize his verses was not unusual for writers of his rank, since most of them had no intention of profiting from publicatiōn. Rochester's engagement in collaborative writing with men of his circle and the libelous nature of many of his satires also precluded his deliberate construction of a unified body of work. But while it reflected an attitude toward writing that had long been prevalent among members of his class, Rochester's negligence toward establishing a poetic identity had new and unforeseen consequences in his own day. During the years following the Restoration, the system of manuscript production—which traditionally had allowed for greater authorial control of circulation and had enabled the restriction of audiences to a chosen circle— grew less exclusionary. Compilers and transcribers increasingly found scribal collections of verse a source of profit, while the manuscripts themselves, although never intended for commercial publication, often wound up in printed volumes: as Harold Love notes, "from the 1670s onward . . . lampoon and libertine verse circulating in manuscript was appropriated by compilers of printed miscellanies, who would cheerfully add any name that would enhance sales."[4] Foremost among these names was Rochester's, for his reputation as a wit and a rake enhanced the aesthetic and commercial value of texts thought to be his. Even clergymen like Robert Parsons and Gilbert Burnet, whose funeral sermons railed against the excesses of Rochester's life, recognized the high esteem that their culture bestowed upon his literary talent, no matter how misemployed in the service of vice. While Parsons praises Rochester's originality ("tho he has lent to many others, yet he has borrowed of none")[5] and Burnet celebrates his inherent genius ("Nature had fitted him for great things"),[6] both men warn against the appeal that such qualities had for contemporary readers. Burnet in particular calls attention to the difficulties that Rochester's verses caused their author:

> He laid out his Wit very freely in *Libels* and *Satyrs,* in which he had a peculiar Talent of mixing his Wit with his Malice, and fitting both with such apt words, that Men were tempted to be pleased with them: from thence his Composures came to be easily known, for few had such a way of tempering these together as he had; so that, when any thing extraordinary that way came out, as a Child is fathered sometimes by its Resemblance, so it was laid at his Door as its Parent and Author.[7]

As both Oldham and Burnet observe, authorship compromised Rochester's public identity; "Rochester" became a shadowy, unstable figure behind the circulation of both manuscripts and printed texts. Moreover, literary production both constituted and eroded the poet's status as a gentleman of parts, for although Rochester's display of wit testified to his superior education and refinement, the circumstances of "amateur" (or nonprofessional) writing left him vulnerable to attributions of work by those inferior in rank and abilities. Recognizing this, Oldham protests that he "could not well believe" that Rochester had written the opening lines of "Bion," for neither the subject nor the faulty style seemed characteristic of "his excellent Pen." During his own lifetime, none of Oldham's volumes carried his name on the title page, yet they explicitly identified him as the "Author of the *Satyrs upon the Jesuits,*" in reference to his most celebrated verses; Oldham also used the advertisements to his volumes to clarify the intent and purpose of his work. While observing some of the same conventions of authorial conduct as Rochester, Oldham was far more inclined to adopt the practices of print culture, in part because he could not afford to do otherwise.

Despite Oldham's admiration for Rochester and Rochester's approval of Oldham, the tensions, even hostilities, that characterized Restoration poetry find representation in the verses of these writers, for they articulate conflicting positions about the direction of English literary culture. Although both poets display a strong ambivalence toward writing and debate whether men of their social class should seriously engage in poetry, they each recognize the prestige and authority that literary production confers and struggle to claim that authority as legitimately their own. That Rochester, an aristocrat whom his contemporaries hailed as "absolutely Lord of Wit"[8] and "one of the most extraordinary Men . . . of the Age"[9] should face a critique of his supremacy as a poet and a gentleman by Oldham, an assistant schoolmaster, is remarkable enough. Yet Oldham's verses construct an authorial identity and offer a view of literary work that challenge those assumptions implicit in the writings of Rochester and other members of his circle. By proposing an alternative to their practice, he threatens to appropriate a measure of the privilege and power belonging to that elite—a threat acknowledged and continued after his death by an emerging class of professional poets.

II

According to Gilbert Burnet, upon returning from his Continental tour, the teenaged earl of Rochester "laid hold on the first Occasion that offered to shew his readiness to hazard his life in the Defence and Service of his Country"; in 1665-66, he went to sea twice in the wars against the Dutch because "he thought it necessary to begin his life with these Demonstrations of his Courage in an Element and way of fighting, which is acknowledged to be the greatest trial of clear and undaunted Valour."[10] Before beginning his life at court, Rochester felt compelled to prove the moral virtue upon which his social distinction supposedly rested. Michael McKeon explains this concern for validation as an element of the aristocratic ideology prevalent in early modern England: "The notion of honor as a unity of outward circumstance and inward essence is the most fundamental justification for the hierarchical stratification of society by status, and it is so fundamental as to be largely tacit. What it asserts is that the social order is not circumstantial and arbitrary, but corresponds to and expresses an analogous, intrinsic moral order."[11] Besides courage and valor in the king's service, another indicator of this "unity of status and virtue" that validated the "rule of the best"[12] was elite participation in, if not dominance over, the literary culture of their time. Despite their reputation for careless (and effortless) composition—a reputation that they actively helped promote[13]—Rochester and other aristocrats of his acquaintance took seriously the tie between writing and social status, maintaining that men of their class should display the kind of wit that does credit to their breeding. By prescribing the proper techniques for upper-class writers—the style and themes of their verse, their form of authorial self-presentation, the mode of production for their work—Rochester and his peers attempted to solidify their group and protect it from external threats, especially the increasing numbers of writers who, professing talent and skill, challenged the prerogatives of their social superiors. In their poems, Restoration aristocrats like Rochester reveal an intense self-consciousness about their position as authors, even while they assert their own prominence against the encroachments of others outside of their coterie.

A month or two after Rochester's death, some of his manuscript verses, along with the verses of his contemporaries, appeared in a printed volume entitled *Poems on Several Occasions by the Right Honourable, the E. of R——*, bearing an imprint of Antwerp; at least nine more editions, separate but related in their sources, followed shortly.[14] Although representatives of the Wilmot family offered a handsome five pound reward for the discovery of the printer, those agents associated with the volume remained unknown (and safe from prosecution)[15]; the family's attempt at damage control having failed, the unauthorized editions provided access to Rochester's verse for an audience far beyond the court and its satellites. Yet while the title proclaims Rochester as the sole author of the 61 poems in the book, the attribution is faulty: the editions include works by Rochester's friends, Charles Sackville (Lord Buckhurst, later earl of Dorset and of Middlesex), Sir George Etherege, and George Villiers (duke of Buckingham); satires on Rochester by Thomas D'Urfey and Sir Carr Scroope; verses by John Sheffield (earl of Mulgrave) and Alexander Radcliffe; and finally, a selection of poems by writers not allied to court circles, namely Aphra Behn and John Oldham.

As John Harold Wilson describes it, the uncertain attributions of such texts amount to a "bibliographical nightmare"[16] for modern readers, or at least a puzzle that has taken years to solve. This difficulty also indicates an enormous gulf between seventeenth-century concepts of writing and modern conventions of print. The 1680 editions of Rochester emerge from a type of literary production that Love calls "Restoration scriptorial satire": state poems on politics, lampoons on courtiers and courtesans, and erotic and pornographic verses that were transcribed and circulated in manuscript by their authors, their readers, or professional scribes working for pay. Whether distributed separately or in miscellanies drawn together from separate texts, these poems favored an exclusive, elite audience, for they assumed a knowledge of circumstances and events that would often seem obscure to those beyond a select circle. For instance, Rochester's "An Epistolary Essay from M.G. To O.B. upon their Mutual Poems" and D'Urfey's "Song" ("Room, room, for a *Blade* of the *Town*")—both included in *Poems on Several Occasions*— depend for their satiric effect on the reader's knowledge of Mulgrave's misplaced pride in his writings, and Rochester's outrages against public order, including a drunken brawl in which a companion died in the poet's defense. While scribally published works in the late seventeenth century were not anachronistic, their function as an alternative to the medium of print implies an oppositional stance: as Love observes, "manuscript publication became a matter of choice rather than necessity and was normally undertaken with the explicit aim of restricting texts to a small group of the like minded. The composition and issuing of these texts might itself become a way of reinforcing the corporate ideology of such groups."[17] Rochester's group included Buckingham, Buckhurst, Etherege, Henry Savile, Sir Charles Sedley, Sir Fleetwood Shepherd, and William Wycherley; while they might have shared a similar political stance against the duke of York's succession, a similar conception of literature and authorship also formed a bond among them. Defending Rochester's verse against the charge of indecency, Robert Wolseley argues that the intimacy of his intended audience—men possessing "the freedom and reflexion of Philosophers"—partly excuses the poems' obscenity: Rochester's lyrics were not designed "for any publick or common Entertainment whatever, but for the private Diversion of those happy Few, whom he us'd to charm with his Company and honour with his Friendship."[18] The privileged class and gender of coterie members gave them the leisure for intellectual and aesthetic "reflexion," and thus the right to more license in their entertainments. Dryden's and Pope's dismissive assessment of "holiday writers" like Rochester—a phrase that attacks status categories in favor of occupational ones—overlooks the purpose of this group: without making poetry their life's work or identifying themselves primarily as poets, they sought to maintain a collective form of cultural authority, particularly by distinguishing the proper subject positions that members of the coterie should adopt. A series of verse epistles from Buckhurst to Etherege printed in the Rochester volume reveals the kinds of rhetorical postures that such membership required.

"The First Letter from B. to Mr. E." takes a form common to scribal texts— that of an epistle from Buckhurst in the country to Etherege in London—but instead of initiating a comparison between town and country, and a political or ethical critique of the former, the "Letter" begins with lines describing the writer's early morning erections and the inconveniences they cause:

> Dreaming last *Night* on Mrs *Farley* [Elizabeth Farley, an actress],
> My *Prick* was up this *Morning* early;
> And I was fain without my *Gown*,
> To rise i'th cold, to get him down.[19]

Rather than the condition of England, the condition of Buckhurst's insistent and highly excitable penis becomes a dominant theme in the poem, and gives the author occasion for writing:"I must intreat you by this Letter,/To enquire for *Whores,* the more the better" (25-26). Calling attention to his parody of a "pretty *Metaphor,*" Buckhurst adopts the time worn comparison of a man to a ship to describe his predicament, concluding that "howsoe're they keep a pudder,/I'm sure the *Pintle* is the *Rudder*" (39-40), and requesting Etherege to provide him with a safe port (or healthy whore) in preparation for his return to the capitol. Buckhurst's second request involves procurement of another kind; this time he asks for bad poetry that might give him raw material for lampoons or satires. Although their "proper uses" are in the privy or the fireplace, verses by "Some lamentable Rhyming *Lover*" (50) or Etherege's fellow knights "Inspir'd with *Love,* and *Grid- Iron Ale*" (60) would keep him abreast of developments in the London literary scene. The failure of these poets at love and verse contrasts explicitly with Buckhurst's success: the deployment of his own pen is authorized by his virility, since he composes his lines in order to locate at least one "fresh *Petticoat*" for his pleasure.

Etherege's response brings out the complexity of this literary and sexual wordplay with Buckhurst. "Mr. E——s Answer" begins with an erotic simile describing Buckhurst's departure from London:

> As Crafty *Harlots,* use to shrink,
> From *Letchers,* dos'd with sleep and drink.
> When they intend to make up *Pack,*

By filching *Sheets,* or *Shirt* from *Back.*
So you were pleas'd to steal away
From me, whilst on your *Bed* I lay. (1-6)

When he awoke and realized his friend's departure, Etherege "stampt and star'd" in a rage, complaining of his stiff limbs and the uncomfortable feel of "poor *Pego*"; the reader only realizes that Etherege and Buckhurst have not been lovers when the former damns the *"Pool of Harlot"* into which he had been dipping. The suggestion of sexual relations between the two poets is somewhat deflected by Etherege's later narration of his visit to a whore, Mrs. Cuffley, yet his tone still suggests an erotic alliance of sorts between the two men, since both had shared Mrs. Cuffley's favors and both exercise their wit upon her.[20] Etherege ends by presenting his friend with the "paultry Rhymes" of poets not in their group; describing their work as "The greatest grievance of our times," he locates them beyond the boundaries of legitimate literary efforts, since they "dayly will invade/*Wits Empire,* both the *Stage,* and *Press,*/And which is worse, with good success" (56-58). These poets, and the audience that supports them, pose a threat to territory that Etherege and Buckhurst mark out for their own, and to the practices of exclusion that their work endorses. "The Second Letter from B— to Mr. E—" continues this critique of their contemporaries. After scolding Etherege for using his "railing, scurr'lous Wit/'Gainst *C*—, and *P*—, the source of it" (4-5), Buckhurst declares that lust inspires all poetic creation, from the lowest to the highest forms of verse:

For what but *C*—*t,* and *P*—*k,* does raise
Our thoughts to Songs, and Roundelays?
Enables us to *Annagrams,*
And other Amorous flim flams?
Then we write *Plays,* and so proceed,
To *Bays,* the *Poets* sacred *Weed.* (5-10)

Unlike the members of Buckhurst's coterie who acknowledge the power of their libido, modern authors' "*Poetique* dizziness" leads them to a kind of aesthetic false consciousness: attempting displacement, they prate "of *Caesar,* in the *Capitol,*/Of *Cinthias,* Beams, and *Sols,* bright Ray" (24-25) as their creative inspiration, when that force actually resides in "*God Priapus,*" or the male phallus. Buckhurst's assertion that promiscuous lust "enables" verse writing discredits literary attempts by those lacking or denying this urge, specifically women and male writers not identified with aristocratic libertines. (Characterized solely as the objects of male sexual conquests, promiscuous women supposedly cannot sublimate lust into literary achievement.) Chastened by Buckhurst's rebuke, Etherege in his second "Answer" protests that "I to C—t am not a *Foe,*/Though you are pleas'd to think me so" (22-23), and reassures his friend that his (hetero)sexual desire has not waned or disappeared: "'Tis strange his Zeal shou'd be in suspicion/Who dyes a *Martyr,* for's *Religion*" (24-25). Etherege, though, unlike Buckhurst, again insists that male homosocial bonds are the most significant result of their libertine activities; describing Buckhurst as "the *Mistress,* that employs our care" (70), Etherege reveals that the group's desire most strongly focuses not on "drink, nor C—t," but rather on the "diviner Charmes" of its members (72-74).

The exchange of manuscript verses, like the exchange of sexual partners, solidifies relationships among upper-class men, for it confirms their sense of belonging to a literary elite above the restrictions of the licensed press. By locating creative instinct in the phallus (Priapus), rather than in the brain or (satirically) in the hands, writers like Buckhurst and Etherege portray poetry as an almost involuntary act of masculine nature rather than a form of mental or manual labor. Although the connection between writing and ejaculation, or poetry and semen, seems to compromise their work by calling to mind contemporary satiric representations of verse as a kind of excretion—an image that Dryden employed to great effect in "Mac Flecknoe" (1682)—coterie writers deliberately risked self-satire to show the little value they placed on their effusions, and implicitly contrasted their carelessness to the painstaking effort that their social inferiors displayed. Only the upper classes, it seems, could indulge themselves in this manner. A letter from Dryden, then poet laureate, to Rochester, his patron at the time, suggests the insularity of this group and the difficulty of outsiders' breaking into it despite their displays of wit. After comparing his own writing unfavorably to Rochester's, Dryden declares himself vanquished, partly by the peer's talent ("You are above any Incense I can give you") and partly by the favorable conditions under which he composes: in his country retreat at Adderbury, Rochester enjoys the freedom from court attendance and the uninterrupted leisure denied to Dryden by his professional responsibilities ("You may thinke of what you please, and that as little as you please").[21] Rochester also has the privilege of engaging in "that dangerous part of wit," the lampoon, which Dryden must forswear: the physical attack on Dryden in Rose Alley (1679) illustrates the hazards that writers of lower rank faced when suspected of lampooning their superiors.[22] Dryden ends this painfully playful letter by offering to entertain his patron with "a thousand bagatelles every week"—an offer that he feels unsure Rochester will accept. Dryden's insecurity had some foundation, for in a letter to Henry Savile, Rochester calls the poet "a rarity which I cannot but be fond of, as one would be of a hog that could fiddle or a singing owl" (*Letters*, 120).

Although Rochester clearly recognized Dryden's genius, he considered the laureate a grotesque anomaly, declaring his talent at odds with his unwieldy appearance and status beneath aristocratic circles. Dryden's forced exuberance signals his discomfort with Rochester as well. By contrast, Rochester's letters to Savile reveal an implicit unity of perspective and interest, whether they discuss political developments, court intrigues, failing health, or material for lampoons and libels. (While in London, Savile sent Rochester possible topics for poetry, stating that "[your] Genius [is able to] shew the world theire follyes as your leasure [serves you to] shew your abilities, for Gods sake, my most [dear Lord, make] this use of your retreat" [*Letters*, 136].) Their collusion extended to sharing sexual partners as well. Toward the end of his life, Rochester bestowed upon Savile his valet, Jean Baptiste de Belle-Fasse, a "pretty fool" whose beauties had been enjoyed by the "greatest and gravest of this Court of both sexes" (*Letters*, 230); Savile later seems to have saved Rochester from blackmail by this enterprising young man (*Letters*, 243). In "Love a *Woman!* y'are an *Ass*," Rochester portrays the dynamics of male erotic and literary relations, like the ones between Buckhurst and Etherege and himself and Savile, depicting wit as something produced apart from the economies of labor and procreative sex. The male speaker in the lyric rejects the "insipid Passion" of heterosexual love, associating intercourse with women with the difficult manual work of the laboring classes:

> Let the *Porter* and the *Groome,*
> Things design'd for dirty *Slaves,*
> Drudge in fair *Aurelias Womb,*
> To get supplies for Age, and Graves. (5-8)

Demoted to the level of objects or "things," the porter and the groom belong to a lower order of human existence; they are enslaved by their subjection to the drudgery both of physical work and reproduction. As Harold Weber points out, the poem's narrator "identifies the world of physical corruption with the female womb"[23]; yet the speaker associates women not only with decay and death but also with the endless, post-Edenic cycle of procurement (getting "supplies"). His resolution to forgo female company in favor of evenings with a "lewd well natur'd *Friend,*/Drinking, to engender *Wit*" (11-12) proposes another kind of economy altogether, one oriented toward leisure, masculine friendship, and poetry: the two men in their cups engender not children or other "supplies" but wit, an act that places them beyond the systems of labor and distinguishes them from the "slaves" and the women entrapped by those systems. The threats that sexual desire poses to this ideal community of gentlemen will be dispelled by their common use of a catamite or their recourse to masturbation over Rochester's manuscript verses ("There's a sweet soft *Page*, of mine,/Does the trick worth *Forty Wenches*" [15-16]): "pages" of both sorts offer erotic gratification, and thus deflect the dangerous, ensnaring need for fair Aurelia.

III

Rochester's view of literary production as part of an alternative, elite sexual and social economy functions as a theme throughout his verse, and contemporaries recognized the will to dominance implicit in this theme. Writing in 1685, Robert Wolseley, an admirer of Rochester, declared that "the vainest Pretenders in his time, the most confident *Essayers,* cow'd and aw'd under the known force of a sence so superiour to their own, were glad at any rate to keep their empty Heads out of Observation, as the Fowl of a whole Countrey creep into the Bushes, when an Eagle hangs hovering above 'em."[24] Published in 1673, Dryden's dedication of *Marriage A-la-Mode* to Rochester articulates a greater discomfort with Rochester's coercive presence. While praising his patron's genius, Dryden claims that wit in Rochester is "so dangerous a quality" that it encourages abuse of power: "from the Patron of Wit, you may become its Tyrant: and Oppress our little Reputations with more ease then you now protect them."[25] Dryden proved all too prophetic on this point, for Rochester's "An Allusion to Horace" (1675-76) repeatedly attacks the laureate in an extended critique of Restoration writers. Rochester begins by voicing his suspicion of Dryden's popularity: he admits that his plays, "Embroider'd" or ornamented with wit and learning, "justly pleas'd the Towne" (6), yet suggests that providing pleasure itself degrades the playwright. Drama, because of its public character, is subject to the judgment of "Clapping-Fooles," whose approval signifies little. While Rochester gives credit to the genius "That can divert the Rabble and the Court" (17), noting that Settle and Otway for all their effort fail at diversion, he prefers the boldness and negligence of Thomas Shadwell, who "scornes to varnish his good touches o're,/To make the Fooles, and Women, praise 'em more" (48-49). Finally, Rochester recommends poets (like himself) who ignore the mass of feminine and effeminate playgoers in favor of pleasing a small and selective masculine audience:

> Canst thou be such a vaine mistaken thing
> To wish thy Workes might make a Play-house ring,
> With the unthinking Laughter, and poor praise
> Of Fopps, and Ladys, factious for thy Plays?
> . . . .
> I've noe Ambition on that idle score,
> But say with Betty Morice, heretofore
> When a Court-Lady call'd her Buckleys Whore,
> I please one Man of Witt, am proud on't too,
> Let all the Coxcombs, dance to bed to you. (104-07; 110-14)

With these lines, Rochester devalues the work of all professional playwrights, since their very survival in the theater depends upon their ability to make the "Play-house ring" with applause. In comparing himself to Betty Morice (or Morris), a courtesan apparently selective in her attachments, Rochester anticipates the charge that his own writing is a source of entertainment, and thus compromises his masculine character. Yet he also insists that pleasing a few men of wit is an occasion for pride instead of shame, as it pays tribute to the knowledge, judgment, and cultural hegemony of his own elite male group; Dryden's performance, by contrast, is unmanning and detracts from his prestige, for it places him under the power of fops and ladies. Another feature of Dryden's work—his rapid pace of composition— also lowers Rochester's assessment of him: if they lack the requisite spirit and grace, "Five Hundred Verses, ev'ry Morning writ,/Proves you noe more a Poet, than a Witt" (93-94). While "Such scribling Authors" include gentlemen (like Robert Boyle, earl of Orrery and author of the tragedy *Mustapha*) as well as professionals like Dryden, the mode of writing that Rochester recommends and his idea of poets' intended audience are especially impracticable to those who earn a living by their pens. For a work to sustain multiple readings by "those few, who know" (103), its author must "Compare each Phrase, examin ev'ry Line,/Weigh ev'ry word, and ev'ry thought refine" (100-01)—in short, give it the kind of attention that Dryden, producing plays for the actors of the King's Company and occasional verses for patrons, often found difficult to bestow.[26] Although Rochester admits that Dryden "best deserves" his position as laureate, the couplet from "A Session of the Poets" (1676)—a lampoon that Rochester helped compose— provides a sense of how aristocrats valued Dryden's appointment: "No gentleman writer that office should bear:/'Twas a trader in wit the laurel should wear."[27] Those poets whom Rochester prefers, including Etherege (for invention), Wycherley (for correctness), Edmund Waller (for panegyrics), Buckhurst (for satire), and Sedley (for erotic lyrics), are conspicuously genteel, and their breeding gives their verses a cast that their social inferiors, whose style is shaped by the requirements of a more plebeian audience, cannot duplicate. For instance, Dryden's attempts to imitate Sedley's "Mannerly Obscene" verses ("That can with a resistlesse Charme impart,/The loosest wishes to the Chastest Heart" [64–65]) end in a public display of impotence; as a poet and a lover, the laureate cannot provide satisfaction: "[W]hen he wou'd be sharp, he still was blunt,/To friske his frollique fancy, hed cry Cunt;/Wou'd give the Ladyes, a dry Bawdy bob" (73–75).

In these passages on Dryden, Rochester in effect condemns the kinds of poetic forms (such as drama) that were profitable, even essential, to professional writers in his time, most of whom depended upon the stage and its public audience for their existence.[28] His imitation of Horace's satire serves a rhetorical function by conferring authority on his aesthetic judgments and emphasizing his ostensibly objective concern for excellence in contemporary verse (a few noble writers do fall under the poet's censure). Yet the political basis for his authority eventually emerges as well, for Rochester ends the poem by positioning himself and his coterie (Sedley, Shadwell, Wycherley, Sidney Godolphin, Samuel Butler, Buckhurst, and Buckingham) as a self-sufficient group of writers and readers who stand as a bulwark against the threatening if ineffectual "Rabble" of inferiors. Writing in 1687, Matthew Prior, himself dependent upon patrons' rewards for his writing, reveals the hegemonic influence of Rochester's stance. His comparison of Rochester to Dryden in *Satyr on the Poets* expresses preference for a model of literary production that Prior himself could never hope to engage in:

> *Sidley* indeed and *Rochester* might Write,
> For their own Credit, and their Friends Delight,
> Shewing how far they cou'd the rest out-do,
> As in their Fortunes, so their Writings too;
> But shou'd Drudge *Dryden* this Example take,
> And *Absaloms* for empty Glory make,
> He'd soon perceive his Income scarce enough,
> To feed his Nostrils with Inspiring Snuff,
> Starving for Meat, nor surfeiting on Praise,
> He'd find his Brain as barren as his *Bays.*[29]

Although Prior exclaims against the paltry rewards that his society bestows upon poets, he rather cynically recommends that poetry should be confined to those who already possess "substantial Happiness" and wealth, or to those who have found a generous patron "To fill their Pockets, and their Title Page" (49).

The exclusive nature of Rochester's masculine community of writers and readers appears not only in his critique of professional poets, but also in "Timon" (1674), his satire on upper-class manners and taste. Based upon the theme of the *repas ridicule* (and following poems in the same tradition by Horace, Regnier, and Boileau), "Timon" is distinguished by its extended assessment of contemporary literary culture.[30] The speaker's reputation as a wit makes him the victim of a "dull dining Sot" who coerces him into a visit; while driving home, the host "*Pulls* out a *Libel* of a Sheet, or two" (14), and, delighted at the piece, charges Timon with its authorship. Despite his denials ("A *Song* to *Phillis*, I perhaps might make,/But never Rhym'd, but for my *Pintles* sake" [21-22]), Timon is "undone" by the host's "officious Lye" or wrongful attribution: the host's confidence in his own abilities as a close reader ("He knew my *Stile*, he sword" [25]) creates a socially damaging incident for the speaker. Worse yet, the host's promise that Timon will dine with some wits of his own acquaintance, or members of his own coterie, falls short, since Sedley, Buckhurst, and Savile reject the invitation and are replaced by boors appropriately named Halfwit, Huffe, Kickum, and Dingboy. The fact that he sees no distinction between the groups confirms the host's lack of judgment: "They're all brave *Fellows* cryes mine *Host*, let's Dine,/I long to have my *Belly* full of *Wine*" (37-38). After an inedible, ill-prepared dinner, the conversation turns to poetry, and the guests betray their ignorance by praising stylistically simple verses with the most bombast and the least sense: the authors whose works they (mis)quote include Orrery, Elkanah Settle, John Crowne, and Dryden, and the passages exhibit doggerel ("There's fine *Poetry!* you'd swear 'twere *Prose*,/So little on the Sense, the Rhymes impose" [119-20]), "rumbling words," and strained conceits. After an hour, the host turns the conversation to foreign affairs, and the evening ends in a brawl, broken up only by exhaustion and "Six fresh *Bottles*" of wine. Timon's representation of the host and his guests as ignorant readers who appreciate and encourage poor writing suggests the dismal state of literary culture and justifies his preference for the elite circle of Sedley, Buckhurst, and Savile; whether or not Timon functions as a reliable spokesman for Rochester, the attention given to satirizing literary taste indicates that the creation and reception of poetry serve as important determinants of masculine social authority.

Yet if the men in "Timon" reveal their inadequacy in discussions of politics and verse, the hostess finds herself altogether silenced on both subjects. In his role as satirist, Timon—and perhaps Rochester as well—asserts that the lady's advanced age disqualifies her from judging poetry: her remarks are ridiculed for their single-minded focus on love lyrics ("*Falkland*, she prais'd, and *Sucklings*, easie Pen,/And seem'd to taste their former parts again" [107-08]), and she is banished from the table before the men begin their serious assessment of verse ("Mine *Host*, drinks to the best in *Christendome*,/And decently my *Lady*, quits the Room" [109-10]). The host's obscene toast indicates the general boorishness of the company, and suggests that his wife receives a rude dismissal, yet the hostess comes under attack as well, provoking Timon's disapproval with her gently flirtatious behavior: "Though nothing else, she (in despight of time)/Preserv'd the affectation of her prime" (53-54).

The lady's exclusion from literary conversation and the contempt shown toward her disparagement of modern wits reflect Rochester's ambivalent treatment of women as writers and readers. One need not agree with Germaine Greer that Rochester was "the best woman poet of the seventeenth century"[31] to recognize his sympathetic understanding of the problems that such poets faced: "A Letter from Artemiza in the Towne to Chloe in the Countrey" (1674) relates the social restrictions set upon female writing, as well as the difficulties that these restrictions created for Rochester's female contemporaries.[32] Commanded by her correspondent to write in verse, Artemiza worries that pursuing the "lofty flights of dang'rous poetry" constitutes trespassing into the sphere of male activities; she compares writing to warfare ("Shortly you'l bid mee ride astride, and fight" [2]) and to adventure on the high seas in search of booty ("How would a Womans tott'ring Barke be tost,/Where stoutest Ships (the Men of Witt) are lost?" [12-13]). Artemiza's reflection on her culture's hostile environment for poetry, let alone female-authored verse, leads to a kind of fragmented consciousness,[33] as she ventriloquizes the words of a grave adviser warning her to give up writing. Noting that "poetry's a snare," the persona of the adviser repeats (in rhyme) the cultural dogma enforcing female silence, and offers a near-parody of the warnings usually given to female writers. Should Artemiza's lines to Chloe be circulated (and the adviser assumes they will be, in keeping with seventeenth-century modes of manuscript transmission), the presumably male reader will discredit her work as a form of hysteria or insanity: "Your Muse diverts you, makes the Reader sad;/You Fancy you'r inspir'd, he thinkes, you mad" (18-19). The adviser also reminds Artemiza of the indiscretion that she commits in making herself "the Fiddle of the Towne" (21), or a source of public entertainment; like a whore, she elects to "fynd th'ill-humour'd pleasure att their need" (22), and can expect to elicit only disgust whether she succeeds or fails. The adviser's warnings go unheeded, though, as Artemiza, resuming her own voice, abruptly decides to go ahead and write: despite being "well convinc'd, writing's a shame" (25), she refuses fully to internalize the ideology that she articulates. Blaming her conduct on her essential nature as an "Arrant Woman" pleased with the "Sin" of transgression (and thus playfully appropriating misogynist sentiments to excuse her behavior), Artemiza deliberately exaggerates the case against women writers—composing verse, if socially improper, was surely not sinful—in order to expose its absurdity. Rochester's treatment of Artemiza throughout the poem supports her perspective. Her criticisms of the degraded state of love are justified by the examples of "that wretched thinge Corinna" (a murderous mistress) and the insightful yet impertinent "fine Lady" (a lover of fools), and while these other female characters become targets of satire, Artemiza's interpretations of their motives, as well as her narrative authority, remain undisputed.

If "Artemiza to Chloe" seems to acknowledge female literary talent, Rochester responds far less generously to a woman writer who is not his fictional creation. "The Earl of ROCHESTER's Answer, to a Paper of *Verses*, sent him by *L.B. Felton*, and taken out of the Translation of *Ovid's Epistles*, 1680" attacks Lady Betty's presumption in intruding upon the "Pleasures of a Jovial Night" (3) spent in male company. Apparently Lady Betty's verses took the form of a reproach or a threat; instead of soliciting Rochester—the recipient—to love, her words "give amaze and fright," and Rochester reprimands her for the misuse of her body in textual aggression:

> Were it not better far your Arms t'employ,
> Grasping a Lover in pursuit of Joy,
> Than handling Sword, and Pen, Weapons unfit:
> Your Sex gains Conquest, by their Charms and Wit. (6-9)

As Edward Burns argues, Rochester's reference to sword and pen might suggest that Lady Betty copied her lines from "Canacee to Macareus," which appeared in the translation of Ovid's *Epistles* edited by Dryden[34]; in this epistle, Canacee writes to her brother/lover just before she kills herself with a sword provided by her father, Aeolus, who was enraged at their incest. The relation between Rochester and Lady Betty remains unclear, yet whatever his offence against her might have been, Rochester insists that she errs in appropriating masculine weapons for self- assertive violence. Rather, for Rochester, the form of writing most suitable for women is an invitation to erotic play, which employs their charms and wit in the service of seduction. Rochester's colloquial, half-comic response to Lady Betty's dramatic gesture deliberately deflates the seriousness of her purpose and exposes it to ridicule: his attempts to regulate the quality and purpose of court verse in this case amounts to repression. In his "Answer," Rochester revises the ending of Lady Betty's copied lines and provides a new script for her; instead of the writer's death by her own hand, Rochester's conclusion features the "death" of Lady Betty in an orgasm that he induces:

> Of Writers slain I could with pleasure hear,
> Approve of Fights, o'er-joy'd to cause a Tear;
> So slain, I mean, that she should soon revive,
> Pleas'd in my Arms to find her self Alive. (10–13)

With these verses, Rochester removes the pen (and the sword) from Lady Betty's possession and transfers it to his own, promising that this shift of power will ultimately leave her "pleas'd."

Despite its casual production and circulation, Rochester's verse establishes him as an arbiter of literary culture, and he confidently denies authority to men like Dryden and Timon's host for their lack of status or merit. Dryden's hopelessly gauche manners and professional orientation limit his capacity for poetry, while Timon's boorish host prefers brawling and warfare to discussions of verse. Lady Betty fares even worse. Reduced to her "natural" role as a primarily sexual creature, she has no business venturing into the masculine preserve of wits like Rochester, unless it were to render an invitation to love. Rochester's insistence on the ideal combination of pen and sword, or the fundamental tie between writing and male aristocratic status, attempts to secure the influence that men like himself exercised over literature as both patrons and poets. Yet the symbiotic relationship between manuscript and print culture that emerged in the late seventeenth century threatened to erase the distinctions between aristocratic writers and their social inferiors.

IV

Anxiety over this development appears in "A Familiar Epistle to Mr. Julian, Secretary to the Muses" (1677), a satire attributed to Buckingham but most likely composed in collaboration with Rochester's circle. Robert Julian, a former naval clerk, probably began his career in manuscript publication by acting as a scribe for Buckingham and his associates; from there he progressed to the entrepreneurial publication of both separate texts and larger compilations. Since this trade in manuscripts, including libels and lampoons, was illegal, Julian most likely received protection for his work, perhaps from Buckingham, who later became his antagonist when Julian took up with the Tory Sir Carr Scroope. By the time that "A Familiar Epistle" appeared, Julian was "well recognized as a professional factor of lampoons,"[35] and the growth of his enterprise, as well as his emerging independence, might have provoked Buckingham and others to satire. The poem begins with an extended metaphor of poetry as excrement, from which Julian—the "common shore of this poetic town"[36]—gathers guineas. Profiting from all poetic forms, including "sonnet, satire, bawdry, [and] blasphemy" (3), Julian shows a lack of discernment in selecting the writers whose works he copies ("All mischief's thine; transcribing, thou dost stoop/From Lofty Middlesex to lowly Scroope" [9-10]); his desire for a salable commodity levels all distinctions among poets, including those of class, and his miscellanies show no concern for aesthetic quality: "What times are these, when in that hero's room/Bow-bending Cupid does with ballads come,/And little Ashton offers to the bum!" (11-13). Buckingham grows outraged that in Julian's collections of verses, poems by Scroope and Edmund Ashton (an officer in the Life Guards) exist alongside of those by Buckhurst (now earl of Dorset and of Middlesex), a companion of Buckingham and Rochester: the context of poetic production—the particular relationships and allegiances that manuscript verses were intended to establish and strengthen—cannot be conveyed in indiscriminately compiled collections, especially if the poems included are anonymous. Julian's services as a scribe, it seems, had unexpected consequences for the aristocrats who employed him, for his compilations often placed them in undesirable company or in the wrong political crowd.

Noting that Julian's need for copy exceeded the output of his aging contributors (among them Etherege and Dryden), Buckingham recommends an alliance with Sir Carr Scroope, a knight "For prowess of the pen renown'd" (26). Buckingham's phrase implies Scroope's descent on the hierarchies of class and gender: his prolific writing reveals that his pen has altogether replaced his sword, an action that emasculates him: although "undaunted in attempts of wit and love" (29), Scroope repeatedly fails at both. Buckingham goes on to portray Scroope as an androgynous, and hence monstrous, creature. His "unfinish'd," almost inhuman face frightens women to the point of miscarriage, but his "inward parts" are even more horrific, for his constant flow of poetry suggests his physical similarity to a menstruating woman: "[B]y his monthly flow'rs discharg'd abroad,/'Tis full, brim-full, of pastoral and ode" (47-48). This comparison would seem especially insalubrious for seventeenth-century readers: medical theory of the time maintained that menstruation was caused by fermentation of the blood, whose monthly "flowers" or discharge took the form of a noisome impurity that could harm living things or inanimate objects coming in contact with it.[37] Buckingham's metaphor designates Scroope's verse a source of public infection as well as a sign of his mental and physical debility. The poem continues to feminize Scroope in its portrayal of his composition style: his "pangs of wit" are "the very symptoms of a breeding muse" (58), and his organ of generation (both poetic and sexual) is the womb and not the penis. Buckingham finally presents Julian with his new supplier of verse ("Thy wit, thy poet, nay thy friend! for he/Is fit to be a friend to none but thee" [89-90]), claiming that Scroope's preoccupation with poetry renders him unfit to associate with men of his own class:

> Laugh at him, justle him, yet still he writes:
> In rhyme he challenges, in rhyme he fights.
> Charg'd with the last and basest infamy,
> His business is to think what rhymes to lie,
> Which found in fury he retorts again.
> Strephon's a very dragon at his pen:
> His brother murder'd and his mother whor'd,
> His mistress lost, yet still his pen's his sword. (93-100)

Buckingham charges that Scroope's writing undermines his status as a gentleman: insults verbal and physical, slights upon his honor, even Sir Thomas Armstrong's killing of his brother during a fight over an actress and his mother's liaison with Henry Savile (Rochester's intimate friend) fail to distract him from verse. For Scroope, poetry has replaced dueling—the conventional aristocratic response to encroachments upon one's moral integrity and social standing—with textual aggression. The symbolic resonance of the sword in seventeenth- and eighteenth-century England illustrates the severity of Buckingham's rebuke: according to J. C. D. Clark, "The small-sword was an article of everyday wear for all gentlemen until the last two decades of the eighteenth century: that gentlemen normally went armed is an important defining characteristic of membership of the elite. The sword, too, was . . . an object of status. Its use was a difficult and aristocratic skill, slowly acquired."[38] By neglecting to employ his sword, Scroope willingly gives over his place in the ruling class: his preferences for verses provides, in Rochester's words, "a revenge so tame" ("Timon," 24) against dishonor that it levels Scroope with tradesmen like Julian.

Scroope himself adopted the same assumptions and vocabulary in his attack on Rochester. His poem "In Defense of Satire" (1677) had charged Rochester with being a source of public entertainment, or "top fiddler of the town"[39]; Rochester's response took the form of another lampoon ("On the suppos'd Authour of a late *Poem* in defence of *Satyr*"), which provoked an answer from Scroope. Addressing Rochester as a "poor feeble Scribbler," Scroope emphasizes his failure as a lover ("full of Pox"), a satirist, and a gentleman: "Thou canst blast noe Mans Fame with thy ill word,/Thy Pen, is full as harmlesse as thy Sword."[40] Here Scroope invokes the belief that proper management of both the pen and the sword are necessary for masculine dominance, and that inadequacy in the deployment of one suggests incompetence in the use of the other. As Warren Chernaik observes, the association of writing, violence, and male social and sexual status had its roots in the decline of aristocratic influence: Scroope's attack "applied not only to Rochester but to a hereditary nobility more and more stripped of real power and reduced to displays of ritual."[41] And these displays often undermined rather than supported the pretensions of Rochester's class. Scroope's attack on his antagonist referred to a violent incident at Epsom, which occurred in June 1676: during a night of revelry, Rochester and Etherege along with two companions (Captain Bridges and Mr. Downs), had assaulted a constable in his own house while mistaking it for the residence of a prostitute. After a "submissive oration" from Etherege, the constable dismissed his watch, whom he had roused in his own defense, but the scuffle erupted again, this time turning deadly:

> Presently after the Lord Rochester drew [his sword] upon the constable. Mr Downs, to prevent his pass, seized on him, the constable cried out murther and, the watch returning, one came behind Mr Downs and with a sprittle staff cleft his skull. The Lord Rochester and the rest run away and Downs, having no sword, snatched up a stick and striking at them, they run him into the side with a half pike and so bruised his arm that he was never able to stir it after.[42]

Downs died from his wounds, and the incident damaged Rochester's reputation so severely that Rochester himself referred to it in "To the Post Boy," a poem that parodies his own conduct and the hyperbole of the lampoons written against him ("Frighted at my own mischeifes I have fled/And bravely left my lifes defender dead" [9-10]).[43] The link between aristocratic prowess in warfare and writing was so pervasive at this time that apologists for Rochester adopted a heroic vocabulary to justify Rochester's often offensive poetic practice. Wolseley argues that Rochester's satiric verse emerged from his duty as a loyal peer to protect his sovereign and his nation: "Never was his Pen drawn but on the side of good Sence, and usually imploy'd, like the Arms of the ancient Heroes, to stop the progress of arbitrary Oppression, and beat down the Bruitishness of head-strong Will; to do his King and Countrey justice upon such publick State-thieves, as would beggar a Kingdom to enrich themselves." But with less accomplished writers, Wolseley states, satire becomes "a Sword in the hands of a Mad-man, it runs a Tilt at all manner of Persons without any sort of distinction or reason."[44]

While Rochester's contemporaries shared the same assumptions regarding the qualities that upper-class men should possess—qualities that support their claim to legitimate social power—his fellow peers also shared the anxiety that bad writing or even writing too frequently might undermine their elite status. Insisting that Scroope's prolific pen makes him an accessory to Julian's enterprise, Buckingham censures the over involvement of men of rank in the production of texts as commodities; the protracted controversy that he and Rochester engaged in with Scroope—which generated six satires and many satiric references to each other—indicates concern over the perceived breach between talent and privilege in their antagonists. While the Etherege-Buckhurst epistles and Rochester's "Allusion to Horace" describe an intimate community of poets who felt secure in their dominance over their social inferiors, other verses emerging from this community reveal the fragility of such a stance. In "A Session of the Poets," for instance, Rochester and his collaborators assert a strict demarcation between genteel and professional writers, agreeing that "Brawny Wycherley," although the best contender, cannot as a gentleman assume the position of laureate. (The honor finally goes to the witty yet modest Thomas Betterton, "For he had writ plays, yet ne'er came in print" [101].) Likewise, the satire in Buckingham's *Rehearsal* rests upon the way in which Dryden/Bayes affects aristocratic manners (by keeping a mistress and writing only for "some persons of quality, and peculiar friends") while boasting of his expertise as a professional dramatist ("I can dispatch you a whole play, before another man, 'egad, can make an end of his plot").[45] As Rochester and his circle perceived, becoming a "Poet of the tymes" ("An Epistolary Essay," 50) also involved becoming a "fiddler of the town" whose verses circulated indiscriminately among audiences of all classes. Rochester's final repudiation of his poetry, and his injunction "to burn all his profane and lewd Writings"—an act recorded in print by Robert Parsons and celebrated in lines by Isaac Watts[46]—may have been a testament to the sincerity of his deathbed repentance, but it also may have been a reaction against the ambivalent position that noble authors occupied in an expanding and increasingly commercial literary culture.

V

Rochester's writing habits—his collaboration with others, his lack of concern for textual accuracy, his disregard for revising, collecting, or even signing his work—suggest that he viewed writing not as a solitary act of genius that celebrates the poetic self, but as a social gesture clarifying and strengthening the relationships among individual men within an elite circle. The commercial market in letters, however, urged a different perspective on composition, and after his death Rochester's work was altered to fit the needs of this system. Jacob Tonson's 1691 edition of Rochester's *Poems on Several Occasions,* intended for a general audience of readers, includes a preface by Thomas Rymer that apologizes for the poet's careless and occasionally obscene style. Rymer argues that unlike Horace, who had patrons to oversee and judge his work (and who prohibited him from circulating it "over hastily"), "My Lord *Rochester* . . . found no Body of Quality or Severity so much above himself, to Challenge a Deference, or to Check the ordinary Licenses of Youth, and impose on him the Obligation to copy over again, what on any Occasion had not been so exquisitely design'd" (preface, n.p.)[47] Besides this lack of discipline, Rochester faced a court audience that demanded "Ribaldry and Debauch" in its verse, a preference that "prove[d] of fatal consequence to a Wit of his Gentleness and Complaisance" (preface, n.p.). Judging Rochester's verses according to formal and moral standards that the poet's coterie of readers did not hold, Rymer concludes that the circumstances of Restoration culture perverted rather than fostered the poet's development as a writer. The standards of print culture, though, prevailed in Tonson's edition, for "the *Publisher* assures us, he has been diligent out of Measure, and has taken exceeding Care that every Block of Offence shou'd be removed" (preface, n.p.): accordingly, the pornographic verses appearing in the 1680 editions (such as "The Imperfect Enjoyment" and "A Ramble in Saint James's Parke") were omitted from Tonson's volume; offending stanzas in the remaining poems were excised; and occasionally obscene words were replaced with milder choices.[48] Tonson's bowdlerization of Rochester's verse is severe, for his editorial practice and the preface's representation of Rochester's shortcomings reveal an alternative set of expectations for poets that conflicted with those of Rochester. The poetry of John Oldham—a protegee of Rochester—provides a sustained example of the challenge posed to aristocratic hegemony by writers working within the system of commercial print.

The 1680 editions of *Poems on Several Occasions* include in the Rochester canon three poems by Oldham, two of them ("Ode. Suppos'd to be spoken by a Court-Hector at Breaking of the Dial in Privy-Garden" and "An Apology for the Foregoing Ode, By Way of Epilogue") satires on Rochester himself. The "Ode," later known as the "Satyr against Vertue," appeared in manuscript by July 1676, and commemorated an incident of June 1675 in which Rochester and other court wits, after a night of drinking, stole into the Privy Garden and came across a phallic-looking sundial belonging to the king. In David Vieth's narration of the incident, Rochester, "seized by an alcoholic inspiration," shouted, "What! Dost thou stand here to [fuck] time?" and in a moment . . . demolished the offending instrument."[49] Intrigued by Oldham's mock celebration of their actions ("We're the great *Roya'l Society* of Vice,/Whose Talents are to make Discoveries,/And advance Sin like other Arts and Sciences" [11.269-71]), Rochester, the earl of Dorset, Sir Charles Sedley, "and other persons of Distinction" visited Oldham at the Whitgift School in Croydon, Surrey, where he held a post as an assistant master.[50] The consequences of Rochester's visit remain unclear. Oldham may have begun a correspondence with Rochester, and an anonymous source records that upon leaving his post as tutor in the household of Sir William Hicks at Reigate, and arriving in London in pursuit of a literary career (1681), "He was found out by his *Croyden-Visiters,* who immediately brought Him acquainted with Mr. *Dryden*" ("Memoirs," x). Despite his reputation among elite coteries and the more general popularity of his *Satyrs upon the Jesuits* (published in their entirety in 1681), Oldham's residence in London proved disappointing; several of his poems describe in detail the miserable life of a writer who lodges in a "Garret near the Sky,/Above five pair of Stairs" ("An Allusion to Martial," 11-12). Sometime in 1682 Oldham left the capitol to take up residence at Holme-Pierrpoint in Nottinghamshire with a new patron, the earl of Kingston. There he continued writing, publishing his final volume of verse—*Poems and Translations*—in 1683, and dying of smallpox at age 30 in December of that year. The accomplishments of his brief career are usually remembered now only because Dryden represented them so vividly in a famous poem to his memory.

Although their patron/client relationship seems to have been casual and intermittent, Oldham acknowledges Rochester's aesthetic influence in "Bion," his pastoral elegy mourning Rochester's death:

> If I am reckon'd not unblest in Song,
> 'Tis what I ow to thy all-teaching tongue:
> Some of thy Art, some of thy tuneful breath
> Thou didst by Will to worthless me bequeath:
> Others thy Flocks, thy Lands, thy Riches have,
> To me thou didst thy Pipe and Skill vouchsafe. (191–96)

As Raman Selden notes, Oldham wrote several pieces in the style of the court libertines even before his initial meeting with Rochester.[51] Yet these poems, with their careful and labored imitation of libertine *jeu d'esprit*, betray Oldham as an outsider consciously trying on a persona that doesn't quite fit. Circulated in manuscript, the ode "Sardanapalus" resembles some of Rochester's verses on the sexual excesses of Charles II, particularly echoing the "Scepter Lampoon" ("His Sceptter and his Prick are of a Length,/And she may sway the one, who plays with th'other" [11-12]) in its obscene and misogynistic satire on the king's subordination to women: "C-t was the Star that rul'd thy Fate,/C-t thy sole Bus'ness, and Affair of State,/And C-t the only field to make thee Great" (1.12-14). Marked similarities also exist between Oldham's "The Eighth Satyr of Monsieur Boileau, Imitated" and Rochester's "Satyr against Reason and Mankind," as well as between their two versions of an ode from the *Anacreontea*, which Rochester entitled "Upon his Drinking a Bowl" and Oldham subtitled "The Cup." Oldham obviously found the libertine style appealing, especially for its evocation of class privilege: adopting the voice and the themes of court wits like Rochester enabled him to experiment with a poetic style favored by a socially dominant group of men whose verses celebrate transgression as a show of power. The "Satyr against Vertue," narrated in the persona of Rochester, examines the aesthetic of vice that regulates the conduct of this group: despising "the unpittied Vulgar" whose uninspired sins are "Scarce worth the Damning, or their Room in Hell" (11.262), the speaker declares "A studied and elab'rate Wickednes" to be a superior form of artistry requiring "Perfection." Oldham's "Dithyrambique on Drinking: Suppos'd to be spoken by Rochester at the Guinny-Club" (1677) also features Rochester as its speaker, and its ventriloquism, like that of the "Satyr against Vertue," gives Oldham the freedom to assume a subject position usually unavailable to an impoverished school usher:

Let the vile Slaves of business toil and strive,
Who want the leisure or the wit to live:
Whil'est we life's taedious journy shorter make,
And reap those joys which they lack sence to take. (18-21)

But while Oldham exaggerated the manner of court wits to the point of parody and implicitly satirized the libertine persona ("Dithyrambique" ends with the speaker's reeling into his tomb to "Sleep out . . . [the] long Debauch of life" [140]), he felt attracted to aristocratic writers like Rochester, and recognized the possibilities that their often outrageous rhetorical self-fashioning offered for verse. Oldham himself, however, lacked the class status that authorized such rhetoric and his imitations of it occasionally appear self-conscious and awkward: "Sardanapalus," for instance, tediously repeats "cunt" (six times in the first stanza alone) in an effort to match the lewdness of court lampoons. Selden argues that "Oldham's attempts to mimic or to assimilate the fashionable wit and obscenity of Rochester's circle seem always to produce a radical ambivalence of stance—a swinging between classical sublimity and mock-seriousness, between heroic libertinism and puritan self-recrimination."[52] Yet Oldham's ambivalence may have arisen from a more concrete and substantial source than the "subconscious drives" releasing "anger and desire" within the constraints of neoclassical poetic forms: one of the century's many frustrated intellectuals whose university education did not provide them with social prestige or financial security,[53] Oldham viewed his writings as an alternative means of achieving cultural authority. Establishing such authority required Oldham to construct an authorial identity and endorse a literary practice very different from those of his noble patron, and while Oldham's changing personae make it difficult to locate a coherent, unified consciousness behind the texts, his verse nevertheless suggests that some forms of self-presentation were more empowering (and more comfortable) for him than others.

VI

Oldham reveals his opposition to Rochester's model of authorship in the "Apology" that followed the "Satyr against Vertue." The poem begins by claiming that Oldham's muse, acting in "Masquerade," articulated not his sentiments but rather those of Rochester: "When she a Hector for her Subject had,/She thought she must be Termagant and mad;/That made her speak like a lewd Punk o'th' Town" (9-11). By contrast, the speaker, representing the "authentic" Oldham, assures readers that he has "a diff'rent Tast of Wit," and stands apart from the "common Vogue" of courtiers like Rochester who "lampoon the State and libel Kings" (24). He also advocates a different form of literary production, insisting on his distinction from possibly treasonous writers who favor manuscript circulation over print:

> He likes not Wit, which can't a License claim,
> To which the Author dares not set his Name;
> Wit should be open, court each Reader's Ey,
> Not lurk in sly unprinted Privacy;
> But Criminal Writers, like dull Birds of Night,
> For Weakness, or for Shame, avoid the Light;
> May such a Jury for their Audience have,
> And from the Bench, not Pit, their Doom receive.
> May they the Tow'r for their due merit share,
> And a just Wreath of Hemp, for Laurel, wear. (27-36)

In these lines the speaker reverses his culture's privileging of scribal over printed poetry, arguing that only incapacity—"Weakness" or "Shame"—keeps writers from openly publishing and circulating their work. Print, associated with "Light," appears as the medium of choice when juxtaposed to the other forms of transmission that attract the dull and the incompetent. The poem's preference for licensed texts available to all readers over "sly," privately-circulated manuscript verses also evokes a measure of class antagonism, for clandestine, scribal publication is less feasible for professional writers whose living depends on the commercial sale of their texts. Oldham's speaker goes on to recommend state regulation of literature: instead of enjoying the protection of anonymity in manuscripts, "Criminal writers" of lampoons and libels who escape the licensor should be subject to the jury and the gallows for their socially disruptive work.

Besides attacking the format of coterie writing, the poem also repudiates the pornographic or licentious content favored by wits like Rochester. The speaker assures readers that Oldham "could be Bawdy too, and nick the Times/In what they dearly love, damn'd Placket-Rhimes,/Such as our Nobles write" (37-39), yet the work of these aristocratic writers does not deserve imitation. Whereas Rochester, Buckhurst, and Etherege had championed "*Cunt* and *Prick*" as the source of their wit—and thus characterized verse-writing as the preserve of libertines—Oldham's speaker associates this "nauseous Poetry" inspired by "the Codpiece and its God" with the bawdry of the lower classes: "If Ribaldry deserv'd the Praise of Wit,/He must resign to each Illiterate Cit,/And Prentices and Carmen challenge it" (47-49). Instead of distinguishing them from their inferiors (whose language is subject to social regulation), the obscenity of "our Nobles" lowers them to the level of common laborers, and thus undermines the allure that their class status bestows upon them. By devaluing the kind of wit exhibited at both ends of the social spectrum, the speaker sets the stage for Oldham's alternative literary practice. Since pleasing contemporary audiences requires the kind of "Wickedness" that Oldham rejects, the speaker instead proposes that he try "noble Satyr" and engages in a fantasy about the kind of power that his verse would give him: "The World should learn to blush,—/And dread the Vengeance of his pointed Wit,/Which worse then their own Consciences should fright" (71-73). Having refused to "submit" himself to the "common Vogue" of writing dominated by Rochester and others of his coterie, Oldham in the "Apology" selects a mode of poetry that would make him an agent of God—"Heav'ns just Plague"—and thus subordinate to no one.

An example of this satire appears in Oldham's "Upon the Author of the Play call'd *Sodom*" (1678), which remained unprinted during his lifetime. Selden refers to this poem as Oldham's "most impressive Rochesterian piece,"[54] since in vulgar language of its own it charges the anonymous author of *Sodom* with lacking wit in his obscenity ("Thou covet'st to be lewd, but want'st the Might" [17]). Yet Oldham's text expresses a kind of violence against the playwright and his subject—homosexual relations at court—that conflicts with Rochester's sexually undiscriminating poetic persona.[55] After censuring the author for his impotent muse that cannot rise to lechery without the extraordinary stimulation of buggery, Oldham changes the gender of this muse to emphasize the playwright's intellectual weakness:

> Thy Muse has got the Flowers, and they ascend
> As in some greensick Girl, at upper End.
> Sure Nature made, or meant at least 't have don't,
> Thy Tongue a Clitoris, thy Mouth a Cunt.
> How well a Dildoe would that place become,
> To gag it up, and make 't for ever dumb!
> At least it should be syring'd—
> Or wear some stinking Merkin for a Beard,
> That all from its base converse might be scar'd:
> As they a Door shut up, and mark't beware,
> That tells Infection, and the Plague is there. (28-38)

Oldham's appeal to his culture's misogynist assumptions about gender and speech is striking in its virulence. References to the author's muse as a "greensick Girl" suggest his mental immaturity and debility: figured as a discharge analogous to menstrual blood, his poetry is the sign of illness and disease in its source. Oldham then associates the writer with the "nothing" of the female genitals. By transforming his antagonist's organs of speech into a "Cunt" and clitoris, Oldham emphasizes his deficiencies in expression as well as sexuality, for the anonymous poet resembles a woman in the absence of meaning, and hence phallic power, from his words. Moreover, Oldham's description of the author's tongue and mouth rather than the more abstract mind and pen as the outlet of his poetry stresses the corporeal locus of the author's creativity: as Michèle Cohen notes, the word "tongue," "inescapably embedded in its materiality, with all the ambiguities—especially sexual—this entails," carries with it associations of female verbal and sexual incontinence, and thus "the very use of the word [has become] uncomfortable."[56] Oldham repeatedly invokes this discomfort: the feminization of *Sodom*'s author allows Oldham to portray his silencing, or censorship of his work, as an acceptable form of the violence customarily inflicted upon unruly women ("How well a Dildoe would that place become/To gag it up"). Anxiety over the anonymous publication of the play surfaces too: the speaker seeks to identify and quarantine the playwright, and proposes marking his offending body part as the site of dangerous sexual/linguistic infection. Oldham's sexualized description of *Sodom* and its author resembles the strategies of Renaissance writers, who, as Wendy Wall points out, identified "unlicensed, unauthorized, textually corrupt, or indiscriminantly circulated poems" with the figure of the harlot.[57] Oldham, however, completely inverts this trope: instead of viewing printed artifacts as culturally disruptive, he labels as feminine and sexually scandalous those texts that remain unpublished, and thus unavailable to an audience of diverse readers. The medium of print, which earlier writers had imaged as violating the integrity of the female text, for Oldham becomes the valorized site of masculine heterosexual activity. As in the "Apology," the speaker's desire to regulate or police literary production entails dismantling the kind of private circulation of texts and coterie relationships among writers and readers that enabled *Sodom,* and the homoerotic behavior the play depicted, to go unchecked and unpunished. Ironically, the obscenity of Oldham's attack on *Sodom* prevented its publication, and thus placed it firmly within the form of literary production that he had set out to denounce.

Oldham's constant praise of Rochester's "excellent Pen" and his declaration of Rochester's influence on his own verse appear somewhat suspect in light of the distinctions his poetry draws between himself and his mentor (or rival). The elegy "Bion," for instance, celebrates Rochester while ignoring the "general Dread" that Wolseley claims his "severe and impartial" satire had aroused. Instead, Oldham praises Rochester's pastorals and lyrics in a way that confines and diminishes him to the status of a harmless swain: in contrast to Edmund Spenser, a commoner and a writer by trade who "sung of Hero's, and of hardy Knights/Far-fam'd in Battles, and renown'd Exploits" (154-55), Rochester "meddled not with bloody Fights, and Wars,/Pan was his Song, and Shepherds harmless jars,/Loves peaceful combats, and its gentle cares" (156-58).[58] Depicting Rochester as a love-obsessed shepherd serves a strategic purpose for Oldham, since it provides a contrast to his own very different self-presentation. Throughout his writings, Oldham claims for himself a literary form—satire—as well as a mode of production—commercial print—that challenges the hegemony of aristocratic writers like Rochester and establishes his own right to an authoritative voice in Restoration culture.

VII

Much of Oldham's verse displays ambivalence over the possibility of such authority, even while it articulates his desire for it. Published in 1683, "A Satyr . . . Dissuading the Author from the Study of Poetry" (also referred to as "Spencer's Ghost") depicts the poet's interview with an apparition of Edmund Spenser, whose diatribe warns the speaker "To shun the dang'rous Rocks of Poetry" (34). Although John Cleveland, Abraham Cowley, Ben Jonson, and the court wits functioned as the strongest stylistic influences upon Oldham,[59] he found in Spenser a precursor to validate his own frustrations with his writing career. Spenser's description of Restoration letters is profoundly discouraging for professional authors: he portrays a culture in which verse writing, along with dueling and whoring, has become a sign of gentlemanly accomplishment or a mark of genteel status instead of an art pursued for its own sake:

> So many now, and bad the Scriblers be,
> 'Tis scandal to be of the Company:
> The foul Disease is so prevailing grown,
> So much the Fashion of the Court and Town,
> That scarce a man well-bred in either's deem'd,
> But who has kill'd, been clapt, and often rhim'd:

The Fools are troubled with a Flux of Brains,
And each on Paper squirts his filthy sense:
A leash of Sonnets, and a dull Lampoon
Set up an Author, who forthwith is grown
A man of Parts, of Rhiming, and Renown. (52-62)

As Spenser complains, among the would-be wits poetry has become a "Fashion" rather than a vocation, and the most insignificant forms of writing (sonnets, lampoons) are sufficient to establish a reputation for literature. Fashion even influences the reception of authors long deceased. Dismantling the myth about the immortality that poetry confers, Spenser argues that in a commercial economy, new commodities inevitably drive out the old: "Poems writ in ancient time" (93) fall out of favor with modern readers, and a glut in the market for print relegates former bestsellers to "wrapping Drugs and Wares" (101). This same economy encourages "All Trades and all Professions" but that of poets. Compared with other sites of traffic in goods, "*Parnassus* only is that barren Coast,/Where the whole Voyage and Adventure's lost" (247-48); in comparison to such contraband as "Dildoes, Lace, and Wine," poetry carries a low exchange value, and exchange value, according to Spenser, has become the measure of all worth. Poets writing for the stage find themselves in similar circumstances. The theater—"That constant Mart, which all the year does hold,/Where Staple Wit is barter'd, bought, and sold" (193-94)— provides a venue for recognition only for those not relying on its third-day profits: the rest, "Whose whole Estate's an ounce, or two of Brains" (204), must cater to an "ill-judging Audience" and lack the independence necessary to produce anything "that's brave and great." Spenser's unrelenting pessimism allows poets no refuge from the aggressive competition of the market, since even patron-client relations are grounded in the economy of consumer choice. The peer who willingly gives "fifty Guinnies for a Whore and Clap" (139) refuses anything "above a Coach-man's pay" for a poet: such a leveling of values leaves writers like Cowley and Samuel Butler with "nothing . . . but Poverty, and Praise" (184). Spenser ends the poem by advising Oldham to "Preach, Plead, Cure, Fight, Game, Pimp, Beg, Cheat, or Thieve;/Be all but Poet" (265-66), and his listing of gamblers, pimps, and thieves along with clergymen, attorneys, and physicians ironically emphasizes the equivalence of profitable occupations—an equivalence that the poem holds responsible for the degradation of writers in Oldham's time.

"A Letter from the Country to a Friend in Town, giving an Account of the Author's Inclinations to Poetry" (1678) voices similar doubts about the feasibility of a poetic career. Addressed to John Spencer, a barrister, amateur poet, and half-cousin of Oldham's patron, Sir Nicholas Carew, the "Letter" situates Oldham on the very margins of literary culture: he represents himself as torn between his conviction that for a country schoolmaster like himself, poetry is a "trifling barren Trade" (85) that would lead him to poverty, and his appreciation of the authority that writing allows him to wield. The poem's language suggests that Oldham considers writing an activity restricted to men possessing leisure and status; he praises Spencer's occasional verses, for "None of your serious pains or time they cost,/But what thrown by, you can afford for lost" (51-52). Like Rochester and his circle, Oldham advocates a poetic style displaying the "easie" lines and "graceful negligence" that supposedly characterize the verses of gentlemen; he also shares the court wits' contempt for the "filthy [or unskillful] Poetry and Rhyme" offered by less privileged writers incapable of imitating the libertines' style. Yet despite recognizing that poetry is a dangerous indulgence that will sap his masculine "vigor," distract his attention from "gainful business," and finally contribute to his financial "Ruine," Oldham cannot turn his attention to the "thriving Arts" instead of rhyme: whether a "darling Sin" or a "foul infection"—Oldham's sense of his own agency as a writer fluctuates—poetry draws him into a way of life he cannot resist yet cannot "afford."

While poetry appears incompatible with Oldham's class position, it seduces him by offering a venue in which he can exercise a "creating power." In a manner resembling the God of Genesis, Oldham transforms the "dark and empty Void" of his mind into a canvas of ordered images, and prides himself on the ability to "make something, what was nought before" (185). The submission of his unwieldy thoughts into rhymes makes him "triumph more, than joyful Warriors wou'd,/Had they some stout and hardy Foe subdu'd" (190-91), while the experience of imaginative contemplation gives him the illusion of regal power:

> Sometimes on wings of Thought I seem on high,
> As men in sleep, tho motionless they lie,
> Fledg'd by a Dream, believe they mount and fly:
> So Witches some enchanted Wand bestride,
> And think they through the airy Regions ride,
> Where Fancy is both Traveller, Way and Guide:
> Then strait I grow a strange exalted thing,
> And equal in conceit, at least a King:
> As the poor Drunkard, when Wine stums his brains,
> Anointed with that liquor, thinks he reigns. (196-205)

Although delusional like dreams or witchcraft, the exaltation that poetry confers on Oldham offers such an attractive alternative to the "vile Drudg'ry" of a schoolmaster's life that he embraces his "secret Feebles" in the "Letter"'s conclusion ("'What ere my fate is, 'tis my fate to write'" [226]). Oldham's unpublished fragment, "In Praise of Poetry"[60] (1678), more seriously celebrates the authority of poets while chastising those detractors who denigrate or disavow the "Great Gift of Heaven":

> Peace then ye dull Blasphemers! who profane
> Our sacred and diviner Strains,
> Who cry tis all Chimerical and vain
> The meer Capricios of unsettled Brains:
> Wit is an Arbitrary Monarch, who
> No Law, but what its self establishes, will know
> Its Pow'r unlimited,—Dominion absolute
> At least tis like our well-form'd State
> Where subject Art may advise and counsell give
> But not encroach upon the great Prerogative. (1-10)

Nearly every stanza of the unfinished ode emphasizes the sovereignty of wit and the exalted standing of the "elected few" who possess it. Counseled by art or the advice of critics but ultimately subject to no external control, the poet enjoys a "prerogative" like that of the king: both exercise dominion in their respective realms, one over literary culture, the other over the state. The speaker's nostalgic recollection of the honor previously given to poets ("Once sacred thought, and crown'd as well as Kings" [47]) suggests a decline in their present status, yet he still desires to be one of heaven's "best Favorites." Although Oldham only tentatively includes himself in the company of Homer, Virgil, Tasso, Pindar, Horace, Cowley, and Jonson, he selectively creates a genealogy of influence that excludes his contemporaries while proposing himself as the heir of both classical poets and their neoclassical English successors.

Triumphant and almost defiant in tone, "In Praise of Poetry" records none of the satiric hostility toward the conditions of writing apparent in both "Spencer's Ghost" and "A Letter from the Country." Yet his constant vacillations between self-admonishment and self-encouragement suggest Oldham's ambivalence about the feasibility of the poetic career he so desired. On the one hand, his "deathless Monuments of Wit," after circulating through the bookshops, may wind up serving as lighters, waste paper, or kites while their creator starves in oblivion; on the other hand, the publication of his verse enables a dispossessed intellectual like himself to gain a measure of prestige and distinguish himself from the "unhallow'd Rabble." Tensions between these two positions also emerge in the advertisements for the three volumes of verse printed during Oldham's lifetime. Apologetic and defensive at the same time, these advertisements convey the poet's uncertainty over engaging in a commercial form of literary production. In the "Advertisement" for *Satyrs upon the Jesuits* (1681), Oldham scornfully ignores the conventions of printed prefaces by refusing to impress readers with his knowledge of poetic theory and thereby establish his qualifications for writing. Dismissing this "laudable custom" as "a vanity he is in no wise fond of" (3), he instead employs his preface to prevent the misinterpretations that arise when his verse progresses beyond manuscript circulation into print. The "Satyr against Vertue" in particular requires clarification:

> 'Twas meant to abuse those, who valued themselves upon their Wit and Parts in praising Vice, and to shew, that others of sober Principles, if they would take the same liberty in Poetry, could strain as high rants in Profaness as they. At first he intended it not for the publick, nor to pass beyond the privacy of two or three Friends, but seeing it had the Fate to steal abroad in Manuscript, and afterwards in Print, without his knowledge; he now thinks it a justice due to his own Reputation, to have it come forth without those faults, which it has suffer'd from Transcribers and the Press hitherto, and which make it a worse Satyr upon himself, than upon what it was design'd. (4)

Oldham's concern for his reputation results partly from a change in this audience: whereas a coterie of gentlemen had "the sence to understand it," the irony implicit in the "Satyr against Vertue" might be lost upon readers unfamiliar with the rants of the court wits. Print also raises anxieties about accuracy. His "Advertisement" for *Some New Pieces* (1681) charges that both "Transcribers and the Press" have mangled his texts, and proposes to remedy these faults with a correct, authorized edition of his work. Oldham's desire to vindicate his transition into print suggests his awareness that this mode of production and circulation implies a descent in social status—a departure from the genteel, careless attitude toward writing expressed by Rochester and others of his rank—and Oldham's resentment against his culture's subordination of professional authors appears in the advertisements' curiously challenging stance toward readers, for the rhetoric of these prefaces seems to dismiss as insignificant the audiences' response to the poetry. Disparaging his translation of Ovid ("The Passion of Byblis") as a "Trifle," Oldham in his first "Advertisement" claims that "The Reader may do as he pleases, either like it, or put it to the use of Mr. *Jordan's Works*" (4); his second "Advertisement" ends with a similar refusal to defend his "Trifles": "[I] leave them wholly open and unguarded to the mercy of the Reader; let him make his Attaques how and where he please" (90). His final "Advertisement" for *Poems and Translations* (1683) openly satirizes the modes of self-presentation that print, and the reading public, require of authors: by the time that Oldham has prepared a comprehensive edition of his works,

> he means to have ready a very Sparkish Dedication, if he can but get himself known to some Great Man, that will give a good parcel of Guinnies for being handsomly flatter'd. Then likewise the Reader (for his farther comfort) may expect to see him appear with all the Pomp and Trappings of an Author; his Head in the Front very finely cut, together with the Year of his Age, Commendatory Verses in abundance, and all the Hands of the Poets of *Quorum* to confirm his Book, and pass it for Authentick. (161)

Dedications, engraved frontispieces, and commendatory verses supposedly validate writers' entry into print by providing them with the marks of distinction and authenticity that readers recognize and accept.[61] But Oldham dispenses with this kind of introduction into literary culture; he contentedly allows his volume to "come abroad naked, Undedicated, and Unprefac'd, without one kind word to shelter it from Censure" and refuses even to arrange its contents to advantage, for "if it be [the poems'] Fate to perish, and go the way of all mortal Rhimes, 'tis no great matter in what method they have been plac'd, no more than whether *Ode*, *Elegy*, or *Satyr* have the honor of Wiping first" (161). The defiant rhetoric in this final preface asserts the poet's independence from the demeaning practices of commercial print, even while the advertisement's very existence confirms his compliance with those practices.

Although Oldham used the medium of print to further his professional career, he resisted being subject to its conventions, and in a poem addressed to his bookseller fashions this resistance as the sign of a masculine sensibility equal if not superior to that of elite authors. "Upon a *Bookseller*, that expos'd him by Printing a Piece of his grosly mangled and faulty" (1680) attacks Joseph Hindmarsh for the printing of a corrupted version of the "Satyr against Vertue." Hindmarsh, who published all of Oldham's subsequent work, probably convinced Oldham that the blame lay with his printer, Mary Clark, for the poem appeared in *Some New Pieces* (1681) with the revised title "Upon a Printer" (*Poems*, 432). The fact that he had found a publisher may have encouraged Oldham's move to London in pursuit of a writing career, yet "Upon a *Bookseller*" depicts only antagonism between the man of genius and the "Dull and unthinking" tradesman. The poem begins by distinguishing Oldham from lyric poets whose verses circulate in manuscript until they are surreptitiously published:

> Had I some tame and sneaking Author bin,
> Whose Muse to Love and softness did incline,
> Some small Adventurer in Song, that whines
> *Phyllis* and *Chloris* out in charming lines
> Fit to divert mine Hostess, and mislead
> The heart of some poor tawdry Waiting-maid;
> Perhaps I might have then forgiven thee,
> And thou hadst scap'd from my Resentments free. (3-10)

Authors of erotic, amorous songs (a group that includes the Rochester of "Bion") whose verses focus on seducing a private female audience receive contempt for their timid choice of form and subject matter. Oldham, by contrast, defines himself as a satirist whose "spleen, and manly rage" compel him to public presentations of his verse: "Born to chastise the Vices of the Age" (13), he attacks "Knaves of all degrees" left unchallenged by agents of reform like the clergy and the stage. Oldham goes on to appropriate and transform aristocratic codes of conduct and the social practices that enforce those codes, for he views wit as an extension of honor and satire as the equivalent of duel fought to vindicate that honor:

> *Satyr's* my only Province and delight,
> For whose dear sake alone I've vow'd to write:
> For this I seek Occasions, court Abuse,
> To shew my Parts, and signalize my Muse:
> Fond of a quarrel as young Bullies are
> To make their mettle and their skill appear.
> And didst thou think, I would a Wrong acquit,
> That touch'd my tenderst part of Honour, Wit? (17-24)

Strictly an expression of upper-class male prerogative, the duel in Oldham's culture "was a deliberate act of rebellion against [the injunctions of law and religion], and a gesture of contempt toward the prudent, rational, calculating values which plebeians might be thought necessarily to hold."[62] For Oldham, however, writing resembles dueling in that both are forms of stylized aggression intended to establish and reinforce male authority. Comparing himself to rakish "young Bullies" like Rochester's Ballers—a group of courtiers whom Samuel Pepys labeled "as very rogues as any in the town"[63]—Oldham emphasizes the dangerous, even terrifying nature of satire, and stresses its association with aristocratic disdain for self-restraint. But while Rochester, Buckingham, and others perceived the pen as an inadequate substitute for the sword and criticized their peers for resorting only to textual violence against insults, Oldham claims these weapons are equivalent:

> I wear my Pen, as others do their Sword,
> To each affronting Sot, I meet, the word
> Is satisfaction; strait to Thrusts I go
> And pointed Satyr runs him thro and thro. (35-38)

Oldham's choice of Archilochus and Ovid as his models for satire and his preference for a style characterized by damaging invective ("Torn, mangled, and expos'd to scorn and shame/I mean to hang and gibbet up thy Name" [43-44])[64] allows him access to the violent assertion of power, legitimate and otherwise, enjoyed by his social superiors: like a bully, he indulges his fondness for personal quarrels; like a justice, he punishes Hindmarsh for his offence against literature (profaning the "genuin Issue of a Poet's brain" [63]) by condemning him to a career in Grubstreet that will end in poverty, disgrace, and finally suicide. The poem's litany of curses resembles the final section of Rochester's "A Ramble in Saint James's Parke," with its vow to plague the unfaithful Corinna, and Oldham's concluding couplet—"And may no sawcy Fool have better fate/ That dares pull down the vengeance of my Hate"—echoes that of Rochester: "And may no Woman better thrive/That dares prophane the Cunt I swive." Yet for Oldham, the bookseller has replaced the jilting mistress as the focus of wrath and revenge, and the torments that he wishes upon Hindmarsh (a stable of unprofitable authors, prosecution for seditious texts) refer to the hazards of the book trade rather than the dangers of promiscuity. While Oldham did unleash misogynist invective against a female target in "A Satyr Upon a Woman, who by her Falshood and Scorn was the Death of my Friend" (1678), he presents himself as the embodiment of "manly rage" only in his attacks on Hindmarsh, for the masculinity of a professional writer is displayed through his poetic productions instead of his sexual performances.

In defining his relations with the book trade and establishing his place among contemporary writers, Oldham asserts the "great Prerogative" that creative intellectual labor bestows upon poets in part by deliberately appropriating traditionally aristocratic expressions of privilege and authority. While he rejected, or was excluded from, the conventions of elite male coteries like those of Rochester—conventions such as the scribal circulation of anonymous verse, homoerotic flirtation, and a disdain for commercial encroachments upon literature—Oldham's writings attempt to establish the cultural significance of professional poets. His unflattering portrayals of upper-class writers (including his mentor, Rochester) consign them to "tame" or low poetic genres, censure their cowardice in avoiding print, and suggest that their talent rests solely upon their possession of estates ("As if a Patent gave [them] claim to sence,/Or 'twere entail'd with an inheritance" ["Horace His Art of Poetry," 634–35]). Oldham himself, however, steps in to fill the void left by their incapacity and, in his satiric persona, appropriates their social role as cultural arbiters. A dispossessed intellectual with little hope for advancement in the customary avenues of the church and state, Oldham belonged to the rapidly expanding group of the "middling sort," professional men identified by Lawrence Stone and Jeanne C. Fawtier Stone as "doctors, apothecaries, architects, dancing masters, musicians, schoolteachers, attorneys, secretaries, [and] clerks" whose emergence during the period from 1660–1800 "is perhaps the most important social feature of the age."[65] As the Stones maintain, the presence of these men, who provided various services for a growing consumer society, "blurred the old distinction between the gentleman and the rest of the population," for the middling sort as a whole were more inclined to imitate the gentry than resent them.[66] Oldham's attempts to mimic elite masculine conduct—his experimentation with libertine personae, his ambivalence toward publication, his equation of the pen with the sword—are a testament to the social influence of aristocratic writers. Yet Oldham's awareness of the cultural power that writing could bestow and his repeated criticism of coterie practices reveal an expanding confidence on the part of writers like himself—a confidence that eventually culminated in their rejection of upper-class dominance over poetry.

VIII

Dryden's "To the Memory of Mr. Oldham" (1684) and Pope's "On lying in the Earl of Rochester's Bed at Atterbury" (1739) indicate how the emerging class of professional writers interpreted the careers of these Restoration poets. Dryden's elegy was one of eight tributes that prefaced the volume of poetry (*Remains*) collected and printed shortly after Oldham's death by Hindmarsh. Yet while it joins the other verses in paying homage to the youthful promise of the deceased, "To the Memory of Mr. Oldham" also contrasts different styles of English poetry, and concludes by endorsing Oldham's manner of composition. In its opening lines, the elegy claims that a common sensibility unites the older laureate to his younger colleague:

> For sure our Souls were near ally'd; and thine
> Cast in the same Poetick mould with mine.
> One common Note on either Lyre did strike,
> And Knaves and Fools we both abhorr'd alike. (3-6)

Oldham's talent for satire allows Dryden to view him as an ally in his campaign against knaves and fools in English politics and letters; as Dryden notes, Oldham even preceded him in publishing his satires ("The last set out the soonest did arrive" [8]), since *Absalom and Achitophel* (1681), "The Medall" (1682), and "Mac Flecknoe" (1682) had all appeared in print at least two years after the pirated text of *Satyrs upon the Jesuits.*[67] The poem emphasizes Oldham's precocity, and Dryden's affinity for him, with a curious reference to the footrace in Book V of the *Aeneid:* "Thus *Nisus* fell upon the slippery place,/While his young Friend perform'd and won the Race" (9-10). Identifying himself as Nisus and Oldham as Euryalus— followers of Aeneas who fought and died together in the war between the Trojans and the Latins—Dryden unleashes many provocative resonances only to suppress most of them in the brevity of his poem's couplet. As Dustin Griffin observes, Dryden translated the Nisus and Euryalus episodes of the *Aeneid* as early as 1684, and these passages from Books V and IX were included in *Sylvae* the following year.[68] The footrace, in which Nisus, by tripping his rival Salius, enables Euryalus to gain victory, and the later self-sacrifice of Nisus as he vainly tries to free Euryalus from his Latin captors, idealize heroic friendship and the "sacred bonds of amity" (5.62). Yet these episodes also idealize homoerotic ties of affection, since Nisus is renowned as the lover of the young and handsome Euryalus. Following Virgil, Dryden's translation acknowledges the sexual nature of their love, as would his readers; Pope later made satiric use of this recognition in the *Dunciad Variorum,* where in Book III he adopts a phrase from Virgil to imply a sodomitical relationship between Thomas Burnet, son of the bishop and author of a weekly newspaper entitled *The Grumbler,* and

George Duckett, author of *The Pasquin,* another newspaper.[69] Dryden, however, seems deliberately to ignore the erotic overtones of his allusion, and thus rejects the Rochesterian associations of verse-writing with homoerotic friendship. Instead, his comparison of Oldham's verse with his own raises nervous doubts about his own commitment to a masculine aesthetic based on gendered differences in poetry. Dryden's assessment of Oldham's "abundant store" of talent breaks the conventions of elegies by including a critique of the poet's early ripeness: the knowledge and reflection that arrives with maturity might have "taught the numbers of thy native Tongue" (14), or enabled Oldham better to understand the techniques of rhyme and meter suited to English verse. Yet Dryden immediately retracts his criticism as insignificant to the rhetorical effect of satire:

> But Satyr needs not those, and Wit will shine
> Through the harsh cadence of a rugged line:
> A noble Error, and but seldom made,
> When Poets are by too much force betray'd.
> Thy generous fruits, though gather'd ere their prime
> Still shew'd a quickness; and maturing time
> But mellows what we write to the dull sweets of Rime. (15-21)

Written nine years later, Dryden's "Discourse concerning the Original and Progress of Satire" proclaimed his preference for the "nicest and most delicate touches of Satire" (*Works,* 4:70) over a rougher style of invective, noting the "vast difference betwixt the slovenly butchering of a Man, and the fineness of a stroak that separates the Head from the Body, and leaves it standing in its place" (*Works,* 4:71). Yet the elegy seems to approve Oldham's own preference for "manly rage" above "charming lines," calling ruggedness a "noble Error" caused by an overabundance of "force," and, in the poem's only triplet, comparing the "dull sweets of Rime" produced by older, more accomplished poets to the state of overripe fruit approaching decay. Dryden's opposition of masculine force with feminine, even effeminate, sweetness reveals a measure of Oldham's influence over his terms of judgment: Oldham's association of his satire with the violence of swordplay and bullies identifies poets as either masculine threats or "tame and sneaking" composers of lyrics, and this construction of authorial identity aroused anxious self-scrutiny even in the very best of England's poets.

Although Pope, nearly 50 years later, preferred Rochester's "delicacy" and "knowledge of mankind" to Oldham's excessive rage and "Billingsgate" style,[70] the verses that he fashioned while lying in the earl's bed show more affinity with Oldham's concept of authorship than with Rochester's. The location of this poem is an estate that had passed out of the Wilmot family into the hands of John Campbell, second duke of Argyle. By 1739, Argyle had joined the patriot Opposition to Robert Walpole, and Pope had already praised his political and military acumen in "Epilogue to the Satires: Dialogue II" ("*Argyle* the State's whole Thunder born to wield,/And shake alike the Senate and the Field" [86-87]). While a guest at Adderbury, Pope commemorated the occasion of his visit with verses that contrast the former owner of the house to the present one. The poem begins with a denial of Rochester's poetic influence: Pope claims that the thought of Rochester's sexual escapades or final repentance—the most notorious scenes enacted in that bedroom—fails to inspire him with "poetic ardours" and "Begets no numbers grave or gay" (4). Rochester's sterility as a source of inspiration contrasts with the potency of Argyle, whose example encourages imitation of his heroic actions:

> But 'neath thy roof, *Argyle,* are bred
> Such thoughts, as prompt the brave to lie,
> Stretch'd forth in honour's nobler bed,
> Beneath a nobler roof, the sky. (5-8)

Argyle's patriotism does not discourage domesticity, or lead to his rejection of hearth and home for the all-male camp, for the "flames" of liberty and honor will even "stoop to bless a child or wife" (10). The exemplary aristocrat, for Pope, is both a man of war and a paterfamilias; Rochester's reputation as a witty transgressor of social norms disqualifies him as a model for masculine conduct and poetic performance in the cultural environment of the mid-eighteenth century. Pope's verses briefly but pointedly allude to his predecessor's decline. Despite his boasted potency, the earl's lineage had become extinct and the symbols of his authority had been appropriated by others. With the death of Rochester's young son Charles in 1681, the Wilmot line ended; his title passed to Lawrence Hyde, and his estate eventually became the property of the Campbells. Moreover, Rochester's bed—which he once termed "loves Theatre" (in "Leave this gawdy guilded Stage")—is occupied by the deformed body of Pope, England's premier poet, who, sleeping alone, conceives an image of masculine perfection that negates the example of Rochester himself. Although numerous editions of Rochester's verse appeared in the early eighteenth century,[71] Pope in 1739 implied that Rochester's aura as the ideal combination of rank and wit had already faded: in his lines the patriot-warrior

Argyle supplants the promiscuous rake and the professional poet supplants the gentleman writer. The shift in sensibility that Pope's verses articulate, with their separation of status from occupation (or "holiday writers" from poets) and their emphasis on an exclusively heterosexual manhood, has its beginnings in Oldham's tentative challenge to aristocratic modes of literary production and the authorial personae that accompanied them.

Chapter Two

FROM THE STAGE TO THE CLOSET:
DRYDEN'S JOURNEY INTO PRINT, MANHOOD, AND POETIC AUTHORITY

> *The main interest in life and work is to become someone else that you were not in the beginning.*
> Michel Foucault, *Technologies of the Self* (1988)

On May 13, 1700, John Dryden's remains were interred in Westminster Abbey, and the mourners attending the funeral agreed that the event bordered on catastrophe. Dryden's admirer, Elizabeth Thomas, recorded the disrespectful treatment supposedly given to Dryden's corpse (she claims the body was left to rot when the Lord Jeffreys, son of the lord chief justice, reneged on his promise to pay for a lavish burial), while Tom Brown, a long-time antagonist of Dryden, described the scene of the internment with gleeful irreverence. Led by Jacob Tonson ("the Muses Midwife"), the "Rhyming Trade" and its motley attendants (fiddlers, cutpurses, whores, pimps, bullies, and beaux) accompanied the funeral procession with a cacophony of noise:

> With Tag Rag, Bob-Tail was the Room full fill'd,
> You'd think another *Babel* to be built;
> Not more Confusion at St. *Batt*'s fam'd Fair,
> Or at *Guild-Hall* at choice of a Lord Mayor.[1]

The "tuneful Rabble" paid its respects by sobbing, weeping, and falling down drunk. In a similar vein, Ned Ward's *London Spy* dutifully records the honor paid to Dryden by the "abundance of Quality in their Coaches"[2] at his burial, but employs his liveliest prose in describing the traffic jam and subsequent brawl occasioned by this entourage. Even a cooler observer like George Farquhar believed that "there was never such another burial seen."[3]

Farquhar, though, moves from description to analysis as he tries to locate the source of this confusion: "And so much for Mr. Dryden; whose burial was the same as his life, variety and not of a piece:—the quality and mob, farce and heroicks; the sublime and ridicule mix'd in a piece;—great Cleopatra in a hackney coach."[4] According to Farquhar, the former laureate himself was an amalgam of incongruous characteristics or ludicrously mixed categories: both the quality and the mob attended his plays; his battles with rival playwrights and opposing political parties contained elements of farce and heroism alike; his writings (as Dryden himself admitted) exhibited passages of rant and bombast along with passages of pathos and strength; and his cultural power as the reigning poet was compromised by his reputation for catering to the taste of an often undiscriminating audience. In Farquhar's phrase, these contradictions render Dryden not "of a piece": not a unified, stable self, but rather a hybrid of conflicting social distinctions and artistic conventions (high and low, poet and hack) whose clash is reflected in the carnival atmosphere of his burial.[5]

Dryden himself articulates these tensions throughout the body of his works. Studies of poets' careers often have made us accustomed to look for a coherence, a unity, or a plan that informs the lives of writers and gives a distinct direction to their work.[6] Yet as many of his contemporaries observed, Dryden's own career was shaped primarily by opportunity and exigency rather than a carefully considered purpose: as a consequence, his prologues and epilogues, poems, and criticism display a sense of the contradictions, or "variety," informing the poet's life. His work also reveals how he employed one such opportunity—the nascent commercial book trade, and the different modes of literary production, expression, and reception that it encouraged—in order to restore (or manufacture) a cohesive class and gender identity that he believed had been compromised by years of writing for the stage. I argue that Dryden's eventual rejection of the theater and growing involvement with print enabled him to distance himself from the carnival atmosphere of the playhouse and the ambiguous constructions of status and sexuality that it fostered, while securing an authoritative position as a professional writer within the emergent literary marketplace.

I

As a young playwright in Restoration London and a member of the landed gentry in Northamptonshire, Dryden may have had a vexed relationship to his craft almost from the start. James Winn traces Dryden's descent from two Puritan families (the Drydens and the Pickerings) who composed part of the squirearchy in Titchmarch, Northamptonshire, since the early sixteenth century.[7] Financial acumen and profitable marriages gradually increased their holdings (although they never yielded more than modest rents), and Dryden was most likely aware of himself as part of a family whose influence extended into the political and religious life of the countryside. In 1663 (the year his first play, *The Wild Gallant,* was staged) Dryden, at age 32, married Lady Elizabeth Howard, daughter of Thomas Howard, earl of Berkshire; the marriage extended his ties to the society of landed wealth and political power, for a number of his in-laws, who had supported the Crown in the Civil War, held significant offices in the state or at court.[8] These social advantages, however, did not always work in favor of Dryden's literary ambitions. The intellectual diversity of Dryden's Puritan background and education might have legitimated his desire to pursue a career in poetry, since Puritan suspicion of visual art did not extend to a condemnation of literature.[9] Yet the dominant model of masculine behavior for Dryden's social class made him acutely self-conscious, even anxious, about his employment in writing verse. For instance, several of Dryden's early works note that serious attention to poetry—the kind of application essential for authors by profession—is incompatible with the responsibilities of adulthood, a conflict particular to men of good family who were expected to exercise the privilege of their station and exert their influence in the world of public affairs. In his verses "To My Lord Chancellor" (1662), Dryden describes the earl of Clarendon as having forsaken the muses—the "Mistresses" whose frivolity he enjoyed in his youth—in favor of duties and concerns crucial to the management of the state.[10] Similarly, Dryden's dedication of *The Rival Ladies* (1664) to the earl of Orrery observes that poetry serves only to fill the idle moments of gentlemen (the "*Muses* have seldome employed your Thoughts, but when some violent fit of the Gout has snatch'd you from Affairs of State" [*Works,* 8: 96]), and, in addressing his patron (Charles Sackville, Lord Buckhurst) before the "Essay of Dramatick Poesie" (1668), Dryden declares verse-writing a task suitable for immature men, "before [they] enter into the serious and more unpleasant business of the world" (*Works,* 17:4). In acknowledging poetry's subordination to such business, Dryden places himself in a role that highlights his patrons' authority but diminishes his own: he continues to pursue for pay an occupation that men of the ruling orders are supposed to abandon after their first youth.

Yet if Dryden could not justify his verse as a form of work appropriate

for men of his background, neither could he excuse it as a form of play.
Contemporaries of Dryden were quick to censure his writing for pay and
saw in the labor he spent upon his poetry the debasement of an upper-class
pastime. Despite his class status, Dryden drew his income almost exclusively
from the profits that his writing brought to him, and his critics charged that
this dependence detracted from the quality of his work. Edmund Hickeringhill, for instance, censures Dryden for making poetry a *"poor dull Trade"*
rather than allowing it to remain an expression of aristocratic *jeu d'esprit*,
and implicitly links Dryden's commercial interest in verse to his sexual
tameness: *"Poetry* (like a *Miss*) is pleasant and *delicious now*, and *then*, (in
some *mens wanton* Fancy) but as *nauseous as a Wife* (is to their liquorish
Humours) *when* made a practice, a Trade, and of *constant use.*"[11] The earl of
Rochester, Dryden's former patron, satirizes the poet in the same terms;
while acknowledging Dryden's great talent ("Nor dare I from his Sacred
Temples teare,/That Lawrell, which he best deserves to weare"),[12]
Rochester condemns him for hasty composition ("Five Hundred Verses,
ev'ry Morning writ" [93]), and, most explicitly, for venturing to imitate the
libertine behavior of his betters:

> Dryden, in vaine, try'd this nice way of Witt,
> For he, to be a tearing Blade thought fit,
> But when he wou'd be sharp, he still was blunt,
> To friske his frollique fancy, hed cry Cunt;
> Wou'd give the Ladyes, a dry Bawdy bob,
> And thus he got the name of Poet Squab. (71-76)

Annoyed by Dryden's pretensions to the risqué wit of aristocratic men,
Rochester describes the poet's inability to perform verbally as a type of
sexual inadequacy: Dryden's inarticulate profanity is an analogue for intercourse that provides no satisfaction for participants. The poet who writes
for a living—whose works are a form of economic production—cannot
be a "tearing Blade" in a linguistic or sexual sense, for engagement in labor
for profit (such as turning out 500 verses in a morning) is at odds with the
"Spirit, and grace" that characterize aristocratic ideals of masculine writing
and behavior. The ethos of leisure and nonproductivity seemed constitutive
of both elegant literature and virile sexuality even to professional writers.
Thomas Shadwell, for instance, satirizes Dryden as a "Heroick Clown" for
trying to imitate the expressions—and the vices—of the "best Company,"
or those courtiers higher in rank than a country gentleman like Dryden:

He boasts of Vice (which he did ne'r commit)
Calls himself *Whoremaster* and *Sodomite;*
Commends *Reeve's* Arse, and says she Buggers well,
And silly Lyes of vitious pranks does tell.[13]

Fornication and sodomy themselves are not the subject of Shadwell's attack here; rather, he resented Dryden's pretensions to the transgressive sexuality and fashionable wit of aristocrats. (The frolics of a "sprightly Horse," Shadwell notes, give pleasure to onlookers, while the frolics of a cow do not.) Writing years later, Samuel Johnson also pointed out the artificiality of Dryden's libertinism. In Johnson's view, Dryden falsified his temperament in order to adopt the manners of his superiors and ingratiate himself with them, since their approval secured his livelihood: "His works afford too many examples of dissolute licentiousness and abject adulation; but they were probably, like his merriment, artificial and constrained—the effects of study and meditation, and his trade rather than his pleasure" (*Lives,* 1:398). Shadwell and Johnson both see Dryden's "studious lewdness" and "laboured impiety"[14] as misguided, unsuccessful attempts at class-climbing whose clumsiness reveals the poet's humbler origins. As Michael McKeon claims, libertine same-sex behavior represents an assertion of class difference: unlike the drudgery of intercourse with women for the production of offspring, sodomy is "a supremely careless *otium* suitably accessory to the gentlemanly Horatian retreat whose central pleasure is to 'engender' not serviceable 'supplies' but insubstantial 'wit.'"[15] According to his critics, Dryden arrogantly overstepped the limitations of his class and aspired to the verse forms, social freedoms, and sexual license appropriate only to aristocrats and gentlemen who could afford to live for pleasure.

In his verse, Dryden also seemed to endorse this masculine ideal even while he acknowledged his distance from it. Dryden's prologue to his revision of *The Wild Gallant* (1667) mocks his own attempts at representing libertine conduct and notes that the relative tameness of his play arises from his ignorance of the town's license. Like "some raw Squire" unpracticed in anything but autoerotic sex, Dryden needs time to gain experience in an unfamiliar milieu before his play can meet the expectations of his audience: "Pray pardon him his want of wickedness:/He's towardly, and will come on apace" (*Works,* 8:6). Dryden's "Letter to Etherege" (1686) also associates writing with sexual assertiveness, and only gently satirizes the "noble Laziness of minde" exhibited by the aristocratic playwright.[16] The poem's conversational, teasing tone is set by its octosyllabic couplets, its absurd rhymes, and its description of Etherege's conduct as an envoy to the Diet at Ratisbon:

> You can be old in grave debate
> And young in Love's affaires of State
> And both to wives & Husbands show
> The vigour of a Plenipo. (*Works,* 3:224)

The Dutch court, with its eternal rounds of drinking and general dullness, provides little occasion for Etherege to display the abilities of an English gentleman: "For here you were his Excellence/For gaming, writing, speaking, keeping,/His Excellence for all, but sleeping" (*Works,* 3:225-26). Writing, like playing at dice, supporting a mistress, or engaging in public debate, is an activity that men of Etherege's class are expected to perform with some degree of competence. But, as Dryden observes, the lack of productivity characterizes upper-class writers, too, for sustained attention to their craft would signal a loss of leisure and a corresponding decline in social rank. Chiding Etherege for his laziness, Dryden requests that he finish his "Trifle call'd a play," even if its completion would compromise his status: "This Truly is a Degradation/But wou'd oblige the Crown & Nation" (*Works,* 3:226); to Etherege's supposed protests regarding his "high Degree," Dryden responds that other aristocrats have written plays, and obliquely derides their efforts ("And you whose Comique wit is ters all/Can hardly fall below [Buckingham's] Rehersall" [*Works,* 3:226]). Yet despite Dryden's mild contempt for the insouciance shown by his social superiors, he recognized the attractiveness and power of leisured men and at times tried to construct a literary persona like theirs. Writing to Etherege around this time, Dryden boasts that he is "gloriously lazy," only to receive a rebuke for affecting to rival the peer: "I cannot endure you shou'd arrogate a thing to yourself you have not the least pretence to. is it not enough that you excelle in so many eminent vertues, but you must be a putting in for a Vice which all the world knows is properly my province" (*Letters,* 28). Etherege's description of indolence as his "province"—a territory over which he has absolute and complete dominion—reinforces Dryden's exclusion from the kind of easy wit and cultural panache that aristocrats claim as their birthright. (Etherege admits that the portly Dryden can claim laziness of the body, but still insists that he has not "obtain'd the perfection" of Sir Charles Sedley, who has grown too lazy to have an erection [*Letters,* 29].)

Etherege's praise of Dryden's incessant "industry" and denial of Dryden's indolence put the poet in his place: his financial need to write for an audience—or, in Hickeringhill's terms, his need to remain eternally wedded to his muse—sets him apart from the libertines whose sexual and literary activities made them a hegemonic model of aristocratic manhood. Unable to emulate men of business like Clarendon, and men of pleasure like Rochester and Etherege—all of whom, in Dryden's own metaphor, used poetry as a mistress—Dryden, despite his attempts, could not identify with forms of masculine authority common to the upper classes or invoke the example of upper-class men to validate his work. Moreover, regardless of the prestige they carried, Dryden's court appointments did not raise him above commercial concerns. His posts as poet laureate (bestowed in 1668) and historiographer royal (bestowed in 1670) promised little security, for the exchequer's unpredictability often left Dryden's annual pension of 200 pounds (300 pounds after 1677) chronically in arrears; this gave the poet an "almost pathetic vulnerability" to patrons, and made him especially dependent upon stage profits.[17] Adding to this dependence was the uncertain value that printed plays held in the literary marketplace of the time. Julie Stone Peters observes that printed plays, unlike sermons or texts by classical writers, brought unreliable returns for playwrights and booksellers: "Because printed play texts were not used as scripts for actors, as performance aids (like our theatre programs), or as re-creations of the theatrical experience at home after the performance, there was little correlation between stage success and publication success."[18] Although collections of plays would later have copyrights of significant value—in 1767, a majority share in the copyright of Dryden's plays sold for 100 pounds[19]—Dryden and the playwrights of his time had to rely principally on performance for their income. The tensions between Dryden's attempts to preserve his status as a gentleman and his pursuit of a career as a professional poet are articulated in tropes of class and gender throughout his writing for the theater.

II

Initially, Dryden seems to have accepted his subjection to playhouse audiences. His epilogue to the first performance of *The Wild Gallant* (1663) allows that English gentlemen and ladies are the best judges of sense in drama ("For he ne'r thought a handsome Garb or Dress,/So great a Crime to make their Judgement less" [*Works*, 8:89]), and the preface to the *Indian Emperour* (1665) states that pleasing the people "ought to be the Poets aim, because Plays are made for their delight" (*Works*, 9:12). Yet after several more years of writing for the theater and constantly facing the challenge of attracting the attention of its audience, Dryden began to portray playwrights like himself as the sexual and literary drudges of a demanding public. In the prologue to *An Evening's Love* (1668), the poet, like a civil husband, must "write in pain" and "strain himself, in complaisance to you" (*Works*, 10:214); the audience, though, responds like frustrated wives by attending to different poets, or "fresh Gallant[s]," who, if not better at pleasing than Dryden, at least promise pleasures of a different variety. This subordination to others not only drains the poet's vitality ("Th' unhappy man, who once has trail'd a Pen,/Lives not to please himself but other men:/Is always drudging, wasts his Life and Blood"),[20] but also compromises his integrity and autonomy—qualities that were definitive of manhood for those in Dryden's social class.[21] The extent of this compromise is suggested in a prologue printed in *Examen Poeticum* (1693), where Dryden introduces a young poet about to lose his "Maidenhead":

> To both [sexes], he wou'd contribute some delight;
> A mere Poetical Hermaphrodite.
> Thus he's equipped, both to be woo'd, and woo;
> With *Arms* offensive, and defensive too;
> 'Tis hard, he thinks, if neither part will do. (*Poems and Fables*, 34-38)

The novice playwright takes on the character of a hermaphrodite because he provides titillating entertainment for both genders: in his active role, he figures as a sexual servant to the women and in his passive role, as a catamite to the men. In light of ongoing debates about the experience of theater, Dryden's contemporaries most likely would have seen the hermaphrodite as an ambiguous, if not disturbing, figure. As Laura Levine points out, for Renaissance antitheatrical writers, "the hermaphroditic actor, the boy with the properties of both sexes, becomes the embodiment of all that is frightening about the self," and his monstrosity lay in his seeming denial that men possess an essential, fixed nature and an inherent gender.[22] This concern over maintaining the boundaries of masculine identity permeated Dryden's culture as well, and surfaces in the ambivalent introduction of the novice playwright as if he were a young prostitute being presented by an experienced bawd: the young man's occupational use of his "parts"—his talents and his genitals—makes him an erotic object for both sexes and thus negates his claims to manhood.

Dryden's anxiety about the poet's equivocal status in his culture, and the sexual metaphors in which this anxiety finds expression, are fueled by his inability to control the response of the spectators in the theater, and by the power of that response to place him on a level with vulgar entertainers. After abjuring the reputation gained from comedy in his preface to *An Evening's Love* (published in 1671), Dryden registers his particular disgust with "low comedy" and his annoyance when audiences find amusement where he intends none:

> [I] am often vex'd to hear the people laugh, and clap, as they perpetually do, where I intended 'em no jest; while they let pass the better things without taking notice of them. Yet even this confirms me in my opinion of slighting popular applause, and of contemning that approbation which those very people give, equally with me, to the Zany of a Mountebank; or to the appearance of an Antick on the Theatre. (*Works*, 10: 202-03)

The leveling nature of applause alarmed Dryden, for it threatened the distinctions between the intellectual humor of his works and the physical humor of professional clowns. To the public at large, the pleasure he gave placed him in the same category as others who pleased with their bodies. While Dryden realized that the audience was the ultimate judge of his plays and understood that "moving laughter" or "raising concernments" in spectators had traditionally been the purpose of drama, he compares the spectators' preferences for low comedy to the "strange appetite" of pregnant women, which is "better satisfi'd sometimes with Loam, or with the Rinds of Trees, than with the wholesome nourishments of life" (*Works*, 10:203). By portraying audiences as women whose physiology renders them depraved in their tastes, Dryden argues for the need to master them rather than please them, curing their feminine distemper by subjecting them to the male poet's healthier imagination:

> The Poet is, then, to endeavour an absolute dominion over the minds of the Spectators: for, though our fancy will contribute to its own deceipt, yet a Writer ought to help its operation. And that the *Red Bull* [a popular theater in Clerkenwell known for unruly spectacles] has formerly done the same, is no more an Argument against our practice, than it would be for a Physician to forbear an approv'd medicine because a Mountebank has us'd it with success. (*Works*, 11:14)

Achieving dominion over the spectators, or regulating both their conduct and their judgment, appears especially difficult for a writer operating in a commercial context. Although his reliance upon stage profits freed Dryden from dependence upon individual patrons—and thus from the need to satisfy their particular aesthetic preferences—it left him subject to the "taste of the Town," or the preferences of elite spectators in the aggregate. Moreover, the very format of theatrical performances invited audience participation, including their vocal approval, criticisms, and interpretations of the play; as Baz Kershaw points out, "however hard the wedge of commodification is driven between producer and consumer in theatre, performance may always have the potential to turn audiences into collective co-producers. . . . Audiences of performance gain power (as a basis for authority) through *not* being [passive] consumers."[23] Dryden's initial strategy for asserting his own authority rested upon the principle of divide and conquer: he identified receptivity to his plays as integral to upper-class manhood, and encouraged men to display this identification by exercising their ideological hegemony and physical force over the weaker elements of the audience. According to Dryden, self-control and independent thought characterize gentlemen, and those spectators who adopt the manners of the irrational and the untamed degrade themselves to the level of women and the lower classes. For instance, Thersites in the epilogue to *Troilus and Cressida* (1679) complains that a "keeping Pit" of "Womens Cullyes" sits in judgment upon poets, and that the sexual infatuation of these men renders their comments nonsensical (*Works,* 13:354). While the harshness of Thersites's speech is in keeping with his misogyny in the play, Charles Blount, a young defender of Dryden in *Mr. Dreyden Vindicated* (1673), also compares theater critics (like the anonymous authors of *The Censure of the Rota*) to finicky, privileged women, and suggests that their demands to poets, whom they treat like "servants," border on absurdity: "The world is now so over-run with *Wits,* that *Poets* have as hard a Task as Women's Parsons or Taylors, not one in ten pleases. So numerous are the Criticks, so frequent is Wit, and so elevated are their Fancies, that as a *great Lady* did, they forget Common Notions, and cry to their servants, *Give me, give me, give me, I think ye call it a Pin.*"[24] In order to discipline these infantile "Pratlers in the Pit," Dryden's "Epilogue to the King and Queen . . . at the Opening of Their Theatre" (1683) offers "Some Laws for publick Welfare" (*Poems and Fables,* 3): the "Vizard Masque[s]," or prostitutes, for whose attention the gentlemen "pretend to Wit" are to be restrained by removal of their disguises, while the "Lacqueys" who attend them are to be silenced by their masters' humble request. Dryden's prologue to Thomas Southerne's *The Disappointment* (1684) similarly upbraids the gentlemen who "so shrewdly judge of Plays" (*Poems and Fables,* 2) by describing their passage through life as coddled children, drunken undergraduates, cullies of town sharpers, and, lastly, the enamoured fools of designing whores. Determined to practice lewdness in the theater's unfashionable "Middle Galleries," "The Doughty BULLIES enter Bloody Drunk,/Invade and grubbel one another's PUNK:/They Caterwaul, and make a dismal Rout" (*Poems and Fables*, 59–61), until the theater becomes bawdier than the conventicles of lower-class dissenters.[25]

Dryden's exhortations to audiences, as Peter Stallybrass and Allon White observe, construct an opposition between high and popular culture by demanding that those in attendance at the playhouse regulate their own behavior and tastes through exclusion: "What is new, and contrasts strongly with the Shakespearean stage, is the urgent attempt to expel the lower sort altogether from the scene of reception, to homogenize the audience by refining and domesticating its energy, sublimating its diverse physical pleasures into a purely contemplative force, replacing a dispersed, heterodox, noisy participation in the *event* of the theatre by silent specular intensity."[26] The "contemplative force" of reason, however, proved difficult to cultivate in the playhouse, for in Dryden's view, the very atmosphere of the theater compromised masculine judgment. His prologues and epilogues insist that the theater's public space is contaminated by desire: the presence of women (respectable and otherwise) encourages a kind of sexual frenzy, and the pre-coital mating ritual enacted by certain members of the audience includes the men's display of wit, often directed against the playwright and actors; moreover, the presence of servants and the lower classes allows for indiscriminate mingling and results in the confusion of hierarchies as they try to imitate their superiors' conduct. After the Revolution of 1688 had deprived Dryden of his laureate status and forced his return to the stage, his writing became increasingly pessimistic regarding the influence poets could wield over infatuated spectators. As he argues in the prologue to *Amphitryon* (1690), the spectators' distaste for correction of their faults robs the playwright (whose income depends upon their approval) of any authority over them:

> The lab'ring Bee, when his sharp Sting is gone,
> Forgets his Golden Work, and turns a Drone:
> Such is a Satyr, when you take away
> That Rage, in which his Noble Vigour lay.
> What gain you, by not suffering him to teize ye?
> He neither can offend you, now, nor please ye.
> The Honey-bag, and Venome, lay so near,
> That both, together, you resolv'd to tear;
> And lost your Pleasure, to secure your Fear.

How can he show his Manhood, if you bind him
To box, like Boys, with one Hand ty'd behind him? (*Works*, 15:227)

Pleasing an audience threatens the poet's masculinity, in fact emasculates him.[27] Deprived of the sting, venom, and blows that comprise a part of satire's arsenal, the poet finds himself reduced to helpless immaturity, for the power to hurt and inflict pain is integral to manhood as Dryden's culture defines it. The audience, figured here as female, also suffers from the poet's castration, since its pleasure depends upon his displaying a potent, productive imagination—or being dangerously fertile—in his attacks upon human vice and folly.

Another threat to the authority of professional writers, though, comes from the writers themselves or, more specifically, from their complicity with the wishes of theater audiences. In "Mac Flecknoe" (1682), Dryden's attack on Thomas Shadwell centers on the latter's supposedly polite and timid plays. Shadwell, "Mature in dullness" (*Works*, 2:54) but intellectually infantile (although in his mid-thirties, he is still a "hopefull boy"), inherits the "Realms of *Non-sense*" from his poetic father, Flecknoe. Shadwell's qualifications for the throne resemble those that were customarily seen as essential to femininity: "gentle," "inoffensive," "mild," and "peacefull," Shadwell's verses provoke smiles and sleep, but never "[i]n keen Iambicks" instill fear or reflection in their audiences (*Works*, 2:59). Flecknoe finally advises Shadwell to "Leave writing Plays," for they require a more masculine, acerbic wit that he possesses: his ineffectual pen cannot transfer his "gall" and "Venom" to their objects. Instead, anagrams, acrostics, and songs ("sing them to thy lute" [*Works*, 2:60]) are more appropriate to Shadwell's feminine genius and modest abilities. (Shadwell employs a similar vocabulary in his self-defense, stating that only "some Women, and some Men of Feminine understanding" dislike the comedy represented in his plays [*Works*, 2:305], and arguing that he, unlike Dryden, was proficient in aristocratic, "Gentleman-like Exercises" [*Works*, 2:316]). Even Shadwell's corpulent body reflects his impotence, and Dryden repeatedly uses the metaphor of pregnancy to describe Shadwell's creative process: "Swell'd with . . . Pride" and "big with Hymn," Shadwell seems to have a fertile imagination, but his "Pangs without birth, and fruitless Industry" (*Works*, 2:58) are a parody of female labor, and this biological analogue suggests Shadwell's ultimate failure as a writer. As Terry Castle notes, Dryden departs from his Renaissance forbears in transforming—and finally rejecting—the trope of childbirth to describe poetic creation, as he insists on the separation between feminine labor of the body and masculine labor of the mind.[28] But this ambivalence regarding the conventional birth motif arises not only from developments in critical theory, as Castle suggests; it also derives from the anxiety that professional writers faced regarding their subjection to audiences. Both Shadwell and Dryden validate their own work with reference to its masculine, gentlemanly character, and both project onto their rivals those traits and behaviors that signify subordination—in terms of class and gender—in their culture.

Despite these attempts to regulate the response of the theater audience, Dryden in the end acknowledged that the financial power of playgoers prevented him from exercising any degree of control over their preferences for entertainment. Dryden's verses "To Sir Godfrey Kneller" (1694) convey his pessimism over the inversion of conventional hierarchies—inversions that occur in a commercial society when the concept of money as a universal equivalent of exchange erodes the regard given to less quantifiable signifiers of worth, such as high birth or talent. Comparing kings with artists like himself and Kneller, Dryden implies that the kind of power that sovereigns, poets, and painters wield is circumscribed by their financial dependence: "But we who Life bestow, our selves must live;/Kings cannot Reign, unless their Subjects give./And they who pay the Taxes, bear the Rule" (*Works,* 4:466). Although they can bestow "Life," or fame, upon the subjects of their poems and paintings, Dryden and Kneller ultimately lack authority over those subjects; moreover, Dryden maintains that subordination to those who purchase their productions limits the potential of artists, and Dryden blames Kneller's milieu for constricting the painter's conception and execution of his work ("Thy Genius bounded by the Times like mine" [*Works,* 4:465]). Both men also face the necessity of relying upon inferior artistic forms to support themselves:

> For what a Song, or senceless Opera
> Is to the Living Labour of a Play;
> Or, what a Play to *Virgil's* Work wou'd be,
> Such is a single Piece to History. (*Works,* 4:466)

Confined to immortalizing his patrons on canvas, Kneller cannot turn his attention to the more prestigious genre of history painting; likewise, Dryden's obligation to entertain playhouse audiences prevents him from composing serious drama, and even more importantly, an epic that would rank him among the most renowned poets.

Written when Dryden was 63 years old and nearly at the end of his life and career, "To Sir Godfrey Kneller" conveys the poet's deep sense of disappointment and frustration. Up to this point, many of Dryden's writings, especially those for the theater, illustrate his conviction that while mastering his audience was impossible, providing it with the kind of pleasure it demanded was the equivalent of prostitution. For a gentleman of Dryden's background, the pursuit of a professional literary career conflicted with the achievement of the masculine social identity valued by the upper classes; as Dryden's prologues reveal, such a career required the playwright's subordination to a heterogeneous audience—a position that was incompatible with the exercise of his cultural authority. Dryden's attacks upon this audience, like his ridicule of Shadwell, his fellow professional, resonate with misogyny as he asserts his differences from the feminine and effeminate public and those artists who catered to its tastes. "To Sir Godfrey Kneller" indicates a kind of resignation to commercial concerns; Dryden seems certain that the lack of reliable patronage and dependence upon the favor of audiences would prevent him from writing the epic poem that might raise him above the need to court popular applause. Yet Dryden began his own Virgilian project (a translation of the *Pastorals, Georgics,* and *Aeneid*) in the same year in which he wrote the poem to Kneller, and his growing involvement with print culture, culminating in the Virgil translation, enabled him to end his career with the status he sought.

III

Dryden first articulated the advantages that print held for poets in the 1680s; by that time, two decades of writing for the stage had resulted in his production of 20 plays, four of them in collaboration with other playwrights. And throughout these years, Dryden's success on stage was mixed: *The Wild Gallant* (1663)—one of the first new plays to be performed in the recently reopened English theaters—proved a rather undistinguished start, but support from members of the court brought attention to *The Rival Ladies* (1664), *The Indian Queen* (1664), and *The Indian Emperour* (1665). The reception of these plays, together with that of his farce *Sir Martin Mar-All* (1667)— whose title role was acted by the popular James Nokes—enabled him to become the house playwright of the King's Company in 1668: he contracted to write three plays annually in return for a share in the company that, as Winn notes, might have given him a yearly income of more than 300 pounds. This contract, together with his appointment as laureate upon the death of William Davenant (1668), seemed to secure Dryden's status as a preeminent poet and guarantee him a genteel social standing.[29] Dryden's experimentation with heroic dramas like *Tyrannick Love* (1669) and *The Conquest of Granada* Parts I and II (1670-71), proved as successful as his comedies, and moreover allowed him to develop new thematic and formal elements in his work: *Conquest of Granada,* for instance, displays philosophical complexity, an intricate mixture of styles (epic, romance), and also some of the linguistic excess that, in Dryden's words, was "bad enough to please" theater audiences (*Works,* 14:100).

Yet even the triumphal performance of this play (which had "swept the stakes" [*Works,* 11: 18] of audience approval, if not critical acclaim) did not shield Dryden's reputation from attack. In response to Dryden's popularity, George Villiers, duke of Buckingham, staged *The Rehearsal:* this farce satirized Dryden as Mr. Bayes, a playwright made ridiculous by his pretensions to wit and genius, his emulation of polite behavior, and his bombastic heroic dramas. In addition to the embarrassment of having Buckingham's play performed by his own theatrical group, Dryden had to face the prospect of insolvency for the King's Company. Set in competition with the Duke's Company and its new theater in Dorset Garden, the King's Company struggled with the destruction by fire of their playhouse (the Theatre Royal) in 1672, and Dryden, a sharer the company's profits, had a considerable financial stake in its distress.[30] These difficulties curtailed Dryden's creative ambition as well. His hasty composition of *Amboyna* (1673) attempted to capitalize on English nationalism in the war against the Dutch, and served as propaganda for drawing in and satisfying patriotic spectators (he admitted to Lord Clifford that "[the play] will scarcely bear a serious perusal . . . the Subject barren, the Persons low, and the Writing not heightned with many laboured Scenes" [*Works,* 12:5]). A more formally and aesthetically ambitious piece, Dryden's *State of Innocence*—a rhymed opera based upon *Paradise Lost*—never made it to the stage, perhaps because of high production costs (instead, his company produced a French opera, *Ariane,* and the *Mock-Tempest* by Thomas Duffet). The inadequacy of audiences, and especially their inability to appreciate unconventional or challenging plays, became a leitmotif in Dryden's writings for the theater at this time. In the epilogue to *Aureng Zebe* (1675), Dryden complains about "Bold *Brittons,*" whose "Bear-garden" behavior betrays a lack of attention to serious drama ("*No Song! no Dance! no Show!* [the playwright] fears you'l say,/You love all naked Beauties, but a Play" [*Works,* 12:249]); turning his criticism upon female spectators, he explains that their promiscuous display of approval discourages excellence in writers:

Who would excel, when few can make a Test
Betwixt indiff'rent Writing and the best?
For Favours cheap and common, who wou'd strive,
Which, like abandon'd Prostitutes, you give? (*Works*, 12:250)

The prologue to *All for Love* (1677), however, also disparages more refined and discerning spectators: confronting the "Flocks of Critiques" hovering like vultures "gaping for the Carcass of a Play" (*Works*, 13:20), Dryden indicates his vulnerability in adopting blank verse:"[Our poet] gives himself for gone; y'have watch'd your time!/He fights this day unarm'd; without his Rhyme" (*Works*, 13:20). Among these critics was Rochester, who earlier had censured Dryden's assumed gentility in his "Allusion to Horace." In the preface to *All for Love*, Dryden strikes back, observing the "wretched affectation" that leads gentlemen to display their "triffling kind of Fancy" in verse; their attacks on professional writers arise out of envy and an inflated sense of their own literary talent: "the Rich are discontented, because the Poets will not admit them of their number. . . . [T]hey have much of the Poetry of *Maecenas*, but little of his liberality. They are for persecuting *Horace* and *Virgil*, in the persons of their Successors" (*Works*, 13:14-15; 16). When aristocrats like Rochester become ambitious for something more than fame as patrons and assume the roles of critic and poet, they forfeit the esteem and courtesy that class hierarchies give them and expose themselves to more democratic, less flattering estimations of their worth. Nonetheless, Rochester's social power allows him to punish Dryden in print for "daring to please without [his] leave" (*Works*, 13:15). But not only the direct hostility of his superiors affected Dryden's professional life. The earl of Danby's impeachment in 1679 left Dryden without a friend in the Treasury to insure prompt payment of his salary, and despite the encouraging reception given to *Oedipus* (1679), the confusion caused by revelations about the Popish Plot was, in Winn's words, "disastrous to the theatre"[31]: the King's Company in part disbanded, its theater closed, and Dryden, a shareholder, faced the "ruine" that had "o'erwhelm'd the Stage" ("Prologue to the University of Oxford" [1679], *Poems and Fables*, 2).

The volatile nature of Dryden's involvement with the theater—which included attacks from critics, unpredictable audience response, and damaging political developments—may have induced his turn toward the medium of print. And, as Winn observes, his preference for the text suggests the lingering influence of Dryden's Puritan upbringing, with its privileging of the word over the spectacle: although Dryden's poems reveal his deep appreciation of visual art, he "never doubted the priority of the art of words, and his witty assertions of poetry's precedence over the other arts betray curious similarities to Puritan polemic."[32] Dryden's later writings show a suspicion of the visual that is rooted in conventional dichotomies between the senses and the intellect. In the dedication to *The Spanish Fryar* (1681), Dryden juxtaposes the experience of viewing a play to reading it, and clearly endorses the latter. Declaring that his "Reverence" for his audience will not permit him to "put a loose indigested Play upon the Publick," Dryden insists that the response of readers, not spectators, matters most to him: "For though it should be taken, (as it is too often on the Stage,) yet it will be found in the second telling: And a judicious Reader will discover in his Closset that trashy stuffe, whose glittering deceiv'd him in the action" (*Works*, 14:99-100). Throughout this prologue, Dryden separates the intellectual qualities of judgment and reflection from the visual seductions of the playhouse. Audiences are lured into an absence of mind by the drama's appeals to their senses, and this sensual abandonment encourages their approval of an unworthy object:

> In a Play-house every thing contributes to impose upon the Judgment; the Lights, the Scenes, the Habits, and, above all, the Grace of Action, which is commonly the best where there is the most need of it, surprize the Audience, and cast a mist upon their Understandings; not unlike the cunning of a Juggler, who is always staring us in the face, and overwhelming us with gibberish, onely that he may gain the opportunity of making the cleaner conveyance of his Trick. But these false Beauties of the Stage are no more lasting than a Rainbow; when the Actor ceases to shine upon them, when he guilds them no longer with his reflection, they vanish in a twinkling. (*Works*, 14: 100)

In Dryden's description, the actors appear as tricksters, while the plays— including some of his own, which he terms "Dalilahs of the Theatre"— take on the qualities of whores. The tropes of madness ("nothing but Madness can please Mad men" [*Works*, 14:102]), deceit, and illicit sexuality characterize the performance of drama, and although Dryden's "Profit" depends upon this performance, he emphasizes his preference for an audience of readers, whose isolation from the glitter of the theater insures their intellectual engagement with the play and critical appraisal of it:"As 'tis my Interest to please my Audience, so 'tis my Ambition to be read; that I am sure is the more lasting and the nobler Design: for the propriety of thoughts and words, which are the hidden beauties of a Play, are but confus'dly judg'd in the vehemence of Action: All things are there beheld, as in a hasty motion, where the objects onely glide before the Eye and disappear" (Works, 14:102).[33] Instead of being dazzled by the "false Beauties" of the drama on stage, the reader in his closet can uncover and scrutinize a play's "hidden beauties"; in other words, the transition from performance to print renders the object of attention subordinate to the audience's surveillance and penetrating analysis.

Dryden's reference to "false Beauties," though, may have had a more flesh-and-blood object. His prologues and epilogues indicate a recurrent fear that the actresses involved in stage productions of his plays undermined the spectators' concentration on the poetry of the lines they spoke. And his complaints did have some basis in fact: among those actresses whose performances captivated male attention were Nell Gwyn, who played Florimell in Secret Love and Valeria in Tryannic Love, and was the mistress of Charles II; Elizabeth Barry, who played Queen Leonora in The Spanish Fryar, and was the mistress of Rochester; and Anne Reeves, who played Esperanza in The Conquest of Granada, Philotis in Marriage A-la-Mode, and Ascanio in The Assignation, and was the mistress of Dryden himself. In the "Epilogue to the King and Queen" that celebrated the union of the King's and Duke's companies in 1682, Dryden implores men in the audience to cease their sexual pursuit of the actresses:

> We beg you last, our Scene-room to forbear,
> And leave our Goods and Chattels to our Care:
> Alas, our Women are but washy Toys,
> And wholly taken up in Stage employs:
> Poor willing Tits they are: but yet I doubt
> This double Duty soon will wear 'em out. (Poems and Fables, 35-40)

Spoken by the actor Thomas Betterton, these lines insist upon the actresses' status as property of the theatrical company ("Goods and Chattels") but also mention their status as professionals dedicated to their craft ("wholly taken up in Stage employs"); although not above servicing the men in the audience, the "Poor willing Tits" are obliged to perform a different "Duty" for their living.[34] Here Dryden displays a sense of actresses' ambivalent cultural position as well as anxiety over how that position affects the reception of his plays: as Deborah C. Payne notes, if their objectification on stage diminished actresses, "in a public sphere with an increasingly pronounced sense of the visual, objectification simultaneously amplified actresses, situating them at the new nexus of power."[35] Such "glittering" might very well obscure the play itself: on stage, actresses mediate between the text and the audience, and have the ability to focus attention exclusively upon themselves, both as sexual objects and as skilled performers. But the threat that the drama will mislead spectators' judgment with lights, scenery, costumes, and actresses disappears when the play becomes a text, for, as Walter J. Ong observes, writing and print exclude "extraneous" materials: "By isolating thought on a written surface, detached from any interlocutor . . . writing presents utterance and thought as uninvolved with all else, somehow self-contained, complete. Print in the same way situates utterance and thought on a surface disengaged from everything else, but it also goes farther in suggesting self-containment."[36] Removed from their delusory settings, "Dalilahs of the Theatre" lose their power over the reader, particularly the masculine "Reader . . . in his Closset," who, alone with the texts, is able to assess their value more dispassionately—and accurately.

This self-containment of the text also implies the self-containment of the playwright: the "nobler Design" of writing for readers insulates Dryden from the demands of the women and effeminate men who, he claims, comprise the theater audience, and rescues him from having to supply satisfaction to that audience. Moreover, the circulation and sale of printed plays enable Dryden to retain his integrity and fully exercise his poetic talent, which the short attention span of spectators prohibits. Forced to return to the stage "against his will" after the Glorious Revolution of 1688 deprived him of his laureate pension, Dryden argues that the performance of *Don Sebastian* (1690) cannot do justice to the "masculine vigour" of the play: "There is a vast difference betwixt a publick entertainment on the Theatre, and a private reading in the Closet . . . [the reader can] find out those beauties of propriety, in thought and writing, which escap'd him in the tumult and hurry of representing" (*Works*, 15:66). According to Dryden, "publick entertainment" necessarily obscures the poet's skills, for a play requires fast-paced action in order to please an undiscriminating audience. By contrast, readers—characterized here as males with sufficient wealth to insure privacy and sufficient leisure and education to read—have the capacity to evaluate and appreciate the poet's work. The silent closet, then, is the only place where poetry truly can be heard.

Dryden elaborates on this opposition between masculine readers and feminine spectators, the closet and the stage, in a poem written to Thomas Southerne consoling him for the failure of his comedy, *The Wives Excuse* (1692). According to Dryden, the play owed its poor reception to the popularity of farces, which have usurped the stage with "Buffoonry"; given this situation, Southerne must turn his expectations to print culture, for readers will allow him the praise that spectators denied him: "The Hearers may for want of *Nokes* repine,/But rest secure, the Readers will be thine" (*Works*,

3:227). Besides the privileging of readers over hearers, Dryden elevates the play as text over the play as performance. Advising Southerne to adopt the style of Etherege and the wit of Wycherley, Dryden envisions Southerne's future plays as a printed archive for study by the next generation of playwrights: "Learn after both, to draw some just Design,/And the next Age will learn to Copy thine" (*Works,* 3:228). Here Dryden characterizes print as a preferable alternative to the playhouse, an alternative that his own poem was written specifically to endorse, for he composed the lines to Southerne in order to assist the bookseller's marketing of *The Wives Excuse.*[37]

Addressing another playwright in "To my Dear Friend Mr. Congreve" (1694), Dryden again takes as his theme the distinctions between printed poetry and drama. Published in part to bolster Congreve's reputation after the disappointing public response to his *Double Dealer,* the verses portray Congreve as the single poet who successfully joins the masculine vigor of his Renaissance forbears to the feminine sweetness of his contemporaries. Although Charles II had "Tam'd us to manners, when the Stage was rude" (*Works,* 4:432) by introducing politeness or art to the native tradition of "boistrous *English* Wit," this refinement involved a loss of strength (an idea Dryden stresses repeatedly in the poem's first part). Congreve, though, combines genius with cultivation; in an architectural metaphor, Dryden describes him as uniting solidity with beauty to improve the structure of English verse: "Firm *Dorique* Pillars found Your solid Base:/The fair *Corinthian* crowns the higher Space;/Thus all below is Strength, and all above is Grace" (*Works,* 4:432). Dryden's praise assumes an even more gendered expression when he places Congreve at the head of the pantheon of English playwrights: Congreve combines the force, judgment, satire, and wit associated with the "Study" to the courtship, "easie Dialogue," and emotive force associated with the "Stage."[38] According to Dryden, Congreve's abilities allow him to excel at drama in its oral and written forms, for he satisfies readers in the study with his judicious "masculine" art and pleases spectators in the theater with his lively "feminine" entertainment. This unique fusion of qualities even allows Congreve to invert the traditional hierarchies within the system of masculine power; although still a "blooming Youth," he is preferred above his older contemporaries who recognize his achievements and submit to his authority ("Thus old *Romano* bow'd to *Raphael's* Fame;/And scholar to the Youth he taught, became" [*Works,* 4:433]).

"To Congreve" exhibits a subtle rhetorical move on Dryden's part: he portrays the disruptive demands of the female (and feminized) theater audience—their demands for polite ease in dialogue and action—as qualities inherent in the poet. That is, Congreve's "sweetness" and "ease" are not a response to the ladies' preferences in drama, but rather derive from internal attributes that find expression in poetic discourse; although the female body is banished as an influence on the poet, its traits are appropriated. Later in his career, Congreve followed Dryden's suggestion and carefully fashioned his plays to suit both reading and theater audiences. In fact, unlike Dryden, he fully recognized the cultural and economic possibilities that print held for playwrights: working closely with his bookseller, Jacob Tonson, and his printer, John Watts, on editions of his *Works,* Congreve took advantage of the medium of print to emphasize his plays' status as significant and important texts—artifacts to be reviewed and studied repeatedly—rather than their function as guides for theatrical performances.[39] By contrast, although the seventeenth-century bookseller Henry Herringman printed (and reprinted) many of Dryden's plays, neither he nor Dryden constructed a visual format for these plays that would suggest their relation to elite literature instead of popular entertainment.[40]

IV

Although Dryden did not use the medium of print to transform his plays into "Works," his growing recognition of print's effect on the cultural status of poets appears throughout his final major project. Begun in 1694— shortly after Dryden composed his poems to Southerne, Congreve, and Kneller—the translation of Virgil initiated Dryden's most sustained discussions of the book's superiority to the stage. In the dedication of the *Aeneid* to the marquis of Normandy, Dryden maintains that "a heroick Poem, truly such, is undoubtedly the greatest Work which the Soul of Man is capable to perform" (*Works,* 5:267); he goes on to illustrate this by observing Virgil's importance as a counselor to Augustus and his politic yet forthright behavior in that role: "He managed both the Prince and People, so as to displease neither, and to do good to both, which is the part of a Wise and an Honest Man: And it proves that it is possible for a Courtier not to be a Knave" (*Works,* 5:283). The implicit comparison between Augustus, who accepted the counsel of his poet, and William III, whose accession to the throne led to Dryden's replacement by Shadwell as laureate, highlights the degeneracy of an ideal relationship, but celebrates the relationship itself. Besides arguing for the usefulness of the epic poet in shaping the policies of the Roman state, Dryden maintains that the didactic purpose of the epic ("to form the Mind to Heroick Virtue by Example" [*Works,* 5:267]) and the unity of action that accompanies this purpose free it from the heterogeneous, mixed style and meandering digressions of lesser verse—features that Dryden associates with novels, and thus effeminacy:

> Even the least portions of [these poems] must be of the Epick kind; all things must be Grave, Majestical, and Sublime: Nothing of a Foreign Nature, like the trifling Novels, which *Ariosto* and others have inserted in their Poems: By which the Reader is miss-led into another sort of Pleasure, opposite to that which is design'd in an Epick Poem. One raises the Soul and hardens it to Virtue, the other softens it again and unbends it into Vice. One conduces to the Poet's aim, the compleating of his Work; which he is driving on, labouring and hast'ning in every Line: the other slackens his pace, diverts him from his Way, and locks him up like a Knight Errant in an Enchanted Castle, when he should be pursuing his first Adventure. (*Works*, 5:267)

The influence of novels and romances (with their feminine, or digressive, literary structure) undermines the linearity of the epic, imprisoning both the poet and the reader within the meanderings of the narrative itself rather than leading them directly to the moral. Dryden finds these "Foreign" (and, given the reference to Ariosto, presumably Italian) diversions suspect, for their laxity of purpose seduces readers into vice—here unspecified, but perhaps sexual—and betrays the heroic virtues associated with self-contained, purposeful, British masculinity.[41]

As a genre, drama (both tragedy and comedy) also proves inferior to the epic, since plays deceive audiences into approving of language and actions that they later reject in the sobriety of the reading experience. After briefly acknowledging that drama may instruct on the stage as well as in the closet, Dryden complains that most plays ultimately disappoint their booksellers financially and their readers aesthetically: "Your Lordship knows some Modern Tragedies which are beautiful on the Stage, and yet I am confident you wou'd not read them. *Tryphon* the Stationer complains they are seldom ask'd for in his Shop. The Poet who Flourish'd in the Scene, is damn'd in the *Ruelle;* nay more, he is not esteem'd a good Poet by those who see and hear his Extravagancies with delight" (*Works*, 5:272). When represented by actors, drama may appear lovely, but readers in the quiet of their chambers recognize the deformity in contemporary plays. Here Dryden, borrowing an image from Horace in "Ars Poetica," criticizes modern tragedies as both puerile and feminine, for their sentiments are immature and undeveloped, and their beauty cannot conceal their monstrous nature: "They are a sort of

stately Fustian, and lofty Childishness. Nothing but Nature can give a sincere pleasure; where that is not imitated, 'tis Grotesque Painting, the fine
Woman ends in a Fishes Tail" (*Works*, 5:272-73).[42] Similarly misogynistic is
Dryden's assertion that the stage (which he characterizes as female) is an
unsuitable and insufficient medium for portraying masculine potency:
whereas the epic can celebrate martial vigor (which appears as "real Beauties in the reading"), "the prowess of *Achilles* or *Aeneas* wou'd appear
ridiculous in our Dwarf-Heroes of the Theatre. We can believe they routed
Armies in *Homer* or in *Virgil*, but *ne Hercules contra duos* in the Drama"
(*Works*, 5:273). Plays, it seems, cut epic heroes down to size by representing
them in the shape of actors; the exaggerations of heroic masculinity are
brought into relief on stage, and Dryden resents this subversion of the
myth of male power.[43]

Dryden's argument in favor of the epic poem in print finally includes
the influence it gives him over the reading public. Even in his very last
plays, Dryden inveighed against the lack of discrimination among theater
audiences. His preface to *Don Sebastian* (1689) complains that his revisions
of the play, which were made to accommodate the attention span of bored
and restless theatergoers, resulted in the drama's loss of "masculine vigour";
his "loathing" of the stage would have kept him from the theater altogether
if his "misfortunes"—his loss of his position as laureate—had not "con-
demn'd [him] to dig in those exhausted Mines" of play-writing (*Works*,
15:66). By contrast, as the translator of Virgil, Dryden expressed confidence in his ability to reach an appreciative public—a public comprised of
educated men. As he admits to Normanby in his dedication of the *Aeneid*,
his "chief Ambition is to please those Readers, who have discernment
enough to prefer *Virgil* before any other Poet in the *Latine* Tongue" (*Works*,
5:326). Dryden then goes on to classify readers according to their intellectual maturity, which he describes in terms of class-based manners. At the
bottom level are "Mobb-Readers" who resemble the "Upper-Gallery
Audience in a Play-House" and who "preferr a Quibble, a Conceit, an Epi-
gram, before solid Sense, and Elegant Expression" (*Works*, 5:326). Comparing this segment of the audience to the politically disenfranchised (the
"Mobb" and immigrants) and the culturally illiterate (the upper gallery of
the playhouse), Dryden disqualifies them from having a voice in determining literary merit: "They are but a sort of *French Hugonots*, or *Dutch Boors*,
brought over in Herds, but not Naturaliz'd: who have not Land of two
Pounds *per Annum* in *Parnassus*, and therefore are not priviledg'd to Poll"
(*Works*, 5:326-27). The trope of polling here suggests that women made up
no part of the reading audience, and this suggestion carries over into Dry-

den's description of the "middle sort of Readers": "A Company of warm young Men, who are not yet arriv'd so far as to discern the difference betwixt Fustian, or ostentatious Sentences, and the true sublime" (*Works* 5:327). These gentleman readers, Dryden implies, will gradually grow out of their bad taste; although "miss-led by their Pedagogue at School, their Tutor at the University, or their Governour in their Travels" (*Works*, 5:327), they will mature beyond the influence of their social inferiors and will improve their aesthetic sense as they develop into manhood and achieve full autonomy. Following Virgil's example, however, Dryden chooses only to please the "most Judicious" audience—a few "Souls of the highest Rank, and truest Understanding" (*Works*, 5:328). This exclusive group, in Dryden's Catholic metaphor, serves as the supreme arbiter of literary merit; the readers' "Magnetism" attracts followers, and "Every day they gain some new Proselyte, and in time become the Church" (*Works*, 5:328).

In these passages, Dryden creates hierarchies of readers based upon the duality of body and soul: members of his audience range from the rabble, mired in their offensive physicality; to poorly trained gentlemen, whose class status insures the eventual growth of their mental faculties; to those with sensibilities so refined that they have shed the body altogether and have become purely spiritual. The act of reading itself, especially its repetitive quality, helps produce this refinement. By making comparisons and distinctions among texts (which, unlike performances, can become the objects of endless reference), readers "improve their Stock of Sense" and eventually shun writers whose books do not reward the expense of time spent upon them. Print and the kind of close scrutiny that it enables also give Dryden's translation a power over the audience that his plays could not exercise on stage; as Dryden notes, "the more [the reader] studies it, the more it grows upon him; every time he takes it up, he discovers some new Graces in it" (*Works*, 5:328). The calm, reflective response of the reader (who is gendered male in this passage) allows the poet a kind of influence prohibited by the boisterous, sexually charged reactions of female-dominated theater audiences.

For Dryden, appealing to the sympathetic male reader was not just a flight of rhetoric or a reference to Milton's invocation of a "fit audience . . . though few." Dryden clearly recognized how print could affect the experience of poetry, and in the Virgil project used the commercial book trade to exert control over the reception of his work. Although Samuel Johnson later commented on the contrast between Dryden's courtly manners and Jacob Tonson's businesslike brusqueness ("To the mercantile ruggedness of that race [booksellers] the delicacy of the poet was sometimes exposed" [*Lives*, 3:407]), Dryden himself used the opportunity conferred by his alliance with Tonson to enlarge, and make distinctions among, his readership. The four volumes of *Miscellany Poems* that he had produced along with Tonson beginning in 1684 proved that an audience of subscribers would support collections of verse, and the success of that venture indicated a source of income for poets that was independent of stage profits and the patronage of theatergoers. Dryden's *Virgil*, though, raised even broader implications for poetic careers, for it was the first highly successful literary project to be completely financed by its sale to readers.

The terms of the contract between Dryden and Tonson reveal the extent to which the Virgil project inaugurated a significant new direction in the commercial production of texts, and articulated a new set of social relationships to accompany this change. This contract (signed 15 June 1694) helps define the modern concept of authorship, for it provides a clear outline of the text's function as a commodity, and suggests how this change in the status of the text would affect the writer's relation to his work and to his reading audience. The contract begins with Dryden's agreement to translate Virgil's works and prepare them for press "with all the Convenient Speed" (*Works*, 6:1179); since Tonson invested a great deal of capital in the venture, he insisted upon a timely return of his money, and Dryden's creative process, whether fast or slow, could not interfere with Tonson's need for a profit. Moreover, Dryden's creative output—his freedom to write what and when he chose—was also curtailed by the requirements of the publisher. "For the more Speedily finishing of the Translation," Dryden agreed not to "write translate or publish or assist in the writing translating or publishing of any other book or thing to be printed"; the allowable exceptions included his translation of Du Fresnoy's *De Arte Graphica*, his assistance with his son John's play, and "any New Originall Poem or book of Prose" . . . not to exceed the price of one Shilling" (*Works*, 6:1179). This clause, which was clearly intended to discourage Dryden from writing anything but the *Virgil*, suggests that both author and bookseller conceived of Dryden's verse in terms of its exchange value and believed that value to be relatively high (the 200 pounds of copy money that Tonson gave Dryden for the translation also confirms the commodity status of his verse). In regulating Dryden's poetic output, Tonson not only attempted to secure the returns on his investment, but also forced the poet to adopt a work discipline previously foreign to him. The supposed subjection of the poet to the man of business signaled

an end to the genteel pretensions that the poet's education and attachment
to patrons of wealth, power, and royal blood had given him. Even Johnson,
despite his professed admiration of booksellers, records with displeasure an
incident relating Tonson's behavior toward Dryden:

> Lord Bolingbroke, who in his youth had cultivated poetry, related to Dr.
> King of Oxford that one day when he visited Dryden, they heard, as they
> were conversing, another person entering the house. "This," said Dryden, "is
> Tonson. You will take care not to depart before he goes away, for I have not
> completed the sheet which I promised him, and if you leave me unpro-
> tected, I must suffer all the rudeness to which his resentment can prompt his
> tongue" (*Lives*, 3:407).[44]

But if Dryden's negotiations with Tonson resulted in the poet's subordination to the requirements of capitalist business practices, they also granted
him increased freedom from the demands of consumers. In contrast to his
plays performed on the stage, the text of the *Virgil* and the conditions of its
commercial sale liberated Dryden from the requirements of pleasing a heterogeneous public and provided him with increased control over his work
and its reception. An item in the contract specifies that the translation's success was not dependent upon the approval of a mass audience: this provision
allowed Dryden to cancel the publication of his work if Tonson could not
procure at least 100 subscribers to the five-guinea edition of the text. In
addition to guaranteeing Dryden all of the profits from this expensive subscription, the contract did not require him to depend upon the reading
public at large for his income. Instead, the elite subscribers—whose "Name
Title & Coat of Armes" were engraved at the bottom of each illustration of
the text—acted as collective patrons for Dryden, and allowed him to address
his work to those gentlemen (and perhaps gentlewomen) who comprised
his most socially-prominent readers.[45] Money collected from the less aristocratic two-guinea subscribers went to Dryden as well, although he had to
pay Tonson a fee for these volumes. Tonson alone received the profits from
the trade edition sold to the general public, but the contract stipulated that
these volumes for commercial sale should not undermine distinctions of
class and wealth. Although anyone with money could purchase the translation, the subscribers' copies boasted an elegant appearance, and the contract
allowed Dryden to advertise this difference by "giv[ing] publick notice that
none but the Subscribers can have books of the fine paper" (*Works*, 6:1182).
Finally, the marketing of the *Virgil* enabled Dryden to distinguish model

readers. Freed from having to solicit the wealthy or politically powerful to support his translation, the poet himself carefully chose the men to whom he dedicated sections of the project; rejecting William III, he selected Lord Clifford for the *Pastorals*, the earl of Chesterfield for the *Georgics*, and the marquis of Normanby for the *Aeneid*. All of these choices emphasize Dryden's independence from the political culture of his day, for they reflect his own long-standing loyalties to particular families, his Jacobite allegiances, and his Catholic faith. And the rhetoric accompanying these dedications indicates the sense of autonomy and authority that the printed commodity made possible for Dryden: as he declared to Chesterfield, "the greatest value, I can put upon my selfe is your favourable opinion of my Verses. I am glad that they have pleas'd the World; but I am proud that they have pleas'd your Lordship" (*Letters*, 90). For the first time in his long career, he was able to forget the temper of the playhouse, and earn a large financial profit while writing for those gentlemen readers whom he esteemed the best judges of his work.

Together, Dryden and Tonson managed the Virgil translation so dexterously that it fulfilled both aspects of the commodity form: its economic value as an item for sale was secured by appeals to the broadest possible consumer audience, and its symbolic value as a literary classic was enhanced by its careful marketing to elite purchasers. By preferring print to the stage, Dryden more actively assisted in commodifying his work, and in doing so, gained a greater degree of influence over its production and reception. The translation's commercial and critical success also redefined Dryden's status as a professional poet; readers' verse and prose responses to the *Virgil* characterize the poet not as a hopelessly bourgeois wit or a sexual servant to the public at large, but as a patriarch whose talent secures his place on the hierarchies of class and gender. For instance, Bolingbroke's praise of Dryden's translation suggests that literary authority and sexual potency arise not from social rank, but from imaginative power. In a metaphor that recalls David (and Charles II) in *Absalom and Achitophel*, Bolingbroke describes Dryden as "Wit's Universal Monarch" whose "Mighty Sway" secures "ev'ry Muse and ev'ry Grace." Instead of remaining, like his predecessors, confined to one "Poetick Wife" (who, growing "stale," would dampen his "appetite," "Fancy," and "Fire"), Dryden enjoys a creative promiscuity with all of the muses:

> To none confin'd, by turns you all enjoy,
> Sated with this, you to another flye:
> So *Sultan*-like in your *Seraglio* stand,

> While wishing Muses wait for your Command:
> Thus no decay, no want of vigour find,
> Sublime your Fancy, boundless is your Mind. (*Works*, 6:61-62)

Dryden's absolute dominion over all types of poetry is figured in political and sexual terms: to Bolingbroke, the range of talent in the poet's translation shows that he possesses the kind of aristocratic prowess in wit and in
seduction that critics like Rochester earlier had censured him for trying to
emulate. And not only male writers used this trope of the poet as successful rake to describe Dryden's accomplishments: in a collection of elegiac
verse organized by Delariviere Manley—*The Nine Muses, or, Poems Written
by Nine Several Ladies Upon the Death of the late Famous John Dryden, Esq.*
(London, 1700)—the female contributors, each representing a muse,
repeatedly employ metaphors linking Dryden's sexual and literary performance. Calliope (Catharine Trotter Cockburn), "The Heroick Muse,"
describes how she and her sisters fell under Dryden's erotic spell and vied
for his attention: "He charm'd us to his Will, each strove which best/Our
Votary cou'd inspire, he all address'd" (15). Even more explicitly, Erato
(Sarah Fyge Egerton), "The Amorous Muse," terms herself a "deserted
Maid" at Dryden's loss (7), while Polimnia (unidentified), the muse "Of
Rhetorick," fondly remembers surrendering herself to his desires: "With
Lovers hands, I lavisht all my Charms,/Gave up my self, to his more Lovely
Arms" (11). Although this language of praise is still primarily physical, the
grotesque body represented in earlier satires against Dryden, with their ref-
erences to him as an unmannerly clown, a frisking cow, or an impotent
"Poet Squab," is replaced by popular insistence on his seductive literary
power and irresistible masculine charm.[46]

In order to sustain the connection between virility and literary talent—
a combination formerly invoked to describe aristocratic wit—admirers of
the Virgil translation either discounted Dryden's aging body and emphasized the brisk qualities of his youthful mind or, more commonly, conflated
his physical and mental state. Charles Brome, for instance, insists that Dryden's advanced years had no harmful effect on his literary (and sexual) performance: like the "Patriarch of old," the poet boasted an "inexhausted
Force" that insured the beauty of his latest production: "This son of *Sixty
Nine* surpassing fair,/With any elder Offspring may compare."[47] Likewise,
Samuel Garth, who was frequently named as a suitable "successor" to Dryden, claimed that Dryden's body and mind suffered no decline in potency
over the years: "As his earlier Works wanted no Maturity; so his latter
wanted no Force, or Spirit. The falling off of his Hair, had no other Con-

sequence, than to make his Lawrels be seen the more."[48] The metaphor of aristocratic and patriarchal dominance requires assertion of Dryden's erotic as well as creative powers, and this tie between literary authority and virility colors discussions of Dryden's works over a century after his death. Writing to George Ellis concerning plans for his own edition of Dryden, Walter Scott declares his abhorrence at sanitizing the text "for the use of boarding schools and colleges": "I will not castrate John Dryden. I would as soon castrate my own father."[49] For Scott, such mutilation of the text is equivalent to the mutilation of Dryden's genitals; a "complete edition" of the poet requires retention of those parts that, although offensive to the sight, guarantee his masculinity. Scott, however, changed his mind with regard to Dryden's translations of Lucretius and Ovid: "What to make of them I know not; but I fear that, without absolutely gelding the bard, it will be indispensible to circumcise him a little by leaving out some of the most obnoxious lines" (*Memoirs*, 1:475).

In applying images of aristocratic patriarchy to a professional poet, these critics reveal the extent to which Dryden had reconstructed popular conceptions of himself. Early in his career, the prevailing model of literary authority proved unsuitable for him; his adoption of the posture of elite amateurs brought him ridicule regarding his social and sexual inadequacy. By the end of his career, he had challenged the exclusivity of this model so effectively that he became a symbol of English national superiority and masculine pride, revered by all classes and both sexes for his accomplishments. Dryden's reputation after *Virgil* thus indicates public recognition of his transgressive claims to cultural power, while the language of his supporters reveals how hegemonic structures of perception curtail the significance of his transgression: as a professional poet, he is esteemed above his titled and privileged competitors, yet praise for his work takes the form of portraying him as an aristocrat secure in his patriarchal dominance. One of Dryden's final poems, "Alexander's Feast; or, the Power of Musique" (1697), examines this transfer of authority from the conventional symbol of masculinity (the warrior-hero) to the unconventional (the poet). Written a few months after the publication of the Virgil translation, the Ode was commissioned on the basis of Dryden's heightened reputation; as Cedric Reverand states, this request from the stewards of the St. Cecilia's Day Feast "must have confirmed the success of [Dryden's] translation and marked a moment of personal triumph" for him.[50] His sense of triumph permeates the Ode, for its stanzas represent the complete subordination of Alexander and his court to the lyrics of the poet Timotheus. Celebrating his conquest of Persia, the monarch is led through a rapidly shifting series of actions and emotional states, none of which suit the character of an imperial ruler: the poet's praise of Alexander's genealogy persuades him that he is a "present Deity"; a song celebrating Bacchus culminates in a round of drunken boasting ("Sooth'd with the Sound the King grew vain;/Fought all his Battails o'er again" [*Poems and Fables,* 66-67]), followed by lachrymose regret for the death of his enemy Darius;"Lydian Measures" provoke Alexander's impotent fumbling with his courtesan Thais ("At length, with Love and Wine at once oppress'd,/The vanquish'd Victor sunk upon her Breast" [114-15]); and, finally, a martial strain on the lyre incites the Greeks to destroy Persepolis by fire. In the last stanza, Timotheus, the "Mighty Master" of the scene—and of Alexander himself—does "divide the Crown" with the "sweet Enthusiast" Cecilia, but the Ode displays his power so well that the female saint's invention of the organ and "Sacred Store" of music hardly seem equal to Timotheus's own superbly manipulative performance.

If artist figures in Dryden's verse serve as his alter egos (and his verses to Southerne, Congreve, and Kneller suggest that they do), then his portrayal of Timotheus may function as an ironic comment on the public's panegyrical response to Dryden's own achievement.[51] Dryden's ambivalence about popular representations of him as an absolute monarch over poetry (and its female attendants, the muses) informs his portrayal of Timotheus, for the influence that the poet exercises over his audience ultimately proves excessive and destructive. (The image of Dryden as the sultan of English verse also might be ironically reflected in the character of Alexander, the conqueror overly susceptible to women and poetry.) Yet the confidence, if not arrogance, which Dryden bestows upon Timotheus reveals something else: the contradictory sense of being "the quality and mob, farce and heroicks; the sublime and ridicule mix'd in a piece" has been shifted from the poet onto the listening audience in these verses. It is Alexander the sovereign, not Timotheus the poet, whose behavior treads the boundaries between farce and heroics, as Dryden effectively displaces onto his betters the satire formerly leveled against himself. Toward the end of his life as a writer, Dryden's growing involvement in commercial print culture helped him present an alternative to "Holiday Authors" and their upper-class hegemony over polite letters. And although the tropes of sovereignty and libertinism used to describe Dryden's success still recall the characteristics of aristocratic manhood, the figure whose literary and sexual prowess they celebrate already had begun to propose a new kind of practice for writers by profession.

Chapter Three

"A GOOD POET IS NO SMALL THING":
POPE AND THE PROBLEM OF PLEASURE FOR SALE

Money dignifies what is frivolous if unpaid for.
Virginia Woolf, *A Room of One's Own* (1929)

In her *Vindication of the Rights of Woman* (1792), Mary Wollstonecraft repeatedly quotes from Alexander Pope's "Of the Characters of Women," agreeing with the poet that women's love of pleasure and sexual power determines the course of their lives: forbidden by men to direct their energies toward an important social purpose, women of the middle and upper classes immerse themselves in gallantry, ornamentation, and other pursuits that extensive leisure makes possible. Wollstonecraft goes on to declare that "people of rank and fortune" resemble leisured women not only in being preoccupied with self-display and amusements, but also in being exempt from the need to exert themselves in productive, character-building employments. A third category of effeminate, useless citizens, however, includes male writers like Pope himself: "A king is always a king, and a woman always a woman. His authority and her sex ever stand between them and rational converse. . . . And a wit [is] always a wit, might be added, for the vain fooleries of wits and beauties to obtain attention, and make conquests, are much upon a par."[1] To Wollstonecraft, wits have much in common with women: lacking any better function, they exist to amuse the idle hours of an audience whose judgment determines their worth.

Writing a decade earlier in 1782, Vicesimus Knox also compares men of wit (specifically poets) to beauties:

> I think it is not difficult to perceive, that the admirers of English poetry are divided into two parties. The objects of their love are, perhaps, of equal

beauty, though they greatly differ in their air, their dress, the turn of their features, and their complexion. On one side, are the lovers and imitators of Spenser and Milton; and on the other, those of Dryden, Boileau, and Pope.[2]

Knox's trope in this passage relegates poets to the subordinate status of women whose attractive charms are observed and evaluated by male readers; the characteristics of the poets' verse—what earlier critics might have referred to as genius, fancy, and style—have become the products of female invention ("air," "dress," "complexion") that are manufactured at the toilette. Although Knox's metaphor of wits as love objects lacks the satiric tone of Wollstonecraft's remarks, the representations of both writers have their roots in a single source: controversies in the early eighteenth century regarding the social usefulness and cultural importance of men composing verse for a living. Pope's writings reveal his centrality to debates over the nature of literary labor and the class and gender status that it conferred upon professional writers; his own financial and social success aroused anxiety in those who feared the influence and prestige that a man engaged in the supposedly trivial business of amusement could claim, while Pope responded to his critics by redefining the basis for literary authority in a commercial culture. Reconstructing the dispute over Pope's sexual and economic position as a purveyor of pleasure for sale displays the extent to which a change in idealizations of manhood accompanied the shift toward the market in literature.

I

The frequency of contemporary attacks on Pope's masculinity can be gauged through Richard Savage's defense of Pope: "*What Evidence* will you produce, in a Point you hint at (doubtless of great Importance to the Commonwealth of Learning) *Whether* Mr. Pope *be, or be not, a Woman's Man?* Since he has no *Wife* of his own to appeal to, can any of *your Wives* or *Daughters* bear Testimony in it?"[3] Savage was replying to pieces such as the anonymous critique of Pope entitled *The Poet finish'd in Prose* (one of Edmund Curll's publications), which reduced Pope's "Fondness for Retirement"—his celebrated retreat from the corruption of urban life and letters—to a fear of rape by Lady Mary Wortley Montagu ("nothing can be more terrible than a Rape, to a Gentleman who has not the least Passion for the Sex") and a preference for masturbation over intercourse with women ("no doubt he has found out some other Amusement, equally entertaining to him in his Solitude, and which makes him less sollicitous about losing the favour of the Ladies").[4] Pope's deviation from normative

sexuality is supposedly evident in the venom of his satire against an emi-
nent object of male desire—the female aristocrat, as personified by Lady
Mary—and the open questioning of his conformity to the dominant standards of masculine behavior was fairly common throughout his career. As
Claudia Thomas notes, Pope's enemies often derided him as "the Ladies'
Play-Thing," charging him with effeminacy for the sweetness or smooth-
ness of his verse, his fragile body, and his appeal to women readers.[5]
According to Colley Cibber, for instance, Pope's success as a poet depended
upon his abstention from the sexual intrigues expected of men; he claims
that he interrupted Pope's dalliance with a "Girl of the Game" in "regard to
the Honour of our Nation": "Would you have had so glorious a Work as
that of making *Homer* speak elegant *English,* cut short by laying up our little Gentleman of a Malady, which his thin Body might never have been
cured of?"[6] Here Cibber implies that Pope's infirm body propels him
toward insignificant literary production ("making *Homer* speak elegant
English") instead of the usual activity of youths—fornication. But according to the author of *The Poet finish'd in Prose,* what really lowers Pope's
position on the hierarchies of both class and gender is his occupation as a
purveyor of entertainment for the public:

> All *Poets* are Tradesmen, from *Stephen Duck* down to Dr. *Young;* they are a
> sort of *Haberdashers of small Ware;* and *Poetry* is a *Trade,* and the most insignif-
> icant of all others. I believe it would be no difficult Matter to prove, that the
> most inconsiderable *Tinker* in *Great-Britain,* who can mend your Kettle, is a
> better Subject, and more valuable Citizen, than either *Farinelli* or *Pope,* tho'
> the two last are so great Masters in the Art of *tickling your Ears,* and the for-
> mer is sure to set your Teeth on edge. How little Reason has a Man to grow
> insolent upon excelling in Trifles! (27-28)

On this utilitarian scale of occupations, poets, like opera singers, rank
low for their frivolity. Aligning Pope with the castrato Farinelli (Carlo
Broschi) was a popular method of discrediting the poet's work by implying
its deviation from a rough, manly, English literary style. Yet aside from its
associations with foreign luxury, Catholicism, and physical deformation, the
figure of the castrato also underscores the loss of masculinity that accompanies the entertainer's status in a consumer culture.[7] Like Farinelli, Pope
becomes effeminate by devoting his life to "Trifles," such as writing verse.
Moreover, contemporaries argued that the effeminacy generated by Pope's
occupation had a malevolent cultural influence. The commercial market in
literature raised new anxieties about the pleasure that poetry and other

forms of writing offered to an indiscriminate reading public: attacks on Swift and Pope's *Miscellanies* charged that an excessive concern with pleasing their readers unmans these writers, who are characterized as indulgent mothers (not fathers, since frivolity is a trait foreign to mature manhood) spoiling the moral fiber of their audience:

> 'Tis too well known, that the Generality of Readers had rather be amus'd than instructed. . . . [B]ut for Authors to tell frivolous Tales, purely for telling-sake, to collect Trifles by Volumes, to deal by their Readers as fond Mothers do by their Children, and give them Toys and Gewgaws, instead of Lessons useful for Life, is wicked, if done with Design to corrupt their Understandings; and if done with no Design, idle and impertinent, unbecoming the Character of a Man.[8]

By pleasing the "Generality of Readers" rather than an elite male group, and by neglecting instruction in favor of turning a profit, writers like Pope supposedly forsake the character appropriate to their gender. Other critics continued this censure of Pope, arguing that the popularity of his verse compromised its masculine qualities. The antagonistic Giles Jacob asks whether "there [is] in his Poems any thing but sinewless Versification, and sonorous Nonsense?,"[9] implying that Pope's verse is flaccid and effeminate because its supposedly easy rhythms and lack of moral message disregard the complex formal structure and lucid expression of sense that educated men were trained to value in poetry. Even a text as classical as the Homer translation aroused suspicion because it provided pleasure to groups of readers who otherwise would have remained ignorant of the original poem: critics declared that the desire for profits from subscribers led Pope to emasculate Homer by putting him in "tawd'ry, Tinsel, fashionable Dress": "He smoothes him o'er, and gives him grace and ease,/And makes him *fine*—the *Beaus* and *Belles* to please."[10] Such criticism continued even after Pope's death. Joseph Warton claims that Pope's ethical verse is a lesser variety of poetry because "it lies more level to the general capacities of men, than the higher flights of more genuine poetry,"[11] while William Cowper maintains that Pope's very strengths—his "nice" ear and "delicate" touch—"Made poetry a mere mechanic art" subject to imitation by "ev'ry warbler" who rhymes.[12] Popularly read and widely imitated, Pope was accused of debasing his work to an act of manual labor and lowering poetry to the status of an effeminate entertainment; his successful engagement in the commercial marketplace—apparent in his appeal to the "Generality of Readers"—aroused cultural anxieties about the commercialization of leisure, anxieties that Pope's critics tried to allay by invoking hegemonic constructions of masculinity and femininity. Pope's attempts to reconfigure the class and gender positions assigned to professional poets appear in his writings throughout his career.

II

Ambiguity toward providing pleasure surfaces in much of Pope's work. As David Morris points out, "many of the difficulties and dangers he recognized in poetry depend upon the central role which Pope grants to pleasure.... The means for pleasing readers, like the readers to be pleased, belong to a continuum ranging from the worthiest to the most contemptible."[13] Yet the "characteristic doubleness" with which Pope responded to pleasure—affirming its power while rejecting it as temporary—may be less a manifestation of Pope's personality than a response to complex political and cultural circumstances. Under constant suspicion both as a Catholic and a friend to Opposition leaders, Pope was alienated from the policies of the state and its rulers, and could not present his work as a source of guidance for those in power. And although Pope later celebrated this alienation for making possible his intellectual independence, he remained constantly aware of his distance from seats of authority and influence: in Leopold Damrosch's words, "aspiring to be a spokesman for his culture, he cannot keep from betraying the fact that he is excluded from that culture."[14]

Prohibited from becoming poet laureate and thus lacking an official role to perform, Pope very early in his career viewed writing for the pleasure of himself and others as a problematic goal. The preface to the first collected volume of his *Works* (1717) reveals his adoption of the indolent, insouciant attitude that aristocratic poets such as Rochester had affected a generation before: "Poetry and Criticism [are] by no means the universal concern of the world, but only the affair of idle men who write in their closets, and of idle men who read there."[15] Here Pope represents the leisured male as composing for the enjoyment of companions of his own class and gender, and portrays poetry as the private "affair" of a learned elite. Yet Pope also appears ambivalent about the retreat from "all the reasonable aims of life" (xxvi) that writing poetry requires, and articulates a sense of the poet's estrangement from more important masculine concerns: "One may be ashamed to consume half one's days in bringing sense and rhyme together" (xxviii). Moreover, the choice of poetry as a vocation at a time when verse was being sold and circulated to an expanding audience of readers places the poet in an illusory state similar to that of royalty and attractive women, whose self-image—based upon the opinions of others—bears no relation to reality: "If he is made to hope he may please the world, he falls under very unlucky circumstances; for from the moment he prints, he must expect to hear no more truth, than if he were a Prince, or a Beauty" (xxvi). Like princes or beauties, poets are the objects of public envy and admiration, both of which contribute to an exaggerated assessment of their qualities, whether good or bad; by contrast, "truth" is located in privacy—in the time before print, or before the poet's indulgence in self-display ranks him among other victims of false consciousness.

Like the 1717 preface, the correspondence written in the early years of Pope's career reveals tensions over poetry's compatibility with masculine conduct and pursuits. Writing to his friend Henry Cromwell in 1710, Pope defends the seriousness of his labor by distinguishing himself from the gentleman amateur Richard Crashaw:

> I take this Poet to have writ like a Gentleman, that is, at leisure hours, and more to keep out of idleness, than to establish a reputation: so that nothing regular or just can be expected from him. . . . [O]nly pretty conceptions, fine metaphors, glitt'ring expressions, and something of a neat cast of Verse, (which are properly the dress, gems, or loose ornaments of Poetry) may be found in these verses. This is indeed the case of most other Poetical Writers of *Miscellanies;* nor can it well be otherwise, since no man can be a true Poet, who writes for diversion only.[16]

Written to display its author's genteel accomplishment, Crashaw's verse disregards the "Soul of Poetry"—elements such as "Design, Form, [and] Fable"—and concentrates instead on its surface qualities; the poems' "pretty," "fine," and "glitt'ring" features indicate their fundamental triviality. Pope's metaphors also portray Crashaw's work as explicitly feminine in nature: composed of dress, gems, and ornaments, the poems, like the items on Belinda's toilette (or like Belinda herself) are constructed to "strike the sight" of their intended audience. Finally, using the language of painting, Pope compares Crashaw's poetic technique to the weaker, less masculine elements of visual art: "Their *Colouring* entertains the sight, but the *Lines* and *Life* of the Picture are not to be inspected too narrowly" (*Corresp.,* 1:110). Like women, the poems of this amateur are "best distinguish'd by black, brown, or fair" ("Epistle to a Lady," 4), for only a masculine style of expression confers individuality, or character, upon an author.

Yet however much Pope tried to contrast his commitment to "establish a reputation," or earn the esteem of the learned, with Crashaw's contributions to leisure-hour miscellanies, Pope remained disturbed by contemporary critiques of poetry as an occupation removed from matters of importance. Throughout his correspondence at this time, Pope repeatedly selected the metaphor of a horse and bells to describe the denigration he felt at employing himself for the amusement of others. In writing to the devout Catholic John Caryll, Pope excuses his attention to verse, maintaining that it does not occupy his entire life: "I really make no other use of poetry now, than horses do of the bells that gingle about their ears (tho' now and then they toss their heads as if they were proud of 'em), only to travel on a little more merrily" (*Corresp.,* 1:191). Always conscious of his audience, Pope may have been humoring or reassuring his rather serious friend, yet the image of the poet as a horse shaking its bells signifies his anxieties about being treated like a menial by those who request his work. In another passage, Pope worries that the "Complaisances" expected of poets by their audiences deprives him of his subjectivity:

> Tis great folly to sacrifice one's self, one's time, one's quiet, (the very Life of Life itself) to Forms, Complaisances, & amusements, which do not inwardly please me, & only please a sort of people who regard me no farther than a meer Instrument of their present Idleness, or Vanity. To say truth, the Lives of those we call Great & Happy are divided between those two States; & in each of them, we Poetical Fidlers make but part of their Pleasure, or of their Equipage. (*Corresp.,* 2:194-95)

Pope borrows from the language of his detractors in envisioning himself as a retainer in the aristocratic households of his audience; occupying a place "next to some *Italian* Chymists, Fidlers, Bricklayers, and Opera-Makers" (*Corresp.,* 1:347), the poet functions as an object of diversion for his patrons' idle hours. Yet Pope himself was never subject to such patrons, and with the fame and profits of the *Iliad* translation supporting him (profits that amounted to more than 4,000 pounds), he did not depend on entertaining the great for his livelihood. Rather, written in 1723, Pope's remarks refer to his work on the *Odyssey,* and to the pressure that he felt to satisfy the friends who were awaiting the text's completion. Although Bernard Lintot's financing of the Homer translation made Pope financially independent of patrons, the rhetoric of Pope's correspondence suggests the limits of this independence: his letters reveal the subordination that accompanied poets' occupational identity, regardless of the source of their income.

Several of Pope's own poems reproduce and validate the subordination enforced upon objects of pleasure, most emphatically when those objects are women. The "Epistle to a Lady" (1735) declares that "Nature" instills into women the "Love of Pleasure" as a ruling passion; in return, they are socialized to provide this pleasure ("[W]here the lesson taught/Is but to please, can Pleasure seem a fault?" [211-12]). Educated from the nursery to arouse and satisfy the senses of others, and possessed of a passion to seek satisfaction for themselves, women, in Pope's view, are by nature and convention the producers and consumers of amusement. Later in the poem, Pope classifies the character traits that distinguish men from women, forming a dichotomy that frees all men, regardless of occupation and status, from contamination by female triviality and lightness:

> Heav'n, when it strives to polish all it can
> Its last best work, but forms a softer Man;
> Picks from each sex, to make its Fav'rite blest,
> Your love of Pleasure, our desire of Rest,
> Blends, in exception to all gen'ral rules,
> Your Taste of Follies, with our Scorn of Fools,
> Reserve with Frankness, Art with Truth ally'd,
> Courage with Softness, Modesty with Pride,
> Fix'd Principles, with Fancy ever new. (271-79)

These lines represent the poet as a man who shares with other men a common desire of rest, scorn of fools, frankness, truth, courage, and pride, all of which complement the more morally ambivalent qualities attributed to the poem's female addressee; this rhetorical move places Pope safely apart from the preoccupation with folly and pleasure that he portrays as inherent to the other sex, and thus saves his work from being aligned with feminine activities and interests.

Pope's male speaker in "Sober Advice from Horace" (1734) likewise naturalizes women's role as providers of pleasure, while advising men to become judicious consumers of the sexual delights they offer. Much of the poem counsels men on their choice of erotic object, and warns against the dangers that attend imprudent selections; the speaker encourages readers to mind "that honest Part that rules us all" (87) and to make no distinction between common women and ladies of quality:

> When sharp with Hunger, scorn you to be fed,
> Except on *Pea-Chicks* at the *Bedford-head?*
> Or, when a tight, neat Girl, will serve the Turn,
> In errant Pride continue stiff, and burn?

I'm a plain Man, whose Maxim is profest,
"The Thing at hand is of all things the *best.*" (149-54)

Characterizing himself along the lines of prudent rakes like Lord
Bathurst ("Who asks no more [right reasonable Peer]/Than not to wait too
long, nor pay too dear" [159-60]), the speaker erases class differences among
women, portraying all of them as similar in their possession of female genitals and in their consequent subjection to the sexual appetites of aristocratic
men. Noting the poem's outrageous innuendo, the critic Thomas Bentley
condemns not only its obscenity, but also its repeated insistence upon the
poet's masculine prowess: "What an *Erection* of Wit, what a *Tentigo* of Parts
in his Note! How he triumphs, and dashes his Sp[erm?] about him! Keep
off, O ye Duchesses and Ladies of Quality; for he is just entered into the
deep Meaning of *Permingere* and *Permolere*" (*A Letter to Mr. Pope*, 16 n.).
Bentley ironically calls attention to the poet's celebration of a physically visible masculinity: Pope bases his claim to manhood upon his possession of
male genitalia—he is included in the sex ruled by its "honest Part"— and his
"Erection of Wit" and triumphal posturing stress his difference from (and
superiority to) the female objects of his satire and lust. But the rhetorical
overkill that Bentley satirizes also suggests the poet's insecurity. According
to Laura Brown, the exposed female body in the poem "indicates the poet's
ambivalence about his own sexuality, his futile attempt to avoid the anxiety
of his own nakedness."[17] This anxiety, though, also arises from Pope's distress
over being perceived by his contemporaries as an object of pleasure. In portraying objectification as the natural condition of women, Pope displaces his
own fear of becoming an item for entertainment and consumption: providing pleasure for others becomes the function of women alone rather than a
task that can be performed by men and women, belles and wits.

In "Sober Advice," Pope's eradication of class categories in favor of gender distinctions distinguishes him from women, portrayed as the natural
seekers and sources of pleasure, and places him in the company of men,
whose essential qualities (or "various Ruling Passions") lead them toward
many different pursuits. Yet this strategy brings Pope to an impasse in his
career as a professional writer, a situation that he details in some of his later
poems. The "Second Epistle of the Second Book of Horace Imitated"
(1737), for instance, begins with a Frenchman offering his clean-shaped,
curly-haired boy as a servant to a gentleman; the boy's expected duties are
vague, but his good looks, pure voice, facility with opera songs, and high
salary suggest that he will provide sexual services: "Sir, he's your Slave, for
twenty pound a year./Mere Wax as yet, you fashion him with ease,/Your

Barber, Cook, Upholst'rer, what you please" (8-10). Urging his son on the gentleman, the father admits that the boy's only fault is thievery. Pope goes on to compare his own situation to that of the "graceless Lad," and asks his audience to believe his declarations of his limited poetic talent: "Consider then, and judge me in this light;/I told you when I went, I could not write" (27-28). Like the boy, the speaker has flaws that compromise his ability to satisfy, and he responds to requests for verse with an annoyance unavailable to the lad whose living depends upon pleasing others: "D'ye think me good for nothing but to rhime?" (32). Pope's distance from the servant or catamite in training—and a sign of his masculinity—is his ability to refrain from performance. In another verse passage, Pope highlights this privilege of refusal by comparing himself to an old soldier who fights only when he needs the money. When he has earned enough, the promise of honors and rewards held out by his commander fails to entice him: "D'ye think me, noble Gen'ral, such a Sot?/Let him take Castles who has ne'er a Groat" (50-51).

The biographical sketch of Pope offered in this poem also endorses the masculine privilege of nonperformance, for it depicts Pope as existing apart from both the London literary market and life at court, and portrays writing for either patrons or the public in general as antithetical to independence and sanity:

> But (thanks to *Homer*) since I live and thrive,
> Indebted to no Prince or Peer alive,
> Sure I should want the Care of ten *Monroes*,
> If I would scribble, rather than repose. (68-71)

As well as being a sign of mental health, repose, or "our desire of Rest," is also a defining characteristic of manhood, for it signifies freedom from trivial acts ("Composing Songs, For Fools to get by heart" [126]) and from subjection to the desires of others. Although he describes writing poetry as integral to his sense of self ("This subtle Thief of Life, this paltry Time,/What will it leave me, if it snatch my Rhime?"[77-78]), the near impossibility of pleasing a varied readership brings Pope to a state of frustration:

> But after all, what wou'd you have me do?
> When out of twenty I can please not two;
> When this Heroicks only deigns to praise,
> Sharp Satire that, and that Pindaric lays?
> One likes the Pheasant's wing, and one the leg;

> The Vulgar boil, the Learned roast an Egg;
> Hard Task! to hit the Palate of such Guests,
> When Oldfield loves, what Dartineuf detests. (80-87)

Pope's metaphor here suggests that such readers respond to literature as if it were literally an item for consumption, like food, and as if he were a cook catering to their palates. Judgment of literature has become a matter of the consumer's individual preference rather than a studied, acquired skill, and poets face the prospect of conforming to, rather than shaping, the audience's tastes. Given this situation, Pope declares his turn toward prose and justifies this choice as a sign of his growth toward adulthood; poetry, associated with the intellectual (and sexual) immaturity of schoolboys laboring for a master, appears incompatible with the autonomy of self-regulated men:

> There is a time when Poets will grow dull:
> I'll e'en leave Verses to the Boys at school:
> To Rules of Poetry no more confin'd,
> I learn to smooth and harmonize my Mind,
> Teach ev'ry Thought within its bounds to roll,
> And keep the equal Measure of the Soul. (200-05)

As Kristina Straub observes, Pope, like many of his contemporaries, associates authorship with certain forms of masculine conduct, and repeatedly "excludes [the schoolboy] from his construction of what [literary authority] should be."[18] Subjected to discipline (and occasionally sexual abuse) by his masters, the schoolboy occupies a place of subordination in the social hierarchy of masculinity; like schoolboys, scribblers are marked by incapacity and provoke correction, even corporal punishment, from their audience or peers. The well-balanced gentleman, by contrast, "keep[s] the equal Measure of the Soul" (and confirms his masculine status) by living to please himself alone.

But repose and prose—both of which would guarantee Pope a rational, independent existence—cannot resolve his dilemma as a poet. How can he, who labors to please readers, retain his authority in a culture where critics disparage verse as an inessential entertainment for leisure hours and classify poets alongside sexually ambivalent purveyors of amusement, like castrati? Yet while Pope's verse declares his anxiety over transgressing norms of behavior derived from aristocratic models, at the same time it challenges these norms by suggesting that masculine identity could accommodate, and perhaps even depend upon, involvement in the "feminizing" consumer economy—specifically, the literary marketplace. Pope constructed this new economic and sexual ideal of authorship through his attacks upon a prominent critic of his professional career—John, Lord Hervey.

III

As Robert Halband notes in his biography of Hervey, this relationship had initially been friendly, but deteriorated as Hervey pursued his career as a courtier aligned with Robert Walpole's party—he eventually rose to the position of lord keeper of the privy seal—and Pope became increasingly identified with the Tory Opposition.[19] The quarrel between them escalated in the early 1730s when Pope repeatedly criticized Hervey as "Lord *Fanny*," a spinner of weak couplets ("The First Satire of the Second Book of Horace Imitated"), and as Fannius, the impudent flatterer of patrons ("The Fourth Satire of Dr. John Donne . . . Versifyed"). Hervey's private reaction to the satire on members of the nobility in Pope's "Epistle to Burlington" (1731) and his "Epistle to Bathurst" (1733)—"it is very probably some of those to whom he pretends to teach the proper use of Riches, may teach him the proper Use of Cudgels"[20]—indicates his outrage at the poet's assault on class hierarchies; he responded to criticism of himself in the anonymously published *An Epistle from a Nobleman to a Doctor of Divinity* (1733), verses that denigrate Pope's talent and satirize his pretensions to the upper-class privilege of using the classics as cultural capital. Hervey found especially impertinent Pope's translation of the *Iliad* and *Odyssey* into English for a profit. Declaring Pope a "Mechanic," Hervey compares his *Homer* to the productions of a corset-maker: "The gaudy *Hinchlif* of some beauteous Mind,"[21] Pope merely provides unnecessary ornamentation for the original text. Even at their best, Hervey argues, Pope's verses remain material for juvenile, not adult, amusement: he charges that Pope's sterile invention and immature style invalidate "This Jingler's Claim/Or to an Author's, or a Poet's Name" (7), since only boys and girls (the least discriminating consumers of literature) appreciate his translation. The motive for Hervey's attack on Pope, though, was not so much a desire to preserve the classics from modern translators and a popular readership as a distaste for what Hervey considered the poet's desire to climb above his rank and aspire to the company of gentlemen:

> I own I have an aversion to those wits by profession, who think it incumbent upon them always to reflect and express themselves differently from the rest of the world; they are a sort of mental poster-masters in company who think they must distort themselves to entertain you, and often give me pain, but

never give me pleasure. Pope is the head of this sect. If he had never talked, one should have thought he had more wit than any man that ever lived, and if he had never written he would have talked much better; but the endeavouring to raise his character as a companion up to the point it stands as an author, has sunk it as much below its natural pitch as he has endeavoured to put it above it. But this is a rock many have split upon as well as him.[22]

To Hervey, the profession of writing was incompatible with the genteel social status that Pope seemingly affected; the poet's "character as a companion" to men of rank suffers from his compulsion to advertise or display his talents (to be a "mental poster-master"). As Hervey saw it, Pope's aspirations to politeness conflicted with his role as an entertainer, a role that Hervey believed Pope internalized to the point where it determined his conduct. And according to the aristocratic Hervey, this conflict within Pope made him unsuitable company. In *A Letter to Mr. Cibber* (1742), Hervey prefers Cibber as a companion over Pope because the actor never mistakes his function or steps out of his subordinate place: "Whilst you in all the Warmth of chearful social connections are trying to amuse and entertain the People you are with; [Pope] is only endeavouring to tax their Admiration. . . . No Wonder then whilst you are sought and introduced into Society, he is shunn'd and excluded from it."[23] Members of his own class apparently agreed with Hervey's assessment of writers, to the point at which they criticized him for composing verse: Hervey's father, the earl of Bristol, reportedly "feared that [his son's] constant rhyming would stand in the way of his advancement in the world," and Hervey's patron, George II, concurred: "You ought not to write verses; 'tis beneath your rank: leave such work to little Mr. Pope."[24] Although secured from the economic need to please the reading public with his work, Hervey was still subject to the censure that such pleasure trivialized, and even unmanned, those who provided it; he responded to potential criticism by treating verse as a form of mindless recreation, insisting that his social superiority and secure class standing enabled him to mock both his own poetic efforts and Pope's satiric appraisal of them:

> Guiltless of Thought, each Blockhead may compose
> This nothing-meaning Verse, as fast as Prose.
> And P——e with Justice of such Lines may say,
> *His Lordship spins a thousand in a Day.* (*Epistle*, 6-7)

Pope, "who at *Crambo* plays with Pen and Ink" (*Epistle*, 7), lacks the confidence and sense of play that characterize the aristocratic writer, and the poet's labored, self-conscious attention to his craft makes him akin to mechanics or laborers whose livelihood depends on catering to the needs and pleasures of others.

A dilettante writer, aristocrat, and courtier, Hervey symbolized the structure of power that relegated Pope, the writer by trade, to the margins of respectability. Pope responded to Hervey's criticism of "this jingler's claim/Or to an author's, or a poet's name" (*Epistle*, 10) in his ironic *Letter to a Noble Lord, On occasion of some Libels written and propagated at Court* (1733), which circulated privately but remained unpublished during Pope's lifetime.[25] In the *Letter*, the rhetorical strategies that Pope employed in his own defense represented the professional poet, rather than the aristocrat, as the upholder of a masculine ideal, and the bourgeois quality of this ideal shows its significant break from previous conventions of male sexual and literary authority. Rather than ignoring Hervey's status and its privileges, Pope— imitating the polite, even unctuous, language of dedications—emphasizes the nobility of his addressee, but only to attack Hervey's pretensions that birth gives him the license to write: "When I consider the *great difference* betwixt the rank your *Lordship* holds in the *World,* and the rank which your *writings* are like to hold in the *learned world,* I presume that distinction of style is but necessary, which you will see observ'd thro' this letter. When I speak of *you,* my Lord, it will be with all the deference due to the inequality which Fortune has made between you and myself: but when I speak of your *writings,* my Lord, I must, I can do nothing but trifle."[26] Stooping beneath his class, Hervey has "modestly" chosen a pen instead of a sword for his attack upon Pope, yet this choice of weapon places him at a disadvantage, since Pope's literary skill more than compensates for the accidental benefits bestowed upon Hervey by fortune: the switch from violence to wit as a means of establishing dominance enables the rise of a new elite who, like Pope, exhibit their masculine superiority by displaying their considerable talents.

The implications of this disparity between amateur and professional production are examined by Jean Baudrillard, who describes the shift toward a "constraint of leisure" or a suspicion of "non-instrumentality as the source of [aesthetic and symbolic] values" that accompanied the development of a capitalist economy: "The current status of the everyday object results from the conflict, or rather, compromise, between two opposed moralities: an aristocratic morality of '*otium*' and a puritan work ethic."[27] Accompanying this change in the nature of the object (including poetry) is an increased emphasis on labor rather than leisure as the basis of social status for men: "Everywhere *homo faber* is the double of *homo otiosus.*"[28] Pope

himself recognized and articulated the superiority of *homo faber* through-
out his work. As early as 1717, in a poem entitled "Sandys's Ghost: Or a
Proper New Ballad on the New Ovid's Metamorphosis, As It Was Intended
To Be Translated By Persons Of Quality," Pope had warned aristocratic
writers that membership in an elite social class does not always result in
"Verses Sterling":

> For not the Desk with silver Nails,
> Nor *Bureau* of Expence,
> Nor Standish well japan'd, avails
> To writing of good Sense. (9-12)

Despite the beauty of their expensive writing implements, the "quality"
ultimately translate Ovid into "Waste-Paper." Yet while the "Lords and
Lordings" described in "Sandys's Ghost" appear bumbling and incompetent, their masculinity still remains unquestioned. By contrast, Pope argues
years later that Hervey's incapacity as a poet embarrasses his audience
because it reveals his intellectual (and, by implication, sexual) immaturity.
Poetry—imaged in the *Letter to a Noble Lord* as Pegasus—requires reserves
of ability and manliness that make it a task too difficult for an effete aristocrat to master: "Should your Lordship be only like a *Boy* that is *run away
with;* and run away with by a *Very Foal;* really common charity, as well as
respect for a noble family, would oblige me to stop your career, and to *help
you down* from *this Pegasus*" (*Prose Works,* 2:443). Pope goes on to assert that
Hervey's status as the son of an earl, which gave him countless advantages
in his upbringing, education, and career advancement, actually hinders the
writing of verse, which demands the sturdy middle-class virtues of incessant study, labor, and perseverance:

> Surely the little praise of a *Writer* should be a thing below your ambition:
> You, who were no sooner born, but in the lap of the Graces; no sooner at
> school, but in the arms of the Muses; no sooner in the World, but you prac-
> tic'd all the skill of it; no sooner in the Court, but you possess'd all the art of
> it! Unrivall'd as you are, in making a figure, and in making a speech,
> methinks, my Lord, you may well give up the poor talent of turning a Dis-
> tich. (*Prose Works,* 2:443)

Coddled and encouraged by female approval, Hervey learns a kind of
assurance that feminizes him: like women, he precociously acquires the
highly artificial manners that enable him to survive and thrive in the

complex, hostile society of the court. (According to Pope, Hervey also shares the linguistic imprecision that presumably characterizes female speech, for the poet notes the confusion in Hervey's attack on mechanics: "Does your Lordship use *Hinchcliff* as a *proper name?* or as the Ladies say a *Hinchcliff* or *Colmar,* for a *Silk* or a *Fan?* I will venture to affirm, no Critic can have a perfect taste of your Lordship's works, who does not understand both your *Male Phrase* and your *Female Phrase*" [*Prose Works,* 2:452].) The *Letter's* catalogue of Hervey's strengths includes his delivery of sycophantic speeches in support of Walpole's government, and his "making a figure," or displaying his body for public admiration and applause—an act that led contemporaries to designate him "Lady of the Lords." Adam Smith's *Theory of Moral Sentiments* (1759) analyzes the purpose of this display, and concludes that the aristocrat's pride in his appearance, by commanding the respect, envy, and awe of spectators, serves as a means of retaining his control over the populace: "His air, his manner, his deportment, all mark that elegant and graceful sense of his own superiority, which those who are born to inferior stations can hardly ever arrive at. These are the arts by which he proposes to make mankind more easily submit to his authority, and to govern their inclinations according to his own pleasure: and in this he is seldom disappointed."[29] (Smith to a great extent shared Pope's contempt for this form of social dominance: "To figure at a ball is [the aristocrat's] great triumph, and to succeed in an intrigue of gallantry, his highest exploit.")[30] While acknowledging the physical defects for which Hervey and Lady Mary Wortley Montagu lampooned him (in their collaborative *Verses Address'd to the Imitator of the First Satire of the Second Book of Horace,* 1733), Pope undermines the connection between masculine authority and aristocratic self-display:

> It is true, my Lord, I am short, not well shap'd, generally ill-dress'd, if not sometimes dirty: Your Lordship and Ladyship are still in bloom; your Figures such, as rival the *Apollo* of *Belvedere,* and the *Venus* of *Medicis;* and your faces so finish'd, that neither sickness nor passion can deprive them of *Colour;* I will allow your own in particular to be the finest that ever *Man* was blest with: preserve it, my Lord, and reflect, that to be a *Critic,* would cost it too many *frowns,* and to be a Statesman, too many *wrinkles!* (*Prose Works,* 2:445)

Pope here employs a tactic that is common in his work: comparing his deformity to the "finish'd" appearance of his two antagonists enables him to contrast his sincerity and moral health with their duplicity and moral decay.[31] This passage, however, goes even further in its indictment of Hervey, for it implies that his handsome face—the "finest that ever *Man* was blest with"— indicates his unfitness for the traditional masculine occupations of criticism and statesmanship. Using one's judgment for the evaluation of literature or for the management of the nation renders one unsuitable as an object of admiring glances; the physical signs of masculine intellectual activity like frowns and wrinkles conflict with the exercise of authority through parading the body—an exercise that aristocrats like Hervey and Lady Mary enjoy. Mental labor, Pope implies, is deforming, but like the deliberate ugliness of Pope's satire—whose "filthy Simile[s]" and "beastly Line[s]" ("Epilogue to the Satires: Dialogue II," 181) expose abuses of power in high places—his body, made ugly through the hard work of thinking, guarantees the integrity of his character. By this logic, the ill-shaped, slovenly, tradesmanlike Pope is more suited to manly endeavors like verse and criticism than the nobleman whose self-conscious attention to appearance makes him a spectacle.

Hervey's effeminacy had long drawn the attention of his critics; the anonymous author of *Tit for Tat* advises the "star of balls and drawing rooms" to avoid literary combat with Pope and Swift, since wisdom and beauty are incompatible: "Ne'er made for use, just fit for show,/ Half wit, half fool, half man, half beau:/Who'd spoil such eyes for any book?"[32] More explicit censure of Hervey as a hermaphrodite, or homosexual, was a staple feature of Opposition pamphlets, and many of these attacks linked his supposed sexual perversions to his involvement in political corruption. For instance, in an abusive tract that eventually led to a duel between them, Opposition politician William Pulteney charged Hervey with being the "Pathick" party in the crime of sodomy; he argues that this "unnatural, reigning Vice" and its associate vices of luxury and effeminacy are personified in Hervey, "a pretty, little, *Master Miss*" whom Pulteney fashions as the antithesis of masculine patriotism.[33] Pope extends this criticism, proposing a relation between Hervey's ambiguous sexuality and the quality of his verse.[34] His *Letter* insists that Hervey lacks the masculine character necessary for authorship and portrays his collaborative work with Lady Mary (on *Verses Address'd to the Imitator*) as a sexual act in which the "natural" roles of men and women are overturned:

> Your Lordship indeed said you had [the poem] from a Lady, and the Lady said it was your Lordship's; some thought the beautiful by-blow had *Two Fathers*, or (if one of them will hardly be allow'd a man) *Two Mothers;* indeed

I think *both Sexes* had a share in it, but which was *uppermost*, I know not: I
pretend not to determine the exact method of this *Witty Fornication:* and, if
I call it *Yours*, my Lord, 'tis only because, whoever *got* it, you *brought it forth.*
(*Prose Works*, 2:447-48)

Here Pope casts doubt upon Hervey's ability to perform the conventionally male, procreative role in his (literary) intercourse with Lady Mary,
and implies that Hervey's lack of masculine prowess reverses the collaborators' positions: Hervey serves as the passive transcriber and publisher of the
verse and Lady Mary as the "uppermost" creative genius whose spark of
wit engenders their illegitimate lampoons. Pope had earlier satirized Lady
Mary for "Father[ing] Her Lampoons upon Her Acquaintance" in "The
Capon's Tale" (1727). The poem portrays Lady Mary as a promiscuous hen
who, having "hatch'd more Chicks than she could rear" (16), foists her
progeny, or her poems, onto an unsuspecting capon (probably Hervey): this
castrated "feather'd Dupe," imagining that he has produced the brood,
"clocks, keeps a Pother,/A foolish Foster-Father-Mother" (25-26). Thus
Hervey finds himself emasculated by being used as a surrogate parent for
Lady Mary's verse, and a mere vehicle for her anger against Pope.

Throughout his *Letter to a Noble Lord*, Pope sexualizes Hervey's literary
production, attributing Hervey's supposed incapacity as a writer to his
indeterminate gender identity; the *Letter* employs a similar strategy to validate Pope's own verse, portraying it as originating in, and drawing strength
from, a normative, bourgeois family life. Unlike Hervey, the successful and
ambitious courtier, Pope "liv'd excluded from all *posts* of *Profit* or *Trust*,"
since he possessed "too *weak a head*, or too *tender a heart*" to renounce the
Catholicism of his parents; poetry, then, provided him with a means of
income acceptable to his father and mother. In response to Hervey's assertion that family life and life at court share the same deceptions and treach-
ery ("Courts are only larger families,/The growth of each, few truths and
many lies:/in private satyrize, in public flatter" [*Epistle*, 8]), Pope emphasizes
his own origins in a respectable if not noble household, headed by "A
Mother, on whom I was never oblig'd so far to reflect, as to say, she *spoiled
me*. And a Father, who never found himself oblig'd to say of me, that he
disapprov'd my Conduct" (*Prose Works*, 2:450). In depicting himself as the
dutiful son of devoted parents, Pope avoids making assertions about his
own sexuality—a necessity occasioned by his antagonists' view that he was
"No more for loving made, than to be lov'd."[35] As Steve Clark maintains,
"Pope seeks to establish not a virile but a wholly desexualised poetic voice,
one whose authority depends upon its own incapacitation."[36] Yet at the

same time, Pope manages to construct a sexual persona in opposition to that of Hervey, and does so by sentimentally portraying himself as the off-spring of an affectionate, fruitful heterosexual union.[37] Through the dis-course of filial piety, Pope attempts to transform his involvement in the commercial marketplace: his insistence that his choice of career upholds the bonds of family life domesticates and naturalizes what is essentially a mode of production for profit. Pope thus invalidates critics' and aristocrats' comparisons of him with showmen like castrati—those emasculated crea-tures who earn their living by providing pleasure for audiences—not by avoiding the commercial sale of his verse, but by locating his poetic activ-ity within the confines of a patriarchal household. Pope's insistence that his work preserves rather than threatens this household forestalls associations of his verse with the effeminacy, luxury, and triviality that the production of commodities for leisure-time consumption was said to encourage.

Published two years after Pope completed the *Letter to a Noble Lord*, his "Epistle to Arbuthnot" refines his attacks on Hervey, broadening them to include the systems of aristocratic privilege—especially patronage—that secured Hervey's power and influence in the state and in the culture at large. Since contemporary opinion of Hervey, and of patronage as an institution, was by no means scornful, the "Epistle" drew attention for its virulence, and especially for its attacks upon Hervey's sexuality. Writing in 1759, W. H. Dilworth—a sympathetic biographer of Pope—puzzled over the poet's hostility toward the courtier: "Whenever our formidable satirist takes this peer in hand, he seems to have a particular delight in touching him to the quick. Nay, he has even perverted the beauty of his person to all the disadvantage he could."[38] The author of *The Poet finish'd in Prose* interprets Pope's animosity against the handsome Hervey to frustrated desire: according to this satire, the "Epistle"'s focus on Hervey's impotence and effeminacy is borrowed from the plebian language and style of a lovers' quarrel between Pope's footman, John, and his dairymaid sweet-heart, Margery ("when Women are in a Passion all will come out, right or wrong" [69]). Like a woman of low rank, Pope uses scurrilous terms to vent his outrage over Hervey's failure to return his ardor, and the "Epistle to Arbuthnot" supposedly reveals how Pope's lack of gentility made impossible any kind of relationship between the two.

The sexual antagonism that contemporaries identified in "Arbuthnot" arises from the poem's investigation of the erotics of patronage, a literary system that Pope juxtaposes to his own emphatically unerotic domesticity. The poem's opening couplet ("Shut, shut the door, good *John!* fatigu'd I said,/Tye up the knocker, say I'm sick, I'm dead") immediately establishes, in Ian Donaldson's phrase, Pope's "own created distinction between public exposure and private space"[39]; by shutting his door to the would-be writers who clamor to see him—"a Parson, much be-mus'd in Beer,/A maudlin Poetess, a ryming Peer/A Clerk" (15-17)—Pope refuses their overtures of courtship. G. Douglas Atkins views Pope as the feminized "sexual object whom the writers pursue," and argues that the poet's seclusion is an attempt to reject "the role of woman they would impose upon him,"[40] a role represented in images of assault and penetration ("What Walls can guard me, or what Shades can hide?/They pierce my thickets, thro' my Grot they glide" [7-8]). Yet beneath Pope's anxiety over the violation of his privacy lies a sense of poetry itself as a sexually disruptive activity. Early in the poem, for instance, Pope discounts the seductive power of his verse in leading both men and women to break the bonds of the patriarchal family:

> *Arthur,* whose giddy Son neglects the Laws,
> Imputes to me and my damn'd works the cause:
> Poor *Cornus* sees his frantic Wife elope,
> And curses Wit, and Poetry, and *Pope.* (23-26)

Disappointed fathers who charge Pope with luring their sons into a literary career and abandoned husbands who accuse him of arousing the adulterous passions of their wives ascribe to Pope attractive and aggressive qualities that he denies possessing. In later passages, Pope insists upon his reluctance—and his physical inability—to become an object of admiration. Although "a hundred Hawkers" spread about his verses for sale, the poet refuses to exhibit himself in person to gather praise: "I sought no homage from the Race that write;/I kept, like *Asian* Monarchs, from their sight" (219-20). Safely ensconced at Twickenham, he retains his authority by avoiding the appraising gaze. Moreover, his very physical defects insure that Pope would be unlikely to provide pleasure to those viewing him: "There are, who to my Person pay their court,/I cough like *Horace,* and tho' lean, am short,/*Ammon's* great Son one shoulder had too high" (115-17). Like the frowns and wrinkles that distinguish him from the effeminate Hervey, Pope's short, thin, crippled body preserves his masculine integrity by protecting him from the onslaughts of sycophantic—and feminizing—courtship.

In "Arbuthnot," the domestic, familial nature of Pope's poetic beginnings also removes the stigma of transgression from his writing. Since he ascribes his talent in part to his parents ("Why did I write? what sin to me unknown/Dipt me in Ink, my Parents', or my own?" [125-26]), poetry does not, for Pope, contradict the ideals of filial duty and obedience with which he identifies himself in this poem ("I left no Calling for this idle trade,/No Duty broke, no Father dis-obey'd" [129-30]). Pope again refers to affective ties in explaining his decision to circulate his work in the marketplace:

> But why then publish? *Granville* the polite,
> And knowing *Walsh,* would tell me I could write;
> Well-natur'd *Garth* inflam'd with early praise,
> And *Congreve* lov'd, and *Swift* endur'd my Lays;
> The Courtly *Talbot, Somers, Sheffield* read,
> Ev'n mitred *Rochester* would nod the head,
> And *St. John's* self (great *Dryden's* friends before)
> With open arms receiv'd one Poet more.
> Happy my Studies, when by these approv'd!
> Happier their Author, when by these belov'd! (135-44)

The choice of verbs in this passage—"lov'd," "approv'd," "belov'd"—and references to gestures such as embracing suggest that Pope's aristocratic supporters responded to his work as if they were an extension of his family; the circulation of his poems generates affection from members of the group that includes, significantly, poets as well as noblemen.[41] And it is the poets who validate the taste and judgment of the peers: acting like literary godfathers in encouraging his career, Charles Talbot (duke of Shrewsbury), John, Lord Somers, John Sheffield (duke of Buckingham), Francis Atterbury (bishop of Rochester), and Henry St. John (Viscount Bolingbroke) earn honorable mention from Pope because they were wise enough to have admired and befriended Dryden in previous years.

According to Brean Hammond, the naming of Pope's noble supporters is an "ideological masterstroke," for it suggests "an aristocracy of rank, wealth, and talent that claimed the poet as its own" and thus distinguished him from other writers who sold their publications for profit.[42] But although references to his "polite," "knowing," and "Courtly" audience certainly set Pope apart from those writers who go to press urged by "hunger and Request of friends" (44), the poet's antagonism in the "Epistle to Arbuthnot" seems not to be directed toward these ordinary scribblers. Rather, this passage describing Pope's initiation as an equal into a social and literary elite pits him against what he later in the poem portrays as a corrupt and even dangerous system of hierarchy—patronage. As Dustin

Griffin observes, Pope's attitude toward the patron/client relationship often contradicted his practices, for he "remained a part of the patronage system, both as supplier of services and as beneficiary, even as he worked to undermine it."[43] Although Pope describes his relations with politically powerful members of the patron class (among them Allen, Earl Bathurst; Henry St. John, Viscount Bolingbroke; Richard Boyle, earl of Burlington; Richard Temple, Viscount Cobham; and Edward Harley, earl of Oxford) in terms of equality ("Above a Patron, tho' I condescend/Sometimes to call a Minister my Friend" ["Epistle to Arbuthnot," 265-66]), he depended upon the protection that such friends could offer him (to the extent of registering the *Dunciad's* copyright in the names of Bathurst, Burlington, and Oxford, whose rank made them immune to prosecution for libel). And while Pope proposed a shift in literary authority from the class of patrons to writers themselves as early as the dedication of the *Iliad* to Congreve (1720), he relied upon the favor of men like Charles Montagu, earl of Halifax to promote the translation's success, and guarantee his own financial independence. Yet in an essay "On Dedications" contributed to the *Guardian* in 1713, Pope characterizes the dedication—a public acknowledgment of the patron's beneficence and the author's indebtedness—as a form of rhetoric peculiarly suited to women: "'Tis observable of the Female Poets and Ladies Dedicatory, that here (as elsewhere) they far exceed us in any Strain or Rant. . . . They adore in the same manner as they would be adored."[44] Early on, Pope seems to have associated the rhetorical posture expected of dedications with an unmanly expression of subservience on the part of authors and vanity on the part of patrons, and Griffin points out that Pope's withdrawal from patronage and its obligations (including dedications) increased in the later stages of his career: "By the 1730s even more than before Pope seems to want to even the score, to pay off old debts, to be as little obliged as possible, even to close 'friends.'"[45] In fact, the stance that Pope takes in the "Epistle to Arbuthnot" indicates an openly antagonistic break with traditional systems of authority, for the poem's investigation of the erotics of patronage not only satirizes the pride of patrons and the sycophancy of clients but implies that their relations are comparable to sodomy— a class-based form of masculine sexuality and power that Pope's contemporaries found increasingly repellent.

Sexual deviance, particularly prostitution, had long been compared to the practice of writing or dedicating books for a reward. In the vocabulary of Pope's contemporaries, the term "hackney" could refer to a horse, a prostitute, or anything let out for hire, and Pope affirms the connection between selling one's body and selling one's wit in his 1743 *Dunciad,* where "a youth unknown to Phoebus" gains his patron's favor by offering the sexual services of his sister (2.213-20). In the "Epistle to Arbuthnot," however, not prostitution but a kind of homoerotic subjugation results from the hierarchy maintained by patronage, and Pope examines this dynamic in representations of three increasingly perverse—and increasingly sexualized—patrons in action. As Hammond notes, the poem's verse portraits of Atticus (Joseph Addison), Bufo (George Bubb Dodington), and Sporus (Hervey) "operate as emotional 'nodes', gathering-places for the poem's intensity"[46]; Griffin describes these portraits as a collection of antiselves against whom Pope defined and clarified his own character for readers.[47] Yet while Pope's satire focuses on the moral degeneracy of both client and patron, the erotic resonance of the passages makes this degeneracy even more problematic, for the "Epistle" repeatedly brings to mind the sexual valence of hierarchical relations among men. There were clear precedents for such insinuations: according to Bruce Smith, "Renaissance Englishmen, like the ancient Greeks and Romans, eroticized the power distinctions that set one male above another in their society,"[48] partly by designating social inferiors as possible sexual objects. In doing so, they (and their Restoration successors, such as the court wits) recognized that homosexual relations, although illicit, were a function of prevailing distributions of patriarchal authority: "Sexual desire took shape in the persons of master and minion; sexual energy found release in the power play between them."[49]

Writing at a time when the commercial sale of literature had offered him an alternative to the dominance and subordination of patronage, Pope stigmatized the more customary dynamics of literary production by hinting at their sexual overtones: all three portraits of patrons reflect the image of master and minion, and this image grows more explicit as the "Epistle to Arbuthnot" progresses. At first, the praise that Pope bestows upon Addison as a writer seems to secure him from criticism: "Blest with each Talent and each Art to please,/And born to write, converse, and live with ease" (195-96), Addison rises to eminence because of his talent rather than his social rank. Yet his need for superiority and flattery transforms him into a dictatorial "Turk" allowing "no brother near the throne" (198); family feeling, or comradery with his fellow authors, fades as Atticus designates himself their master: "Like *Cato,* give his little Senate laws,/And sit attentive to his own applause" (209-10). To Joseph Spence, Pope confided his more private reservations about Addison, calling him and Richard Steele "a couple of H[ermaphrodites]."[50] Pope characterizes their relationship as homosexual because Addison's supposed need for dominance draws suspicion upon his close collaboration with Steele. Pope, by contrast, celebrates his own reluctance to encourage the band of minions who besiege him ("I sought no homage from the Race that write" [219]) or even to preside over coteries of "Wits or Witlings" to advance his reputation. Rather, Pope resigns "the whole *Castalian* State" to Bufo, the subject of his second, more critical and sexually explicit verse portrait.

Traditionally considered a composite portrait of a patron, Bufo maintains his power over the writers who court him by granting them favors ranging from government posts to dinners. Pope describes him as inflated in body and ego ("full-blown *Bufo*, puff'd by ev'vy quill" [232]), ostentatious in his display of wealth ("Much they extoll'd his Pictures, much his Seat" [239]), and essentially passive in the hands of his "undistinguish'd" admirers ("Fed with soft Dedication all day long" [233]). By giving him these characteristics, Pope indicts Bufo's moral as well as aesthetic sense, for this description perfectly recalls the Renaissance stereotype of the sodomite: defined for purposes of prosecution in Edward Coke's *Institutes of the Laws of England,* buggery or sodomy are abominations rooted in "pride, excesse of diet, idlenesse, and contempt of the poor,"[51] qualities grotesquely emphasized in the verse portrait of Bufo. Although not specifically charged with sexual deviance in "Arbuthnot," Bufo uses his social status and wealth to create a relationship of hierarchy and dependence between master and minions; despite their constant flattery of his judgment, the wits receive little sustenance in exchange, for he alone—not the marketplace—determines the value of their work: "He pay'd some Bards with Port, and some with Praise,/To some a dry Rehearsal was assign'd,/And others (harder still) he pay'd in kind" (242-44).

For Pope, the commerce in literature provided an alternative to the eroticized relations of patronage. As the "Epistle to Arbuthnot" asserts, maintaining a "Poet's Dignity and Ease" (263) requires a kind of self-possession that only men independent of masters (and patrons or other employers) can attain; rather than subordinating him to the pleasure of others, Pope's production of verse for the marketplace offers him financial— and therefore intellectual and physical—autonomy: "I was not born for Courts or great Affairs,/I pay my Debts, believe, and say my Pray'rs,/Can sleep without a Poem in my head" (268-70). Venues of aristocratic power such as courts and ministries, and participation in those "Affairs" that define ruling-class masculinity are, paradoxically, beneath Pope's concern, for his rejection of systems of patronage (such as that of the court) makes him subject only to God ("say my Pray'rs") and to economic contracts with other men ("pay my Debts"). Moreover, the poet's ability to refrain from verse functions as a sign of his independence; unmotivated by the need to produce pleasure for others, he can rest from his employments undisturbed. By contrast, the model for Bufo—George Bubb, who adopted the name of his benefactor, Dodington—was entrenched in the system of patronage, functioning as both a client (of Robert Walpole) and a benefactor of writers for the Whig interest (including Edward Young, James Thomson, and James Ralph); according to Horace Walpole, Dodington's own writings unwittingly "left him to be viewed as a courtly compound of mean compliance and political prostitution."[52] In emphasizing his deliberate withdrawal from such concerns, Pope negates their importance as elements in the construction of manhood.

The final figure implicated in the corruptions of the patron/client relationship is Hervey, heir to the earldom of Bristol and vice-chamberlain and lord privy seal at court. Pope begins his attack by describing in explicitly sexual terms Hervey's dual role in the hierarchy of dependence: Hervey's dominant status as a male peer is at odds with the feminizing implications of being a servant to the court, and Pope articulates the debasement that attends submission to kings in his characterization of Hervey as Sporus, the catamite and favorite of Nero. Pope's references to Hervey as a "Curd of Ass's milk," a butterfly, a bug, a "painted Child of Dirt," a "Puppet," a toad, and a reptile are also indicative of his culture's symbolic economy: as Cameron McFarlane maintains, "the [eighteenth-century] sodomite is frequently represented as having sunk into a filthy and bestial nature associated with dirt, mire, offal, and animality."[53] In a rhetorical move that mirrors the confusion of contemporary attitudes toward sodomites, Pope portrays Hervey as both impotent and dangerous, as the political tool or "Puppet" of Walpole, whose policies he consistently advocated, and the influential advisor of Queen Caroline ("Eve"), at whose ear he spitted froth and venom. The Miltonic resonances point to the fact that in Pope's time, "inversion—and the chaos that will inevitably result from upsetting the order of things—[was] the structuring principle of almost all representations of the sodomite."[54] Yet instead of suggesting that Hervey undermines an ideal order, Pope implies that he emblematizes an already corrupted system; Hervey's bisexuality becomes, for Pope, an analogue for the perverse dominance and subordination inherent in patronage itself :

> His Wit all see-saw between *that* and *this*,
> Now high, now low, now Master up, now Miss,
> And he himself one vile Antithesis.
> Amphibious Thing! that acting either Part,

The trifling Head, or the corrupted Heart!
Fop at the Toilet, Flatt'rer at the Board,
Now trips a Lady, and now struts a Lord. (323-29)

Hervey's embodiment of the contradictory characteristics necessary for
success in this system—he is proud and sycophantic, tempter and puppet,
active and passive—is physically expressed in his uncertain gender identity. Both lord (husband to former maid of honour Mary Lepell, and father
of their eight children) and lady (lover of Stephen Fox and Francesco
Algarotti), Hervey represented, in Pope's view, the unsettling and possibly
dangerous instability of character encouraged by the established hierarchy
of dependence. In defining himself against Hervey and the system of
social and sexual relations that he symbolized—"Not proud, nor servile,
be one Poet's praise" (336)—Pope emphasizes his liberation from all
forms of patron/client ties. His insistence upon the equivocal enjoyment
provided by his verses ("[I]f he pleas'd, he pleas'd by manly ways" [337])
links masculinity to the ability to refrain from giving pleasure—a with-
holding of self denied to those engaged in economies of patronage.

The "Epistle to Arbuthnot" ends with a wish that "each Domestick
Bliss" will crown Arbuthnot's last days, and that retirement will prove as
profitable as his previous years of court service:"Preserve him social, chearful, and serene,/And just as rich as when he serv'd a QUEEN!" (416-17).
Self-sufficient domesticity offers the proper setting for poetic activity as
well. Unlike the "Two Curls of Town and Court" (380)—the bookseller
Edmund and Lord Hervey—who furnish titillating lampoons about the
poet for scandal-loving audiences, Pope locates his literary production in a
self-sustaining, insular household. His sentimental depiction of this household seems to exemplify the ideological shift in which "the family, as the
primary location of the social, replaces the *polis* as the sphere of both [mas-
culine] virtue and humanness."[55] Derived neither from town commerce
nor court patronage, Pope's family income has no visible source, no connection at all with the state or its markets ("'What Fortune, pray?'—Their
own,/And better got than *Bestia's* from the Throne" [390-91]). But the idealized retirement of Pope's parents offers him, as their son, only two roles:
imitating his gentle, self-effacing father ("Oh grant me thus to live, and thus
to die!/Who sprung from Kings shall know less joy than I" [404-05]) and
nurturing his ailing mother ("Me, let the tender Office long engage/To
rock the Cradle of reposing Age" [408-09]). While serving as a refuge from
booksellers and patrons, domesticity allows the poet no influence beyond
the sphere of the home: acting like an obedient son requires being quiet

and serviceable—qualities incompatible with writing satiric verse.[56] Appearing nearly a decade after the "Epistle to Arbuthnot," the 1743 *Dunciad* reinvestigates at length the position of retired ease from which Pope pretended to write, and concludes with a more emphatic association between manhood and the rigors of mental labor.

IV

Although Pope's earlier verse had satirized the moral and intellectual short-comings of the upper classes, his challenge to the cultural authority of leisured, aristocratic males receives its most sustained articulation in the *Dunciad*'s fourth book.[57] Once the main focus of Pope's attacks, Hervey is mentioned only briefly here; rather, the systems of power that sustain the dominance of peers like Hervey come under scrutiny for their encourage-ment of effeminacy in ruling-class men—an effeminacy that eventually infects and weakens the entire nation. One of these systems, patronage, lies at the root of aristocratic influence, and Pope displays patrons' corrupting force through their support of Italian opera:

> [A] Harlot form soft sliding by,
> With mincing step, small voice, and languid eye;
> Foreign her air, her robe's discordant pride
> In patch-work flutt'ring, and her head aside.
> By singing Peers up-held on either hand,
> She tripp'd and laugh'd, too pretty much to stand;
> Cast on the prostrate Nine a scornful Look. (4.45-51)

Aficionados of opera and amateur performers themselves, the "singing Peers" encourage opera through subscriptions, since its frivolity prohibits it from standing on its own, or facing rejection from the general, ticket-buying public. Pope's note to this passage emphasizes the threat of sexual indeterminacy that accompanies opera. Although he assigns it female pro-nouns in his verses, his commentary censures its "affected airs" and "effem-inate sounds" (n. 45), terms that imply an exaggerated or simulated femininity and that perhaps allude to the presence of castrati on the stage.[58] The performance of opera erases other distinctions as well: "Chromatic tortures soon shall drive them [the muses] hence,/Break all their nerves, and fritter all their sense:/One Trill shall harmonize joy, grief, and rage" (4.55-57). As Pope's note indicates, this chaos of sound appeals only to effete nobles: "That harmony which conforms to the Sense, and applies to

the Passions"—a harmony exemplified in the music of "Giant Handel"—
"proved . . . too manly for the fine Gentlemen of his age" (n. 54). The
masculine understanding that would appreciate sense in music and bold,
martial sounds has disappeared, and Handel's attempts to revive it—"'To
stir, to rouze, the shake the Soul he comes' " (4.67)— result in his banish-
ment by Dulness "to th' Hibernian shore."

Years earlier, critics had compared Pope to Farinelli and implied that
those who provide entertainment for the public jeopardize their masculinity; here Pope reverses this criticism, for Handel, the paid performer,
attempts to preserve a manly spirit in music while the peers introduce and
protect art forms that promote effeminacy. Patronage, or the network of
relationships between benefactors and dependents that maintains aristocratic influence over the church, the state, and the arts, cooperates with
Dulness in Pope's verses ("There march'd the bard and blockhead, side by
side,/Who rhym'd for hire, and patroniz'd for pride" [4.101-02]). This
exchange of patrons' financial support for influence over their clients not
only erodes the integrity of both parties, but also infects English culture at
large with the degraded tastes of the ruling elite.

Like patronage, education also reproduced ruling-class masculine power,
most explicitly through university training. Pope himself, we have seen,
faced criticism from Hervey and others for a kind of intellectual poach-
ing—that is, his translations of Homer appropriated the classics in a manner presumptuous for a commoner who had never studied at Oxford or
Cambridge. The *Dunciad,* however, reveals that life at school, instead of
guiding noblemen into mental and physical maturity, actually emasculates
them. Book IV's portrayal of aristocratic education and its crippling effects
begins with a speech by the ghost of Dr. Busby, past headmaster of Westminster School, regarding classical translation:

> We ply the Memory, we load the brain,
> Bind rebel Wit, and double chain on chain,
> Confine the thought, to exercise the breath;
> And keep them in the pale of Words till death.
> Whate'er the talents, or howe'er design'd,
> We hang one jingling padlock on the mind:
> A Poet the first day, he dips his quill;
> And what the last? a very Poet still. (4.157-64)

The students' confinement to verse translation without a chance to
exercise the "quick springs of Sense" (4.156) in analysis and criticism leaves

them intellectually stunted.[59] Moreover, Busby's methods—teaching languages through flogging—produces generations of mentally cowed men; upon hearing Busby's voice, "The pale Boy-Senator yet tingling stands,/And holds his breeches close with both his hands" (4.147-48). Pope's note details the political consequences of such fear: "Let it not be imagined the author would insinuate these youthful Senators (tho' so lately come from school) to be under the undue influence of any *Master*" (n. 148). Of course, Pope is very obviously insinuating the subjugation of the young lords to Walpole, their "Master" in Parliament. Busby's teaching, both in content (rote repetition) and in method (physical punishment) ensures that his boys will be boys forever.[60]

The perpetual adolescence of aristocrats remains unchallenged through their European travels; in fact, the Continental tour, which was supposed to add cosmopolitan sophistication to the English gentleman (and prepare him for his future role in governing the state), instead guarantees his immaturity ("[H]e ne'er was Boy, nor Man" [4.288]). A member of the "gay embroider'd race" (4.275), the "young Aeneas" passes undistinguished through school and college, but makes a spectacle of himself abroad:

> Intrepid then, o'er seas and lands he flew:
> Europe he saw, and Europe saw him too.
> There all thy gifts and graces we display,
> Thou [Dulness], only thou, directing all our way! (4.293-96)

Being the object of the gaze and attracting admiration through display of one's graces were usually functions performed by women; here, the noble youth engages in feminine conduct that the tour only encourages. He learns to act obsequiously from the "silken sons" of France (4.298); to be contentedly oppressed from "lands of singing, or of dancing slaves" (4.305); and to prefer effeminate (and perhaps homoerotic) pleasure over martial rigor and commerce from Venice: "Where, eas'd of Fleets, the Adriatic main/Wafts the smooth Eunuch and enamour'd swain" (4.309-10). The tour degenerates into an orgy of consumption, as the passive youth is led by his governor from vice to vice; Pope's ironic adverbial phrases—"with spirit whored," "Judicious drank," "greatly-daring din'd"—emphasize, in order, the pupil's depressing lack of spirit, judgment, and daring. Finally, the aristocrat exchanges "Classic learning"—the "dull lumber of the Latin store" (4.319) that legitimizes his cultural and sexual superiority—for familiar knowledge of the opera. This exchange effectively nullifies his claims to manhood:

> See now, half-cur'd, and perfectly well-bred,
> With nothing but a Solo in his head;
> As much Estate, and Principle, and Wit,
> As Jansen, Fleetwood, Cibber shall think fit. (4.323-26)

As Pope observes, the now complete English gentleman remains incapable of handling his patrimony and exercising his moral character; although mature in years, he lives dependent upon the guardianship of showmen and gamblers such as Sir Henry Jansen, Charles Fleetwood, and Colley Cibber, "who, tho' not Governors by profession, had . . . concern'd themselves in the Education of Youth; and regulated their Wits, their Morals, or their Finances, at that period of their age which is the most important, their entrance into the polite world" (n. 326). In the political rhetoric of Pope's time, careful management of one's paternal estate signified a measure of self-control, or the subordination of individual desire for the good of the nation; from this perspective, the youth and the race he represents are unfit for the ruling-class privileges their birth and gender assign to them.

In the *Dunciad's* final lines, Pope investigates the concept of aristocratic leisure, or the freedom from the need to spend one's life in production of pleasure for others. Pope's upper-class detractors (and critics who adopted the rhetoric of their betters) maintained that the poet's commercial sale of his verse demoted him to the level of a mechanic; moreover, as one whose livelihood involved providing amusement for vacant hours—an act perceived as feminine in his culture—Pope found his gender identity threatened, too. Yet the *Dunciad* challenges this criticism by portraying the masculine elite engaged in leisure pursuits that are a parody of work. Notably, the peers do not (or cannot) compose verse; rather, inspired by Dulness, they play at a kind of labor that levels them with the lowest of commoners:

> The Cap and Switch be sacred to his Grace;
> With Staff and Pumps the Marquis lead the Race;
> From Stage to Stage the licens'd Earl may run,
> Pair'd with his Fellow-Charioteer the Sun;
> The learned Baron Butterflies design,
> Or draw to silk Arachne's subtile line. (4.585-90)

In an effort to while away unproductive time, a duke turns jockey, a marquis becomes a footman, an earl drives a stagecoach, and a baron tries his hand at weaving spider webs. To contemporary readers, the aristocrats' engagement in manual labor would indicate their negligible talents and degraded sensibilities: imitating a worker not only meant adopting an inferior social status, but also a subordinate sexual position, for in Pope's day, masculinity was gauged in terms of class distinctions among men. Those on the bottom of the hierarchy, including laborers, found themselves lowered to the ranks of boys for their lack of economic clout and social influence. In the *Dunciad,* then, the gentlemen's déclassé pastimes demean them to the level of their subordinates, whose menial occupations conferred the stigma of immaturity. These trivial pursuits, though, grow more serious and more damaging when they engage the nation's rulers: "Others import yet nobler arts from France,/Teach Kings to fiddle, and make Senates dance" (4.597-98). In his note to this couplet, Pope describes fiddling as "an ancient amusement of Sovereign Princes, (viz.) Achilles, Alexander, Nero," and explains that senates dance "either after their Prince, or to Pontoise, or Siberia" (n. 598); this list of warlords and tyrants who called the tunes for legislators suggests that indulgence in pleasure is a sign of their destructive willfulness, while the enforced performance of the people's representatives signifies their subservience. In the worst scenario, amusement becomes a privilege of the powerful who seek their satisfaction at the cost of the nation as a whole. The "Unfinish'd Treaties," "Chiefless Armies," and yawning navies depicted in the *Dunciad's* final lines reveal the collapse that occurs when masculine activity gets diverted from its proper channels. Yet poets like Pope are not responsible for such diversions; rather, the text suggests that the fault lies with ruling-class men who cannot fulfill the expectations for their status and gender, and instead, through boredom generated by incapacity, become poor imitators of the mechanics (including fiddlers, singers, and dancers) whom they vilify. Pope's depiction of male aristocrats demeaning themselves in pursuits of pleasure indicates a growing cultural disdain for *homo otiosus,* and a corresponding elevation of men like himself, whose engagement in difficult intellectual labor—including the work of poetry—testifies to their superior manhood.

As part of Pope's response to the devaluation of his work, the *Dunciad* hit its mark. The comments of his posthumous biographers reveal how his indictment of aristocratic masculinity, and the institutions that preserved its authority, helped to revise popular perceptions of the poet's own status and vocation. In his *Life of Alexander Pope* (1769), Owen Ruffhead celebrates Pope's independence from his aristocratic supporters ("though he lived among the great and wealthy, he lived with them upon the easy terms of reciprocal amity, and social familiarity"),[61] but gives even more praise to his commitment to productive intellectual work. Ruffhead extols his "persevering industry" in study and verse-writing as well as his abstention from "the violent agitations of licentious pleasures" (*Life*, 1:20) and gluttony that tainted the elite households where he visited. Pope, Ruffhead notes with approval, found satisfaction in his writing alone rather than with women or at table. Johnson in his "Life of Pope" was more skeptical about the poet's abstemious nature ("He was too indulgent to his appetite"),[62] and located other signs of aristocratic frailty in Pope's preoccupation with his health: "The indulgence and accommodation which his sickness required had taught him all the unpleasing and unsocial qualities of a valetudinary man. He expected that every thing should give way to his humour, as a child whose parents will not hear her cry has an unresisted dominion in the nursery" (*Lives*, 3:198). While critical of Pope's occasional lapses into effeminacy and even childishness, the tenor of Johnson's remarks indicates how much he took for granted the bourgeois ideal of manhood that Pope struggled to legitimize. With approval rather than apology, Johnson foregrounds Pope's involvement in the literary market; Pope, he observes, "considered poetry as the business of his life; and, however he might seem to lament his occupation, he followed it with constancy" (*Lives*, 3:218). And whereas Pope could only try to mitigate the dangers of defining himself as a producer of texts for the amusement of audiences, Johnson argues that Pope's claim to notice lies solely in his works and in the pleasure they give: "One of his favourite topicks is contempt of his own poetry. For this, if it had been real, he would deserve no commendation, and in this he certainly was not sincere; for his high value of himself was sufficiently observed, and of what could he be proud but of his poetry?" (*Lives*, 3:208). Yet Johnson's annoyance with Pope is a testament to Pope's ultimate success rather than to his failure. The affectation and insecurity that Johnson criticizes in Pope arose from tensions about charges of triviality that accompanied his participation in commercial print culture—tensions that Johnson, writing in 1779, no longer had to face. Although Pope himself remained uncertain about whether a consumer economy made possible the poet's masculine independence, his writings effectively attacked the cultural hegemony of gentlemen amateurs. As Johnson points out, Pope's attachment to aristocratic systems of value compromised his claims to independence ("His admiration of the Great seems to have increased in the advance of life" [*Lives*, 3:205]). Yet while Pope himself did not completely embody the bourgeois model of authorship and manhood, he helped inaugurate this model. The remarks by Wollstonecraft and Knox that began this chapter, then, are residual reminders of sentiments that faded away under the challenge, and eventual dominance, of Pope's alternative constructions.

Chapter Four

"I SHALL BE BUT A SHRIMP OF AN AUTHOR":
GRAY, THE MARKETPLACE, AND THE MASCULINE POET

> *To be a poet is a school thing, a skirt thing, a church thing.*
> Saul Bellow, *Humboldt's Gift* (1975)

In 1767, an anonymous pamphlet appeared entitled *The Sale of Authors, a Dialogue, in Imitation of Lucian's Sale of Philosophers*. Written by naval official Archibald Campbell, this pamphlet features Apollo and Mercury conducting an auction among booksellers for the premier writers of the day, including James Macpherson, John Wilkes, Charles Churchill, and Thomas Gray. With its magnified sense of poets' powerlessness in the commercialized literary culture of midcentury England, Campbell's text seems a typical attack on the vigorously expanding book trade. Yet while satirizing the transformation of writers into commodities, and emphasizing the diminished social stature that accompanies this change, Campbell manages to capture with some accuracy the defining features of Gray's literary career. Most obviously, he calls attention to the poet's departure from current norms of masculine behavior:

> *Apollo.* I see this good company are not a little surprised, that so eminent a poet is wrapt up in a watchman's coat. Pray, Mercury, inform them how it happened. . . . .
>
> *Mercury.* You must know, having made many unsuccessful attempts to catch this great poet, I was at last obliged to have recourse to stratagem. Though he has a great deal of poetical fire, nobody indeed more, yet is he extremely afraid of culinary fire, and keeps constantly by him a ladder of ropes to guard against all accidents of that sort. Knowing this, I hired some watchmen to raise the alarm of fire below his windows. Immediately the windows were

seen to open, and the Poet descending in his shirt by his ladder. Thus we caught him at last, and one of the watchmen, to prevent his nerves from being totally benumbed by frigorific torpor, lent him his great coat. Here you have him, watchman's coat, ladder of ropes, silver tea tongs and all.[1]

The tale of Gray's capture that Mercury relates was based on an incident that various Cambridge men exaggerated and embellished; undergraduates out for a good time supposedly alarmed the poet (who indeed had a fear of fire) in his rooms at Peterhouse College. In some versions of the story, Gray responded to their warnings of fire by appearing at the window in a "delicate white night cap"; in others, he descended by means of his ladder (a rope "soft as the silky cords by which Romeo ascended to his Juliet") into a tub of water.[2] All versions, however, strongly hint at the poet's effeminacy; these tales were considered so damaging to Gray's reputation that Horace Walpole warned William Mason to omit the event of Gray's removal from Peterhouse to Pembroke College in his memoirs of the poet's life.[3] Yet despite the precautions of Gray's friends, this incident was seen as illustrative of Gray's character. England's greatest lyric poet of that period was ridiculed as a "butterfly" too feminine to accept the rigors of life at Cambridge—that training ground where privileged youths learned to exercise their social and cultural power.

Gray's effeminacy, moreover, was not considered a mere personal idiosyncrasy. According to Campbell, it also affected his choice of poetic form and subject matter: "The *sweetly plaintive* G[ray], the divine Author of Elegies in a Church-yard, and a Cat" (*Corresp.*, 3:1217) stood accused of producing sentimental, lachrymose verses on trivial subjects. The mention of the "Ode on the Death of a Favourite Cat," with its seemingly unimportant subject matter (Samuel Johnson, like Campbell, considered it a "trifle"),[4] appears to rank Gray with poets whose work privileges feeling over breadth and scope of thought, or emotional display over the concept and design exhibited by heroic poets such as Homer and Milton. And when Gray does attempt the heroic, as in "The Bard," Campbell charges that his poetry consists solely of commonplace sentiments expressed in inflated rhetoric. Praising the "Pindarick *Powers*" evident in "The Bard"'s opening line ("Ruin seize thee, ruthless king!"), Mercury invites the booksellers to "observe with what sublimity he has expressed the very vulgar phrase of Devil take ye" (*Corresp.*, 3:1218). The poet's function as a moral or intellectual monitor for his culture—a "merciful substitute for the legislature,"[5] in the words of his contemporary, Goldsmith—seems abandoned in favor of emotional or imaginative indulgence, a move that Campbell censures in the feminizing epithet ("sweetly plaintive") he repeatedly bestows upon Gray.

Finally, the very form of Campbell's satire suggests the diminution of poets and their verses to a purely ornamental function. Campbell portrays the market in texts as resulting not only in needy writers' sale of copyrights to mercenary booksellers, but in the exchange of the authors themselves for a price. After reciting some of his verses, Gray is auctioned off to Robert Dodsley at the bargain rate of half a guinea; Dodsley defends his bid for Gray's "plaintive poetical *powers*" by noting the low market value of verse: "Poetry is a mere drug now-a-days. It seldom pays for paper, print, and advertising. That I know both to my cost and sorrow" (*Corresp.*, 3:1218). Although the model for this satire—Lucian's *Philosophers for Sale*—dates back to around A.D. 160, the prospect of authors on the auction block calls to mind the contemporary auctions of luxury goods that provided the English upper classes with an opportunity for both entertainment and conspicuous consumption.[6] Like paintings, sculpture, or china vases, writers and their works exist as objects whose exchange is intended to enrich their sellers and adorn the lives of consumers. (Mercury emphasizes Gray's ornamental function, commending both his "elegant" verses and silver tea tongs.) But poetry, unlike the other items at auctions, confers neither wealth nor prestige. As Dodsley complains in Campbell's satire, poetry is a "mere drug"—a worthless commodity that in some ways resembles the patent medicines that also graced the shelves of booksellers' shops. As items for sale, medicines and poems are commonplace and cheap; as narcotics, they endeavor to promote pleasure and reduce pain for a short time, bestowing no real benefits upon consumers who come to crave the sensations they induce.

The criticisms raised in *The Sale of Authors* concerning Gray and his verse are by no means peculiar to Campbell. Rather, anxieties about the increasing marginality of poets and the supposedly trivial and ineffectual nature of their verses were an integral part of the literary culture of the mid-eighteenth century and characterize what Suvir Kaul terms "the public vocational crisis" experienced by poets of the time.[7] As Kaul argues, the increased professionalization of writing threatened to erode hierarchies of distinction among poets—or the boundaries between hacks and gentlemen—since participation in the commercial book trade leveled them all to the status of commodity producers. Yet this crisis in poets' search for a vocation was articulated through socially sanctioned hierarchies of gender as well as class. We have seen that for Augustan writers such as Pope, participation in the book trade compromised poets' authority and masculinity alike, for it rendered them hacks, or literary prostitutes; dependent upon and subjected to the desires of others (particularly booksellers and readers), commercial writers in no way resembled the self-sufficient, disinterested gentlemen who formed the aristocratic ideal of civic virtue.[8] Yet the example of Pope's career also suggests that the steady expansion of the commercial book trade made cultural attitudes toward involvement in the literary market more complicated: regardless of their class backgrounds or political allegiances, writers frequently began to associate masculinity and cultural power with commercial success, while characterizing poets' detachment from the market as an infantile, or effeminate, dependence upon others. (Samuel Johnson and Charles Churchill exemplify this trend; although he detested Churchill's politics and disliked his verse, Johnson admired his fertile invention: convinced that Churchill "cannot produce good fruit," he nevertheless concedes that "a tree that produces a great many crabs is better than a tree which produces only a few.")[9] The following chapter will examine Gray's response to this productivist ethic, and will investigate his attempts to resist the emerging sexual and economic models of authorship.

I

In an essay entitled "Gray Among the Victorians," Malcolm Hicks observes that the censure of Gray's small poetic output by critics such as Matthew Arnold and Leslie Stephen was "as much a moral as an aesthetic" judgment against the poet, for it implied that Gray's "scantiness" arose from his personal failure to realize or develop his talents; Stephen, for instance, "attributes Gray's 'singular want of fertility' largely to the fact that 'he belonged to the class fop or *petit-maître,* mincing, precise, affected, and as little in harmony with the rowdy fellow-commoners [at Cambridge] as Hotspur's courtier with the rough soldiers on the battle-field.'"[10] To Victorian critics like Stephen, Gray's handful of poems not only signified a transgression against the ideal of industry, but against the ideal of masculinity, as well: his sterility as a poet reflects his lack of virility as a man. Contemporaries of Gray voiced a similar censure. His admirers and critics alike viewed writers' active marketing and promoting of their works as the norm, and their reactions to Gray's indifference toward completing his poems and getting them into print ranged from outright disgust to embarrassed apologies. Johnson, who took pride in his own professionalism, deplored the poet's "fantastick foppery" in insisting that he required certain "happy moments" for composition.[11] Percival Stockdale also criticized the dilettante in Gray, stating that his talents were checked by "an unmanly timidity to appear, in the character of an Authour, before a generous publick."[12] Even William Mason, Gray's most devoted partisan, found his reluctance to publish disturbing. While acknowledging that "Mr Gray's life was spent in that kind of learned leisure, which has only self-improvement and self-gratification for its object," Mason described the poet's aloofness as a "foible" in his character, arising from "a certain degree of pride, which led him, of all other things, to despise the idea of being thought an author professed."[13] By way of explanation, however, Mason carefully noted that Gray's "effeminacy" was a contemptuous gesture affected "before those whom he did not wish to please" (*Memoirs,* 403) rather than an inherent trait.[14]

Yet whether written in the spirit of defense or detraction, these assessments of Gray identify masculinity not with aristocratic detachment from the volatile exchange of commodities (as civic humanists had earlier implied), but with active participation and success in the commercial arena. For many of Gray's contemporaries, the social esteem given to male writers depended upon their proper circulation of texts in the literary market. In light of this perspective, Gray's retreat from the market appeared to demonstrate his deficiency as a poet—and his effeminacy. Gray himself repeatedly renounced the role of public writer, and did so in part because he opposed the commodification of literature. Writing to Walpole, he disdainfully compares the bookseller Dodsley's marketing of his poems to the selling of goods: "I promised to send him an equal weight of poetry or prose: so, since my return hither, I put up about two ounces of stuff" (*Corresp.*, 3:1017). In a similar vein, his ironic comment on the rewards of publishing the "Eton Ode"—that he will "relish and enjoy all the conscious pleasure resulting from six pennyworths of glory"—shows his dislike for evaluating poetry in terms of cash (*Corresp.*, 1:282). Self-promotion of any sort disgusted him as well. Gray refused Dodsley's offer to print his picture before his scanty volume of poems, claiming it "would be worse than the Pillory" and shunned publication, lest he be known as a mercenary "fetcher and carrier of singsong" (*Corresp.*, 1:372, 1:343). Only the repeated persuasions of his friends induced Gray to send his work to press. For instance, Gray allowed Walpole to print his best-known poem—the "Elegy Written in a Country Churchyard"—solely to preempt its appearance in the *Magazine of Magazines,* and describes the episode to Walpole with a trope that implies a breach of chastity, as if he had produced a bastard child: "You have indeed conducted with great decency my little *misfortune:* you have taken a paternal care of it, and expressed much more kindness than could have been expected from so near a relation. But we are all frail; and I hope to do as much for you another time" (*Corresp.*, 1:342).

For Gray, publicly circulating one's text is a sign of frailty: a falling away from silence, integrity, and self-containment. Poets, in his view, compromise their reputation not just by publishing too much (or circulating themselves like prostitutes) but by venturing to publish at all. What Gray opposes is, in Jean Baudrillard's words, "the identity that man dons with his own eyes when he can think of himself only as something to produce, transform, or bring about as value"; this "productivist ego" develops because a capitalist political economy not only defines the individual as the possessor of labor power that is sold and exchanged, but "produces the very conception of labor power as the fundamental human potential."[15] By contrast, in a letter to Thomas Wharton, Gray describes his own mode of composition as an unpredictable process that is unsuited to the regulated operations of a market:

> I by no means pretend to inspiration, but yet I affirm, that the faculty in question is by no means voluntary. it is the result (I suppose) of a certain disposition of mind, which does not depend on oneself, & which I have not felt this long time. you that are a witness, how seldom this spirit has moved me in my life, may easily give credit to what I say.[16]

In resisting pressure to define himself as a maker of commodities, Gray lays claim to a type of labor that cannot be represented in commodified form: his talent comes to him as an involuntary state of consciousness whose fluctuations he cannot control and whose products he cannot easily view as items with exchange value.[17] Gray's reasoning here suggests that characterizations of poets as professionals subordinate the individual writer's creative powers to an economy that emphasizes the production and circulation of goods. Several of Gray's poems (particularly those that critics of his day considered his least successful) attempt to imagine forms of literary work that are alternatives to a commercial market in texts, while they take issue with models of the poet as producer. These poems, including the "Sonnet [on the Death of Richard West]," "A Long Story," and the "Ode for Music," all dramatize Gray's resistance to the concepts of literary labor and literary property, along with the configurations of masculinity that such concepts encouraged: in contrast to the growing contemporary emphasis on a "manly" engagement with the market, Gray's early poetry deliberately attempts to reconstruct the noncommercial systems of literary relations prominent in the Renaissance and Restoration. For Gray, the intimacy afforded by exclusively male coteries of writers and readers not only served as a refuge from popular expectations for literary production, but also provided a relatively safe forum for one of his insistent themes: the expression of desire and love for other men, and the anxiety generated by this expression.

Recent scholarship on Gray has given much attention to his homoerotic attachments, from his early involvement with Thomas Ashton, Horace Walpole, and especially Richard West—all members of the Etonian "Quadruple Alliance"—to his late infatuation with Charles Victor de Bonstetten, and has noted the different ways in which this affects the structure and content of his verse.[18] Yet the erotic component of Gray's verse—in Robert F. Gleckner's evocative phrase, "his heroic struggle to come to terms with his own sexuality"[19]—is not wholly responsible for the contours of his career as a poet. As Kaul points out, the dilemma represented in Gray's verse—"the contradictory vocational attractions of the public and the private, of the anonymous market and of the self-selecting coterie"[20]—has its roots in hierarchical systems of value that transcend Gray's individual position. However, these different vocational stances are themselves eroticized in Gray's culture, and his verse exhibits this: while Gray's sensibility had little in common with that of Dorset, Etherege, Savile, Sedley, and Rochester, he shared the court wits' attachment to coterie writing in order to circumvent conformity to the dominant public expectations for both authorial and sexual conduct. In particular, the "Sonnet," "A Long Story," and the "Ode for Music" attempt to evade the increasing emphasis on a masculine literary identity defined by commodity production, while at the same time reflecting on why such an attempt is impossible.

II

Written in August 1742—two months after the death of his beloved West— Gray's "Sonnet" first appeared in print in Mason's edition of Gray's works (*The Poems of Mr. Gray, to which are prefixed Memoirs of his Life and Writings,* 1775), and achieved some notoriety when Wordsworth criticized its use of poetic diction in his preface to *Lyrical Ballads.* The "Sonnet" has not lacked defenders against Wordsworth's charge that it favors a "family language" of literary devices common to poets over the "very language of men" who read the verses.[21] Yet Wordsworth's criticism of this poem, despite its disapproving tone, points out a crucial feature of the "Sonnet'''s structure, rhetoric, and subject matter. The exclusive "family language" used in the poem distances Gray from contemporary readers more than Wordsworth realized, for it encourages private, even eroticized literary exchanges over public, commercial ones.

While West remains the principal object of Gray's sorrow in the "Sonnet," his death also signified the breakup of a nurturing literary community for Gray. West and Gray, together with Horace Walpole and Thomas Ashton, became intimate friends as the "Quadruple Alliance" during their days at Eton. Adopting various pseudonyms, this select group (West, Walpole, and Gray especially) corresponded regularly to share news and gossip; as William Epstein maintains, their elite "intelligence community," with its emphasis on the covert relaying of information, suggests the selective disclosure and "secret understanding" of undercover agents.[22] Yet in their exchange of literary manuscripts, they resembled the coteries of aristocratic male writers prominent in the Renaissance and Restoration more than modern spies. What West, Walpole, and Gray created was a set of literary and affective relationships fostered and cemented by their circulation of texts. Whether West or Walpole were sexually involved with Gray still remains uncertain, but their emotional intimacy clearly rested on their sharing in the creation of each other's work. And the assistance that Gray, Walpole, and West gave to each other's compositions is figured in sexual terms. Gray not only describes Walpole's printing of the "Elegy" with a trope that implies an illegitimate birth, but also inquires about his own "godsons and daughters" borne by Walpole, who "can slip away, like a pregnant beauty . . . into the country, be brought to bed perhaps of twins, and whisk to town again the week after with a face as if nothing had happened" (*Corresp.*, 1:257). Descriptions of the poet as a childbearing woman and of the poet's friend (who helps edit or publish the text) as a paternal guardian appear repeatedly in Gray's letters to Walpole, and suggest a familial dimension to their involvement in each other's work. In these metaphors, Walpole and Gray assume both masculine and feminine identities as they give life to and protect a set of poems, which, like children, are evidence of their union. For these poets, literary production did not require proving their virility through engagement in the market, but instead, emerged from (and sustained) an intimate network of sympathetic friends.[23]

The degree of creative collaboration and emotional intimacy was even greater between West and Gray. Gray constantly revised West's poems, and the very theme of Gray's "Sonnet"—the contrast between the speaker's inner desolation and the rebirth of nature in springtime—reworks the theme of West's "Ad Amicos," whose own origins lay in an elegy by Tibullus and a letter from Pope to Steele printed in *The Guardian*.[24] According to Peter Manning, "these and other literary echoes place Gray's lament within the exchanges of a circle of men of letters. . . . The reader who recognizes the allusions is urbanely complimented, drawn into the band of initiates."[25] Yet the original audience for the "Sonnet" was even smaller than the number of readers who appreciated this "intimate gesture" of inclusion: although Mason added the "Sonnet" to his edition of Gray's poems, during Gray's lifetime it remained concealed from all eyes in his Commonplace Book. For his memorial to West, Gray was reluctant to set up the boundary assumed by publication, and distinguish his work from that of his friend: when Gray first considered publishing his own poems—upon Walpole's suggestion, in 1747—the volume was to have included works by West as well, and only the small size of their "Joynt-Stock" impeded the project (*Corresp.*, 3:1200). The intercourse between Gray and West takes place within what Hélène Cixous terms the realm of the gift: the poets' inclination to continue the "circuit of an exchange"[26] with each other is opposed to the patriarchal economy, which favors the strict demarcation of property boundaries—boundaries essential to the commercial market in print. The structure and content of Gray's "Sonnet" show not only his rejection of the proprietary view of his work that the market encouraged, but also his cultivation of the affectional, even erotic ties with readers that accompanied the private circulation of texts.

Gray's choice of the sonnet for his poem—a form neglected throughout most of the eighteenth century—seemed to determine that it would not be circulated for sale. If, as Paul Oppenheimer suggests, the sonnet "marks a turning point in the history of the lyric—away from the poem as pure public performance [addressed to others]" and toward introspection, then Gray's using the sonnet signals his resistance to the very public nature of literary culture in his day.[27] The only other lament written by Gray for his friend appears in Book II of "De Principiis Cogitandi," a "Metaphysic" poem dedicated to West: written in Latin and circulated only among Gray's intimate friends, the verses, like the "Sonnet," remained inaccessible to contemporary readers until Mason printed them in the *Memoirs*. Besides being fashioned in deliberately unpopular styles, the "Sonnet" and "De Principiis Cogitandi" are also distinguished by their homoeroticism. The elegy on West (addressed by his Eton pseudonym of "Favonius") that begins Book II of "De Principiis" consists of 29 lines written shortly after West's death on 1 June 1742. In them, Gray expresses anguish at West's suffering, somewhat misleadingly implying his presence at the sickbed of his friend, watching the heaving of "a breast never slow to respond to another's pain."[28] As Gleckner notes, the elegy is suffused by a "heart-wrenching guilt . . . coupled with an equally powerful self-lamentation that [barely] escapes self-pity" since Gray had neglected seeing his friend for years before his death.[29] Yet the poem insists upon the fiction of Gray's attending West, providing line upon line of details regarding West's decline ("eyes grow[ing] dull," a "loving face grow[ing] pale") and creating the impression of their physical as well as emotional intimacy. Gray then portrays himself as the victim of West's desertion, asking the "inspiration" of his verse to "look back on these tears, also, which, stricken with love, I pour out in memory of you . . . while my only wish is to mourn at your tomb and address these empty words to your silent ashes" (332). Much of Gray's later verse, particularly the "Sonnet" and the "Elegy Written in a Country Churchyard," continue this mourning; in George E. Haggerty's words, "[i]t is almost as if Gray finds himself in this moment of regret and realizes his own poetic capabilities in this moment of loss."[30]

Yet even if, as Haggerty argues, the culture of sensibility encouraged his self-representation as "the melancholy figure of male-male desire,"[31] Gray's most explicit portrayals of love and loss remained in his Commonplace Books, inaccessible to all but a few (male) readers. Composed two months after the Latin elegy, the "Sonnet" likewise mourns the breakdown of community. Fluent in Italian, Gray knew the work of Petrarch, and his "Sonnet" imitates Petrarchan verses in form (the rhyme scheme and stanza breaks) and content (an imitation of Sonnet 310, describing the contrast between the return of spring and the poet's desolation over Laura's death). Gray adopts the persona of a lover in brooding over the renewed life and awakened sexuality of the natural world: amid the teeming "cheerful fields" and the birds' "amorous descant," the poet remains isolated and sterile in his grief: "I fruitless mourn to him that cannot hear,/And weep the more because I weep in vain" (13-14). The usual forms and devices of the Petrarchan sonnet are employed to express an unconventional affection in Gray's poem, for the object of Gray's grief and longing is male; yet the homoerotic resonances of the "Sonnet" extend beyond the mere change in the gender of the love object. For Gray, writing is a function of relationships between men (his "Sonnet" circles back on itself, beginning and ending with the words "in vain" since West cannot respond to it); as Kaul states, "the loss it mourns is actually the passing of a shared, enabling poetic credo, cultural discourse, social tradition"[32]—a tradition of coterie writing that would prevent from being "fruitless" the poet's gesture toward a sympathetic, loving auditor. Moreover, Gray's adopting a literary form that seemed archaic—a form associated with the exchanges of manuscripts among

social and intellectual elites that preceded commercial print culture—
reveals his nostalgia for a model of authorship that depends upon and solidifies affectional, sometimes erotic ties. Yet this model of interdependence
became increasingly devalued as effeminate by the reading audiences of
Gray's age, and their suspicion of it informs their reception of his two
poems concerning patronage—"A Long Story" and the "Ode for Music."

III

One of Gray's complaints against writing for pay centers on the alienation
of author from audience that commercial print encourages. In his perception, the market in letters posed a threat to the control that classically educated readers and writers had exercised over literary culture, for he feared
that a mass audience was replacing the genteel patrons who had been the
source of support for writers in previous years. As Gray told Walpole in
1768, "When you first commenced an author, you exposed yourself to pit,
box and gallery. Any coxcomb in the world may come in and hiss, if he
pleases; aye, and (what is almost as bad) clap too, and you cannot hinder
him" (*Corresp.*, 3:1009). Gray's anxieties had some basis in fact, for his reading audience included not only the usual educated men and (occasionally)
gentlewomen, but also literate members of other classes, such as petty merchants, artisans, yeomen, middle-class women, and servants and laborers of
both sexes; the pit, box, and gallery of this audience could all potentially
influence the direction of literary culture through their purchase of texts.
Yet this heterogeneous group of readers had been in existence since at least
the late seventeenth century,[33] and Gray's response to the possible exercise
of its influence was remarkably reactionary for his time: he called for a
revival of patronage to reimpose aristocratic authority over literary production and high aesthetic standards for writers. Gray himself felt allegiance to
England's patron class: born in 1716 into a well-to-do and socially established family of merchants, he attended Eton and Cambridge, afterward
embarking on the grand tour with Walpole, which lasted nearly two years.
After returning to Cambridge in 1741, he resided at Peterhouse as a fellow-
commoner, refusing to submit himself to the demands of a profession.
Later in life, Gray numbered among his friends people of high social rank
and high position in the church and state, most of them attached to the
Whig party interest;[34] his ideal of a union between poets and men of
power emerges from this background. In a letter to Count Francesco
Algarotti, chamberlain to Frederick the Great of Prussia, Gray optimistically envisions a kind of renaissance emerging from the court's regulation

of culture: "I see with great satisfaction your efforts to reunite the congenial arts of Poetry, Musick, & the Dance, which with the assistance of Painting & Architecture, regulated by Taste, & supported by magnificence & power, might form the noblest scene, and bestow the sublimest pleasure, that the imagination can conceive" (*Corresp.*, 2:810).

Despite his endorsement of aristocrats' curatorship of the arts, Gray's experiences with the politics of patronage—detailed in "A Long Story" and "Ode for Music"—display how participation in this kind of literary economy results in a loss of authority for male poets. By the time Gray started writing, cultural prestige was beginning to follow from writers' successful competition in the literary marketplace instead of competition for the favors of patrons. Johnson, for instance, argues that the decline in patronage bolsters writers' integrity: "If learning cannot support a man, if he must sit with his hands across till somebody feeds him, it is as to him a bad thing. . . . While a man is in equilibrio, he throws truth among the multitude, and lets them take it as they please; in patronage, he must say what pleases his patron, and it is an equal chance whether that be truth or falsehood" (*Life*, 5:59). The public trade in ideas that Johnson describes, and the independence that this trade presumably granted to authors, had so influenced writers' representations of themselves that Gray's "A Long Story" and "Ode for Music" reveal his embarrassment over being the object of patronage. And part of this embarrassment was sexual. Johnson's remarks indicate how, in the era of commercial print, male writers were increasingly expected to act as independent economic agents—that is, to support themselves by selling their commodities without waiting "till somebody feeds [them]," like infants, women above the trading classes, and the idle rich. Gray's characterization of the poet as the hen-pecked, infantile plaything of aristocratic women in "A Long Story," and his own ambivalence toward myths of unity between intellectuals and the state in "Ode for Music" display how commercial print culture discredited residual modes of literary production along with the forms of authorial self-presentation that accompanied them.

"A Long Story" bears the distinction of being, in Mason's words, the "least popular of all [Gray's] productions" (*Memoirs,* 227). Written in 1750, the poem was published only once with Gray's approval, in *Designs by Mr R. Bentley, for Six Poems by Mr T. Gray* (1753); upon Gray's request, Dodsley omitted it from the 1767 edition of his poems, and Mason included it in his *Memoirs* rather than printing it alongside of Gray's other verses. Part of the public's dislike for the poem arises from the private nature of the events it narrates. "A Long Story" owed its genesis to a particular instance of aristocratic condescension: residing near Gray at Stoke Poges, Lady Cobham sent her niece, Henrietta Speed, and her companion, Lady Schaub, to relay her compliments on the "Elegy Written in a Country Churchyard." Gray, who was absent at the time, returned their visit and wrote "A Long Story" to commemorate the event.

Yet while these verses originated in circumstances recalling the days of patron-client relations, they question received wisdom about the benefits of such relations. In the poem it immediately becomes clear that the implied audience—the aristocratic ladies and gentlemen assembled to hear the tale—and not the speaker controls the poem's discourse. After four stanzas about the manor house and its history, a voice interrupts the narrator, chastising him for his loquacity: responding to the commanding tone of the interrupter, the speaker adopts a plainer, more direct narrative style: "A house there is (and that's enough)" (21). The poet's subordination appears even more plainly in the following stanzas. Lady Schaub and Henrietta Speed are described as "Amazons" commissioned by Lady Cobham to "rid the manor of such vermin" (52) as verse writers; Gray, by contrast, assumes the form of a "wicked imp" whose diminutive size enables him to escape the clutches of the masculine warrior-women: ("Under a tea-cup he might lie,/Or creased, like dogs-ears, in a folio" [67-68]). His safety, however, proves brief. Unable to resist the spell of the ladies' calling card, Gray finds himself whisked to the manor house where the wealth and status of the peeress and her entourage (which includes the ghosts of her female ancestors) so awe the poet that "his rhetoric forsook him" (117); his power of persuasion is ineffectual before the majesty of class prerogative. He can only defend his verse-making to the polite circle by disclaiming his talent and subordinating his authority to theirs:

"He once or twice had penned a sonnet;
"Yet hoped that he might save his bacon:
"Numbers would give their oaths upon it,
"He ne'er was for a conjurer taken." (125-28)

Despite the advice of the "ghostly prudes" who were her forbears, Lady Cobham possesses sufficient noblesse oblige to forgive the poet and invite him to dinner. Aristocratic conduct has changed since the time of "fierce Queen Mary": the social power of upper-class women in Gray's day reveals itself through civility instead of severity, and condescension replaces corporal punishment in keeping the poet, like other social inferiors, in line.

"A Long Story" suggests that the poet's role as a dependent of the aristocracy is outmoded to the point of parody. The Amazons' attempts to lure Gray to the manor house—and into a conventional patron-client relationship with high-born, cultured women interested in the arts—trivializes his work and renders him a pitiable victim of female aggression. Gray's playful tone in "A Long Story" does not obscure the point of his satire: patronage by wealthy women (who were an increasing part of the mid-century reading public) emasculates the poet, quelling the force of his speech and rendering him a harmless form of entertainment for leisure-hour consumption.

The public's general dislike for "A Long Story" demonstrates how far patronage had fallen into disrepute. Gray's readers resented the poem's topicality: Gray himself notes that the "Verses . . . were wrote to divert that particular Family, & succeeded accordingly, but, being shew'd about in Town, are not liked there at all" (*Corresp.*, 1:335). Composed on a private occasion, the poem seemed remote and even incomprehensible to those who had no part in the exchange of pleasantries between the poet and Lady Cobham. And it must have seemed incongruous for the author of the "Elegy Written in a Country Churchyard"—a work criticizing the arrogance of the rich—to record in verse the hospitality of aristocrats. The "Elegy"'s reputation, which first aroused Lady Cobham's interest in Gray, suggests that poets were no longer dependent on the patronage of elite circles for recognition. Gray's ironic treatment of relations between poets and patrons exposes how these exchanges render poets the object of feminine amusement rather than masculine respect; moreover, with its extensive satiric evocation of Renaissance personages and customs, "A Long Story" implies that these customs (including private support of authors) are hopelessly anachronistic. In removing "A Long Story" from subsequent editions of his work, Gray implicitly acknowledged that cultural power had shifted from titled coteries of readers to a mass audience served by the book trade.

The production and reception of Gray's "Ode for Music" show this shift in cultural power even more explicitly. Written in 1769 to celebrate the installation of Augustus Henry Fitzroy, duke of Grafton, as the chancellor of Cambridge University, the ode exemplifies the reciprocity between patron and client: Grafton the year before had secured Gray's appointment as Regius Professor of Modern History at Cambridge, and the "Ode for Music" was Gray's expression of gratitude. Like the "Sonnet" and "A Long Story," the ode recalls and recreates earlier modes of literary production. But whereas Gray's Petrarchan lament for West and "A Long Story" both posit a break with the past (whether through mourning for previous times or satirizing them), the "Ode for Music" suggests a continuity.

The vision the poem offers is one of mutual support between state power and English culture, a relationship that Grafton is called upon to cultivate. Gray celebrates Cambridge as the place where patronage by England's ruling class helps create a national culture (in the person of a "bard divine" like Milton and a "sainted sage" like Newton); bards and sages, in turn, help buttress the British empire by providing examples of genius that will forever illustrate England's cultural superiority ("There sit the sainted sage, the bard divine,/The few whom genius gave to shine/Through every unborn age and undiscovered clime" [15-17]). Ambivalence toward the waste of talent in a stratified society—a sentiment infused throughout the "Elegy"—finds no expression in the triumphal "Ode for Music." Conspicuously revising the "Elegy"'s much-noted flower and gem stanza (53-56), Gray predicts that Grafton's bounty will descry "[t]he flower unheeded" and "raise from the earth the latent gem," enabling gifted but obscure scholars and poets to serve the church and state (71-76). The poem ends with a voice from the tomb (that of Margaret, mother of Henry VII) assuring Grafton that George III's prudent political course will prove a model for Grafton's term as chancellor.

After the performance of the "Ode for Music" at Grafton's installation, critics descended upon Gray, declaring him a "venal Muse" for prostituting his talent in praise of the rich (*Corresp.*, 3:1070-71). To Gray's contemporaries, the prospect of bards and sages flourishing under Grafton's management of Cambridge seemed unlikely, and the conventional rhetoric of this panegyric appeared almost ludicrously timeworn: a prominent Whig statesman who served as a secretary of state in the Rockingham ministry and as head of the treasury under William Pitt, Grafton was also known for his lax morality and occasional inattention to business (exasperated at Grafton's troublesome lack of resolution, Walpole complained that he behaved "like an apprentice, thinking the world should be postponed to a whore and a horse race" [Walpole, *Corresp.*, 39:100-01]). A parody of the epitaph from Gray's "Elegy" that appeared in the *London Chronicle* illustrates the source of critics' disgust with Gray's ode: in contrast to the "Elegy"'s much-admired portrayal of the "authentic" poet (who secludes himself from the avenues of official power), Gray's actions seem a throwback to the degrading cultural practices of former times:

> Here rests his head upon the lap of earth,
> One nor to fortune nor to fame unknown;
> Fair science frown'd not on his humble birth,
> And smooth-tongued flatt'ry mark'd him for her own.[35]

Gray himself felt reduced to servitude in composing the ode: after accepting Grafton's patronage the year before, he thought himself "bound in gratitude" to perform the "task of writing those verses," although he realized that because of its subject matter, the "Odicle" was "by nature doom'd to live but a single day" (*Corresp.*, 3:1070).[36] Although two editions of the ode were printed for the university, Gray himself had no hand in preparing them for publication and his name did not appear on the title page;[37] while he confided to James Beattie that he expected "abuse" from "news-paper parodies, & witless criticism" (*Corresp.*, 3:1070), he obviously felt no need to solicit more of it.

Public response to the "Ode for Music" suggests how the alternatives to commercial print had diminished by Gray's time. Although Gray maintained that circulation of texts on the literary market reduced them to the level of mere commodities, avoiding the market appeared impossible, or even morally suspect, for male writers. His evocation of earlier forms of literary production in the "Sonnet [on the Death of Richard West]," "A Long Story," and "Ode for Music" results not in these forms' successful revival, but in a sense of irrevocable loss, parody, or cynicism: West's death brings an end to the shared creation of poems among gentlemen; the aristocrats' admiration of the poet in "A Long Story" transforms him into a feminized ladies' companion, and paying his debt of gratitude to the duke of Grafton gives him the character of a venal hanger-on. While commodified print seems to have provided authors with more diverse audiences and readers with more varied texts, it also worked to discredit other modes of circulating literature, particularly those founded upon social relationships like patronage: as Gray's experience shows, opposition to commercial practices carried with it the stigma of effeminacy, and this combination of capitalist and patriarchal discourse clearly articulated emergent cultural expectations for the careers of male poets. Yet not all sites of resistance against commercial print were closed off for Gray. In composing his most popular odes, from "Ode on the Spring" (written in 1742) to the "Progress of Poesy" and "The Bard" (both published in 1757), Gray attempted to recover an authoritative role for poets that avoided the stigma of effeminacy and dependence, while resting on something other than writers' success as men in the marketplace.

IV

Gray's efforts to create this position of authority for poets have been obscured by modern accounts of poets' marginality in mid-eighteenth-century culture. Following John Sitter's thesis describing poetry's retreat from political and historical themes—a retreat that includes a switch from memory to fancy as the basis for composition—Wallace Jackson and Paul Yoder argue that in the midcentury "literature of crisis," and particularly in Gray's work, "the cost of the visionary experience . . . is marginality or death."[38] Likewise, Henry Weinfield reads the "Elegy Written in a Country Churchyard" as a formal and thematic expression of Gray's "consciousness of a lost center" in society, and his "sense of the separation of the poet from the public sphere."[39] Contemporaries of Gray also perceived—or imagined—an increasing disregard for poets and a decline in their influence over public and private conduct. Charles Churchill, writing in 1763, nostalgically recalls the more responsive audiences of Pope's age ("Is this the Land, where, in those worst of times,/The hardy Poet rais'd his honest rimes/ . . . /Bade Pow'r turn pale, kept mighty rogues in awe"), while Robert Lloyd compares the Romans' awed distinction of Horace in the Forum with the recognition given to the "modern breed" of writer: like Horace, contemporary poets are singled out from the crowd, "But 'tis by way of wit and joke,/To laugh, or as the phrase is, *smoke.*"[40]

These statements of despair over poetry's declining importance, however, circulated along with texts insisting on poets' centrality in English life, particularly on their function as custodians of a public spirit that seemed endangered in an increasingly pluralistic society. Thomas Cooke asserts that "a good Poet and a good Critic are public Benefits" for improving taste and manners, while for Aaron Hill, the "Public Interest" of England requires subsidizing the poet by "taking him off from all Cares, and Inquietude; and then [putting] him upon Subjects, most likely to do Honour to his Country."[41] The basis for such concern over poets lies in their supposed ability to rise above factions in political and social life to advocate the welfare of the nation as a whole. For writers like Percival Stockdale, "the bard's quick, and comprehensive soul" brings before him "the universe, and all created things," enabling him to transcend the more constricted views of those pursuing their particular interests ("The Poet feels not for himself alone;/He makes the cause of human kind his own").[42] In these accounts the poet replaces the gentleman, whose rule over English society had been justified by the independence, learning, and leisure that enabled him to comprehend the totality of national life.[43]

Yet assuming this controlling stance proved difficult for midcentury poets like Gray, who confronted an increasingly heterogeneous audience unaware of the traditional canon, conventions, and social significance of poetry. By the late 1740s—shortly after he began writing his odes—Gray was convinced that polite society had voluntarily abandoned the task of upholding literary standards, forgetting all distinctions in its desire to consume commodified print. As he complains to Walpole, "Litterature (to take it in its most comprehensive Sense, & include every Thing, that requires Invention, or Judgement, or barely Application & Industry) seems indeed drawing apace to its Dissolution" (*Corresp.*, 1:265). An illiterate aristocracy appears to be at fault for this decline: "Mr. Bedingfield in a golden shower of panegyrick writes me word, that at York-races he overheard three People, whom by their dress & manner he takes for Lords, say, that I was impenetrable & inexplicable, and they wish'd, I had told them in prose, what I meant in verse, & then they bought me (which was what most displeased him) & put me in their pocket" (*Corresp.*, 2:532). Even though the lords purchased Gray's work, they were not attracted to him by a shared aesthetic sensibility; despite their birth and education, Gray found them to be ignorant and thoughtless consumers. Churchill joins Gray in blaming a neglectful aristocracy for poetry's decline and in his nostalgia for a time "When Nobles, with a lore of Science bless'd,/Approv'd in others what themselves possess'd"; while he charges the social elite with relinquishing its duty as the guardian of English literary culture, he represents the bourgeoisie, who rival the elite in wealth, as "men of narrow souls" preoccupied with the "dull drowsy track of business" ("The Author," 29-30; 93; 95). Untrained in liberal arts, the middle-class reading public supposedly lacked the skills to comprehend and the confidence to judge poetry; as Stockdale notes, members of this class wholeheartedly relied on periodicals like Ralph Griffiths's *Monthly Review* to formulate their taste:

> [M]onthly readers, ever daily fools,
> Adopt his nonsense for true critic rules;
> Fit only, o'er the coffee's gentle stream,
> Of Nabobs, and of India-stock to dream,
> Presume to try the Poet as their peer,
> Enjoy the malice, and applaud the sneer. (*The Poet*, 20-21)

It is uncertain whether the quality of audiences actually had declined, but the perception at midcentury was that things were getting worse, as poets more bitterly and more frequently acknowledged the social and intellectual differences between themselves and their readers.[44] One of these differences lay in their conception of literary labor and its products. To many writers of the period, consumers of commercial print proved an inadequate audience for poetry, in part because they viewed verse as one commodity for entertainment among others. It seemed that for aristocrats and bourgeoisie alike, poetry's didactic and moral function had been subsumed by its function as an amusement "[t]o sooth, with change, the idle, and the vain" (Stockdale, *The Poet,* 23). Some critics of contemporary letters traced this decline in the status of poetry to the pursuit of luxury, which, fueled by advances in trade and manufacturing, supposedly encouraged the expansion of the market in letters. John Brown, in *An Estimate of the Manners and Principles of the Times* (1757) argues that only reading "that can . . . prevent the unsupportable Toil of *Thinking*" is able to "entertain the languid Morning-Spirit of modern Effeminacy"; this "refined Indulgence" of the reading public (all classes included) is fed by booksellers, who promote "weekly Essays, amatory Plays and Novels, [and] political Pamphlets" over the less-appealing rigors of classical verse accessible only to educated men.[45] More moderate in tone, Goldsmith's *Enquiry* (1759) also traces the decline of English letters to a corruption of taste and an undue regard for sensual pleasure on the part of the Great, as "a jockey, or a laced player, supplies the place of the scholar, poet, or the man of virtue" (*Collected Works,* 1:311).

While not directly addressing the claims of cultural critics, Gray took part in this attempt to link the decline of aristocratic dominance over letters to an encroaching effeminacy of taste and the success of popular literary forms; his odes repeatedly articulate his concern over how the consumer market in texts trivializes poetry. From his early "Ode on the Spring" to his final major poems—"The Bard" and "Progress of Poesy"—Gray questions the kind of communication possible between poets and their audiences and debates the extent of poets' control over the reception of their works. The speakers in the odes are often poets, and the odes repeatedly thematize the issue of whether poetry can influence thought or arouse emotion in those whom it addresses.[46] While acknowledging that commercial print had removed poets from a sympathetic coterie of readers and defined them as purveyors of entertainment for noblemen, nabobs, and the masses at large, Gray tried to reclaim a cultural position for poets that would render them not marginal but central, not mercantile but heroic. And in doing so, he defined resistance to commerce, not participation in it, as the truly masculine stance for writers.

V

Much of Gray's poetry consists of odes, a genre conventionally believed to distance poets from their audiences.[47] Yet Gray's odes also make this distance their theme, articulating specific concerns about whether poets and readers can ever share a community of understanding: the views they present challenge the "pragmatic" poetic theory endorsed throughout the eighteenth century,[48] for instead of taking for granted the popular Horatian dictum that literature should please and instruct, the odes question whether poets can in fact interpret experiences for readers or affect them with their words. The first of these poems, Gray's "Ode on the Spring," is in part about a failure of sympathy between the speaker, who is a poet, and his hearers. In the opening stanzas, the spring, with its "untaught harmony" of voices—the birds and the zephyrs—occupies one spatial frame ("Lo! where the rosy-bosomed Hours,/Fair Venus' train, appear" [1-2]), and the speaker's commentary on it takes place in another:

> Where'er the oak's thick branches stretch
> A broader browner shade;
> Where'er the rude and moss-grown beech
> O'er canopies the glade,
> Beside some water's rushy brink
> With me the Muse shall sit, and think
> (At ease reclined in rustic state)
> How vain the ardour of the crowd,
> How low, how little are the proud,
> How indigent the great! (11-20)

The poet exists apart from the temporal, eroticized realm of "rosy-bosomed Hours" and apart from the "crowd" whose actions he judges. In contrast to the fluttering, dancing, time-bound insects and their human counterparts, the speaker—identifying himself with "Contemplation"—concerns himself with eternal, permanent truths and rehearses the conventional wisdom of retirement poems like John Pomfret's "The Choice" or Pope's "Ode on Solitude" ("How low, how little are the proud,/How indigent the great!"). Self-consciously adopting the stance of an Augustan poet, the speaker finds universal meaning in particular circumstances and instructs his audience with it: his ability to stand back and derive maxims from what he sees appears to justify his portrayal of the action within the framed picture that he creates, and his point of view seems authoritative because he can extract a useful moral from the insects' play. But the poet's authority is dramatically undermined by an unexpected voice that interrupts his reflections. A fly—one of the "sportive kind"—replies to the speaker, reminding him of his own likeness to the objects of his musings:

> Poor moralist! and what art thou?
> A solitary fly!

Thy joys no glittering female meets,
No hive hast thou of hoarded sweets,
No painted plumage to display:
On hasty wings thy youth is flown;
Thy sun is set, thy spring is gone—
We frolic, while 'tis May. (43-50)

The fly disputes the poet's assumed superiority to the life he contemplates by proclaiming that he is inside, not outside, the scene of ephemeral erotic play that he depicts; the speaker is just another short-lived fly, and a lonely, aging one at that.

Gray's treatment of the speaker in this ode is often explained as an expression of his isolation from the life around him.[49] Yet even if it is autobiographical, the ode does more than expose Gray's private dilemma of loneliness; it also questions whether poets can stand above a knowable audience and address it with confidence and authority. The speaker's pronouncements, made with the help of his muse, resemble the stock poetic sentiments of Augustan humanism, which supposedly apply to all people in all times: retirement is the ideal state, people can metaphorically be compared to insects, and all bustle and pride end in death. But instead of appearing as the source of ageless truths about the scene before him, the speaker is revealed to have an incomplete, limited perspective, no different from anyone else's. The unexpected reaction of an unintended, dissenting audience—the fly—challenges his assumption of a privileged level of sensibility.

In his "Ode on the Spring," Gray portrays a disruption of the dynamics expected between the speaker and the object of contemplation. The speaker's control over the scene, which he assumes from his stance as a poet, is contested by an audience rejecting his attempts to impose significance upon its actions. Gray's "Ode on a Distant Prospect of Eton College" also dramatizes the failure of the speaker's rhetorical strategies. The ode is a topographical poem; like others of its kind, it portrays the impressions of an observer gazing at the distant landscape from a height while ordering and organizing the scene that is passive under his eyes. Gray's speaker uses his distant, superior stance to present his version of Eton life. The boys "disporting" on the lawns, enjoying the health, cheer, wit, and invention that come with youth, preserve their happiness by being unaware of the misfortunes that the speaker, unconfined by the limited vision of childhood, sees awaiting them. The ode ends with the speaker being forced into silence; he cannot relate what he knows to the boys playing in the fields below him. In concluding that "where ignorance is bliss,/'Tis folly to be wise" (99-100), Gray's speaker suppresses his urge to alert and warn them about their future.

Gray represents the distance between speaker and intended audience as unbridgeable. And the rhetorical figures that he employs throughout the poem stress the impossibility of communication. The first three stanzas of the ode begin with apostrophes: first, the speaker invokes "Ye distant spires, ye antique towers,/That crown the watery glade" (1-2); then turns to the features of the landscape ("Ah, happy hills, ah, pleasing shade,/Ah, fields beloved in vain" [11-12]); and finally asks Father Thames to identify the boys at play (21-30). Critics of the poem have viewed these speeches to inanimate objects as lapses in Gray's artistic power. Johnson, for one, regards as "useless" the speaker's supplication to Father Thames because he asks the river something that it cannot possibly know (*Lives,* 3:435). Landscape in the poem never does respond to the speaker's articulated needs: the gales from the hills and fields only "seem to soothe" his "weary soul" (18), and the river is unable to answer his questions about the boys. But while Johnson assumes that communication is the speaker's intent, establishing contact with another is probably not apostrophe's function in the ode. Instead, as Jonathan Culler suggests, the address to "thou" common to apostrophe "can in fact be read as an act of radical interiorization and solipsism," as objects of the speaker's remarks "function as nodes or concretizations of stages in a drama of mind."[50] The objects that Gray's speaker addresses are not expected to react to him; rather, the "happy hills," "pleasing shade," and "fields beloved in vain" are invoked to show his nostalgia for childhood and inescapable distance from his past. Instead of initiating relations between the speaker and scene surrounding him, the repeated use of apostrophe in the ode works to forestall communication by its emphasis on expressing the speaker's emotional state.

Halfway through the ode, the speaker's modes of address become even more self-expressive and result in a kind of confusion over the audience to whom he directs his remarks. After celebrating—and idealizing—the schoolboys' carefree life, he abruptly begins a description of the evils that he sees already upon them:

> Yet see how all around 'em wait
> The ministers of human fate,
> And black Misfortune's baleful train!
> Ah, show them where in ambush stand
> To seize their prey the murtherous band!
> Ah, tell them, they are men! (55-60)

The object of these imperative verbs is uncertain here, but it seems that the speaker is exhorting himself to represent and communicate his perceptions to the boys ("show them," "tell them"). In the following stanzas, he goes on to name the misfortunes that await them: "These shall the fury Passions tear" (61); "Ambition this shall tempt to rise" (71); "The stings of Falsehood those shall try" (75). The vale in which the children are playing is then transformed into the "vale of years," populated by the "painful family of Death"—illness, hardship, physical decay—that the speaker on his promontory observes and describes. The speaker presents his action in the passive voice ("A grisly troop are seen" [82]), as if effacing himself as the one who envisions the scene and who can relay that vision to the schoolboys. In the concluding lines, he decides not to alert the students to their destiny, choosing silence instead.

Despite his expressed desire to relate what he knows to the boys, the speaker ends the poem—as he began it—by talking to himself. By constantly addressing himself with imperatives ("see," "show," and "tell") with rhetorical questions ("why should they know their fate?"[95]) and with commands ("No more"), by repeatedly using apostrophes that demand no response, and finally by refusing to tell what he knows of the future, Gray's speaker makes himself both the source and target of his discourse. What Culler terms the "circuit of communication"[51] between speaker and audience is thus constantly, and deliberately, interrupted. Of course, one could argue that Gray's readers, and not the schoolboys, are the speaker's intended audience. Yet even if readers appreciate the poem's message about the hazards of maturity, within the poem itself communication is all but impossible. The devices of the speaker's rhetoric, rather than being directed toward the Eton schoolboys, refer back to the speaker; he eventually persuades himself that representing and relating their futures to them would be worthless. The distance between speaker and audience that his speech seems intended to narrow ("tell them," "show them") is both emphasized and left intact.

Like the "Ode on the Spring," Gray's "Eton Ode" questions whether a speaker's interpretations of experience can be shared or understood by others, or whether his perspective is confined to himself alone. When he wrote these poems, Gray was confronting the same problem faced by his speakers—that of reaching a responsive, appreciative audience—and he located the source of this problem in the culture that commodified print fostered. To Gray, the market in texts did not enhance communication, but rather deprived poets of their authority to interpret experience, for instead of writing to a circle of like-minded friends, they found themselves directing their verses to an unfamiliar public whose class background, education, and taste varied widely. Gray's uncertainty about addressing his readers and his pessimism about the future of literature signal his disillusion over the loss of an intimate, elite community of men—an idealized union of writers and their audiences that had been supplanted by the commercial literary system. Gray's later odes continue to articulate this pessimism, constructing images of ideal receptive audiences but at the same time disputing the importance of the role that any audience plays in the creation and interpretation of verse.

VI

For a decade after his first two odes appeared, Gray published nothing in that genre. In the meantime, his "Elegy Written in a Country Churchyard," which Dodsley printed in February 1751, established Gray's fame as a poet. Five editions of the poem were sold by the end of 1751 (four of them within two months of the poem's appearance), and ten came out by 1756.[52] Virtually all readers and critics praised the "Elegy"; as the *Monthly Review* remarked just after its publication, "the excellence of this little piece amply compensates for its want of quantity."[53] Part of the poem's appeal no doubt arose from Gray's apparent self-portrait in the closing lines. Given the "popular preoccupation with the artistic sensibility"[54] that took root in midcentury, readers of the "Elegy" most likely beheld Gray in the epitaph that the poet-speaker creates for himself:

> Here rests his head upon the lap of earth
> A youth to fortune and to fame unknown.
> Fair Science frowned not on his humble birth,
> And Melancholy marked him for her own. (117-20)

An obscure genius and man of feeling ("He gave to Misery all he had, a tear,/He gained from Heaven ('twas all he wished) a friend" [123-24]), the speaker is distinguished by his sympathy for the dead rustics. Yet in the "Elegy," the qualities that define the poet's character include not only imaginative identification with people lacking social importance (the speaker elegizes the cottagers "far from the madding crowd" [73]), but also separation from all human community: alienated by poverty from the "Proud" whose remains are interred in cathedrals, and by knowledge from the laborers buried in the moldering graves, the speaker exists apart from the society he describes. His audience in the poem, who reads his epitaph and listens to the "hoary-headed swain['s]" narrative of his life, consists of a sole "kindred spirit"—an outsider like himself led by "Contemplation" to the churchyard (95-96). Gray's portrayal of the isolated speaker seems to voice, and indeed validate, his own feeling of detachment from an understanding public; the "Elegy" mystifies and personifies this alienation, transforming it from a result of commodified print to a feature of the sensitive poet's temperament.

In light of this, the public's enthusiastic response to the "Elegy" understandably embarrassed and annoyed Gray. He believed that readers liked the poem only because its theme fit the current vogue for graveyard verse: it "owed its popularity entirely to the subject . . . [for] the public would have received it as well if it had been written in prose."[55] Yet something more subtle (and, for Gray, more insidious) than literary fashion accounted for the "Elegy"'s success. Reflecting on Johnson's assessment of the poem ("The 'Churchyard' abounds with images which find a mirrour in every mind, and with sentiments to which every bosom returns an echo" [*Lives,* 3:441]), John Guillory points out that the "Elegy" was a "linguistically anomalous production" for Gray because of what its very "commonness"—or its departure from his usual style of poetic diction—signified: readers barely educated could find the poem accessible while remaining unaware of its sources in classical and Renaissance texts. Thus the "Elegy" "effaces the struggle for cultural capital" by presenting its acquisition as the realization of an innate human potential: "The cultural entitlement that for Gray is defined by classical literacy, by his immense learning, is thus acquired by his readers at a *discount,* at the cost only of acquiring the vernacular literacy requisite to reading the poem."[56] The approval and enthusiasm evoked by Gray's "Elegy" indicate how easily various classes (and both sexes) were able to understand and appropriate its statements. For instance, Thomas Gisborne in his *Enquiry into the Duties of the Female Sex* (1797) advises women in their leisure time to adopt "the custom of committing to the memory select and ample portions of poetic compositions . . . for the sake of private improvement," and recommends Gray's work to "kindle benevolence by pathetic narrative and reflection."[57] (Gisborne forbids public recitation of poetry, since propriety dictates that women should be consumers of literature, not performers actively reproducing the text.) Moreover, the tone of Gray's "Elegy"—the nostalgic and sentimental conception of the anonymous poor and the anonymous poet—also increased the poem's popularity with a wide reading public. According to Colin Campbell, modern consumerism has its roots in "longing as a permanent mode [of being], with the concomitant sense of dissatisfaction with 'what is' and a yearning for 'something better.'"[58] The rise of consumerism in the book trade was only one aspect of this trend. By bringing to consciousness the problem of thwarted talents and frustrated abilities—a unique feat for a poet in Gray's time—the "Elegy" thematizes the sensation of wishfulness that is an integral element of consumption.

Although the "Elegy" provided him with an attentive, sympathetic audience, Gray found the applause of readers at large to be more humiliating than gratifying; the poem's unexpected success in the marketplace ranked him among the vulgar, crowd-pleasing writers whom he despised. And Gray associated this kind of success with effeminacy on the part of writers and readers alike. Writing to Walpole, he traces the decline of literature to texts like Joseph Spence's "pretty Book," *Polymetis* (1747)—a collection of dialogues intended to introduce Roman poetry and art to an audience composed of people other than scholars and antiquarians. Gray's deliberately bad spelling and grammar, and his imitation of foppish, fashionable chatter indicate his contempt for the simplification—and the marketing—of classical culture:

> [I]f you ask me what I read; I protest I don't remember one Syllable; but only in general, that they were the best-bred Sort of Men in the World, just the Kind of *Frinds* one would wish to meet in a fine Summer's Evening, if one wish'd to meet any at all. the Heads & Tails of the Dialogues, publish'd separate in 16ᵐᵒ, would make the sweetest Reading in Natiur for young Gentlemen of Family & Fortune, that are learning to dance. (*Corresp.*, 1:265)

Gray himself seemed determined to dismantle the image the "Elegy" earned him as a popular author by publishing the "Progress of Poesy" and "The Bard" in August 1757. Although readers bought about 1,200 copies of the odes within two weeks (*Corresp.*, 2:524), and although the poems were reviewed or reprinted in nearly every major magazine, not everyone favored them. Admirers of Gray including Walpole, Mason, "Estimate" Brown, Richard Hurd, and Henrietta Speed enjoyed them, as did Bishop Warburton, David Garrick, and the poets William Shenstone, Mark Akenside, and Anna Seward. Yet Gray knew very well what most of his audience thought:

> Ld Lyttelton & Mr Shenstone admire me, but wish I had been a *little clearer.* Mr (Palmyra) Wood owns himself disappointed in his expectations. . . . Dr Brown, says I am the best thing in the language. Mr F[o]x, supposing the

Bard sung his song but once over, does not wonder, if Edward the Ist did not
understand him. this last criticism is rather unhappy, for tho' it had been sung
a hundred times under his window, it was absolutely impossible, Kg Edward
should understand him: but that is no reason for Mr Fox, who lives almost
. 500 years after him. 'tis very well: the next thing I print shall be in Welch.
that's all. (*Corresp.*, 2:523-24)[59]

Despite Gray's supposed indifference to his poems' reception ("nobody
understands me, & I am perfectly satisfied" [*Corresp*, 2:522]), the "vanity of
an Author" was hurt by the public's judgment. And criticisms by "people of
condition" (particularly the statesmen and divines whose remarks he continually repeats) troubled him most, for he expected that out of all readers,
they would most likely appreciate the learned, highly allusive odes. Public
response to the poems, however, could have been predicted; perhaps composing them with the "Elegy" in mind, Gray deliberately fashioned the
odes to exclude as readers women and, by extension, men lacking a liberal,
university education:

[O]ne thing I must say, (but this is sacred, & under the seal of confession) there
is no Woman, that can take pleasure in this kind of composition. if Parts only
& Imagination & Sensibility were required, one might (I doubt not) find them
in that Sex full as easily as in our own: but there is a certain measure of learning necessary, & a long acquaintance with the good Writers ancient & modern, which by our injustice is denied to them. and without this they can only
catch here & there a florid expression, or a musical rhyme, while the Whole
appears to them a wild obscure unedifying jumble. (*Corresp.*, 2:477-78)

Although he acknowledges the patriarchal "injustice" toward women,
Gray was determined that his intended audience for the odes remain educated men; disregarding the advice of his friends, he refused to provide
explanatory notes for obscure passages, stating his reluctance to insult his
readers' understanding. The motto prefixed to the odes declared these
poems "vocal to the Intelligent alone," and Gray claimed that his ambition
"was terminated by that small circle" of cognoscenti (*Corresp.*, 2:797)—"a
few Men of sense & character" who would comprehend and appreciate his
work (*Corresp.*, 1:447).[60]

In the sister odes, Gray attempted to recreate a precommercial past.
Their obscurity, which takes the form of elaborate allusions to mythology
and history, challenged the contemporary fashion for literature of sensibility: their difficulty was meant to frustrate the easy consumption of Gray's

work by alienating a popular audience accustomed to accessible texts. Moreover, Gray's odes were directed to men whose education and class status enabled them to recognize the conventions of elite culture, a culture threatened by the rise of commercial print and the consequent increase in supposedly inept readers (like women and the middle classes). His list of the people who commented on the odes includes (with rare exceptions) only the names of men holding important civil and ecclesiastical offices, such as George Lord Lyttelton, member of the privy council and chancellor of the exchequer; William Wildman Barrington-Shute, treasurer of the navy, secretary at war, and chancellor of the exchequer; Henry Fox, secretary of state, paymaster general, and leader of the House of Commons; Richard Hurd, bishop of Lichfield and Worcester; and Robert Wood, under-secretary of state. Unfortunately, though, most of these elite readers proved deficient in their knowledge of both classical mythology (necessary for "The Progress of Poesy") and English history (necessary for "The Bard"). As Gray commented, "we are almost all Lords, & the commonest events of English History are to us impenetrable & inexplicable. . . . [Y]ou see what my *celebrity* . . . is come to" (*Corresp.*, 2:538). The Lords to whom Gray refers—the peers at the races who found him "impenetrable & inexplicable"—resemble women readers in their ignorance, and the increase in such an audience signified, to Gray, the end of an intellectual, male-oriented literary milieu.

Gray's elitism, his obscurity, and his disillusionment with finding an appropriate audience agree with the concept of poetry's creation and reception presented in the sister odes. "The Progress of Poesy," for instance, opens by celebrating the power of verse. In the "Progress," poetry is spoken and heard, not written and read; the listeners and the poet are present to each other. The ode's opening lines show poetry being performed this way in an ideal time and place:

> Enchanting shell! the sullen Cares
> And frantic Passions hear thy soft control.
> On Thracia's hills the Lord of War
> Has curbed the fury of his car,
> And dropped his thirsty lance at thy command.
> Perching on the sceptered hand
> Of Jove, thy magic lulls the feathered king. (15-21)

In Gray's allegory, the force of Poesy works its effects on a responsive mythological audience—Mars, Jove, and later, the Graces—who have no

reciprocal influence on the sounds that "control" them. Poesy has an immediate and irresistible effect. Its "command" curbs the fury of Mars; its magic
"lulls" Jove into calm; and its "warbled lay" initiates a dance among the
"rosy-crowned Loves" (25-31). In contrast to the "Ode on the Spring" and
the "Eton Ode," Gray's "Progress of Poesy" reveals no breach between
poets and audiences. The earlier odes had questioned whether speakers
could communicate with their hearers; the "Progress" circumvents this
question by describing the "melting strains" and "tuneful echoes" of poetry
as having a kind of "command" over an audience that "obeys" the poet's
voice. Because the poet can determine the audience's reaction, there is no
failure of understanding or sympathy that alienates speakers from hearers.
Yet in the "Progress," poets achieve this perfect empathy with a special kind
of audience: those who fall under poetry's "control" are supernatural beings
existing out of human time and circumstances.

The very later in the poem, Poesy—represented as an abstraction—is traced in its
advance from primitive lands to Greece, Rome, and finally England, where
it is embodied in Shakespeare, Milton, and Dryden. These poets, however,
are primarily praised not for the rhetorical effect of their work, but for
their skill at description, and their talents are stated, not dramatized. Shakespeare can "[r]ichly paint the vernal year" (90), Milton spies the "secrets of
the abyss" (97), and Dryden composes with images from "bright-eyed"
Fancy's "pictured urn" (108-109). As Patricia Meyer Spacks points out, the
"Progress of Poesy," unlike Gray's earlier odes, presents no dramatic situations and no conflict.[61] Similarly, Jean Hagstrum argues that the sister odes
"consist so exclusively and rigorously of picture and music as to eliminate
virtually all rhetorical statement."[62]

The very form of Gray's "Progress" in part encourages its pictorialism.
According to R. H. Griffith, nearly all eighteenth-century progress
pieces—whether featuring Beauty, Wit, Language, Fear, or Civil Society—
involve "an imaginary tour of an allegorical abstraction"; Griffith notes
that "The Progress of Poesy" "marked the crest" of the "fad" for these
poems.[63] Through his use of allegory and description, and avoidance of
rhetoric, Gray offers a theory of poetry that excludes a dialectic involving
audience and poet. In the "Progress," Poesy is entirely the creation of
authors. The reception of poetry does not decide its effect, meaning, or
value, for listeners play no part in ascertaining these; mythological figures
respond instantly and unconsciously to verse, and Gray's less pliable contemporary audiences are not represented in the poem. Moreover, Poesy
evolves and progresses without being affected by the expectations or desires
of specific audiences in specific historical contexts. Instead, this power is

inherited from poet to poet, from Shakespeare to Milton to Dryden, and then to a "daring spirit" (presumably Gray) who now wakes the "lyre divine" (112). Gray concedes that the environment for Poesy is important: it survives only among free people, since the muses "scorn the pomp of tyrant- power,/And coward Vice that revels in her chains" (79-80). But this is the extent of society's influence on poetry's development. For in the "Progress," Poesy is integral to itself; it remains, in essence, wholly separate from the audience that receives it. Poets, too, are removed from interaction with others. The speaker's "distant way" leads him into a sphere of his own "Beyond the limits of a vulgar fate,/Beneath the Good how far—but far above the Great" (122-23).

Standing alone on a rock above the hostile King Edward and his army, Gray's Welsh Bard—in the sister ode to the "Progress"—also finds himself isolated. His immediate audience intends to murder him as they have his fellow bards: Gray's poem resurrects the traditional story that Edward I, after invading and conquering Wales, hanged all the bards in that country to prevent sedition. In Gray's version of the legend, poetry is seen as a hindrance to unlawful authority, for the invaders literally drive the Bard to his death. But the Bard triumphs over those who try to silence him; he transforms Edward and his noble henchmen from threatening enemies into passive objects of his discourse by incorporating them into a prophecy that they cannot dispute or contradict.

"The Bard" centers on a contrast between two acts of speech. Given before the poem's action begins, King Edward's decree had led to the slaughter of the Welsh poets. In response to this, the Bard unites his voice with those of his comrades for revenge upon the King: "'With me in dreadful harmony they join,/And weave with bloody hands the tissue of thy line'" (47-48). Pointing out the difference between his speech and that of Edward, the Bard declares that Edward's words are limited in their effect to a particular moment and place:

> "Fond impious man, think'st thou yon sanguine cloud,
> Raised by thy breath, has quenched the orb of day?
> Tomorrow he repairs the golden flood,
> And warms the nations with redoubled ray." (135-38)

The Bard's words, by contrast, have effects that transcend the context of their delivery.[64] Joined by the other poets, he creates a prophecy that determines England's future: "'Weave the warp and weave the woof,/The winding-sheet of Edward's race'" (49-50). Gray borrows this image of fate being woven from Norse mythology, but adds a significant change. In the Norse, the weavers are supernatural women, or "Weird Sisters," who represent fate; in Gray's "Bard," the weavers are male poets. This change of gender identifies lyric poetry as the ultimate form of masculine power, for the Bard and his fellows, not the king and his army, determine the country's future. "The Bard"'s alteration of the Norse myth also enables a transformation of Gray's poetic personae from ineffectual, insignificant, even henpecked figures to heroic ones. Earlier, Gray's image of the persecuted poet was the comic, harmless "imp" of "A Long Story," terrorized by Amazonian patrons and the chorus of their ghostly female ancestors; in "The Bard," the poet is a figure of awe instead of ridicule, triumphing over Edward's army and declaiming the fate of his country. By replacing the Weird Sisters with a chorus of bards, Gray reestablishes the connection between poets and social power, a connection that his previous poems had questioned or declared lost.[65] And this power is predicated on the displacement of female agents by male ones.

After weaving the course of English history from the death of Edward to the reign of Elizabeth, the Bard predicts the return of poetry to England during the Renaissance—a return that coincides with the demise of Edward's line and the ascent of the Tudor dynasty. He constructs an image of the Elizabethan court populated by bold barons, " 'gorgeous dames,' " and majestic statesmen surrounding the " 'form divine' " of their queen (111-15): " 'strains of vocal transport' " (120) play around Elizabeth and her entourage as if validating their power. In this atmosphere of comity between poetry and the state, English talent revives. " 'Fierce war and faithful love' " (126) enliven dramatic verse through Shakespeare, while Milton's " 'voice as of the cherub-choir' " (131) sounds along with the "'distant warblings'" of later poets. The Bard's vision of a cultural renaissance inspired by the restoration of " 'genuine kings' " to Britain portrays the audience for poetry as an ideal, enlightened court; these verses recall Gray's enthusiasm at Algarotti's efforts to bring the arts under the control of the Prussian crown. But the Bard's immediate audience of a murderous king and nobility becomes an object that he manipulates in his verse-making. His words mold and shape the future of Edward and his men, and they are helpless to resist or challenge what he says; their hostility has no effect on his prophecy, for history will inevitably bring it to pass. Although the Bard's voice has "scattered wild dismay" (10) among Edward's followers, leaving them frightened and mystified, his prophecy is constantly affirmed by another audience—the poem's readers—who know that his predictions have been fulfilled. Criticisms that "The Bard" consists of panorama rather than clashes between antagonists, and that it fails to continue the conflict and action promised by its opening lines, overlook the idea of poetry implicit in the ode. No real conflict is dramatized because the Bard and his persecutors are unequal adversaries: that is, Gray's "Bard" displays the same confidence about the authority of poetic speech that is evident in the "Progress of Poesy," for like its sister ode, "The Bard" shows the poet's words captivating an audience unable to oppose them. Moreover, "The Bard," like the "Progress," suggests that poetry's creation is wholly author-centered. Made into the passive object of his prophecy, the Bard's audience is deprived of any influence in determining the effect or meaning of his verses. The concern that the early odes display with speakers' interpretations of events and with their failure to impart their message to an audience is replaced in the sister odes by a theory of poetry that makes communication unproblematic: while the early poems represent the audience as a responsive force, even as something that offers a threat to the speaker's authority, the later ones altogether deny its significance to and involvement in poetic creation.

Both "The Progress of Poesy" and "The Bard" register Gray's response to his alienation from the reading public and from the social context of literary production in his day. The odes' concept of poetry exhibits the same disregard for audiences that Gray evinced when he deliberately made them too complex to please his contemporaries; predictably, his readers gave the odes a mediocre reception. Yet in verses written to console Gray, David Garrick contends that the audience's effeminacy, not the odes' obscurity, was responsible for the poems' failure with most readers; he argues that the market in literature, with its emphasis on providing material for leisure reading, undermines the classical canon and thus makes appreciation of Gray's verses difficult:

> The gentle Reader loves the gentle Muse,
> That little dares & little means,
> Who humbly sips her learning from *Reviews*
> Or flutters in the *Magazines.*
>
> No longer now from Learning's sacred store
> Our minds their health & vigor draw;
> Homer & Pindar are revered no more,
> No more the Stagyrite is Law. (*Corresp.*, 2:535)

Reviews and magazines, with their requirements for poems that easily fit the space allotted them and match the abilities of a general, heterogeneous audience, feature poems whose sameness guarantees their success as commodities. Analyzing commercial print's effect on modernism, Frank Lentricchia calls this "standardization" of verse "a relentless attack on the historical sense, with the history of literary invention relegated to the junk heap of antiquarian interest (that is, an outmoded product)."[66] Garrick discovers the public's disregard for history in the declining authority of classical models like Homer and Pindar; at one time the lawgivers of literary culture, the ancients are rendered obsolete by the workings of the book trade. Supporting this trade and the popular culture it fosters is an effeminate (and predominantly female) audience that finds literature a mere object of consumption. Such "gentle Reader[s]" reject the masculine canon of epic and lyric verse, perhaps in part because of this canon's exclusivity. The laws of composition derived from Homer and Pindar would preempt women and lower-class readers and writers, whose cultural predispositions are implicitly figured in images of disease (the opposite of the "health & vigor" derived from classical learning). Garrick goes on to implore Gray—who, "nurst" by the ancients, is one of the last custodians of a heroic culture—to "[w]ake slumb'ring virtue" in his countrymen by appealing to their masculine pride and patriotism:

> With ancient deeds our long chill'd bosoms fire,
> Those deeds which mark Eliza's reign!
> Make Britons, Greeks again—then strike the Lyre,
> And Pindar shall not sing in vain. (*Corresp.*, 2:536)

Evoking nationalistic feelings in male readers causes a transformation in their sensibilities: when effeminate Britons return to the simplicity of their Greek forbears, Gray will discover a newly receptive audience for his poems.

Yet while Garrick's verses declare that Gray's rhetorical powers could refashion his readers' consciousness and establish his authority over English letters, Gray's experience with the odes convinced him otherwise: the "Progress of Poesy" and "The Bard" were virtually the last new pieces that he published. The theory of poetry expounded in the sister odes may have liberated Gray from an audience of consumers by discounting that audience's role in establishing the value and significance of verse, but this liberation had its price—a nearly complete estrangement from readers male and female, learned and unlearned. In declaring that he felt himself the Bard when composing his ode (*Corresp.*, 3:1290), Gray perhaps identified with the poet's mistreatment by the ruling orders; his advice to James Beattie about Beattie's poem *The Minstrel* wistfully recalls the esteem and honor formerly given to poets:

> Why may not young Edwin, when necessity has driven him to take up the harp, and assume the profession of a Minstrel, do some great and singular service to his country? . . . such as no General, no Statesman, no Moralist could do without the aid of music, inspiration, and poetry. This will not appear an improbability in those early times, and in a character then held sacred, and respected by all nations. (*Corresp.*, 3:1140)

In earlier times, the poet's work was revered and heeded by a powerful masculine audience. In his own time, Gray found his verse reduced to a commodity purchased by people he believed only barely literate or effeminate in understanding, like the lords at the races ("they bought me . . . and put me in their pocket"). Poets, it seems, lost their function as curators of the nation's culture when the generals, statesmen, and moralists who made up their audiences were replaced by common readers or became common readers themselves. To Gray, retreat from the market in letters and from the mass audience that print culture created was necessary for both composition and the writer's integrity, since in his view, "the *still small voice* of Poetry was not made to be heard in a crowd" (*Corresp.*, 1:296).

VII

Yet to his argument that poetry's voice is stifled in the public sphere, Gray makes an important exception: "Satire will be heard, for all the audience are by nature her friends" (*Corresp.*, 1:296). A contributor to the *London Magazine* agreed. Comparing the poems of mourning written after the death of Gray (1771) and after the death of satirist Charles Churchill (1764), the writer concludes that Churchill, although less deserving, commanded a greater share of the limelight in his day: "[Gray's] poetry was in so superior a stile, that it could be relished only by the few, whose taste is exquisite, and whose minds are cultivated to a high degree. . . . And hence we may remark that upon the death of Churchill, who was a popular poet, a poet who wrote to the times, there were many occasional publications: whereas, upon the death of Mr. Gray, there has been only one."[67]

Churchill himself, though, offered a different analysis of his contemporaries' "taste" in literature. Throughout his career he deplored poets' preference of lyric to satire, and maintained that by this choice of genre they abandoned their political roles and compromised their manhood. In "The Author," for instance, he charges poets like Gray with having voluntarily relinquished their influence as monitors over powerful figures in the church and state (and, thus, as preservers of English liberty) by lapsing into the quietism of lyrics. The "daring Muse" whose satire had once chastised corruption in all forms has been persuaded by critics to adopt a more innocuous form and content for her poetry:

> Bids her frequent the haunts of humble swains,
> Nor dare to traffick in ambitious strains;
> Bids her, indulging the poetic whim
> In quaint-wrought Ode, or Sonnet pertly trim,
> Along the Church-way path complain with GRAY,
> Or dance with MASON on the first of May. (117-22)

To Churchill, pastorals, odes, sonnets, and verses like Gray's "Elegy" are not only characterized by their disregard for political affairs; the poems' retreat into stylized art also exposes the feminine nature of the lyric. Described as "quaint" and "trim"—slang signifying both female genitalia and frippery—these lyrics, unlike satire, are suited to the private (and, by implication, insignificant) realm of female experience. The poetry of earlier writers whose sense-laden, pointed verses "Bade Pow'r turn pale, kept mighty rogues in awe,/And made them fear the Muse, who fear'd not Law" ("The Author," 91-92) was, in Churchill's view, abandoned in favor of soothing, melodic lines that (like castrating "Italian fathers") "mangle vigor for the sake of sound" ("The Apology," 349). The loss of its masculine, English harshness undermined poetry's function as an agent of social reform, and, in Goldsmith's words, foretold a time "when the muse [should] seldom be heard, except in plaintive elegy, as if she wept her own decline" (*Collected Works*, 1:337).

In editing Gray's poetry for publication, Mason, with Walpole's assistance, constructed an image of the poet that reproduced this dichotomy between lyric and satire, private and public, feminine and masculine verse. Although Gray's corpus includes several satires, none appear in the *Poems* section of Mason's 1775 edition[68]; while Gray never sought publication for these satires, or for any of his other verses, Mason's table of contents does not exclude other poems that Gray left hidden in his Commonplace Books, like the "Sonnet [on the Death of Richard West]." Mason and Walpole seem to have compiled this collection of 15 poems (11 of them odes) and reserved others for the *Memoirs* with the intention of attracting the largest possible consumer audience. As Walpole advises Mason on the selection of materials for the volumes, all potentially scandalous or politically charged items—anything with a venomous "sting"—should be expunged:

> You know my idea was that your work should consecrate his name. To ensure that end, nothing should be blended with it that might make your work a book of party and controversy. By raising enemies to it, you will defeat in part your own benevolent purpose of a charitable fund; when so numerous a host are banded against it, the sale will be clogged; reflect how many buyers you will exclude. . . . [I]f the book appears without its sting, Gray's character will be established, and unimpeached. (Walpole, *Corresp.*, 28:151-52).

Mason's comments at the beginning of the *Memoirs* reveal his adherence to this policy; he justifies his selection of Gray's letters to Walpole on the basis of whether they would "please the generality of readers," excluding the "more sprightly and humourous sort" whose style and content "did not seem so well adapted to hit the public taste" (*Memoirs*, 16-17). In an effort to avoid offending readers, Mason's edition presented Gray as the "sweetly plaintive" recluse that Campbell's *Sale of Authors* depicted some years earlier, for it emphasized those qualities of Gray's verse that an audience composed of different classes and sexes could understand and enjoy—especially its pathetic qualities that, to be appreciated, required little awareness of social or political contexts and references. The poet's work, as Mason describes it, is best appreciated by "those who have feeling hearts" while "the unfeeling," after reading the verses, "will, perhaps, learn to respect what they cannot taste" (*Memoirs*, 157). Yet while Gray himself distinguished between the efficacy of satire and lyric in eliciting a response from readers ("Satire will be heard, for all the audience are by nature her friends"), he employed both poetic modes to address a coterie of male initiates, using satire to display his (masculine) opposition to abuses of political power. A reading of Gray's satires in light of Mason's editorial policy reveals the marketing strategy that removed this objectionable exclusivity, and created a poetic persona suitable for consumption by general audiences.

In his *Memoirs* of Gray, Mason so often characterizes him as "melancholy" that he introduces Gray's humorous or satiric verse with an apology, and justifies printing a few of these texts by referring to the undeveloped aesthetic judgment of his contemporaries: Gray's fragmentary "Hymn to Ignorance" appears because "it will give the generality of Readers a higher opinion of his poetical Talents, than many of his Lyrical Productions have done. I speak of the Generality; because it is a certain fact, that their taste is founded upon the ten-syllable couplets of Dryden and Pope, and upon these only" (*Memoirs,* 175). Gray, however, considered satire, and his recent literary forbears, in a more favorable light. His admiration for Dryden ("[He] could not patiently hear him criticized" [*Corresp.,* 3:1290]), and Pope ("the finest Writer, one of them, we ever had" [*Corresp.,* 1:229]) stands out against Mason's assessment of them as somewhat common, and Gray also followed Dryden and Pope in his conviction that poets had a legitimate concern in the progress of public affairs. As he writes to Walpole regarding midcentury political intrigues, "the present times are so little like any thing I remember, that you may excuse my curiosity: besides I really interest myself in these transactions, & can not persuade myself, that Quae supra nos, nihil ad nos" (*Corresp.,* 2:817).

Gray's allegiance to traditions of Augustan satire is manifest in the "Sketch of his Own Character" (1761), which Mason relegates to a footnote illustrating Gray's piety. The "Sketch," however, portrays Gray as the ideal poetic persona for satire: he is alienated from avenues of power ("Too poor for a bribe"); independent ("Too proud to importune"); modest and religious ("No very great wit, he believed in a God" [4]); and proud of his stance as a political outsider ("A post or a pension he did not desire,/But left church and state to Charles Townshend and Squire" [5-6]). As Roger Lonsdale's edition of the poem details, shades of Pope inhabit the "Sketch" throughout: the verses paraphrase lines from Pope's correspondence, the "Epistle to Arbuthnot" ("I was not born for Courts or great Affairs,/I pay my Debts, believe, and say my Pray'rs" [267-68]), *Imitations of Horace* ("Unplac'd, un-pension'd, no Man's Heir, or Slave" [Satire II.i. 116]), and *Imitations of Donne* ("I bought no *Benefice,* I begg'd no *Place*" [iv.12]). The lines that Mason uses as evidence of Gray's religious faith established, for Gray, a position from which to criticize eminent figures in both church and state: unlike those dependent on places and pensions, Gray retains his impartiality and liberty of thought that, in the symbolic language of civic humanism and Augustan satire, signify heteronormative manhood as well. This political and sexual stance repeatedly appears in Gray's satires, and challenges his contemporaries' claim that Gray's performances in lyric verse indicate his retreat from the political and ethical responsibilities of male writers.

First printed surreptitiously in the *London Evening Post* (February 1777), "The Candidate" satirizes John Montagu, earl of Sandwich, first lord of the admiralty, secretary of state, and well-known libertine, for aspiring to the post of high steward of Cambridge University in 1764. While the current steward lay dying, Sandwich ran a hard campaign for election, and, since he could provide extensive ecclesiastical patronage, he won the support of the faculty of divinity—a circumstance that disgusted Gray, who deplored Sandwich's candidacy from his residence at Pembroke Hall.[69] Joining writers like Churchill as well as anonymous journalists attacking Sandwich in the newspapers, Gray composed his verses against the candidate, and circulated them in manuscript form. Sandwich appears in the poem as Jemmy Twitcher (the turncoat who impeaches Macheath in the *Beggar's Opera,* and an oblique reference to Sandwich's hypocritical attack on John Wilkes for obscenity), courting the "three sisters of old"—the faculties of Physic, Law, and Divinity. Physic rejects him for his "'sheep-biting look,'" his "'pick-pocket air'" (6), and his general lewdness. Law objects to his character and morals: "'They say he's no Christian, loves drinking and whoring,/And all the town rings of his swearing and roaring,/His lying and filching, and Newgate-bird tricks'" (15-17). Divinity alone accepts the earl as a suitor, excusing his behavior with reference to biblical precedents ("'What a pother is here about wenching and roaring!/Why David loved catches and Solomon whoring'" [23-24]). The controversy over Gray's satire on Sandwich, and the basis for Mason's censorship of it, lies in the last four lines:

> "Never hang down your head, you poor penitent elf!
> Come, buss me, I'll be Mrs Twitcher myself.
> Damn ye both for a couple of Puritan bitches!
> He's Christian enough that repents and that stitches." (31-34)

A vulgar term for sexual intercourse, "stitches" rendered the poem unprintable in the eyes of Gray's editors. Writing in elation to Mason in 1774 upon rediscovering his copy of "The Candidate" ("Why what should I have found, but the thing in the world that was most worth finding?"), Walpole nevertheless recommended suppressing the poem ("I think your decorum will not hold it proper to be printed in the life, nor would I have it" [Walpole, *Corresp.,* 28:168]), or at the very least revising the final couplet out of deference to women readers: "Methinks I wish you could alter the end of the last line, which is too gross to be read by any females, but such cock bawds as the three dames in the verses" (Walpole, *Corresp.,* 28:170). After several attempts at rewriting the last rhyme, Mason and Walpole decided to exclude the poem entirely from the 1775 edition. Subsequent editors as late as 1898 followed suit in omitting either the whole poem or the offending couplet; their rationale was their reluctance to expose the indecency of a poet "through whose whole volume was not, ere this, one line which could raise the slightest blush on the cheek of virginity."[70]

Editorial reaction to Gray's most lively satire reveals the censorship that followed from the expansion of reading audiences, particularly those including women.[71] Churchill addresses the dampening effect of such restraint in *The Times* (1764), a poem attacking sexual license, and, at great length, sodomy. He apologizes for wounding "the nice, and chaster ear" and raising "blushes in the maiden's cheek," but excuses his graphic verses on the grounds that they revile homosexual behavior and thus redirect male desire onto women: "The Cause of Woman is most worthy Man—/For You I still will write, nor hold my hand/Whilst there's one slave of SODOM in the land" (688-90). But sexually explicit language and themes that were barely permissible for an acknowledged satirist like Churchill seem to have been wholly inappropriate for Gray, with his reputation for (in Richard Sheridan's words) the "chaste and moral lay."[72] By midcentury, descriptive categories like satire and lyric seem to have become categories for marketing and consumption as well—in Gray's case, exclusive categories, for as his editors' comments reveal, his satire was suppressed as a deviation from the usual polite tone of his verse. Like "The Candidate," Gray's lines "On Lord Holland's Seat near Margate, Kent" were left in obscurity for commercial reasons. Before being created Baron Holland, Henry Fox had served as secretary of state, leader of the House of Commons, and paymaster general of the troops (in which position he amassed a fortune); "On Lord Holland's Seat" echoes the popular resentment against Fox for misconduct and breach of public trust. Written in 1768 and first published a year later without Gray's permission in the *New Foundling Hospital for Wit,* the poem establishes a likeness between the statesman and his dwelling, and investigates architecture's relation to human morality in a manner common to Augustan humanists.[73] Built with money embezzled during Fox's term as paymaster general and thus constructed at the expense of the English state, Fox's seat is remarkable for its atmosphere of desolation, decay, and ruin. The "congenial spot" where "sea-gulls scream and cormorants rejoice" (7) symbolizes Fox's rapaciousness; the absence of whispering trees and singing birds mirrors Fox's emotional isolation after being "abandoned by each venal friend" (1) who formerly courted his power. The "mimic desolation" that Fox creates corresponds to the ruin that he had hoped to inflict on the nation before the defection of his allies; for Gray, the triumph of Fox's politically corrupt party would have ended in the total destruction of the state.

Although no evidence exists that Gray disparaged this satire, Walpole advised Mason against including the verses for fear of damaging Gray's reputation and as a courtesy to the ailing Fox ("As Gray too seems to have condemned all his own satirical works, that single one would not [?give] a high idea of his powers, though they were great in that walk; you and I know they were not inferior to his other styles" [Walpole, *Corresp.*,28:118]). As Walpole advised, making the edition "a classic"—that is, marketing a text that readers would consider authoritative—required presenting a character of Gray that contemporary audiences would recognize and approve; Walpole and Mason, then, reduced Gray's resistance to commercial print to an expression of his melancholy quietism, and omitted those texts that suggest his interest in polemical forms of verse, like satire. Later editors adopted this image of Gray without question. In 1814 Thomas Mathias, revising Mason's edition, justifies suppressing Gray's "*jeux d'esprit*" on the grounds that they were circulated only among friends instead of being published commercially, and then proceeds to praise some lines from "On Lord Holland's Seat."[74] "All political and personal reflections being set aside and forgotten," Mathias believes that the "descriptive stanzas" of this poem are worth relating (*Works*, 2:617), even if such a reading ignores the poem's rhetorical purpose. Mathias's extraordinary disregard for the satire present in the verses is in keeping with the unworldly, apolitical character that he assigns to Gray: "*Such a mind* respects the important distinctions of rank, of wealth, and of fortune; it understands their use, their necessity, and their specific dignities, and it neither despises nor disdains them; but calmly, and without a murmur, *leaves* them to the world and its votaries" (*Works*, 2:627).

For Mathias, "the retirement of *private* life is the true scene in which *such* transcendent abilities can alone appear in their proper dimensions" (*Works*, 2:627); his catalogue of great poets who performed, like Gray, "*in the depths of privacy*" includes Virgil, Dante, and Milton. Mathias's purging of satire from his collection of Gray's works and his creation of a poetic genealogy for Gray enables him to rationalize and approve the poet's ostensible retreat from the public sphere. The stance of alienation that, for Gray, was a means of questioning poets' authority over audiences and preventing the easy sale and consumption of his work, was removed from its roots in Gray's hostility to commercial print by editors eager to establish Gray's place in the English canon. Similarly, writers like Virgil and Milton—who embodied Gray's ideal of poets with influence over generals, statesmen, and moralists—became in Mathias's account figures immersed in aestheticism and retirement. Created by Walpole and Mason and intensified by Mathias, this image of Gray triumphed: reviewing Mason's 1775 edition, a writer for the *London Magazine* concluded that Gray's "powers of ridicule . . . were by no means forcible" and that he "appears to manifest disadvantage when he aims at pleasantry or merriment."[75] The writer had reason to endorse Mason's perspective on Gray, since Mason earlier had adopted the *London Magazine*'s own assessment: at the end of his volumes on Gray's life and writings, Mason incorporated the Reverend William Johnson Temple's character sketch—a paragraph of remarks about Gray written in a letter to James Boswell, who later made them available for publication in the *London Magazine*. The reviewer of Mason's volumes exulted over Mason's reliance on Temple, realizing that it gave a measure of authority and respectability to the journal:

> It has become fashionable with many to treat *Magazines* in a slighting man-
> ner, as fit only for the ignorant and the frivolous: but although *the mob of*
> *Magazines written with ease,* may have occasioned such a censure, the honour
> done by Mr. Mason to the *London Magazine,* is a proof that an Established
> Monthly Miscellany may be useful and agreeable not only to less informed
> readers, but to masters in literature. And let it be remembered, that a charac-
> ter of Mr. Gray in *our* Magazine has been thought worthy of being placed
> by the hands of Mason as an *apex* upon the top of the *monument of Gray.*[76]

This vindication of the *London Magazine* represents, ironically, the tri-
umph of the market in literature over Gray's strategies of resistance. The democratic, popular, profitable miscellany of the sort Gray despised had the last word on his career, generously praising his work but also noting his reputation among "many of his contemporaries as an effeminate conceited being with a great deal of learning"; his "feebleness" in all but lyric verse; and, quoting Temple, his failure to use his talents for the purpose of sus-
tained literary production: "He could not bear to be considered himself merely as a man of letters: and though without birth, or fortune, or station, his desire was to be looked upon as a private independent gentleman, who read for his amusement. Perhaps it may be said, what signifies so much knowledge, when it produced so little? Is it worth taking so much pains to leave no memorial but a few poems?"[77]

While Temple defends Gray's small output, arguing that the poet was "at least innocently employed" by his studies, his questions themselves articu-
late the differences between Gray's writing career and the one encouraged by commercial print. Lacking the rank, fortune, and gender that justified noncommercial (or "innocent") dabbling in the arts, Gray was expected to conform to the model of the poet as a bourgeois professional who is

willing and able to sell his productions, and whose masculinity depends upon his doing so; aware of these expectations, his editors and critics explained his noncompliance as an expression of an inherently withdrawn, melancholic sensibility, and either defended this sensibility as poetic or denounced it as effeminate. But Gray's rejection of the emerging sexual and economic model for authorship was not merely temperamental. By relying on male coteries for encouragement and support, writing odes comprehensible only to classically-educated gentlemen, and, in his satires, violating contemporary standards for inoffensive politeness in print, Gray advanced an alternative concept of the poet's role. This repudiation of the literary market, albeit nostalgic, articulated desires—for intimate community with sympathetic readers, for influence over a social elite, for a self (and a sexuality) not defined through the manufacture of commodities— that the operations of a commercial economy, and its emergent ethos of productivity, could not fulfill.

Chapter Five

"I ALSO AM A MAN":
JOHNSON'S *LIVES* AND THE GENDER OF THE POET

> *In a modern, industrial nation, the ability to act without relationship is still a mark of the masculine gender; boys can still become men, and men become more manly, by entering the marketplace and dealing in commodities. A woman can do the same thing if she wants to, of course, but it will not make her feminine.*
>
> Lewis Hyde, *The Gift* (1979)

In a conversation with Samuel Johnson shortly after the initial volumes of his *Lives of the English Poets* (1779-81) appeared, James Boswell raised the touchy issue of Johnson's subordination to the London booksellers who initiated the project: "I asked him if he would [provide a preface] to any dunce's works, if they should ask him. Johnson. 'Yes, Sir; and *say* he was a dunce.'"[1] Johnson's reply asserts the complete autonomy of his critical judgments, declaring that even the economic concerns of those who financed the *Lives* would have no effect on the content of his prefaces. Most readers of the *Lives* agreed that Johnson maintained his intellectual independence, surpassing the work of his predecessors and transforming the "not very extensive or difficult"[2] undertaking into something much more complicated: as Robert Halsband observes, the *Lives* represented "the culmination of his career as well as the art and craft of literary biography up to that time."[3] Yet despite Johnson's declarations, the ethos of the marketplace certainly pervades the *Lives* (albeit in a subtler way than Boswell had envisioned), and this influence is nowhere more apparent than in the specific configurations of class and gender that accompany the *Lives*'s construction of a model of professional conduct for poets. In determining the nature of their literary work and the occupational identity that this work confers, the *Lives* provides a rationale for constricting the developing canon of English verse: Johnson's dismissive treatment of aristocratic poets and his omission of women poets from the *Lives* strengthened a cultural practice that was not, at the time, inevitable—the practice of defining poetry as the exclusive province of male writers engaged in commercial literary production.

I

The commercial origins of the *Lives* itself were obvious to Johnson's contemporaries. As Lawrence Lipking points out, "the work that climaxed Johnson's career was sparked by a booksellers' war"—a conflict between competitors with profit as its objective[4]—and Johnson proved an invaluable weapon in the arsenal of the London conger. The *Lives* began as "little prefaces" to the *Works of the English Poets* (1779-81), a 68-volume collection initiated by 36 London booksellers to compete with an impressively ambitious, 109-volume series published by the Apollo Press in Edinburgh—John Bell's *The Poets of Great Britain* (1776-82). Thomas Bonnell notes that although "both collections aspired to be definitive," they represented few poets outside of the 140 year period from Cowley to Lyttelton (Bell, however, did include Chaucer, Spenser, and Donne, while the London proprietors did not).[5] In an effort to outclass and outsell Bell's edition, the London booksellers called on Johnson and solicited him to provide "a few dates and a general character" (*Lives*, 1:xxvi) of each poet for the sum of 200 guineas, which Johnson himself set. As the booksellers anticipated, Johnson's prestige drew readers to the collection, some of whom complained that they could not purchase the prefaces apart from "a perfect litter of poets in fillagree" (*Lives*, 1:xxvi, n.2).

But while Johnson was allowed to name his price for his labors, he was not allowed to determine the selection of poets. Rather, "the first self-conscious declarations of an English poetic canon in published form" owed their genesis to the market: only the booksellers possessed the funds needed to print and distribute such collections, and they concentrated on a group of writers whose works they could sell as a complete set or representative group.[6] Johnson himself added only four poets (Richard Blackmore, John Pomfret, Isaac Watts, Thomas Yalden) to the booksellers' set of 48, and appeared to have exercised little control over this canon-forming project: recognizing his minor role in the edition, Johnson resented its being popularly called "Johnson's *Poets*" (*Life*, 4:35). But Johnson's dismissal of his influence on the project is misleading: as Lipking argues, the prefaces, together with the *Works,* offered "an occasion for Johnson to coach the public in his way of reading," for "in order for readers to assimilate the tradition of English poetry, a good guide had first to invent it."[7] Johnson's response to his precursors in literary biography—particularly to those sources from whom he gathered information—provides a sense of how he shaped the defining features of that tradition.

The precedents for the structure of the *Lives* have long been a focus of scholarly interest: Johnson's combination of historical life-writing, psychological character analysis, and literary criticism has been linked in part to classical writers (Diogenes Laertius), seventeenth-century French sources (Fontenelle), and contemporary English authors of texts similar to Johnson's (Giles Jacob, Theophilus Cibber, Robert Shiels).[8] By contrast, the sources from which Johnson derived the details of his *Lives* have received far less attention. In an essay on Johnson and biographic dictionaries, Pat Rogers identifies four texts that provided material for the *Lives:* Giles Jacob's two-volume *Poetical Register* (1719-20); the ten-volume *General Dictionary* (1734-41) edited by John Peter Bernard, Thomas Birch, John Lockman, and others; the seven-volume *Biographia Britannica* (1747-66), edited by Henry Brougham, John Campbell, William Harris, and others; and Theophilus Cibber and Robert Shiels's five-volume *The Lives of the Poets of Great Britain and Ireland* (1753). According to Rogers, Johnson's use of these works was more than casual; he emphasizes Johnson's reliance on them *"even where a single life* [of the author] *was available"* for reference.[9] Yet despite their importance to the *Lives* and Johnson's own esteem for them— he declined an invitation to prepare the second edition of the *Biographia Britannica,* and later regretted it—these sources (especially the volumes produced by Cibber and Shiels) usually receive only disparagement from scholars comparing them to Johnson's performance. Their differences from the *Lives,* however, are more complex than these comparisons suggest.

Compiled by Shiels—who had served as an amanuensis on Johnson's *Dictionary*—and revised in part by Theophilus Cibber, the *Lives* was, in William Keast's phrase, "by far the most ambitious" biographical and critical collection before Johnson's project.[10] Shiels and Cibber included 202 poets from Chaucer to John Banks: two of the lives (Savage and Roscommon) were derived from earlier texts by Johnson, and acknowledge him as their author. Although Johnson in general commended the usefulness of individual compilers ("tho' he exerts no great abilities in the work, he facilitates the progress of others")[11] and in particular praised Shiels as "a man of very acute understanding" (*Lives,* 2:312), modern assessments of this collaborative project are less generous: they accuse Cibber and Shiels of producing the kind of unoriginal hack work that casts a shadow over Johnson's similar but superior labors. Calling attention to the qualities that distinguish Johnson's "respectable literary biographies" from those of his predecessors, Lipking, for instance, compares the veracity of Johnson's "Life of Lyttelton" to the flattery apparent in Cibber and Shiels's entry on Mary Chandler: "The small insistent voice of truth makes all the trouble, and all the difference."[12] Like Lipking, Keast ridicules the entries on women poets in Cibber and Shiels's *Lives*, calling them "hilarious in their fussy, moralizing gallantry."[13] Johnson's biographies are undoubtedly superior instances of literary criticism and life-writing, yet such comparisons unwittingly reveal a troubling difference between the *Lives* and its precursors: Cibber and Shiels follow a long tradition of including women in the ranks of English poets, whereas the *Works of the English Poets,* like Bell's *Poets of Great Britain,* excludes them completely, and Johnson apparently concurred with their exclusion.

Johnson's break with traditions of literary biography is surprising, for his respectful, supportive treatment of contemporary women writers makes it difficult to account for his failure to follow precedent and acknowledge the contributions of their forbears. Johnson's encouragement of Charlotte Lennox, Frances Burney, Anna Williams, and Elizabeth Carter is well-known: he provided them with the same kind of assistance—revising their manuscripts, writing proposals and dedications for their projects, helping them negotiate with publishers—that he gave to male writers. In fact, Johnson's generosity had become so legendary that "a woman of the town"—an occasional whore and thief named Bet Flint—visited him requesting a preface to an account of her life in verse (*Life,* 4:103). But Isobel Grundy notes that despite his esteem for the talent of female writers and his willingness to help them, Johnson "made no move . . . either by direct or indirect means to revise the canon."[14] Elizabeth Rowe, for instance, received his verbal praise for being the first to complete the "great design" of employing "the ornaments of romance in the decoration of religion" (*Life,* 1:312), but Johnson overlooked Rowe and instead chose Isaac Watts—her successor in composing religious verse—for inclusion in the *Lives.* Clearly Johnson possessed some discretionary power over the edition, yet chose not to exercise it on behalf of women poets. Moreover, references to these poets in the *Lives* repeatedly downplay their importance, either by mentioning them very briefly or describing them in a pejorative tone: Margaret Cavendish serves as an example of the vanity of authors and women; Katherine Philips is mentioned solely as a member of the earl of Roscommon's coterie; Aphra Behn is distinguished above Dryden for her extreme flattery of patrons; Delariviere Manley gets recognition only for her work on *The Examiner;* and Mary Barber is characterized as a beggar for subscriptions to her poems. Whether they appear in a comment about the careers of their male counterparts or in anecdotal asides about the faults of writers in general, women poets have no "Lives" of their own and are merely supporting players in the lives of others.

Female writers had not been always so easily dismissed, for they received considerable recognition and praise in eighteenth-century anthologies of notable women, as well as in many of the sources that Johnson used for the biographical part of his prefaces. From her study based on the appearance of women's names in bibliographies, collective biographies, and dictionaries of authors, Judith Philips Stanton concludes that in the period from 1660-1800, "the number of women starting to write, decade by decade, increased steadily but slowly . . . to the 1730s," decreased somewhat in the 1740s, but later "increased dramatically in the last four decades of the century . . . far outstrip[ping] the population growth rate."[15] Of the 913 women listed in Stanton's sources, 263— 28.8 percent—wrote poetry, with the largest increase occurring in the period from 1770-1800 (prose fiction was the next most popular genre, adopted by 22 percent of the women authors recorded).[16] As the number of female poets grew substantially throughout the century, recognition of their work increased, too: Giles Jacob gives an account of 19 female poets and dramatists ranging from Mary Sidney to Elizabeth Rowe in his *Poetical Register* (1719-20); George Ballard's *Memoirs of Several Ladies of Great Britain* (1752) records the lives and accomplishments of 62 women from medieval times until the death of Constantia Grierson (1732), including those of selected female poets and playwrights; the *General Dictionary* (1734-41) and *Biographia Britannica* (1747-66) feature accounts of women poets such as Aphra Behn, Katherine Philips, and Elizabeth Rowe; Cibber and Shiels provide entries for 15 women writers in their *Lives* (1753), beginning with Margaret Cavendish and ending with Mary Chandler; and a two-volume anthology compiled by Bonnell Thornton and George Colman—*Poems by Eminent Ladies* (1755)—offers verse selections and brief biographies of 18 female poets from Margaret Cavendish to contemporary women such as Mary Barber, Elizabeth Carter, Mary Jones, Judith Madan, Mary Masters, and Lady Mary Wortley Montagu, all of whom were alive, if not still writing, at the time of the volumes' publication. These sources featured information and commentary on women poets to a degree that equaled, and often surpassed, the attention given to male writers of similar stature. In the *General Dictionary*, for instance, Aphra Behn is allotted eight pages of commentary—more than Edmund Waller (six), Nicholas Rowe (six), and William Congreve (two)—while the less notorious and less prolific Katherine Philips received two pages of commentary, placing her on a par with poets such as John Philips (three), Charles Montagu (two), and Thomas Otway (two). Likewise, Cibber and Shiels devoted 15 pages of description to Elizabeth Rowe's poetic career, while Matthew Prior received 14 and John Gay received only nine. The most celebrated female poets—those who appear in at least three of these biographic dictionaries or anthologies—were Aphra Behn, Margaret Cavendish, Mary Chudleigh, Catharine Trotter Cockburn, Anne Finch, Constantia Grierson, Anne Killigrew, Mary Monck, Katherine Philips, and Elizabeth Rowe; Susannah Centlivre and Delariviere Manley were the playwrights most often recognized. Johnson, then, had several resources at hand for the biographies of the female poets who wrote during the period covered by his *Lives;* moreover, their poetry mostly existed in collected form, which would have facilitated its reprinting by the London booksellers. Even the mode of biography that Johnson himself practiced, and believed most valuable, encouraged attention to writing women's lives. As Robert Folkenflik observes, Johnson's interest in portraying the domestic life of poets—such as Milton's neglect of family prayer and Pope's care of his aging mother—originated from his belief that character reveals itself most fully in private.[17] Upon this theory *Rambler* No. 60 justifies biographies of obscure or undistinguished figures: "The business of the biographer is often to pass slightly over those performances and incidents, which produce vulgar greatness, to lead the thoughts into domestick privacies, and display the minute details of daily life, where exterior appendages are cast aside, and men excel each other only by prudence and virtue" (*Works*, 3:321). Johnson's emphasis on detailing characteristics and experiences that all readers could comprehend and learn from suggests that women writers' more restricted sphere of action and relative absence from public affairs would not render them unsuitable subjects for biography. In theory, the "Life of Behn" could be as instructive as the "Life of Dryden"; in fact, Johnson's "Life of Behn" went unwritten.

Finally, as literary property, the works of many female poets and playwrights held a value equal to that of their male counterparts. The rhetoric of national pride in native talent infuses descriptions of *Works of the English Poets* as well as Bell's *Poets of Great Britain,* but both projects were undertaken primarily for the sake of profit.[18] The booksellers' strategy involved marketing the volumes as a set so that readers' demand for the more popular poets would help finance the printing of those less in vogue. This strategy, however, held no particular disadvantage for female poets: although few of them could match the sales appeal of Milton, Dryden, Gay, Pope, and Thomson, several did provide booksellers with impressive returns on their copy money and printing costs. Throughout the century, poems and plays by Behn, Centlivre, and Rowe had lengthy publication or production records, both as individual texts and as collected works; Behn's poetry, drama, and prose, for instance, went through multiple editions and performances, particularly *The Rover* (produced 51 times from 1677 to 1800) and *Emperor of the Moon* (produced 32 times from 1687 to 1800); Centlivre's plays, especially *The Gamester* (1705), *The Busy Body* (1709), *The Wonder! A Woman Keeps a Secret* (1714), and *A Bold Stroke for a Wife* (1718) appeared on stage and in print in nearly every decade after their debut; and Rowe's poetry and prose enjoyed steady popularity from 1696 to 1796, with reprints and new editions appearing almost annually, especially after her publication of *Friendship in Death, or Letters from the Dead to the Living* (1728).[19] At the other end of the spectrum, poems by Margaret Cavendish, Katherine Philips, and Anne Killigrew never made it to press after 1685, while most of their successors—Mary Barber (1690-1757), Mary Chandler (1687-1745), Mary Chudleigh (1656-1710), Mary Leapor (1722-46), Mary Masters (1706-59), Mary Monck (1678-1715)—published only a volume or two of verse with few or no reprints. This pattern was hardly gender-specific, for it characterized the careers of many male poets as well. Yet their limited appeal to readers did not automatically exclude male writers from the London and Edinburgh editions; publication records from the *English Short Title Catalogue* show that little or no demand existed for works in English by Richard Blackmore (d. 1729), William Broome (1689-1745), Elijah Fenton (1683-1730), George Granville (1667-1735), William King (1663-1712), Charles Montagu (1661-1715), Christopher Pitt (1699-1748), Thomas Tickell (1686-1740), and Thomas Yalden (1670-1736), all of whom have a place in the booksellers' canon-making collections.[20] The exclusion of female poets did not arise entirely from the profit motive, for many of their works were at least as valuable—and vendible—as those of their male counterparts.

Given their strong presence within contemporary literary culture, female poets' absence from the *Works of the English Poets* and from Johnson's prefatory *Lives* is difficult to explain, and most Johnsonian scholarship evades the issue altogether.[21] Johnson's encouragement of female writers in his literary circle only complicates matters, for it prohibits an easy dismissal of the problem as an instance of gender prejudice. Yet in the years between 1750 and 1779, women writers lost their place alongside of men in biographical accounts of English poets and dramatists: the consideration that they had been given as late as midcentury by Cibber and Shiels (successors of Jacob) and the editors of the *General Dictionary* and *Biographia Britannica* eroded to the point of their complete disappearance from the London and Edinburgh collections of verse. This critical period, which saw an exponential increase in publications by women poets, novelists, and dramatists, also saw a relatively sluggish growth in the commercial book trade overall, as the number of booksellers and titles printed rose slowly from a severe decline at midcentury.[22] But although they grew more visible on the contemporary literary scene, female writers paradoxically lost what recognition they had earlier received as participants in and creators of that scene. Apparently, a new history of English poetry had emerged: the London and Edinburgh editions, together with Johnson's *Lives,* actively revised an existent tradition, or produced a selective version of an already interpreted past. And as Raymond Williams observes, the social position of those revising the past influences the changes made to it: "Any tradition . . . is an aspect of *contemporary* social and cultural organization, in the interest of the dominance of a specific class. It is a version of the past which is intended to connect with and ratify the present."[23] Written at the end of Johnson's 40-year career, the *Lives of the English Poets* offers its own ratification of a particular hegemonic development: the identification of writing, and especially poetry, as an activity best practiced by professional authors. Although the increasing commercialization of eighteenth-century life complicated the distinctions between professionals and pseudoprofessionals, Geoffrey Holmes argues that during Johnson's time, a profession was still characterized as a lifelong vocation requiring extensive training and application and resulting in "services in which the hands normally played a subordinate part to the brain."[24] The *Lives's* preoccupation with the nature of literary labor, the social status of poets, and the relation of poets to the audiences whose needs they presumably served reveal Johnson's concern with detailing the distinguishing features of his profession. In repeatedly asserting what Magali Larson calls "the monopoly of competence"[25] of nonaristocratic literary men, the *Lives* articulates and codifies new expectations for poetic careers—expectations that could not be met by writers whose class and gender required them to operate under an alternative economy.

II

While the *Lives* are hardly systematic in describing the criteria for professional writing, they display an unprecedented focus on the theme of literary labor, or the kind of productivity that according to Johnson distinguished the poet from the versifier, the professional from the amateur. Moreover, this emphasis functions as means of controlling access to literary authority: Johnson's classification of writers' labor attempts to restrict their pretensions to the title of poet, and in doing so, initiates a form of cultural regulation foreign to previous compilers and biographers. Written 60 years before the *Lives*, Giles Jacob's *Poetical Register* makes no distinctions between gentlemen authors composing in their leisure time and authors of lower rank who wrote for a living, but recommends them all fairly indiscriminately for possessing qualities such as genius, wit, fancy and judgment. If anything, Jacob seems markedly more deferential to polite authors, concealing their moral and aesthetic deficiencies under hyperbolic praise: without irony, he refers to the earl of Rochester as "the Wonder of the Age wherein he liv'd" (1:230), and praises the earl of Roscommon as "a Gentleman and a Poet" (1:44), joining what he believed were two complementary and mutually reinforcing categories. Significantly, the most effusive entries detail the accomplishments of Granville ("a fine Gentleman, and an admirable Poet" [1:266]) and John Sheffield, duke of Buckingham ("the greatest Honour to his Country, and the *Mecoenas* of this Age" [1:179]), both of whom served as Jacob's patrons for his project.[26] By contrast, Jacob bestows rather muted praise upon Milton, calling him "the fullest and loftiest Poet we ever had" (1:106), and claims that the applause of aristocrats validates the merit of Pope's writing: "What can Criticisms avail when the great *Sheffield* asserts his Work?" (1:145). Writing 30 years after Jacob, Cibber and Shiels depart from his pattern to a degree. They are bolder than Jacob in censuring the faults of aristocratic poets like Rochester (although they devote 31 pages to anecdotes of his wickedness); more respectful of the talents of writers by profession like Gay and Pope; and more forthright in detailing the hardships of destitute writers like Richard Savage and literary "hacks" like Samuel Boyse ("unfit to support himself in the world, he was exposed to variety of distress, from which he could invent no means of extricating himself, but by writing mendicant letters" [*Lives,* 5:167]). Yet by assigning commentaries of roughly equal length to Sheffield and Addison (15 pages), Granville and Gay (ten pages), and Dryden and Philip, duke of Wharton (30 pages), Cibber and Shiels reveal a residual bias toward genteel poets, who claim more attention than the quality (and quantity) of their works or their influence on English letters warranted.

Johnson's *Lives* significantly departs from these models by replacing the deference given to gentlemen with an esteem for the activity—remunerated work—that gentlemen were exempted from, and Johnson's emphasis on the continual, deliberate labor required of poets partly responds to and partly endorses the pressures and requirements of the commercial book trade. Sustained productivity emerges as an important criterion of value throughout the *Lives*, much to the surprise (and dismay) of contemporary critics like Robert Potter, who accused Johnson of estimating "poetical merit, as Rubens did feminine beauty, *by the stone.*"[27] Johnson's treatment of Restoration poets, particularly his attention to their process of composition, illustrates his insistence on writing as work. In his "Life of Milton," he examines theories of genius in order to demystify them: reviewing Milton's early manuscripts, Johnson emphasizes the revision and corrections that these poems required more than their display of inspiration and extraordinary talent: "Such reliques shew how excellence is acquired: what we hope ever to do with ease we may learn first to do with diligence" (*Lives*, 1:162). Johnson commends Samuel Butler for the same careful application to his craft, suggesting that the time and effort that writers spend in their occupation is as significant as their display of imagination and judgment:

> *Hudibras* was not a hasty effusion; it was not produced by a sudden tumult of imagination, or a short paroxysm of violent labour. To accumulate such a mass of sentiments at the call of accidental desire or of sudden necessity is beyond the reach and power of the most active and comprehensive mind. I am informed by Mr. Thyer of Manchester . . . that he could shew something like *Hudibras* in prose. He has in his possession the common-place book, in which Butler reposited, not such events or precepts as are gathered by reading; but such remarks, similitudes, allusions, assemblages, or inferences as occasion prompted or meditation produced; those thoughts that were generated in his own mind, and might be usefully applied to some future purpose. Such is the labour of those who write for immortality. (*Lives*, 1:213)

Butler earns Johnson's respect for the constant mental activity that results in materials for his poems; instead of merely gathering images or sentiments from others, Butler reflected upon experience, and with this expense of labor, generated thoughts that became his own property—property that was stored in commonplace books and later "usefully applied" in the production of verse. William Congreve, by contrast, aroused

Johnson's suspicion for his denial of labor, his insistence on writing only for amusement, and his "strange affectation . . . of appearing to have done every thing by chance" (*Lives,* 2:214). While admiring the "very powerful and fertile faculties" evidenced in *The Old Bachelor* (a play written in Congreve's 21st year), Johnson challenges the boy wonder's claims to the kind of worldly knowledge that comedies of manners require:

> If *The Old Bachelor* be more nearly examined, it will be found to be one of those comedies which may be made by a mind vigorous and acute, and furnished with comick characters by the perusal of other poets, without much actual commerce with mankind. The dialogue is one constant reciprocation of conceits, or a clash of wit, in which nothing flows necessarily from the occasion, or is dictated by nature. The characters, both of men and women, are either fictitious and artificial . . . or easy and common . . . and the catastrophe arises from a mistake not very probably produced, by marrying a woman in a mask. (*Lives,* 2:216)

The discipline and sustained labor that Johnson finds essential to a poetic career is noticeably absent from the aristocratic contemporaries of Milton and Butler (and from those who, like Congreve, aspire to that rank). Johnson acknowledges the "sprightliness and vigour" of Rochester's poems, and sees in them the "tokens of a mind which study might have carried to excellence"; Rochester's libertine habits, though, prevent his talent from flowering: "What more can be expected from a life spent in ostentatious contempt of regularity, and ended before the abilities of many other men began to be displayed?" (*Lives,* 1:226). Here Johnson replaces a previously dominant set of cultural values with those of a different social class. The aristocratic ideal of poetry as the spontaneous effusion of wit (a view championed by Rochester himself) gives way to a professional, bourgeois insistence upon sustained intellectual labor as the foundation of exceptional verse. Although less licentious than Rochester, poets like Sheffield, Granville, William Somervile, and George Lyttelton all receive Johnson's criticism for lacking a serious approach to their work. Dismissing previous assessments of Sheffield as the result of "favour and flattery," Johnson declares his verses "at best but pretty"; as a poet, Sheffield "hopes, and grieves, and repents, and despairs, and rejoices, like any other maker of little stanzas" (*Lives,* 2:175). Granville's stature is diminished as well. With the advantages of illustrious birth, elegant manners, and party loyalty, Granville, after learning how to rhyme, "declared himself a poet"; to Johnson, however, this title was undeserved, for Granville's verses "are trifles written by idleness, and published by vanity" (*Lives,* 2:295). Similarly, Johnson judges Somervile as exceptional only in comparison to men of his class— although beneath notice as a poet, "*he writes very well for a gentleman*" (*Lives,* 2:318)—and sums up Lyttelton's poems as the barely acceptable efforts of leisure hours: although "cultivation might have raised [his verses] to excellence," without it "they have nothing to be despised, and little to be admired" (*Lives,* 3:456-57). (A decade before the *Lives* appeared, Archibald Campbell predicted the treatment that Lyttelton's work would receive from Johnson; dedicating his satire *Lexiphanes* [1767] to Lyttelton, Campbell identifies professional jealousy as the source of Johnson's antipathy toward writers "of fortune and quality": "Authors by profession . . . reckon a gentleman that writes, or in the language of the shop, makes a book, an interloper who takes so much of the trade out of their hands. . . . They look upon him with no friendlier eyes, than a taylor would on a man of fashion, who should take a fancy to cut out and make his own cloaths.")[28]

The value that Johnson sets upon the expense of labor in poetry, and his insistence, in the "Life of Roscommon," that literary productivity in the form of published verse—"large volumes and numerous performances"— is the sole reliable proof of "genius, knowledge, and judgement" (*Lives,* 1:234-35), renders aristocratic writers marginal to literary history. The *Lives* in effect erects a double standard for criticism or reverses the one that had prevailed earlier: the gentleman writing from idleness and leisure inhabits a category separate from and inferior to that of the professional man of letters, who lives upon his talents. High birth has been replaced as a guarantee of excellence by a supposedly more empirical measure—that is, a record of accomplishments performed without the advantages of wealth and rank. Johnson's preference for merit over class status also influenced his assessment of performance in other occupations: speaking of Lord Shelburne, a rising young statesman, Johnson observes that "'His parts . . . are pretty well for a Lord; but would not be distinguished in a man who had nothing else but his parts'" (*Life,* 3:35-36).

More than any other poet in the *Lives,* Pope exemplifies the triumph of the man of parts. Boswell notes that "The Life of Pope was written by Johnson *con amore,* both from the early possession which that writer had taken of his mind, and from the pleasure which he must have felt, in for ever silencing all attempts to lessen his poetical fame, by demonstrating his excellence" (*Life,* 4:46). Part of Johnson's fascination lay in Pope's consummate professionalism: like Dryden (whom he finally preferred over Pope), Johnson himself "was no lover of labor," yet Pope's own "incessant and unwearied diligence" impressed him as the poet's most valuable and characteristic quality—one that made the most of his good sense, genius, and memory:

> He had recourse to every source of intelligence, and lost no opportunity of information; he consulted the living as well as the dead; he read his compositions to his friends, and was never content with mediocrity when excellence could be attained. He considered poetry as the business of his life, and, however he might seem to lament his occupation, he followed it with constancy: to make verses was his first labour, and to mend them his last. (*Lives,* 3:217-18)

Pope departed from the convention of his aristocratic predecessors by defining himself primarily through his work, and by making its perfection the main object of his existence: poetry became the "business of his life" in that his verses allowed him to assume a public identity unavailable to him before he wrote, and enabled him to enjoy the authority that accompanied his self-creation as patriot, social critic, moralist, and leading man of letters. (Lady Mary Wortley Montagu realized with disgust that textual self-creation threatens established hierarchies; discussing Pope and Swift, she charged that "these two superior beings were entitled by their birth and hereditary fortune to be only a couple of link-boys" [*Lives,* 3:178 n.5].) To Johnson, Pope's superiority lay in his single- minded focus on his "occupation": "From his attention to poetry [Pope] was never diverted" (*Lives,* 3:218), for he viewed everything—remarks made in conversation, occasional thoughts and expressions, fragments of lines, couplets—in terms of its potential use in his verse. Finally, what Johnson found most significant about Pope's career was his control over the process of literary production; the fortune that he amassed from the Homer translation gave him the freedom to write when and what he pleased: "His independence secured him from drudging at a task, and labouring upon a barren topick: he never exchanged praise for money, nor opened a shop of condolence or congratulation" (*Lives,* 3:219). Johnson's marketplace metaphors suggest the possible debasement awaiting the poet who too literally treats his texts like commodities; the transition from bard to shopkeeper implies a loss of integrity and status, as fulfilling consumers' occasional requests becomes the poet's main objective. By choosing when and what to write, Pope experienced no sense of alienation from his poetry, no sense of its being a task imposed upon him by external forces (like patrons or booksellers). Johnson recognized that Pope's mastery of commercial practices insulated him from their worst effect—the artistic limits they impose; untroubled by "pecuniary interest," Pope "was not content to satisfy" his readers' expectations, but rather wrote to surpass his own standards of excellence, and in doing so achieved a great measure of autonomy from the demands of audiences and the requirements of the book trade (*Lives,* 3:221).

In a move that distinguishes them from their predecessors, Johnson's *Lives* proposes labor as a defining characteristic of a poet's career: his critical vocabulary, with its repeated stress upon diligence, suggests that the time and effort that writers spend in their occupation is as significant as their display of imagination and judgment. This vocabulary also offers a class-based critique of the booksellers' literary canon; if Johnson actually calls no poet a dunce, he accuses more than a few of being noble triflers. For the first time in the history of literary biography, aristocrats whose writing, according to Johnson, takes the form of self-indulgent play, are subordinated to poets by profession, whose writing represents the prolonged labor of genius that is tested and confirmed in a competitive marketplace. While Johnson valued politeness as a social accomplishment—"no praise was more welcome to [him] than that which said he had the notions and manners of a gentleman"[29]—he distinguished between genteel behavior and poetic talent, and insisted that poets possess their authority over English literary culture from their productions rather than their rank.

Besides declaring labor an essential component of poetry, Johnson throughout the *Lives* attacks those cultural conventions that hinder the development of a professional identity for writers. The pose of aristocratic insouciance especially irritated Johnson. In the "Life of Pope," he accuses the poet of deception for denying the importance of his verses: "One of his favourite topicks is contempt of his own poetry. For this, if it had been real, he would deserve no commendation, and in this he certainly was not sincere; for his high value of himself was sufficiently observed, and of what could he be proud but of his poetry?" (*Lives,* 3:208). Pope's habits of composition—his retiring from the company of his closest friends and incessant calls for paper in the middle of the night "lest he lose a thought"—declare him a poet preoccupied by his craft, not an aristocrat who versifies "when 'he has just nothing else to do'" (*Lives,* 3:208-09). Congreve receives Johnson's criticism for a similar affectation. Although Giles Jacob had noted with approval that "Mr. Congreve does not shew so much the Poet as the Gentleman" (*Poetical Register,* 1:42), Johnson interprets Congreve's preference for the latter persona as a betrayal of his profession: "Having long conversed familiarly with the great, he wished to be considered rather as a man of fashion than of wit; and, when he received a visit from Voltaire, disgusted him by the despicable foppery of desiring to be considered not as an author but a gentleman; to which the Frenchman replied, 'that if he had been only a gentleman, he should not have come to visit him'" (*Lives*, 2:226). For Johnson, the danger increased when false consciousness turned into falsehood—that is, when the poses that writers adopted to conform to aristocratic values and modes of conduct led them to overlook the realities of their economic condition and misrepresent the motives behind their actions. The "Life of Dryden" dismisses apologias for publication because they deny the poet's legitimate self-assertion; Dryden's excuse for printing his *State of Innocence*—manuscript circulation had supposedly corrupted the text, making a correct printed version necessary—incurs a rebuke for prevarication: "An author has a right to print his own works, and needs not seek apology in falsehood" (*Lives*, 1:360). This "right" refers to authors' exclusive possession of their work, which had been legally upheld by the House of Lords in 1774; for Johnson and his contemporaries, the conception of literature as alienable property produced for exchange had superceded the convention of aristocratic writers' disdain for seeking profit, and rendered obsolete the practice of surreptitious publication. Yet Dryden's apology also annoyed Johnson for what it implied about the author's cultural status—that he required an excuse to enter into public discourse. In Johnson's time, apologies for addressing readers were ludicrous in light of authors' material circumstances, and, more disturbingly, diminished the "dignity of wit" that professional writers had to assert within these circumstances.

Boswell observes that "no man had a higher notion of the dignity of literature than Johnson, or was more determined in maintaining the respect which he justly considered as due to it" (*Life*, 3:310). If many of the *Lives* detail the frustrated schemes and ambitions of poets—focusing, in Paul Fussell's words, on "the pathology of literary hopes"[30]—others portray the rise to influence, wealth, and distinction (although perhaps not happiness) experienced by writers such as Milton, Dryden, Addison, Prior, Congreve, and Pope. For Johnson and his contemporaries, literary talent provided one significant avenue of social advancement, and, as Dustin Griffin states, the use of that talent in the service of virtue (however that was defined) insured the "dignity" of the writer's profession.[31] Yet the *Lives* also depicts the struggles and uncertainties involved in achieving such dignity, and illustrates the tensions that arose when traditional hierarchies of birth and rank conflicted with emergent concepts of the writer's authority. The "Life of Savage," first published in February 1744, portrays a subject who internalized that conflict: Johnson interprets Richard Savage's career as a constant and often comic struggle between competing identities. At least in part,

Savage, who was 12 years older than Johnson, adhered to the residual ideal of the gentleman-author: declaring himself the natural son of the Earl Rivers and the countess of Macclesfield, Savage wrote in an effort to resume his position among the titled elite. His repeated appeals for patronage—many of them successful—in the character of an abject orphan suggest "that he mingled in his own mind the legal and moral precept that a son deserves to inherit from his parents with the traditional idea (shared by Dryden) that a poet deserves to be supported by men of position and wealth."[32] Johnson's sympathetic account of Savage, however, stops short of endorsing this strange conflation of birthright and the right of genius, and repeatedly forces readers to acknowledge the distinction between the writer and the gentleman. In Johnson's narrative, Savage's participation in two opposing systems of value leads to his failure in each. After years of "accidental favours and uncertain patronage" (including assistance from fellow professionals, like the actors Robert Wilks and Anne Oldfield, and the poet Aaron Hill), Savage determined "to endeavour after some settled income," in effect forcing his putative mother and her kin to give him a pension with threats of textual harassment—namely, lampoons and a "copious narrative of her conduct" (*Lives*, 2:357). But the pension of 200 pounds granted to Savage by Viscount Tyrconnel (nephew to Savage's mother) eventually led to a quarrel between the two men and their complete alienation from each other. Reasonably expecting some gratitude in exchange for his patronage, Tyrconnel resented Savage's preference for tavern life over presence at his table; upholding his dignity as a gentleman and a genius, Savage in turn resented these (rather moderate) intrusions upon his liberty, and "declared it as his resolution 'to spurn that friend who should presume to dictate to him'" (*Lives*, 2:369). Although Johnson blames both parties for the rupture—"it was undoubtedly the consequence of accumulated provocations on both sides" (*Lives*, 2:372)—he locates the source of Savage's humiliation in the system of rank and privilege that Savage himself endorsed, and yearned to (re)enter: Savage should have reflected that "he was only a dependant on the bounty of another, whom he could expect to support him no longer than he endeavoured to preserve his favor by complying with his inclinations" (*Lives*, 2:373). In contrast to his censure of Savage's behavior as a client of Tyrconnel, Johnson approves of his deportment as a man of letters, particularly Savage's insistence on the leveling effects of talent upon social hierarchies:

> His distresses, however afflictive, never dejected him; in his lowest state he
> wanted not spirit to assert the natural dignity of wit, and was always ready

to repress that insolence which superiority of fortune incited, and to trample on that reputation which rose upon any other basis than that of merit: he never admitted any gross familiarities, or submitted to be treated otherwise than as an equal. (*Lives,* 2:401)

The competition for precedence between ability and rank affected Johnson as well; replying to Boswell, who felt that he deserved more public recognition, Johnson explained why the elite avoided his conversation: "'I never courted the great; they sent for me; but I think they now give me up. . . . [G]reat Lords and great Ladies don't love to have their mouths stopped'" (*Life,* 4:116). If Johnson's assertion of intellectual power led to his neglect by those possessing social power, Savage's vacillation between these two bases of authority led to his undoing. In his final assessment, Johnson suggests that Savage's sense of entitlement made him unfit to maintain the prestige of his profession, and instead left him permanently dependent and infantile: "He appeared to think himself born to be supported by others, and dispensed from all necessity of providing for himself; he therefore never prosecuted any scheme of advantage, nor endeavoured even to secure the profits which his writings might have afforded him" (*Lives,* 2:431). Savage's pretensions to gentility sabotaged rather than advanced his literary ambitions by making it difficult for him to view poetry as the "business of his life"—a business that requires disciplined application and a willingness to pursue profitable "scheme[s] of advantage" in the marketplace.

Writing in the period from 1717 to 1743, Savage could not have predicted that the esteem conferred upon literature by high rank (either the author's or the patron's) eventually would be dispersed through a complex network of booksellers, readers, authors, reviewers, and critics like Johnson himself. But to Johnson, who began his career in 1738 as a contributor, and later a staff writer, for Edmund Cave's *Gentleman's Magazine,* Savage's assertion of his aristocratic lineage—whether authentic or spurious— ultimately had no bearing on his performance as a poet, and actually hindered his ability to function in the literary marketplace. By repeatedly insisting on the distinctions between gentlemen and men of letters, Johnson in the *Lives* draws boundaries between categories that had traditionally been merged: he defines poets as intellectual laborers (and not necessarily members or retainers of the genteel classes) whose productions, circulated by the book trade, give them possession of a prestige equal to, if different from, that of aristocrats. As Michael McKeon states, "writing for the public constituted the man of letters as the industrious producer of a value related to but more authentic than that conferred by traditional accomplishments."[33] But for Johnson, the cultural value of a literary text also emerged as part of an exchange between author and audience. And Johnson had in mind audiences far more extensive and diverse than the coteries of aristocratic men whom Rochester preferred in his "Allusion to Horace" and Gray attempted to address in his odes. In the *Lives*, the authority of peers, patrons, subscribers, and critics in deciding the merit of a text is secondary to the power that commercial print bestows upon readers in general. Recommendations of poems that are unsupported by popular approval provoke a rebuttal from Johnson: despite critics' esteem for Christopher Pitt's translation of the *Aeneid* (1736), Johnson maintains that a comparison between Pitt and his predecessor Dryden would reveal "that Dryden's faults are forgotten in the hurry of delight, and that Pitt's beauties are neglected in the languor of a cold and listless perusal; that Pitt pleases the criticks, and Dryden the people; that Pitt is quoted, and Dryden read" (*Lives*, 3:279). Similarly, Johnson ends his assessment of Gray—and the *Lives* as a whole—with an expression of confidence in the "common reader"'s judgment, "for by the common sense of readers uncorrupted with literary prejudices, after all the refinements of subtilty and the dogmatism of learning, must be finally decided all claim to poetical honours" (*Lives*, 3:441). To Johnson, the physical, emotional, and psychological makeup that men and women supposedly share proves the most valid, least biased ground for textual evaluation: common readers living apart from the coteries and factions of the literary world (and untainted by the entrenched opinions that distort critical judgments) respond to literature with an immediacy that offers an accurate measure of an author's performance.[34]

Johnson's *Lives* puts these principles into practice. His axiom that "the end of poetry is pleasure" (*Lives*, 1:175) allows him to recommend the work of Pomfret (a poet whom he added to the London bookseller's collection); although limited in talent, Pomfret "has been always the favourite of that class of readers, who without vanity or criticism seek only their own amusement" (*Lives*, 1:302). Likewise, Pomfret's "Choice," despite being completely pedestrian in form and content, demands critical attention for its longstanding appeal ("perhaps no composition in our language has been oftener perused" [*Lives*, 1:302]); his other poems earn praise for their "easy volubility" and uncomplicated sentiments. Johnson concludes that a favorable reaction from audiences redeems even commonplace verses like Pomfret's, for "he who pleases many must have some species of merit" (*Lives*, 1:302). But Johnson reserves his highest praise for authors, like Dryden, who have a more aggressive relation to their readers. Justifying the public esteem given to Dryden's translation of Virgil, Johnson argues that Dryden balances the reader's ultimate control over the fate of the text with his own kind of influence:

> Works of imagination excel by their allurement and delight; by their power of attracting and detaining the attention. That book is good in vain which the reader throws away. He only is the master who keeps the mind in pleasing captivity; whose pages are perused with eagerness, and in hope of new pleasure are perused again; and whose conclusion is perceived with an eye of sorrow, such as the traveller casts upon departing day. (*Lives*, 1:454)

Portrayed as seductive objects, texts entice the reader's attention with a promise of infinitely new pleasures for consumption; the author, by contrast, manages this seduction and eventual domination of the reader without making himself an object of desire and pleasure. Whereas Dryden himself had represented the poet as enslaved to (and emasculated by) the theater audience's demands for entertainment, Johnson reverses this dynamic of power, entirely severing the connection between the poet's body and his text. Providing pleasure to readers remains a crucial element of poetry's aesthetic and exchange value, but in Johnson's criticism, the poet retains his authority over readers through his mastery of their response.

The state of "pleasing captivity," however, is difficult to produce and maintain, for Johnson insists on hierarchical distinctions among levels of enjoyment. Competent readers, according to Johnson, gradually mature in judgment and learn to reject easy verses in favor of more substantive, intellectually challenging works; poets, he implies, must mature along with them: "Compositions merely pretty have the fate of other pretty things, and are quitted in time for something useful . . . they are blossoms to be valued only as they foretell fruits" (*Lives*, 1:284). Occasional poems, most often addressed to women or children and nearly always on domestic topics, fall into the category of such ephemeral "pretty things." Some of Edmund Waller's *vers d'esprit* ("To a Lady, who can sleep, when she pleases"; "On a tree cut in paper") is dismissed as insipid, contemptible nonsense ("Little things are made too important" [*Lives*, 1:287]), while Ambrose Philips—whose simple, informal topics and singsong rhymes have "added nothing to English poetry" (*Lives*, 3:325)— receives no acclaim for the pleasure that he does contribute: "If [the short tetrameter poems] had been written by Addison they would have had admirers: little things are not valued but when they are done by those who can do greater" (*Lives*, 3:324). Johnson's apparently egalitarian endorsement of pleasure as the test of poetry becomes less inclusive as he narrows the range of poets qualified to provide pleasure: "little things" produced by little talents ought to be beneath the notice of readers, for they offer no promise of greater things in store and imply no amusing descents from higher flights of genius. Despite championing the common reader's responses to texts, Johnson, in a contradictory and ultimately conservative move, prescribes what readers should enjoy, and privileges complexity over artlessness, public topics over private and personal ones, useful verses over pretty trifles, and poets who master audiences over those who divert them.

III

Radically revising the stance of its predecessors, Johnson's *Lives of the English Poets* offers a version of literary history and a concept of authorship that endorse and legitimize the practices of the commercial marketplace. Johnson's insistence that writing is work rather than play; that the quality and number of poets' productions, not their class backgrounds, determine their cultural status; and that readers rather than patrons or even critics ultimately decide literary merit all advance the bourgeois ethos of the book trade while offering a professional identity for poets that secures their autonomy from hierarchies of value based on birth and rank. Yet in Johnson's day, this new configuration of poetic careers applied to men only, for as aristocratic models of literary production lost authority throughout the eighteenth century, they became associated primarily with women's writing: as Raymond Williams maintains, to validate a specific present order, tradition has "to discard whole areas of significance, or reinterpret or dilute them, or convert them into forms which support or at least do not contradict the really important elements of the current hegemony."[35] For tradition-makers like Johnson (and some other contemporary biographers) one such area of significance involved residual attitudes against incipient commercialism—attitudes once displayed by aristocratic male writers— which over time were "diluted," or made less threatening, by being ascribed to women poets. Although cultural constructions of femininity before, during, and after publication of the *Lives* did not prevent women from writing, anthologies, collective biographies, and literary dictionaries increasingly represented their work as something produced apart from the requirements of the marketplace, thus removing women poets from the commercial economy that initiated the booksellers' collections of the 1770s and informed Johnson's prefatory *Lives*. Biographical accounts of female poets and playwrights included in Johnson's sources for the *Lives*—

Jacob's *Poetical Register* (1719-20), the *General Dictionary* (1734-41), the *Lives* of Cibber and Shiels (1753), and *Biographia Britannica* (1747-66)—along with accounts that appeared in the years just before the *Lives's* publication, collectively worked to designate a separate, exclusively feminine (and feminized) economy of literature.

Jacob's essay introducing the second volume of *The Poetical Register* adopts the model of supply-and-demand to explain what he sees as a recent decline in poetry's reputation: as the number of poets and poems increases, they command less esteem, "for Poems, like beautiful Women, are undoubtedly most valu'd, where there is the greatest Scarcity" (2:xix). This comparison of women and poetry as objects of desire, however, does not prevent Jacob from including female poets and playwrights in his listing of English authors: the first volume provides entries for 13 female dramatists (out of 306 total entries), ranging from Mary Sidney, to Susannah Centlivre, Delariviere Manley, and Catharine Trotter Cockburn, who were still alive and writing; the second volume features seven female poets (out of 217 total entries), including Susannah Centlivre, Mary Chudleigh, Anne Finch, Martha Fowke, Mary Monck, Elizabeth Rowe, and Anne Wharton. Despite the aristocratic bias of Jacob's biographies (lineage is featured prominently, and literary talent often appears linked to high rank), women who wrote for pay, like Behn, Centlivre, and Manley, receive the same praise given to women ostensibly disinterested in or repulsed by publication, like Katherine Philips and Elizabeth Rowe. Moreover, Jacob refused to conflate his subjects' writing and their morality: since he generally abstains from bestowing any criticism upon the writers listed, he commends the "strong Natural Genius" of Behn (*Poetical Register*, 1:14), the "Conduct and Beauty" of Centlivre's comedies (*Poetical Register*, 1:32), and the "Affability, Wit and Loyalty" of Manley (*Poetical Register*, 1:167) without qualifying comments about their sexual misconduct. Instead, in *The Poetical Register*, major and minor poets of both sexes earn praise for displays of wit, genius, and fancy; this troubling lack of distinction made Jacob a dunce to writers like Pope, who sought to "guard the sure barrier" separating modesty from impudence, merit from incapacity.[36]

Published by subscription in 1752, George Ballard's *Memoirs of Several Ladies of Great Britain* quietly draws some distinctions, and in doing so calls attention to changing representations of female literary talent.[37] Social class, and the virtues supposedly linked to gentle birth, apparently determined the selection of subjects for his brief biographies of 64 female intellectuals from Juliana, anchoret of Norwich, to Constantia Grierson. In Ruth Perry's description, all of the entries "were cut on the same pattern:

genteel—for who but a gentlewoman could obtain the leisure and training for such unremunerative pursuits?—conservative, quietly studious, decorous, devout."[38] Ballard's own intellectual insecurity might have influenced his choices; bred to the profession of mantua-maker, he lacked the formal learning that his antiquarian pursuits required, and perhaps fearful of censure, he declined to challenge conventional opinion concerning female conduct or accomplishments.[39] As a result, all female poets and playwrights who earned a living from the sale of their work were conspicuously absent from the *Memoirs;* unless dignified by their rank, other unconventional women such as prophets and Quakers also received no mention.[40] To Ballard, professionalism, or active engagement in the literary marketplace, seemed to carry with it a moral taint; he not only omitted mention of Behn, Centlivre, and Manley (all of them popularly reviled for their sexual conduct), but also unobjectionable playwrights like Mary Davys, Catharine Trotter Cockburn, and Mary Pix; reputable poets like Mary Chandler and Mary Leapor; and, most surprisingly, the devoutly religious Elizabeth Rowe. (Rowe's immense popularity with readers purchasing her work might have eroded her gentility in Ballard's view.) The connection that he draws between modest self-effacement and literary talent in women appears throughout his life of Katherine Philips. Philips's horror at seeing an unauthorized version of her poems in print (*Poems by the Incomparable Mrs. K.P.* [1664]) had become legendary by Ballard's time, and Ballard dutifully notes her reaction without skepticism: "This ungenteel and ungenerous treatment proved so oppressive to her great modesty that it gave her a severe fit of illness."[41] Yet despite her protestations ("This is the most cruel accident, that could ever have befallen me") that early editions of her work recorded at length,[42] Philips's physical collapse upon seeing a published copy of her verses aroused disbelief in other eighteenth-century biographers: in their *Lives*—published a year after Ballard's *Memoirs*—Cibber and Shiels assert that "no body who reads the human heart" could credit the tale of her print-induced illness: "Surreptitious editions are a sort of compliment to the merit of an author; and we are not to suppose Mrs. Philips so much a saint, as to be stript of all vanity . . . which arises from the good opinion of others, however aukwardly it may be discovered" (2:151). Ballard's persistent adherence to myths of female modesty—and his persistent denial of female authorial ambition—not only provoked readers' amusement at his chivalry, but also compromised the value of his work as a record of intellectual and literary (rather than moral) achievement. Although Margaret Ezell states that "Samuel Johnson would have heartily approved of Ballard's design to diffuse the example of the virtuous learned lady by showing her in her true and proper eighteenth-century light,"[43] virtue and learning did not earn women poets a place in the *Lives.*

Unlike Ballard, Cibber and Shiels admit women writers by profession into their *Lives of the Poets,* and discuss their careers with the same loquacious and anecdotal style that they employ for male poets and playwrights. Yet despite their acknowledgment of Behn's "fine understanding" (*Lives,* 3:25), Manley's "high [natural] powers" (*Lives,* 4:18), and Elizabeth Thomas's "soft and delicate" verses (*Lives,* 4:161), Cibber and Shiels fall short of endorsing women's participation in the commercial economy. Instead, their lives of women writing for money take the form of a seduction narrative, with circulation in the marketplace (rather than illicit sex) being the dangerous step leading to their loss of reputation. Cibber and Shiels repeatedly describe circulation as an act of force, or as women writers' submission to an overwhelming economic necessity; their apologies for their subjects' commercial transactions exceed their excuses for the women's apparent sexual indiscretions. For instance, after exonerating Behn's personal conduct from the slanders of "supercilious prudes, who had the barbarity to construe her sprightliness into lewdness" (*Lives,* 3:27), Cibber and Shiels admit that her plays are "full of the most indecent scenes and expressions" (*Lives,* 3:26), yet blame their indecency on the demands of writing for the seventeenth-century public: "Let those who are ready to blame her, consider, that her's was the sad alternative to write or starve; the taste of the times was corrupt; and it is a true observation, that they who live to please, must please to live" (*Lives,* 3:26). As Cibber and Shiels admit, the dilemma of professional writers—those who must please to live—is especially problematic for women, since their gender makes them even more vulnerable to the charge of prostituting their talents.[44] The defensive presentation of professional female poets and playwrights in the *Lives* (what Keast called the text's "fussy, moralizing gallantry")[45] blames the system of commercial literary production more than the writers' moral characters for displays of transgressive behavior in an attempt to sever misogynistic cultural connections between promiscuity and female literary expression of all kinds: Delariviere Manley's decline in virtue and public reputation was occasioned not by her sexual seduction, but by her forced reliance on the stage for a living, since it brought her "adulation from such wretches . . . who would be ready to boast of favours they never received" (*Lives,* 4:13-14); Laetitia Pilkington's misfortunes in London were "such as commonly happen to poets in distress," not only to poets whose husbands had divorced them for adultery (*Lives,* 5:322); and the impoverished Elizabeth Thomas, far from deserving the scurrilous epithet of "Curll's Corinna" (which linked her to Ovid's courtesan as well as the Theban poet),[46] "innocently offended" Pope by allowing the bookseller Edmund Curll to "wheedle" his letters from her possession (*Lives,* 4:161). In contrast to Behn, Manley, Pilkington, and Thomas, women writers who engaged in the marketplace less aggressively, if at all, receive the unqualified endorsement of Cibber and Shiels: while doubting Katherine Philips's shyness as a poet, they praise her self-effacement as a wife ("This lady had too much piety and good sense to suffer her superior understanding to make her insolent; [and in her verses] always speaks of her husband with the utmost respect" [*Lives,* 2:150]); they politely regret that titled women like Anne Finch were secured from the necessity of more frequently "exercising [their] genius" (*Lives,* 3:325); and they distinguish Elizabeth Rowe, with her disdain for celebrity, from the "present race of females . . . who rake the town for infamous adventures to amuse the public" (*Lives,* 4:340)—probably a reference to amatory memoirs such as *An Apology for the Conduct of Mrs. Teresia Constantia Phillips* (1748-49), and Lady Anne Vane's *Memoirs of a Lady of Quality* (1751). The admiration that Cibber and Shiels display for Rowe's reticence echoes the praise given to her resolute antiprofessionalism in their source, the *Biographia Britannica.* In the *Biographia,* Rowe appears as a paragon of Christian femininity whose rather dreary virtues included "a distaste for every thing, that bears the name of diversion and amusement," including novels and romances (5:3527); her ambivalence toward the public self-assertion that authorship entails, and her refusal to engage with either patrons or booksellers, are represented as exemplary instances of female modesty:

> She could not be persuaded to publish her works by subscription, or even to accept some advantageous terms offered her by the Bookseller, if she would permit her scattered pieces to be collected and published together. She wrote no dedication to the Great, and the name of no minister of state is to be found in her works. She never saw a court. She wrote no preface to any of her works to prepossess the public in her favour, nor suffered them to be accompanied by the panegyrics of her friends. She would not indeed so much as allow her name to be prefixed to any of them, except some few poems in the earlier part of her life: and though this was the occasion that a beautiful pastoral of her's was ascribed to another hand, she would not alter the modesty of her conduct. (*Biographia Britannica,* 5:3527)

Caring nothing for money, recognition, nor even literary property, Rowe seems to have rejected every aspect of the contemporary literary system. Part of the confusion over critical principles that scholars perceive in Cibber and Shiels's *Lives* may arise from its ambivalence toward its female subjects. Despite its attempts to deny the connection between sexual promiscuity and female literary talent, the *Lives,* in imitation of its sources, articulates suspicions and anxieties about the effect of the marketplace upon women writers, and asserts a preference for a type of career that is removed from commerce altogether.

Appearing in 1755, Colman and Thornton's two-volume *Poems by Eminent Ladies* reveals a similar ambivalence toward the 18 female poets whose verses comprise the anthology.[47] Its range (from the Restoration to the time of publication) resembles the scope of the later editions by Bell and the London booksellers, but Colman and Thornton included poetry by living writers as well. Perhaps anticipating readers' rejection of such a unique project, the preface assures us that "this collection is not inferior to any miscellany compiled from the works of men" (1:iv): the poems themselves "are a standing proof that . . . genius often glows with equal warmth, and perhaps with more delicacy, in the breast of a female" (1:iii). In their brief biographies, Colman and Thornton also take pains to validate the poets' talents by mentioning their favorable reception by the social and literary elite: Mary Barber gained the approval of Jonathan Swift, the earl of Orrery, Thomas Tickell, "and many other persons of eminence in *Ireland,* as well as of Mr. *Pope,* and most of the Nobility in England" (1:1); Mary Jones boasts "an intimacy with many of our *English* nobility" (2:254); and Katherine Philips's writings "procured her the friendship and correspondence of many learned men, and persons of the first rank in *England*" as well as Ireland (2:214). These reassuring introductory remarks attempted to dispel the climate of doubt surrounding women's poetry: some years earlier, for instance, the editors of the *General Dictionary* archly suggested that Behn's sexual allure tipped the scales of critical judgment in her favor ("great deductions ought often to be made from the applauses of a Writer of our sex, when bestowed on a beautiful woman of genius, with whom he is intimate" [3:143]). In Colman and Thornton's anthology, however, the mention of support from male aristocrats certifies the value of the collected verses while it urges readers to follow the chivalric example of the higher classes. Colman and Thornton's critical vocabulary also calls attention to the gender of the writers under scrutiny. Ezell points out that despite references to the genius, wit, and judgment of female poets—qualities they share with male writers—the term "delicacy" establishes a crucial difference between the sexes, for "delicacy" (meaning moral and social propriety) would later be invoked as a touchstone for determining female literary merit.[48]

The construction of distinct critical standards for women's writing appears in other parts of the anthology as well. Colman and Thornton justify their decision to print selections from "these ingenious females" rather than their entire works, arguing that the latter would have been "less satisfactory":

> For as most of their poems were first published by subscription, the bulk as well as merit of the volume, was necessary to be considered: on which account several pieces were thrown in merely to fill up so many pages. Besides, most of these Ladies (like many of our greatest male writers) were more indebted to nature for their success, than to education; and it was therefore thought better to omit those pieces, which too plainly betrayed the want of learning, than to insert them merely to disgrace those others, which a writer, with all the advantages of it, could not have surpassed. (*Poems,* 1:iv)

According to the editors, a complete collection of poetry by women lacked the appeal needed to guarantee sales: that is, the verses in their entirety, without judicious pruning, could not command sufficient attention or respect from the reading public. Colman and Thornton justify their editorial decision by arguing that the form of literary production employed by most women poets—subscription publication—allowed the circulation of texts that could not sell on their own merits. Women, they imply, operate outside of a competitive literary marketplace. Yet as Dustin Griffin observes, both male and female writers continued to rely on subscriptions throughout the century: from 1720-1760, around 250 books were published each decade by subscription; after 1760, the average number increased to 300, with 420 published during the 1780s and 498 during the 1790s.[49] Colman and Thornton, however, characterize subscription—a type of collective patronage often based upon networks of friends and mentors—as a polite form of charity for the author or her family, and, more seriously, as a threat to the overall quality of literature in print: regardless of their merit, "several pieces were thrown in merely to fill up so many pages" of the volumes produced for well-meaning subscribers. Another threat lay in women writers' "want of learning," which must be concealed by the editors' selection of examples of innate genius unmediated by art. Although it celebrated (and circulated) poetry by women, Colman and Thornton's anthology also reflected midcentury hesitations about the proper status of women writers: while recommending their verses to readers, it suggested that no market (and no need) existed for a canon-making collection of their complete works.

If biographies and critical assessments of women poets insisted upon their protection, or exclusion, from the commercial literary system, they also emphasized the denial of professional aims by the poets themselves. The Reverend John Duncombe's *Feminiad* (1754)—a popular defense of women's literary accomplishments—neatly sums up contemporary attitudes. While rejecting as barbarous and "eastern" the "slavish" prejudice that kept women ignorant, and while championing the true Britons who allowed their "nymphs" to adorn their minds as well as their bodies, Duncombe views women's poetry not as a profession, but as a wholesome pastime:

> Pleas'd with domestic excellence, [she] can spare
> Some hours from studious ease to social care,
> And with her pen that time alone employs
> Which others waste in visits, cards, and noise;
> From affectation free, tho' deeply read,
> 'With wit well natur'd, and with books well bred.'[50]

"The modest Muse"—represented by Katherine Philips, Anne Finch, Catharine Trotter Cockburn, Elizabeth Rowe, Mary Leapor, and Elizabeth Carter—unlike the "bold unblushing" Aphra Behn, Susannah Centlivre, and Delariviere Manley, does not solicit circulation and audience approval of her work, especially not at the cost of virtue. *The Feminiad's* link between wanton sexuality and professional writing, and its advocacy of "contempt" for those "who prize/Their own high talents, and their sex despise" (11), were reflected in the tactics adopted to defend women writers from the taint of ambition and self-assertion. In her study of prefatory remarks to verses by women, Rebecca Gould Gibson estimates that the modest apology for poetic trifles composed in leisure hours "appeared in at least half" of the samples she observed between 1667-1750; while acknowledging that male writers also employed this convention—which Swift satirized at length in his preface to *A Tale of a Tub*—Gibson observes that "female poets of the period used the formula with particular insistence and frequency," and with constant reference to their gender.[51] This convention seems to have been especially useful in presenting a new talent to the reading public or in excusing the "incorrectness" of new and established poets. The editor of the *Biographia Britannica,* for instance, claims that Rowe's inattention to her poetry is pardonable for a female amateur: "She did not set so high a value on her works, as to employ much labour in finishing them with the utmost accuracy; and she wrote verses through inclination, and rather as an amusement, than as a study and profession, to excel in which she should make the business of her life" (5:3528). Unlike Pope, whom Johnson applauds for making poetry "the business of his life," female poets receive praise for rejecting a professional stance toward their verse. In their prefatory remarks on Mary Barber, Colman and Thornton reprint Swift's letter introducing her to the earl of Orrery: after praising Barber's "wit and good sense" (along with her humility and gratitude), Swift assures Orrery that "no woman was ever more useful to her husband in the way of his business. Poetry hath only been her favourite amusement" (*Poems*, 1:4-5). The portrayal of women's verse as a pastime subordinate to domestic concerns (or a diversion for the author and the reader alike) also appears in prefaces to texts by Mary Jones, Mary Leapor, and Mary Masters—prefaces reprinted and circulated widely by the *Monthly Review*. The review of Mary Jones's *Miscellanies in Prose and Verse* (1750) accepts as truth the rhetoric of her "modest apology" for publication, and applauds both her "very slight regard" for her verses and her consequent "dread" of printing them: "The respect she had for [her friends], the world, and herself, always kept such a thought at the greatest distance imaginable,"[52] but the subscriptions to her volume enabled her to assist a decrepit old relation. Perhaps misled by these rhetorical commonplaces, the reviewer cannot reconcile Jones's careful imitation of Pope's style and sentiments with a view of her poetry as "accidental ramblings of her thought into rhyme," and appears puzzled by the contradiction between her "extensive reading" and her apparent "aversion to studious or laborious writing."[53] What emerges from the review is a conventional portrayal of the female poet that is obviously and humorously at odds with Jones's actual performance. Mary Leapor's achievements were contained more successfully. In an article examining Leapor's second volume of verse (*Poems on Several Occasions*, published posthumously in 1751), the *Monthly Review* printed a letter from Leapor's patron, Bridget Freemantle, praising the poet's "virtuous principles," dutiful housekeeping, and consequent disregard for her writing: "Nothing could pique her more than peoples imagining she took a great deal of pains, or spent a great deal of time, in such composures; or that she set much value on them."[54] Freemantle's letter also assures readers that Leapor wrote to entertain herself, not impress the public ("She told me, that most of them were wrote . . . purely to divert her thoughts from dwelling upon what was disagreeable"),[55] and states that filial piety, not authorial pride, induced Leapor to publish her verse (by subscription, for her aging father's benefit). The poet's diffidence and self-disparagement are also leitmotifs in the *Monthly Review*'s assessment of Mary Masters's second volume (*Familiar Letters and Poems on Several Occasions*, 1755). In a quotation from her preface justifying her work, Masters entreats readers "to remember, that my appearance as an author, is neither the effect of vanity, nor of unreasonable fondness of any thing that has been the product of my pen"; rather, when the "little stock" of money that she accumulated from *Poems on Several Occasions* (1733) declined, "[she] was prevailed upon to make a second attempt" by promises from "several gentlemen and ladies" to secure subscribers to her work.[56] The gentlemen assisted her even further, padding her slender volume with verses of their own composition to justify its publication and sale. After praising Masters as a "chaste, moral, and religious" writer, the reviewer states that the quality of her poetry is less important than the nature of her relationship to subscribers: "Certain daughters of the muses have been less eminent for their virtue than their wit; but Mrs. *Masters*'s character, as a woman, is such as must have had a considerable share in inducing her numerous friends to subscribe to the Poetess: for which she hath sufficiently repaid them in grateful acknowledgments, even were her book out of the question."[57] Exclaiming "What a glorious thing is humanity!," the reviewer celebrates Masters's verse for providing an occasion for subscribers to feel good about their own generosity, and thus justified in their benevolent expenditures.

Besides assuring readers of women's natural reticence—a shrinking from notice common even to published poets—the apologias and prefaces, like the anthologies and biographic dictionaries appearing at midcentury, situate women's writing in opposition to commercial practices even while recommending their texts to a consumer audience. Ballard, the most conservative (and perhaps most influential)[58] of the lot, persistently equated merit with docile gentility; professional poets and dramatists—often the most prolific female writers of their age—disappear from his history, along with other women who disrupted class and gender hierarchies. Although more accepting of these professionals, Cibber and Shiels viewed involvement in the literary marketplace as morally compromising for women, while Colman and Thornton implied that, because its printing costs were most often subsidized by subscription, women's poetry was insulated from marketplace realities: without extensive editing, they argued, it could not successfully compete in the bookshops for readers' attention and money. Nearly all comments by biographers, patrons, and poets themselves during the century's middle decades characterize women's verse as an amusement secondary to their more serious domestic obligations: for the most part, their familial roles take precedence over their identity as authors. This chorus of remarks fundamentally shaped the public personae of female poets in a direction opposite to the one delineated for male writers in Johnson's

Lives. As Cheryl Turner observes, attempts to desexualize and sanitize women's literary production—to break the metaphorical connection between the text's, and the body's, circulation and sale—elevated women's propriety and femininity over their literary talents: the emphasis on respectability "undermined their authorial autonomy, confining the creative process within narrow boundaries and authorizing critical responses to their work which concentrated upon sentiment rather than literary skill."[59] By 1750, living upon the profits of their commodified intellectual labor was a definitive feature of professional authorship for men. Women, by contrast, were relegated to the residual economy of noncommercial literary production: the nature of their poetry as a gift of thanks for patrons' generosity toward themselves or their relatives is continually emphasized to clear them from the sexually transgressive taint of profit seeking. And while their ability to negotiate the literary marketplace verified the masculinity of professional male writers, the reverse was true for women, as contemporary constructions of femininity valorized their absence from that marketplace.

Johnson's familiarity with the rhetoric employed by female poets and their supporters appears in the "Proposals" and "Advertisement" that he wrote for Anna Williams's *Miscellanies in Prose and Verse* (1766). Impoverished and blind, Williams (whose father Johnson also assisted) took up residence in Johnson's household after his wife's death in 1752; over the years Johnson attempted to alleviate her circumstances with suggestions for various literary projects. In 1750, Johnson printed his "Proposals" calling for subscriptions to her volume of poetry (then entitled *Essays in Prose and Verse*), and, assuming Williams's identity, self-consciously relied upon the customary disclaimers in offering her work for sale:

> When a Writer of my sex solicits the regard of the publick, some apology seems always to be expected . . . [and] how little soever I may be qualify'd either by nature or study, for furnishing the world with literary entertainments, I have such motives for venturing my little performances into the light, as are sufficient to counterballance the censure of arrogance, and to turn off my attention from the threats of criticism. . . . Censure may surely be content to spare the compositions of a woman, written for amusement, and published for necessity.[60]

Besides fashioning Williams as a conventionally feminine poet—self-deprecating and motivated by need rather than ambition—Johnson also assumed the role of editor for her work: he revised some of Williams's verse, solicited friends (Hester Thrale, Thomas Percy, Frances Reynolds, and

John Hoole) to contribute pieces to fill up the volume, and even added some of his own material—most notably, "The Fountains: A Fairy Tale"—to justify the book's publication.[61] Johnson's "Advertisement" for the sale of the *Miscellanies*, which finally appeared 16 years after the "Proposals," firmly locates Williams's writing in the noncommercial economy, as work performed in exchange for kindness received: "I . . . would not mention the misfortunes of my life but to return my thanks for the kind endeavours to alleviate them, exerted by those who have subscribed, and procured Subscriptions, and those who by contributing their Compositions, have left my friends less reason to repent their solicitations."[62] While the subscription brought Williams about 300 pounds, no second edition was called for, and copies remained for sale as late as 1770.[63] *Miscellanies in Prose and Verse*—and Johnson's efforts on its behalf—thus perfectly followed the pattern established for women's verse of this period.

Yet at the time Williams's poems appeared in print, cultural expectations for and assumptions about female poets had begun to change. Many still published by subscription, and adopted the usual modes of self-presentation: like Lady Dorothy Dubois (*Poems on Several Occasions*, 1764), they pleaded that necessity, or "Affliction," had forced them to write for the public; like Catherine Jemmat (*Miscellanies, in Prose and Verse*, 1766), they acknowledged the inclusion of poems by "a friend or two" to lengthen their rather thin books; and like Mary Whateley (*Original Poems on Several Occasions*, 1764) and Priscilla Pointon (*Poems on Several Occasions*, 1770), they claimed that the gratification of benefactors, rather than the pursuit of literary fame, was the purpose of their writing.[64] But in the late 1760s and 1770s, women poets recognized a somewhat different climate of reception for their verse. Although she dedicated her *Original Poems on Several Occasions* (1769) to the Honorable Mrs. Stratford, thanking her for her "esteem and protection," Clara Reeve indicates later in her preface that such protection may no longer be necessary: she had once believed that her "sex was an insuperable objection" to "pretensions to literary merit," yet found that the public now respected and rewarded women writers.[65] Critical response to Mary Savage's two-volume *Poems on Various Subjects and Occasions* (1777) also indicated a greater public acceptance of female poets, along with higher expectations for their performances. While Savage, following the customary style of the apologias, protested that she "never intended [her poems] for publick Inspection," lacked "a learned Education," and "never yet neglected [her family or business] for the sake of writing," her attempts "to prevent all Criticism" of her work failed entirely.[66] An article on her poems in the *Critical Review* reveals how badly Savage misjudged her audience: congratulating contemporary Britons on their increasing cultural refinement and consequent rejection of outdated "prejudices" against women writers, the reviewer celebrates the variety and sheer volume of the literature they produced: "Instead of the single Sappho of antiquity, we can muster many names of equal, and some of superior value, in our little island, who, far from confining their abilities to the narrow limits of lyric poetry, stand foremost in various species of writing, both in prose and verse."[67] The reviewer's praise of female talent, though, shortly turns into censure of Savage's negligence and "inexcusable" self-indulgence in venturing into print without the skills and education required for writing:

> Mrs. Savage is conscious of being "a stranger even to the grammar of her native tongue," and calls herself a "woman of business, who is not five minutes alone from morn to night." Her poems are such as justify this assertion, without any of those qualities, which, though undeserving of commendation, might at least withhold the tongue of censure. We summon the whole sex to exercise their talents, and invite them to partake of that liberal approbation, and that heartfelt praise, which a really enlightened and indulgent public has in store for them:—but let them beware lest they make their appearance in a slatternly undress.[68]

The reviewer's insistence that female poets appear in proper dress—or adorn their verses with the appropriate use of language and poetic devices—sexualizes his criticism of Savage and thus reinforces the constraints that femininity imposed upon women writers. Yet the complaints about Savage's inattention to her craft also signal a growing demand for competence: unlike earlier critics and biographers who considered women's poetry merely an innocent pastime (and thus indulgently excused its faults), the writer for the *Critical Review*—whose essay on Savage appeared just before Johnson's *Lives*—holds female poets to a more rigorous professional standard. While it retains its focus on the gender of the poet (praising women for their mastery of "soft and engaging" verse), the critique of Mary Savage insists that nothing can excuse sloppiness in writing produced for "the public's eye"; whereas previous accounts of women poets had tried to shield them from the requirements of the commercial literary system, the *Critical Review* insisted that women's acceptance as writers depended upon their being judged in accordance with that system.

Johnson might have approved of the *Critical Review*'s rigor, for it corresponded to his own model of professional conduct for poets—a model fundamentally different from contemporary constructions of female authorship, and from aristocratic practices of a century before. Throughout the *Lives*, poetry becomes characterized as work requiring constant attention and diligence; the social identity of poets rests solely upon their productions; and the circulation and sale of their verse to the general public determines poets' reputation. By contrast, depictions of female poets in Johnson's time associate them with the characteristics that Johnson derisively ascribed to aristocratic male writers, and show them operating in an economy similar to that of aristocratic amateurs: their verse is described as a diversion to occupy leisure hours rather than the business of life; their identity primarily depends upon their fulfillment of class and gender roles rather than upon their literary performances; and their avoidance of publicity rather than their aggressive captivation of readers certifies their merit. This divergence in the representation of male and female poets—a divergence that accompanied the eighteenth century's growing interest in literary history and biography—reached its peak with the London and Edinburgh collections, as professional behavior, which was coded as masculine, became the norm against which all writers were measured, and alternative forms of behavior, which were coded as amateurish or feminine, became the aberration. In articulating and validating these changes, Johnson's *Lives* offers a revisionist reading of the past, a ratification of the present, and a prescription for the future: the *Lives*'s idealization of the man of letters as an independent economic agent negotiating the terrain of the commercial marketplace legitimized women's unprecedented exclusion from literary history and from a place of prominence in the ranks of contemporary poets. The continued difficulty of reclaiming and reassessing the poetry of these women attests to the hegemony of the professional ideal, whose features Johnson helped define.

AFTERWORD ∽

In the early 1830s, an edition of Boswell's *Life of Johnson* by John Wilson Croker received surprisingly detailed and thoughtful reviews by both Thomas Babington Macaulay and Thomas Carlyle. After noting Croker's numerous editorial errors, Macaulay and Carlyle turn their attention to the significance of Johnson's career, and a offer a lengthy reassessment of his place in literary history. Johnson's reputation badly needed this boost.[1] After his death in 1784, writers increasingly questioned his status as a critic, poet, and moralist. Johnson, they claimed, failed to look and act the part of the sage: his nervous ticks, dirty clothes, voracious appetite, and combative conversational style appeared completely at odds with contemporary expectations for a distinguished author's appearance and behavior. Blaming Johnson's bodily contortions on the "solitude and low breeding, to which he was long condemned in the early part of his life," the Reverend William Johnson Temple maintained that his class origins, along with his unseemly physical presence, inhibited public acceptance of him as a writer: "You would rather take him for an Irish chairman, London porter, or one of Swift's Brobdingnaggians, than for a man of letters."[2] Likewise, Robert Potter argued that Johnson's corporeality blunted his critical acumen: "His vigorous mind being perhaps vitiated or degraded by the grossness of his body, vibrated not to the delicate touches of a Shenstone and a Hammond, nor even to the stronger hand of a Gray, but gravitated by the weight of that in which it was inclosed to earth."[3] Other critics charged that the system of literary production in Johnson's time promoted his intellectual debasement. To the dramatist Richard Cumberland—whose attitudes were fueled by a lingering distrust of commercial print and an emerging romantic aesthetic—Johnson's subjection to the operations of the book trade and the demands of publishers lowered him to the level of a mechanic whose labor is initiated and directed by forces beyond his control:"The variety we find in his writings was not the variety of choice arising from the impulse of his proper genius, but tasks imposed upon him by the dealers in ink, and contracts on his part submitted to in satisfaction of the pressing calls of hungry want."[4] Finally, his detractors argued that Johnson's own endorsement of the commercial ethic (an endorsement famously articulated in his remark that "No man but a blockhead ever wrote, except for money") undermined his ability to judge literature with the requisite taste and impartiality. James Thomson Callender charged that "in the true spirit of a mercantile author, [Johnson's] pen blackens every species of merit, which can admit of a comparison with his own"[5]; paradoxically, Johnson's very success in the market economy compromised his authority over English literary culture.

The reviews by Macaulay and Carlyle completely transform this image of Johnson: although they agree with the assessments of earlier critics that his writings "are becoming obsolete for this generation,"[6] their main focus is on Johnson's significance as a liminal figure in the history of authorship and a prototype for future generations of writers. Macaulay begins his distinctly Whiggish account by describing the bleak social context for Johnson's triumphal career. Borrowing details from some of Johnson's *Lives*, Macaulay represents early eighteenth- century writers by trade as delusional creatures driven to pathological behavior—behavior he believed was motivated by the economic instability that accompanied the developing market in literature. For Macaulay, the poets Samuel Boyse and Richard Savage displayed most vividly the symptoms of the "moral disease" that afflicted all professional writers of their time: their association of authorship with aristocratic identity led them to imitate the practices and preferences of upper-class males, which profoundly conflicted with the realities of their class situations. Unaccustomed to disciplined work—and completely averse to the bourgeois habits of cleanliness, regularity, sobriety, frugality, and temperance that such work requires—these authors existed on the unregulated and precarious margins of their culture:

> Sometimes blazing in gold-laced hats and waistcoats; sometimes lying in bed because their coats had gone to pieces, or wearing paper cravats because their linen was in pawn . . . they knew luxury; they knew beggary; but they never knew comfort. These men were irreclaimable. They looked on a regular and frugal life with the same aversion which an old gipsy or a Mohawk hunter feels for a stationary abode, and for the restraints and securities of

civilised communities. . . . If [the writer's] friends gave him an asylum in
their houses, those houses were forthwith turned into bagnios and taverns.
All order was destroyed; all business was suspended. The most good-natured
host began to repent of his eagerness to serve a man of genius in distress
when he heard his guest roaring for fresh punch at five o'clock in the
morning.[7]

Of course, this "untameable" band admits no female members:
Macaulay, following Johnson, altogether excludes women writers from his
literary history. Instead, the hacks' drinking, whoring, and carousing reveals
their unreformed masculinity, and Macaulay compares them to other male
"primitives" (the gipsy, the Mohawk hunter) whose undomesticated, if
somewhat romantic existence cannot withstand the spread of "civilised
communities." For Macaulay, the bourgeois life of order and business is
synonymous with society itself, and he sees early eighteenth-century writers as a disruptive, atavistic group that cannot be "broken into" the
"restraints and securities" of modern life—or, in other words, made to
accept middle-class mores and norms.

Civilization, however, ultimately took hold, and Johnson's experiences
provide an outline of its progress. According to Macaulay, as the century
wore on, the advance of capitalism turned the improvident, dissipated hack
into a self-disciplined man of letters, characterized by his careful management of both his finances and his sensuality: booksellers acknowledged and
supplied the public's "demand for amusement and instruction," and authors,
receiving higher and more frequent payments for their work, developed into
men who could be "admitted into the most respectable society on an equal
footing" (*Works*, 5: 523-24). Johnson's long involvement with the commercial marketplace—his bargains with booksellers and his attempts to assert the
high value of literary labor—make him a paradigmatic figure in Macaulay's
progressivist myth. But although he helped construct a new, bourgeois model
of authorship, Johnson himself remained a "specimen of the past age"
(*Works*, 5:524) irrevocably shaped by his early experiences: his sloppy appearance, irregular hours, and uncouth habits prevented him, in Macaulay's view,
from attaining the normative manhood of "civilised beings" (*Works*, 5:524).

For Carlyle, however, Johnson's residual wildness certified his masculin-
ity. Contrasting Johnson's roughness with the "Pharisaical Brummellean
Politeness, which would suffer crucifixion rather than ask twice for soup,"
Carlyle asserts that Johnson exhibited "the noble universal Politeness of a
man that knows the dignity of men, and feels his own" (*Essays*, 3:131).
Manliness, for Carlyle, is an innate rather than acquired or performative

quality; a "genuine Man" is by nature a visionary leader of the "dull host" (*Essays*, 3:89). Yet he argues that engaging in the literary marketplace—an arena populated by hacks and "dull oily Printer[s]"—enabled Johnson to display his manhood by rising above his difficult circumstances. In turn, the force of Johnson's character as a "Man of Letters, and Ruler of the British Nation" (*Essays*, 3:97) transformed the mode of production for literature, guiding it from its "boyhood and school-years" under the "Bookseller-System" to its assumption of the "*toga virilis*" under professional authors who manage and control their own careers (*Essays*, 3:101). Johnson helped effect this transition by providing the model for self-directed, disciplined labor: "Animated by the spirit of a true *workman*, resolute to do his work well" (*Essays*, 3:116) for his daily wage, Johnson cast himself forth into "that waste Chaos of Authorship" (*Essays*, 3:109) while resisting the subordination of his opinions and morality to the demands of the booksellers and their audiences. Instead of compromising Johnson's integrity, his involvement in a commercial economy and his eventual success within it confirmed his masculine status: Carlyle claims that "a Truth had been revealed to him: I also am a Man; even in this unutterable element of Authorship, I may live as beseems a Man!" (*Essays*, 3:110).

The attention that early Victorian writers like Macaulay and Carlyle paid to Johnson—whose reputation had been decidedly in decline—has its roots in the anxieties about authorship and manhood present in their own culture. Male intellectuals possessed an uncertain authority in a society dominated by the practices and principles of industrial capitalism. Lacking the capital—and hence the economic power—that was replacing rank as the foundation of social influence, and confronted by the growing numbers of middle-class women who desired a share in the dignity and independence that work provided, writers and other professionals faced the problem of legitimizing their masculinity and their right to the privileges attendant upon that status.[8] The "destabilization of gender by the various social forces of the day"[9] led to anxious assessments of the labor that confers manliness; increasingly, men of the professional classes identified energetic self-discipline and self-regulation—or a "strenuous psychic regimen" and commitment to the work ethic[10]—as the attributes that distinguished them from women and male laborers, and thus justified their claims to cultural authority. These forms of symbolic capital, however, proved hard to quantify and almost impossible to represent. For instance, Ford Madox Brown's well-known painting of Victorian labor, entitled *Work* (first exhibited in 1865), portrays Carlyle and the Reverend Denison Maurice, principal of the Working Men's College, leaning against a railing observing men, women, and children sweating at their manual tasks. Contemporary concerns about intellectual labor surface in the supplementary text of the exhibition catalogue, which assures readers that despite appearances, Carlyle and Maurice are not casual loafers: while "seeming to be idle, [they] work, and are the cause of well-ordained work and happiness in others."[11]

Early Victorian writers turned their sights to Johnson precisely because of how he represented intellectual work: he enabled them to associate a literary career with the bourgeois model of masculinity, a model that privileges successful involvement in the world of commerce (such as the book trade) and technology (such as print culture). However imperfect his actual conduct may have been, Johnson's emphasis on the rigorous exertion required for serious literary production and his characterization of poetry as an occupation exclusive to men provided a precedent for Victorian configurations of authorial labor. In Boswell's *Life* and in Johnson's own *Lives of the English Poets,* nineteenth-century intellectuals found a means of justifying their claim to a dominant social position: Johnson's economic success and his adherence to the moralized "gospel of work" suggest that writers could in fact meet Victorian standards for male achievement. Implicit in the masculine poetic that Johnson sketches is an acceptance, and eventual mastery, of marketplace practices. This includes a distaste for alternative practices, which are derided as feminine. Declaring that Johnson (unlike John Keats, perhaps) "was no man to be killed by a review," Carlyle compares Johnson's "healthy" commercialism and regard for profit to other writers' sickly—and effeminate—concern with reputation: the outcome of an intense self-consciousness is hysteria, as writers overly protective of their work resemble nothing more than a "brood goose" feverishly "flapping and shrieking" over her eggs (*Essays,* 3:116). Even the characteristics that repulsed Johnson's contemporaries became reinterpreted as evidence of his manhood, or of his fitness as a "muscular" Christian who successfully managed a fierce and potentially dangerous male energy. According to Carlyle, Johnson's occasional violence arose from a rough expression of tenderness rather than ill nature: "He was called the Bear; and did indeed too often look, and roar, like one; being forced to it in his own defence: yet within that shaggy exterior of his there beat a heart warm as a mother's, soft as a little child's" (*Essays,* 3:127). Johnson's shagginess actually confirmed the sincerity of his affection; the heroic man of letters without embarrassment appropriated conventionally feminine sentiments and behavior because his prowess had been tested and proved in the commercial world: "No Penny-a-week Committee-Lady, no manager of Soup-Kitchens, dancer at Charity-Balls was this rugged, stern-visaged man: but where, in all England, could there have been found another soul so full of Pity?" (*Essays*, 3:128). Accounts of Johnson written later in the century echo Carlyle's representation. In 1878, George Birkbeck Hill and Leslie Stephen extolled Johnson's tender nature and "acutely responsive heart"; his charity toward fallen women, servants, street urchins, and animals figures prominently in Sarah Boulton's 1885 essay on Johnson for children; and George Dawson's 1886 lecture concludes that "Nothing in history is more touching than this man's tenderness," for "he was merciful even to his cat."[12] For these writers, the ample evidence of Johnson's "robust nature" or "Valour"—his capacity for work, endurance, and hardship—enabled them to celebrate his "Mercy," which is the other necessary component of Victorian masculinity.

But Johnson's manhood was not only confirmed by his acts of tenderness. Assurances of his physical virility and considerable sexual magnetism surface repeatedly in Victorian texts. Stephen argues that the "charm" of "deep tenderness in a thoroughly masculine nature" made Johnson "singularly attractive" to women.[13] Elaborating more fully on this "charm," Thomas Hitchcock reminds readers that Johnson's body was as well developed as his mind: despite Johnson's "repulsive appearance and behavior," his "compensating physical advantages ["colossal stature," brawny strength, and "manly courage"] . . . amply reenforced by his intellectual gifts," impressed women "with that sense of power which is so attractive to their sex."[14] Like the famously ugly John Wilkes, Johnson "was 'only half an hour behind the handsomest man in England'" in arousing female passion—a passion that, as an "ardent" admirer of women, he fully returned.[15] Stephen's and Hitchcock's portrayals (or fantasies) of the virile, amorous man of letters confirm Johnson's adherence to heterosexual norms while allaying potential anxieties about his strange household "seraglio" and apparent commitment to celibacy; they also assure readers that potency of mind and body (in that order), rather than wealth and rank, establish male sexual dominance.

By the end of the nineteenth century, Carlyle's and Macaulay's assertions that writing is a man's work—a form of labor that requires and develops qualities peculiar to one sex—seem to have prevailed, as Johnson, the pivotal figure in these narratives, is transformed into a prototype of masculine excellence. The title of Sarah Boulton's book of essays, *Lives of Poor Boys Who Became Famous,* suggests the extent to which Carlyle's account of Johnson's heroism had been vulgarized into a Horatio Alger story, yet it also illustrates Johnson's successful integration into myths of middle-class advancement. By contrast, Johnson's onetime patron—Philip Dormer Stanhope, earl of Chesterfield—whose *Letters* (1774) comprised a manual for genteel conduct in his era, became synonymous with frivolity and impotence: for instance, Charles Dickens's version of Chesterfield, Sir John Chester in *Barnaby Rudge,* is described as one who "never compromised himself by an ungentlemanly action, and never was guilty of a manly one."[16] Over the course of a century, the aristocrat who had considered Johnson beneath his regard had been replaced as a model of masculine behavior by Johnson himself. And perhaps much of the affection for Johnson expressed in our own century arises from our culture's continued endorsement of the type of manhood that he as an author came to embody.

NOTES ⌐

Introduction

1. James Boswell, *The Life of Samuel Johnson*, ed. George Birkbeck Hill, rev. L.F. Powell, 6 vols. (Oxford: Clarendon Press, 1934-50), 3:311.

2. Lord Camden was one of the justices who voted against perpetual copyright in the 1774 case of Donaldson vs. Becket, and his juxtaposition of those authors who write for fame and "Glory" and those "Scribblers for bread, who teize the Press with their wretched Productions" and "traffic with a dirty Bookseller" reveals his disdain for professionals like Goldsmith. See *The Cases of the Appellants and Respondents in the Cause of Literary Property, Before the House of Lords* (London, 1774), reprinted in *The Literary Property Debate: Six Tracts 1764-1774*, ed. Stephen Parks (New York: Garland, 1975), 54.

3. Alexander Beljame, *Men of Letters and the English Public in the Eighteenth Century*, ed. Bonamy Dobrée, trans. E. O. Lorimer (London: Kegan Paul, Trench, Trubner, 1948), 385.

4. A. S. Collins, *Authorship in the Days of Johnson* (New York: E. P. Dutton, 1929), 193.

5. J. W. Saunders, *The Profession of English Letters* (London: Routledge and Kegan Paul, 1964), 145; 95; 175.

6. Siskin argues that during this period, the concept of work was "rewritten" from an activity beneath the concerns of gentlemen "to the primary activity informing adult identity; the tales that tell of it and the features associated with it were altered to produce a myth of vocation." *The Work of Writing: Literature and Social Change in Britain, 1700-1830* (Baltimore: Johns Hopkins University Press, 1998), 107. As Geoffrey Holmes observes, what gives a profession its "distinctive social stamp" is the "particular body of specialised knowledge" that it requires and its association with intellectual rather than manual labor; as a sign of his distinction, the professional man in eighteenth-

century England "was entitled to nothing less than the prefix "Mr", . . . [and] he quite frequently earned the label of 'gentleman,'" *Augustan England: Professions, State and Society, 1680-1730* (London: Allen & Unwin, 1982), 3; 9. Magali Sarfatti Larson dates the emergence of professions in their modern sense from the end of the eighteenth century, and defines professionalization as "the process by which producers of special services sought to constitute *and control* a market for their expertise"; this process also involves "a collective assertion of special social status and . . . a collective process of upward social mobility" (xvi). See *The Rise of Professionalism: A Sociological Analysis* (Berkeley: University of California Press, 1977).

7. These studies include Elizabeth Eisenstein's *The Printing Press as an Agent of Change: Communications and Cultural Transformations in Early-Modern Europe,* 2 vols. (Cambridge: Cambridge University Press, 1979); Alvin Kernan's *Printing Technology, Letters & Samuel Johnson* (Princeton: Princeton University Press, 1987); and Brean S. Hammond's *Professional Imaginative Writing in England, 1670-1740* (Oxford: Clarendon Press, 1997).

8. See Martha Woodmansee, "The Genius and the Copyright: Economic and Legal Conditions of the Emergence of the 'Author,'" *Eighteenth-Century Studies* 17 (1984): 425-48; and *The Author, Art, and the Market: Rereading the History of Aesthetics* (New York: Columbia University Press, 1994); David Saunders and Ian Hunter, "Lessons from the 'Literatory': How to Historicise Authorship," *Critical Inquiry* 17 (1991): 479-509; David Saunders, *Authorship and Copyright* (London: Routledge, 1992); and Mark Rose, *Authors and Owners: The Invention of Copyright* (Cambridge, MA.: Harvard University Press, 1993).

9. Frank Donoghue's *The Fame Machine: Book Reviewing and Eighteenth-Century Literary Careers* (Stanford: Stanford University Press, 1996) and Dustin Griffin's *Literary Patronage in England, 1650-1800* (Cambridge: Cambridge University Press, 1996) both examine how writers' careers were shaped by institutional practices.

10. Investigations of how female authors negotiated the gender ideologies of their time include, on fiction, Jane Spencer, *The Rise of the Woman Novelist: From Aphra Behn to Jane Austen* (Oxford: Basil Blackwell, 1986); Dale Spender, *Mothers of the Novel: 100 Good Women Writers before Jane Austen* (New York: Pandora, 1986); Janet Todd, *The Sign of Angellica: Women, Writing and Fiction, 1660-1800* (New York: Columbia University Press, 1989); Cheryl Turner, *Living by the Pen: Women Writers in the Eighteenth Century* (London: Routledge, 1992); Catherine Gallagher, *Nobody's Story: The Vanishing Acts of Women Writers in the Marketplace 1670-1820* (Berkeley: University of California Press, 1994); on poetry, see Donna Landry, *The Muses of Resistance: Laboring-Class Women's Poetry in Britain, 1739-1796* (Cambridge: Cambridge University Press, 1990); Claudia Thomas, *Alexander Pope and His Eighteenth- Century Women Readers* (Carbondale: Southern Illinois University Press, 1994); Moira Ferguson, *Eighteenth-Century Women Poets: Nation,*

Class, and Gender (Albany: State University of New York Press, 1995); and Carol Barash, *English Women's Poetry, 1649-1714: Politics, Community, and Linguistic Authority* (Oxford: Oxford University Press, 1996); on drama, see Jacqueline Pearson, *The Prostituted Muse: Images of Women and Women Dramatists, 1642-1737* (New York: Harvester Wheatsheaf, 1988); Mary Anne Schofield and Cecilia Macheski, eds., *Curtain Calls: British and American Women and the Theater, 1660-1820* (Athens, OH: Ohio University Press, 1991); and Laura J. Rosenthal, *Playwrights and Plagiarists in Early Modern England* (Ithaca: Cornell University Press, 1996).

11. Gallagher, *Nobody's Story*, xxi.
12. Jill Campbell, *Natural Masques: Gender and Identity in Fielding's Plays and Novels* (Stanford: Stanford University Press, 1995), 8.
13. James Thompson, *Models of Value: Eighteenth-Century Political Economy and the Novel* (Durham: Duke University Press, 1996); Catherine Ingrassia, *Authorship, Commerce, and Gender in Early Eighteenth-Century England: A Culture of Paper Credit* (Cambridge: Cambridge University Press, 1998).
14. Michael Roper and John Tosh, "Introduction: Historians and the Politics of Masculinity," in *Manful Assertions: Masculinities in Britain since 1800*, ed. Michael Roper and John Tosh (London: Routledge, 1991), 18.
15. Mark Breitenberg, *Anxious Masculinity in Early Modern England* (Cambridge: Cambridge University Press, 1996), 2.
16. George L. Mosse argues that this stereotype "was closely linked to the new bourgeois society that was in the making at the end of the eighteenth century." *The Image of Man: The Creation of Modern Masculinity* (Oxford: Oxford University Press, 1996), 17. My own investigations into emergent constructions of masculinity have been shaped and influenced by the work of Randolph Trumbach, in "The Birth of the Queen: Sodomy and the Emergence of Gender Equality in Modern Culture, 1660-1750," *Hidden from History: Reclaiming the Gay and Lesbian Past*, ed. Martin Bauml Duberman, Martha Vicinus, and George Chauncey, Jr. (New York: New American Library, 1989), 129-40; and "Sodomy Transformed: Aristocratic Libertinage, Public Reputation and the Gender Revolution of the 18th Century," *Journal of Homosexuality* 19 (1990): 105-24; G.J. Barker-Benfield, *The Culture of Sensibility: Sex and Society in Eighteenth-Century Britain* (Chicago: University of Chicago Press, 1992); Anthony Fletcher, *Gender, Sex and Subordination in England 1500-1800* (New Haven: Yale University Press, 1995); Michael McKeon, "Historicizing Patriarchy: The Emergence of Gender Difference in England, 1660-1760," *Eighteenth-Century Studies* 28 (1995): 295-322; and Shawn Lisa Maurer, *Proposing Men: Dialectics of Gender and Class in the Eighteenth-Century English Periodical* (Stanford: Stanford University Press, 1998).
17. Hammond, *Professional Imaginative Writing*, 73.
18. Tonson complained that Dryden had offered Peter Motteux, editor of the *Gentleman's Journal*, a greater number of lines per guinea than he had

offered Tonson. *The Letters of John Dryden,* ed. Charles E. Ward (Durham: Duke University Press, 1942), 49-52.

19. These figures are cited in Harry Ransom's "The Rewards of Authorship in the Eighteenth Century," *University of Texas Studies in English* 18 (1938): 47-66.

20. As quoted in *The Poems of Gray, Collins, and Goldsmith,* ed. Roger Lonsdale (London: Longman, 1969), 409-10. Five years after offering no copy money for Collins's *Odes,* Millar paid Henry Fielding 800 pounds for the copyright to *Amelia*—twice the amount that he had given for *Tom Jones* in 1749.

21. Ransom, "The Rewards of Authorship," 52. As Ransom notes, "The price of poetry does not seem to have increased measurably during the century" (54).

22. James Prior, *The Life of Oliver Goldsmith,* 2 vols. (London, 1837), 2:276-77.

23. *The Life and Errors of John Dunton, Late Citizen of London; Written by Himself in Solitude* (London, 1705), 244.

24. Dunton, *Life and Errors,* 243.

25. For nearly a century, the precarious existence of poets by trade remained a common topic for writers who either satirized or sympathized with their subject; some of the texts generated by this discourse include: John Oldham's "Spencer's Ghost" (1683); Ned Ward's "The Author's Lamentation" (1691); Tom Brown's "The Poet's Condition" (1700?) and "The Mourning Poet" (1700?); Swift's "The Progress of Poetry" (1720) and "Advice to the Grub-Street Verse-Writers" (1726); Pope's *Dunciad* (1728; 1743) and "Epistle to Arbuthnot" (1735); Fielding's *The Author's Farce* (1730); Aaron Hill's *Advice to the Poets* (1731); Bezaleel Morrice's "A Satirical Essay on Modern Poets" (1734); Samuel Foote's *The Author* (1757); William Whitehead's "The Danger of Writing Verse" (1741) and "A Charge to the Poets" (1762); Charles Churchill's "The Author" (1763); James Scott's "The Perils of Poetry" (1766); William Dunkin's "The Poet's Prayer" (1734); and Percival Stockdale's *The Poet* (1773). To his contemporaries, William Hogarth's *The Distressed Poet* (1736) became a visual emblem of the professional writer's pathetic self-delusion; as M. Dorothy George reports, Benjamin Disraeli's grandfather, recalling this image, grew alarmed when his son Isaac declared his desire to write, for "his idea of a poet was formed from one of the prints of Hogarth hanging on his wall." *Hogarth to Cruikshank: Social Change in Graphic Satire* (New York: Viking, 1967), 126.

26. *The Poems of Alexander Pope,* ed. John Butt (New Haven: Yale University Press, 1963), 321.

27. James Scott, *The Perils of Poetry* (London and Cambridge, 1766), 16. References to this poem are cited by page number.

28. Percival Stockdale, *The Poet* (London, 1773), 24. References to this poem are cited by page number.

29. John Brewer, "'The most polite age and the most vicious': Attitudes towards Culture as a Commodity, 1660-1800," *The Consumption of Culture 1660-*

1800: Image, Object, Text, ed. Ann Bermingham and John Brewer (London: Routledge, 1995), 345.

30. Pat Rogers, in *Grub Street: Studies in a Subculture* (London: Methuen, 1972), notes that the locale of Grub Street, particularly Lewkner's Lane, had long been identified as a "haunt of tarts" as well as a place of business for Pope's dunces (73).

31. William Dunkin, *Select Poetical Works of the Late William Dunkin, D.D.*, 2 vols. (Dublin, 1769-70), 2:294. References to this poem are cited by page number.

32. Pope's addresses to women readers in his notes to the Homer translation, and the hostility that these addresses evoked from critics, provide a sense of his culture's ambivalence toward women as consumers of literature. Dryden's Virgil translation, published two decades before Pope's *Iliad*, made no references to a female audience. For an account of Pope's "appeals to the ladies," see Claudia Thomas, *Alexander Pope and His Eighteenth-Century Women Readers*, 19-67.

33. Richard Helgerson presents this argument in *Self-Crowned Laureates: Spenser, Jonson, Milton and the Literary System* (Berkeley: University of California Press, 1983), 21-54, and in *The Elizabethan Prodigals* (Berkeley: University of California Press, 1976).

34. Helgerson, *Self-Crowned Laureates*, 29. Kevin Pask observes a similar consensus about the role of poetry in aristocratic life-narratives of the Renaissance: these narratives portray verse writing "as the avocation of youthful courtship and thus courtiership," which must be forsaken for the administrative or military duties of manhood, as in the case of Philip Sidney. *The Emergence of the English Author: Scripting the Life of the Poet in Early Modern England* (Cambridge: Cambridge University Press, 1996), 54.

35. Wendy Wall, *The Imprint of Gender: Authorship and Publication in the English Renaissance* (Ithaca: Cornell University Press, 1993), 185.

36. Robert Lloyd, "To George Colman, Esq. A Familiar Epistle," *Poems* (London, 1762), 154-59.

37. Morris Golden, "Goldsmith's Reputation in His Day," *Papers on Language and Literature* 16 (1980): 222. Samuel H. Woods also suggests reasons for the undervaluation of Goldsmith in "The Goldsmith 'Problem,'" *Studies in Burke and His Time* 19 (1978): 47-60.

38. Michèle Cohen, *Fashioning Masculinity: National Identity and Language in the Eighteenth Century* (London: Routledge, 1996), 1. Cohen goes on to note that "the unrestrained tongue was inescapably female and had to be contained and controlled" (32)—a practice advocated by Boswell in relation to his rival biographer, Hester Thrale, whose verbal "inaccuracy" he delighted in exposing (*Life*, 3:226).

39. Goldsmith was not always so egalitarian, for like Boswell, he realized the prestige that could be gained by adopting aristocratic social practices, including that of making one's body a spectacle. In one passage, Boswell

records the ridicule that Goldsmith provoked after "bragging of his dress," when his pride in the attention attracted by his "bloom-coloured coat" drew a rebuke from the plainly-attired Johnson: "'Why, sir, . . . [the tailor] knew the strange colour would attract crouds to gaze at it, and thus they might hear of him, and see how well he could make a coat even of so absurd a colour'" (*Life*, 2:83). Boswell thus relies upon Johnson (who was noticeably careless of his clothes) to censure Goldsmith's self-display as an inappropriate trespass on the prerogatives of gentlemen.

40. Sir John Hawkins, *The Life of Samuel Johnson, LL.D.*, Johnsoniana 20 (1787; reprint, New York: Garland, 1974), 420.

41. According to Hawkins, Goldsmith insultingly rejected the earl's patronage, preferring instead to rely on commercial exchanges for a living : "'I have no dependence on the promises of great men: I look to the booksellers for support; they are my best friends, and I am not inclined to forsake them for others'" (*Life of Samuel Johnson*, 419).

42. As quoted in Prior, *Life of Oliver Goldsmith*, 2:272.

43. *Monthly Review* 42 (1770): 445; *St. James's Chronicle*, as quoted in Prior, *Life of Oliver Goldsmith*, 2:273.

44. Thomas Davies, *Memoirs of the Life of David Garrick, Esq.* (1780), in *Goldsmith: The Critical Heritage*, ed. G.S. Rousseau (London: Routledge and Kegan Paul, 1974), 194-95.

45. The phrase is Edmund Malone's from the biographical preface to *Poems and Plays by Oliver Goldsmith* (1780), in *Critical Heritage*, 186.

46. *Collected Works of Oliver Goldsmith*, ed. Arthur Friedman, 5 vols. (Oxford: Clarendon Press, 1966), 1:3. Subsequent references to Goldsmith's writings are to Friedman's edition.

47. John Ginger, *The Notable Man: The Life and Times of Oliver Goldsmith* (London: Hamish Hamilton, 1977), 102.

48. Ginger, *The Notable Man*, 102.

49. Henry Fielding, *The Author's Farce*, *The Complete Works of Henry Fielding*, ed. William Ernest Henley, 16 vols. (New York: Croscup and Sterling, 1902), 8:222.

50. James Ralph, *The Case of Authors by Profession or Trade* (1758) (Gainesville, FL: Scholars' Facsimiles & Reprints, 1966), 21; 22.

51. *Critical Review* 1 (1756): 97-98.

52. William Kenrick, another of Griffiths's writers for the *Monthly*, charged Goldsmith with duplicity for being one of the very "Literary Understrapper[s]" whom he condemns (*Monthly Review* 21 [1759]: 389).

53. Donoghue, *The Fame Machine*, 91.

54. *Works*, 2:377. Ralph also distinguishes between professional and amateur writers, arguing that the "Writer by Trade" is superior to the "Holiday Writers," for the former "obtains that Mastery in Matter, Method, Stile and Manner, which is hardly to be obtained any other Way" than by constant composition (*Case*, 8-9).

55. Ralph, *Case*, 47; 19.
56. *Case*, 71. Ralph invokes the need for a revival of the Society for the Encouragement of Learning and for the continued function of the Premium Society, or Society for Encouraging Arts and Sciences, as forms of collective patronage for commercially inept authors (*Case*, 62).
57. Zeynep Tenger and Paul Trolander, "Genius versus Capital: Eighteenth-Century Theories of Genius and Adam Smith's *Wealth of Nations*," *Modern Language Quarterly* 55 (1994): 172.
58. Adam Smith, *An Inquiry into the Nature and Causes of the Wealth of Nations*, ed. Edwin Cannan, 2 vols. (Chicago: University of Chicago Press, 1976), 2:352.
59. John Barrell, *English Literature in History 1730-80: An Equal, Wide Survey* (New York: St. Martin's Press, 1983), 44; 47.

Chapter One

1. The line is from "Timon." *The Poems of John Wilmot, Earl of Rochester,* ed. Keith Walker (Oxford: Basil Blackwell, 1984), 22. All references to Rochester's poetry are to this edition.
2. *The Poems of John Oldham,* ed. Harold F. Brooks with Raman Selden (Oxford: Clarendon Press, 1987), 90. All references to Oldham's poems and prose are to this edition.
3. *The Letters of John Wilmot, Earl of Rochester,* ed. Jeremy Treglown (Oxford: Basil Blackwell, 1980), 251. Rochester's mother Anne, the dowager countess, reported rumors of this lampoon with annoyance, fearing it would compromise her narrative of Rochester's final repentance.
4. Harold Love, "But Did Rochester *Really* Write Sodom?," *Publications of the Bibliographical Society of America* 3 (1993): 319. Love's *Scribal Publication in Seventeenth- Century England* (Oxford: Clarendon Press, 1993) also provides an extensive account of coterie writing practices, and I am indebted to his study throughout my discussion of Rochester. For an analysis of the literary scene earlier in the century, see Arthur F. Marotti, *Manuscript, Print, and the English Renaissance Lyric* (Ithaca: Cornell University Press, 1995).
5. Robert Parsons, *A Sermon Preached at the Funeral of the Rt Honorable John Earl of Rochester* (Oxford, 1680), 8.
6. Gilbert Burnet, *Some Passages of the Life and Death of the Right Honourable John Earl of Rochester* (1680), in *Rochester: The Critical Heritage,* ed. David Farley-Hills (New York: Barnes and Noble, 1972), 86.
7. Burnet, *Critical Heritage,* 51.
8. Nathaniel Lee, dedication to *The Tragedy of Nero* (1675), *The Works of Nathaniel Lee,* ed. Thomas B. Stroup and Arthur L. Cooke, 2 vols. (New Brunswick, NJ: Scarecrow Press, 1954), 1:24.
9. Burnet, *Critical Heritage,* 86-87.
10. Burnet, *Critical Heritage,* 50.

11. Michael McKeon, *The Origins of the English Novel, 1600-1740* (Baltimore: Johns Hopkins University Press, 1987), 131.
12. McKeon, *Origins,* 169.
13. According to Harold Love, "amateurism . . . was not the mark of untrained dabblers but an aesthetic and a system of literary production in its own right, which . . . was premised on the notion of the inherent superiority of an upper-class culture which validated its writing skills by reference to the art of spontaneous, polished conversation and natural elegance" ("Shadwell, Rochester and the Crisis of Amateurism," *Restoration: Studies in English Literary Culture, 1660-1700* 20 [1996]: 122). Marianne Thormahlen's very helpful study, *Rochester: The Poems in Context* (Cambridge: Cambridge University Press, 1993), also aims to dispel the pervasive "wicked-Earl-who-wrote-with-ease image" by analyzing Rochester's poetry as "the work of a complex and serious artist" (8); Simon Dentith, in "Negativity and Affirmation in Rochester's Lyric Poetry," in *Reading Rochester,* ed. Edward Burns (Liverpool: Liverpool University Press, 1995), calls attention to the carefully constructed nature of this image: "The 'ease,' the deftness, the speed, the wit of those holiday writers is a crucial part of their social self-presentation, as much as the tying of Dorimant's cravat" (91). Dustin Griffin's "Rochester and the 'Holiday Writers,'" in *Rochester and Court Poetry,* Papers presented at a Clark Library Seminar, 11 May 1985 (Los Angeles: William Andrews Clark Memorial Library, 1988), 35-66, distinguishes Rochester's work from that Etherege, Dorset, and Sedley, while Peter Porter's "The Professional Amateur," in *Spirit of Wit: Reconsiderations of Rochester,* ed. Jeremy Treglown (Oxford: Basil Blackwell, 1982), 58-74, examines how Rochester's work conflates these two opposing categories of writers.
14. Bibliographic accounts of these editions include James Thorpe's introduction to *Rochester's Poems on Several Occasions,* Princeton Studies in English 30 (Princeton: Princeton University Press, 1950); and David M. Vieth's *Attribution in Restoration Poetry: A Study of Rochester's Poems of 1680* (New Haven: Yale University Press, 1963). Vieth also identifies the authors of individual poems in the 1680 text.
15. Vieth, *Attribution,* 60-61.
16. John Harold Wilson, *The Court Wits of the Restoration: An Introduction* (Princeton: Princeton University Press, 1948), 111.
17. Love, *Scribal Publication,* 224.
18. Robert Wolseley, preface to *Valentinian, a Tragedy as 'tis Alter'd by the Late Earl of Rochester* (1685), in *Rochester: The Critical Heritage,* 155.
19. *Poems on Several Occasions,* 1-4. References are to Thorpe's edition of the volume.
20. The verse correspondents, however, seem far more interested in courting each other than in pursuing women: as Eve Kosofsky Sedgwick observes in *Between Men: English Literature and Male Homosocial Desire* (New York: Columbia University Press, 1985), "wit is an important mechanism for

moving from an ostensible heterosexual object of desire to a true homosocial one" (61).

21. Dryden to Rochester, Rochester's *Letters*, 88. Love explains the importance of country houses as sites of upper-class literary production: landowners' facility at writing "was frequently put to work in user or author publication, and was reflected in a habit of reading that was serious, attentive and solitary" (*Scribal Publication*, 198). Rochester's own serious reading at Adderbury included Livy and the Bible.

22. James Anderson Winn speculates that Louise Keroualle, duchess of Portsmouth, might have orchestrated the Rose Alley assault in revenge for an abusive reference to her in "An Essay upon Satire," a manuscript poem written by the earl of Mulgrave (Dryden's patron), perhaps with Dryden's assistance (*John Dryden and His World* [New Haven: Yale University Press, 1987], 326). Rochester himself had threatened corporal punishment for Dryden's satire: "If he falls upon me at the blunt, which is his very good weapon in wit, I will forgive him if you please and leave the repartee to Black Will with a cudgel" (*Letters*, 120).

23. Harold Weber, "'Drudging in Fair Aurelia's Womb': Constructing Homosexual Economies in Rochester's Poetry," *The Eighteenth Century: Theory and Interpretation* 33 (1992): 111.

24. Wolseley, *Critical Heritage*, 145.

25. *The Works of John Dryden*, ed. Edward N. Hooker, H. T. Swedenberg, Jr., et al., 20 vols. (Berkeley: University of California Press, 1956-), 11:224. Unless otherwise indicated, references to Dryden's writings are to the California edition.

26. In "'An Allusion to Horace', Jonson's Ghost, and the Second Poets' War," Brean S. Hammond observes that "for the professional writers of the time, who experienced at first hand, as Rochester did not, the pressures that gave rise to such expedients [as plagiarism and hurried composition], his Horatian advice was difficult to take" (*Reading Rochester*, 180). Hammond's essay very usefully modifies Howard D. Weinbrot's dismissal of the poem as "not only personal and unjustified, but unconvincing" ("The 'Allusion to Horace': Rochester's Imitative Mode," in *John Wilmot, Earl of Rochester: Critical Essays*, ed. David M. Vieth [New York: Garland, 1988], 330).

27. "A Session of the Poets" (1676), *Poems on Affairs of State: Augustan Satirical Verse, 1660-1714*, ed. George deForest Lord et al., 7 vols. (New Haven: Yale University Press, 1963- 75), 1:353.

28. Since the standard rate that booksellers offered for printed plays was often quite low, the profits from the third day's performance were crucial to playwrights' survival, along with the remuneration gained from dedicating a play to wealthy patrons. See Terry Belanger, "Publishers and Writers in Eighteenth-Century England," in *Books and Their Readers in Eighteenth-Century England*, ed. Isabel Rivers (New York: St. Martin's Press, 1982),

5-25; Graham Pollard, "The English Market for Printed Books," *Publishing History* 4 (1978): 7-48; and Marjorie Plant, *The English Book Trade: An Economic History of the Making and Sale of Books* (1939; reprint London: George Allen & Unwin, 1965). Even Dryden, who was a sharer in the King's Company and thus more financially secure than most writers, had to draw an audience to his plays to keep profits up.

29. Matthew Prior, "Satyr on the Poets" (1687), *The Literary Works of Matthew Prior*, ed. H. Bunker Wright and Monroe K. Spears, 2 vols., 2nd ed. (Oxford: Clarendon Press, 1971), 1:32-33.

30. Thormahlen examines the sources of "Timon" and the extent of Rochester's indebtedness to them in *Rochester: The Poems in Context* (274-77).

31. Edward Burns quotes Greer in his introduction to *Reading Rochester* (4).

32. Some excellent studies of women's writing in the seventeenth century include Margaret J. M. Ezell, *The Patriarch's Wife: Literary Evidence and the History of the Family* (Chapel Hill: University of North Carolina Press, 1987); Isobel Grundy and Susan Wiseman, eds., *Women Writing History: 1640-1740* (Athens, GA: University of Georgia Press, 1992); Elaine Hobby, *Virtue of Necessity: English Women's Writing 1649-88* (London: Virago, 1988); Mary Prior, ed., *Women in English Society 1500-1800* (London: Methuen, 1985); and Helen Wilcox, ed., *Women and Literature in Britain, 1500-1700* (Cambridge: Cambridge University Press, 1996). Analyses of Rochester's feminism usually focus on his representations of female sexuality, not his attitude toward women as writers. For studies of his sexual politics, see Stephen Clark, "'Something Genrous in Meer Lust'?: Rochester and Misogyny," in *Reading Rochester*, 21-41; Carole Fabricant, "Rochester's World of Imperfect Enjoyment," *Journal of English and Germanic Philology* 73 (1974): 338-50; Helen Wilcox, "Gender and Artfulness in Rochester's 'Song of a Young Lady to Her Ancient Lover,'" in *Reading Rochester*, 6-20; Reba Wilcoxon, "Rochester's Sexual Politics," *Studies in Eighteenth-Century Culture* 8 (1979): 137-49, reprinted in *John Wilmot, Earl of Rochester: Critical Essays*, 113-26; and Sarah Wintle, "Libertinism and Sexual Politics," in *Spirit of Wit: Reconsiderations of Rochester*, 133-65.

33. James Gill discusses the appearance of the split subject in Rochester's poems, arguing that his best work "distrusts the privileging of single subject positions or 'fictions' just as some contemporary critics are distrustful of all 'master narrative fictions.'" "The Fragmented Self in Three of Rochester's Poems," *Modern Language Quarterly* 48 (1988): 37.

34. Edward Burns, "Rochester, Lady Betty and the Post-Boy," in *Reading Rochester*, 73.

35. Love, *Scribal Publication*, 250. Love's assertion that "the print medium was [the] enemy" (297) of aristocratic writers is not altogether accurate, for his account of Robert Julian shows that they were ambivalent toward any "professional" circulation of their work.

36. George Villiers, duke of Buckingham, "A Familiar Epistle to Mr. Julian, Secretary to the Muses" (1677), *Poems on Affairs of State*, 1:388.

37. Patricia Crawford, "Attitudes to Menstruation in Seventeenth-Century England," *Past and Present* 91 (1981): 47-73.

38. J. C. D. Clark, *English Society, 1688-1832: Ideology, Social Structure and Political Practice during the Ancien Regime* (Cambridge: Cambridge University Press, 1985), 114.

39. Sir Carr Scroope, "In Defense of Satire" (1677), *Poems on Affairs of State*, 1:367.

40. "The Author's Reply" (1677), *Poems on Affairs of State*, 1:373.

41. Warren Chernaik, *Sexual Freedom in Restoration Literature* (Cambridge: Cambridge University Press, 1995), 80. The analogy between pen and sword appears throughout libertine writing, and usually suggests a dangerously easy access to both weapons on the part of incompetents.

42. Charles Hatton to Christopher Hatton, 29 June 1676, *Correspondence of the Family of Hatton*, ed. E.M. Thompson, 2 vols. (Westminster: Camden Society, 1878), 1:133-34. As quoted in Burns, "Rochester, Lady Betty and the Post-Boy," in *Reading Rochester*, 69.

43. Vieth discusses some of these satires, most of which characterize Rochester as a drunkard, bully, buffoon, whoremaster, and coward, in *Attribution in Restoration Poetry*, 164- 203.

44. Wolseley, *Critical Heritage*, 140; 146.

45. George Villiers, duke of Buckingham, *The Rehearsal* (Great Neck: Barron's Educational Series, 1960), 1.1; 3.3.

46. Parsons, *A Sermon*, 28. Watts's "Lines on the Death of the Earl of Rochester" commemorates "Strephon"'s repentance while excoriating his verse: "But, O indulgent Heaven!/So vile the Muse, and yet the man forgiven!" *The Repentance and Happy Death of the Celebrated Earl of Rochester* (Nottingham: Sutton and Son, 1814), 8. As quoted in Johannes Prinz, *Rochesteriana: Being Some Anecdotes Concerning John Wilmot Earl of Rochester* (Leipzig: privately printed, 1926), 71.

47. Thomas Rymer, preface to *Poems, &c. On Several Occasions: with Valentinian, a Tragedy*, Written by the Right Honourable John Late Earl of Rochester (London, 1691), n.p.

48. Thorpe's introduction to the 1680 *Poems on Several Occasions* catalogs the changes that Tonson made to the text (xxxvi). These changes may also have been made in compliance with the revival of licensing legislation after 1680, which reinforced booksellers' responsibility for the content of the texts they published and sold. See Jim McGhee, "Obscene Libel and the Language of 'The Imperfect Enjoyment,'" in *Reading Rochester*, 42-65.

49. David M. Vieth, introduction to *The Complete Poems of John Wilmot, Earl of Rochester* (New Haven: Yale University Press, 1968), xxvii.

50. Biographical information about Oldham is scanty, but accounts of his life are provided in Raman Selden's "Rochester and Oldham: 'High Rants in

Profaneness,' " in *Reading Rochester,* 187-206; in the "Memoirs" prefixed to the first volume of *The Works of Mr. John Oldham Together with his Remains,* 2 vols. (London, 1722); and in Brooks and Selden's introduction to *The Poems of John Oldham,* (xxv-lxx). James Zigerell's *John Oldham,* Twayne's English Authors Series 372 (Boston: Twayne, 1983), also offers a helpful overview of Oldham's verse and career.

51. Selden, "Rochester and Oldham," 194.

52. Selden, "Rochester and Oldham," 204.

53. Roger Chartier's "Time to Understand: The 'Frustrated Intellectuals,' " *Cultural History: Between Practices and Representations,* trans. Lydia G. Cochrane (Ithaca: Cornell University Press, 1988), 127-50, observes the anxiety that déclassé parvenus "who had become learned in vain" (139) aroused in members of the established order. Lawrence Stone identifies the prestige given to learning, and the "demand by the State for an administrative *elite* of proved competence, irrespective of the claims of rank," as some of the factors behind the growing crisis of confidence in the aristocracy. See *The Crisis of the Aristocracy 1558-1641* (Oxford: Clarendon Press, 1965), 748-49.

54. Selden, "Rochester and Oldham," 195.

55. Love's "But Did Rochester *Really* Write *Sodom?*" argues against attributing the play to Rochester, since he viewed sodomy as an expression of personal power-politics rather than a metaphor for the degeneracy of relationships at court: "The kinds of power implied, and indeed freely acknowledged [in Rochester's poems], are those by which one kind of individual—the aristocrat—is able to exploit the bodies of other individuals for his private diversion: apart from this the sodomitic relationship is not endowed with a wider metaphorical significance" (332).

56. Michèle Cohen, *Fashioning Masculinity: National Identity and Language in the Eighteenth Century* (London: Routledge, 1996), 2.

57. Wendy Wall, *The Imprint of Gender: Authorship and Publication in the English Renaissance* (Ithaca: Cornell University Press, 1993), 185.

58. Oldham's "Bion" contrasts with the elegies of other writers such as Aphra Behn, who celebrates the power of Rochester's satiric verse:

> Satyr has lost its Art, its Sting is gone,
> he Fop and Cully now may be undone;
> That dear instructing Rage is now allay'd,
> And no sharp Pen dares tell 'em how they've stray'd.

"On the Death of the late Earl of *Rochester,*" *The Works of Aphra Behn,* ed. Janet Todd, 2 vols. (Columbus: Ohio State University Press, 1992), 1:161.

59. Raman Selden, "Oldham, Pope, and Restoration Satire," in *English Satire and the Satiric Tradition,* ed. Claude Rawson (Oxford: Basil Blackwell, 1984), 110.

60. Oldham's lines "In Praise of Poetry" exist only in the form of several drafts,

which Brooks and Selden have arranged to form a more coherent text; for an explanation of their editorial decisions, see *Poems*, 524.

61. Ironically, prefatory verses praising Oldham were included in Hindmarsh's *Remains* (1684), and an engraved likeness of the poet by Van der Gucht served as the frontispiece to a volume entitled *Works and Remains* (1703). Even Oldham's published attacks on such "Trappings" could not prevent booksellers from adopting them.

62. Clark, *English Society*, 109.

63. 30 May 1668, *The Diary of Samuel Pepys*, ed. Robert Latham and William Matthews, 11 vols. (Berkeley: University of California Press, 1976), 9:218. G.J. Barker-Benfield notes the deep cultural roots, and attractiveness, of such unregenerate masculinity: "In his 'frollicks,' his drinking, his participation in gang attacks on the watch and on accessible women, together with his expressions of misogyny, the rake symbolized the public manners of an older male leisure culture." *The Culture of Sensibility: Sex and Society in Eighteenth-Century Britain* (Chicago: University of Chicago Press, 1992), 45.

64. Ken Robinson discusses Oldham's relation to these satiric models in "The Art of Violence in Rochester's Satire," in *English Satire and the Satiric Tradition*, 95-96.

65. Lawrence Stone and Jeanne C. Fawtier Stone, *An Open Elite? England 1540-1880* (Oxford: Clarendon Press, 1984), 408. Nancy Armstrong and Leonard Tennenhouse argue for a more contentious relation between these social groups; they propose that through its skill at writing and growing control over determinations of literacy, the "class emerging in the wake of the English Revolution"—a class composed of "the owners of knowledge" rather than the owners of capital—over time "acquired the power to displace permanently the aristocracy." *The Imaginary Puritan: Literature, Intellectual Labor, and the Origins of Personal Life* (Berkeley: University of California Press, 1992), 138.

66. Stone and Stone, *An Open Elite?*, 408.

67. Dustin Griffin makes this point in "Dryden's 'Oldham' and the Perils of Writing," *Modern Language Quarterly* 37 (1976): 138.

68. Griffin, "Dryden's 'Oldham,'" 138.

69. The allusion to Virgil's homosexual lovers was so unmistakable and so offensive that Pope removed the couplet ("Fam'd for good-nature, B[entley] and for truth;/ D[uckett] for pious passion to the youth" [3.175-76]) from the *Dunciad*'s final version. *The Poems of Alexander Pope*, ed. John Butt (New Haven: Yale University Press, 1963). All references to Pope's poetry are to Butt's edition.

70. Pope to Joseph Spence, 1-7 May 1730, in *Anecdotes, Observations, and Characters of Books and Men*, ed. J.M. Osborn, 2 vols. (Oxford: Clarendon Press, 1966), 1:473. Paul Baines examines Pope's relationship to his predecessor in "From 'Nothing' to 'Silence': Rochester and Pope," in *Reading Rochester*, 137-65.

71. David Farley-Hills's introduction to *Rochester: The Critical Heritage* observes
     the gradual decline in Rochester's reputation throughout the eighteenth
     century, as editions of his verse became more and more infrequent (3);
     Horace Walpole's appraisal is representative of critical opinion after 1750:
     "Lord Rochester's poems have much more obscenity than wit, more wit
     than poetry, more poetry than politeness" (*A Catalogue of the Royal and Noble
     Authors of England,* 2 vols. [Strawberry Hill, 1758], 2:37-39).

Chapter Two

1. Although suspicious of Thomas's "wild story," Johnson still recorded it in
    his "Life of Dryden." See *Lives of the English Poets,* ed. George Birkbeck Hill,
    3 vols. (1905; reprint, New York: Octagon, 1967), 1:390-92. Tom Brown
    provides his burlesque version of the event in *A Description of Mr. Dryden's
    Funeral* (London, 1700), 6.
2. See Ned Ward, *The London Spy* 2.6 (April 1700):

    > The great Number of Qualities Coaches that attended the Hearse,
    > so put the *Hackney* Whore-drivers out of their Biass, that against the
    > *Kings-head Tavern* there happen'd a great stop, occasion'd by a Train
    > of Coaches which had block'd up the narrow end of the Lane,
    > obstructed by an intangled number of moveable Bawdy-houses,
    > who waited to turn up the same narrow Gulph, the others wanted
    > to go out of; some with their Poles run into the Windows of anoth-
    > ers Coach, wherein sat *Bawd* and *Whore,* or *Mother* and *Daughter*
    > squeaking out for the Lords sake, that some merciful Good Man
    > would come in to their assistance. (8)

3. Quoted in *The Critical and Miscellaneous Prose Works of John Dryden,* ed.
    Edmond Malone, 3 vols. (London, 1800), 1.1:363.
4. *Prose Works,* 1.1:363. Writing much later, Horace Walpole blamed Dryden's
    heterogeneous style on the promiscuous climate of Restoration culture:
    "Wycherley, Dryden, Mrs Centlivre, etc., wrote as if they had only lived in
    the Rose Tavern—but then the Court lived in Drury Lane too and Lady
    Dorchester and Nel Gwyn were equally good company." "To Lady Ossory,"
    14 June 1787, *Horace Walpole's Correspondence,* ed. W. S. Lewis, 48 vols. (New
    Haven: Yale University Press, 1937-83), 33.2:564.
5. Swift continues this vein of criticism against Dryden in "The Battle of the
    Books," where he describes the poet in his armor confronting Virgil: "The
    Helmet was nine times too large for the Head, which appeared Situate far
    in the hinder Part, even like the Lady in a Lobster, or like a Mouse under a
    Canopy of State, or like a shrivled Beau from within the Pent-house of a
    modern Perewig: And the voice was suited to the Visage, sounding weak
    and remote." *The Prose Works of Jonathan Swift,* ed. Herbert Davis and Irvin

Ehrenpreis, 14 vols. (Oxford: Basil Blackwell, 1941-68), 1:157. Exposing the difference between the idealized constructions and actual manifestations of pastoral innocence, valor, and love, Dryden's own verses in *The Secular Masque* view the farcical union of high and low as a defining characteristic of his time:

> All, all, of a piece throughout;
> Thy [Diana's] Chase had a Beast in View;
> Thy [Mars's] Wars brought nothing about;
> Thy [Venus'] Lovers were all untrue.
> 'Tis well an Old Age is out,
> And time to begin a New. (92-97)

The Poems and Fables of John Dryden, ed. James Kinsley (Oxford: Oxford University Press, 1962). All references to poems in this edition are cited by line number.

6. While Lawrence Lipking argues that "we can't ignore the evidence that the development of a great many poets follows a consistent internal logic," I propose that Dryden offers an important exception to the idea that "the great poet . . . makes his own destiny." See Lipking, *The Life of the Poet: Beginning and Ending Poetic Careers* (Chicago: University of Chicago Press, 1981), viii, ix.

7. James Anderson Winn, *John Dryden and His World* (New Haven: Yale University Press, 1987), 2. I am deeply indebted to Winn's biography throughout my study of Dryden's career.

8. For background on the earl of Berkshire's family and its relation to the court of Charles II, see Winn, *John Dryden*, 119-23.

9. Winn, *John Dryden*, 20-22.

10. John Dryden, "To My Lord Chancellor," *The Works of John Dryden*, ed. Edward N. Hooker, H. T. Swedenberg, Jr., et al., 20 vols. (Berkeley: University of California Press, 1956-), 1:38. Unless otherwise indicated, references to Dryden's writings are to the California edition.

11. Edmund Hickeringhill, *The Mushroom: or a Satyr Against Libelling Tories and Prelatical Tantivies* (London, 1682), 17. Similarly, in *La Muse de Cavalier, or, An Apology for such Gentlemen, as make Poetry their Diversion, not their Business* (London, 1685), John Cutts declares his muse "My Mistress, not my Wife" (3), and argues that amateur poets like himself possess the financial independence (and personal integrity) denied to professional "Brother[s] of the Quill" (3).

12. John Wilmot, earl of Rochester, "An Allusion to Horace," *The Poems of John Wilmot, Earl of Rochester,* ed. Keith Walker (Oxford: Basil Blackwell, 1984), 79-80.

13. Thomas Shadwell, *The Medal of John Bayes* (London, 1682), 4.

14. Samuel Johnson, *Rambler* 77, *The Yale Edition of the Works of Samuel Johnson,*

15 vols. (New Haven: Yale University Press, 1958-), 4:43. James Eli Adams examines at length Johnson's emphasis on the "acute conflict between the economic and moral burdens of authorship"; see "The Economics of Authorship: Imagination and Trade in Johnson's *Dryden*," *SEL* 30 (1990): 467-86.

15. Michael McKeon, "Historicizing Patriarchy: The Emergence of Gender Difference in England, 1660-1760," *Eighteenth-Century Studies* 28 (1995): 309. Randolph Trumbach also analyzes the transgressive implications of sodomy for gentlemen libertines in the Restoration:

> It is as though sodomy were so extreme a denial of the Christian expectation that all sexual acts ought to occur in marriage and have the potential of procreation, that those who indulged in it were likely also to break through all other conventions in politics and religion. The unconventionality of that minority of rakes who were sodomitical was therefore frightening to society at large; but they were not held in contempt. It was, instead, that they were secretly held in awe for the extremity of their masculine self-assertion, since they triumphed over male and female alike. (130-31)

"The Birth of the Queen: Sodomy and the Emergence of Gender Equality in Modern Culture, 1660-1750," in *Hidden from History: Reclaiming the Gay and Lesbian Past,* ed. Martin Bauml Duberman, Martha Vicinus, and Geroge Chauncey, Jr. (New York: New American Library, 1989), 129-40.

16. *The Letters of John Dryden,* ed. Charles E. Ward (Durham: Duke University Press, 1942), 28.

17. Winn, *John Dryden,* 253.

18. Julie Stone Peters, *Congreve, the Drama, and the Printed Word* (Stanford: Stanford University Press, 1990), 13.

19. Terry Belanger, "Publishers and Writers in Eighteenth-Century England," in *Books and Their Readers in Eighteenth-Century England,* ed. Isabel Rivers (London: St. Martin's Press, 1982), 18.

20. Prologue to *Caesar Borgia* (1680), *Poems and Fables,* 1-3.

21. J. G. A. Pocock describes the civic ideal as entailing the ownership of property, which guaranteed the gentleman's authority, independence, and autonomy—and hence virtue, or "goodness as an actor within the political, social, and natural realm or order" (103). By contrast, in eighteenth-century political thought, "production and exchange are regularly equated with the ascendancy of the passions and the female principle" (114), and men who engaged in commercial practices were considered too much influenced by their egoism—their individual appetites and desires—to exercise their judgment for the good of the whole. "The Mobility of Property and the Rise of Eighteenth-Century Sociology," *Virtue, Commerce, and History: Essays on Political Thought and History, Chiefly in the Eigh-*

teenth Century (Cambridge: Cambridge University Press, 1985). In somewhat different terms, Anthony Fletcher details the conflict between the value placed on courage and independence (or a "heroic spirit") and the increasing emphasis on refinement, or politeness and civility, in eighteenth-century constructions of masculinity; see *Gender, Sex and Subordination in England 1500-1800* (New Haven: Yale University Press, 1995), 322-46.

22. Laura Levine, *Men in Women's Clothing: Anti-Theatricality and Effeminization, 1579-1642* (Cambridge: Cambridge University Press, 1994), 19.

23. Baz Kershaw, "Framing the Audience for Theatre," in *The Authority of the Consumer,* ed. Russell Keat, Nigel Whiteley, and Nicholas Abercrombie (London: Routledge, 1994), 184. An incident recorded in Joseph Spence's *Anecdotes* shows the critical and financial disaster that audience participation could generate:

> In one of Dryden's plays there was this line, which the actress endeavoured to speak in as moving and affecting a tone as she could: "My wound is great—because it is so small," and then she paused and looked very distressed. The Duke of Buckingham, who was in one of the boxes, rose immediately from his seat, and added in a loud ridiculing tone of voice—"Then 'twould be greater were it none at all," which had such an effect on the audience, who before were not very well pleased with the play, that they hissed the poor woman off the stage, would never bear her appearance in the rest of her part, and as this was the second time only of its appearance, made Dryden lose his benefit night.

Quoted in Sir Walter Scott, *The Life of John Dryden,* ed. Bernard Kreissman (Lincoln: University of Nebraska Press, 1963), 414.

24. Charles Blount, *Mr. Dryden Vindicated* (1673), reprinted in *Dryden: The Critical Heritage,* ed. James Kinsley and Helen Kinsley (New York: Barnes and Noble, 1971), 80.

25. Of course, as Harold Love reminds us, prologues and epilogues are always "thoroughly practical pieces of rhetoric whose aim is to secure a favourable hearing for the play" (23), and their description of audiences must be analyzed with this purpose in mind. "Who Were the Restoration Audience?," *The Yearbook of English Studies* 10 (1980): 21-44.

26. Peter Stallybrass and Allon White, *The Politics and Poetics of Transgression* (Ithaca: Cornell University Press, 1986), 87.

27. According to David Kramer in *The Imperial Dryden: The Poetics of Appropriation in Seventeenth-Century England* (Athens, GA: University of Georgia Press, 1994), Dryden's loss of the laureateship changed the sexual dynamic of his entire career, for "the poetic phallus that Dryden had so proudly displayed as a symbol of his poetic strength [was] now ripped from his body by the censors, by the bad times, by ill health, by advancing age" (123). Yet

while the loss of privilege certainly finds representation in Dryden's later verse, the erotic anxiety of his earlier writings for the stage and critics' attacks on his pretensions to libertinism suggest that possession of the "poetic phallus" always proved tentative for Dryden.

28. Terry Castle, "Lab'ring Bards: Birth *Topoi* and English Poetics 1660-1820," *Journal of English and Germanic Philology* 78 (1979): 193-208.

29. Dryden's salary, however, was more impressive on paper than in actuality: in an appendix to his biography of Dryden (525-31), Winn records Treasury payments on the laureate's salary that were often several years in arrears.

30. Winn, *John Dryden*, 232.

31. Winn, *John Dryden*, 316.

32. Winn, *John Dryden*, 21.

33. Dryden's objections to the theater later found an echo in eighteenth-century denunciations of the opera. John Dennis, for instance, complained that "Opera after the Italian Manner is monstrous . . . [and] prodigiously unnatural," while Swift worried that English spectators would be "overrun with Italian effeminacy and Italian nonsense." Eric Walter White records these reactions in *A History of English Opera* (London: Faber and Faber, 1983), 151-52.

34. Elizabeth Howe observes that theatrical companies "exploited the sexual availability of their women as a means of attracting audiences" to the point where "the actress's sexuality—her potential availability to men—became the central feature of her professional identity as a player." See *The First English Actresses: Women and Drama 1660-1700* (Cambridge: Cambridge University Press, 1992), 34.

35. Deborah C. Payne, "Reified Object or Emergent Professional? Retheorizing the Restoration Actress," in *Cultural Readings of Restoration and Eighteenth-Century English Theater*, ed. J. Douglas Canfield and Deborah C. Payne (Athens, GA: University of Georgia Press, 1995), 16. Howe also notes the power that actresses' popularity bestowed upon them: "In the Restoration theatre, as in film and television today, it was the star performer whom people remembered and wanted to see, not the writers, and as such the actresses were certainly more than 'mouthpieces'" (*First English Actresses*, 172).

36. Walter J. Ong, *Orality and Literacy: The Technologizing of the Word* (New York: Methuen, 1982), 132.

37. D. F. McKenzie notes that the "passage from auditor to reader, from stage to study, had already begun in the meticulous editing of [Ben Jonson's] plays for a reading public in the 1616 folio" (*The London Book Trade in the Later Seventeenth Century*, Sandars Lectures Typescript [Cambridge University, 1976], 14). Yet Jonson, unlike Dryden, desired to retain the sense of a play's performance in print, and attempted to do so by means of typographic pointers, the arrangement of texts, the division of scenes, and descriptive stage directions. As his admiration for masques indicates, recapturing the glamour of stage productions and their hypnotic effect on the audience was important

to him: "Such was the exquisit performance, as (beside the *pompe, splendor,* or what we may call *apparelling* of such *Presentments*) that alone (had all else beene absent) was of power to surprize with delight, and steale away the *spectators* from themselves" (as quoted in McKenzie, 14).

38. Laura Runge offers an extended discussion of how gendered categories structure Dryden's critical thought in *Gender and Language in British Literary Criticism* (Cambridge: Cambridge University Press, 1997).

39. For studies of Congreve's relation to print, see McKenzie's *London Book Trade* and Peters's *Congreve, the Drama, and the Printed Word.*

40. John Feather provides an account of Herringman's publications in *A History of British Publishing* (London: Croom Helm, 1988), 56-57. Despite the precedent that Jonson had set, Dryden evinced no interest in collecting and publishing his dramatic works; often writing his plays in haste and for specific occasions, Dryden perhaps was reluctant to spend as much time with revisions as would be required for success with a reading audience.

41. Taylor Corse presents an intriguing analysis of how the Virgil translation contributes to early modern constructions of gender in his essay entitled "Manliness and Misogyny in Dryden's *Aeneid,*" in *The Image of Manhood in Early Modern Literature: Viewing the Male,* ed. Andrew P. Williams (Westport, CT: Greenwood Press, 1999), 73-94.

42. See Horace, *Epistulae, Liber 2,* ed. Niall Rudd (Cambridge: Cambridge University Press, 1989), 58.

43. Dryden's attempts to preserve the majesty of epic poetry included barring writers of insufficient talent or low reputation from attempting it; in his dedication to Normanby, he suggests that "some Lord Chamberlain should be appointed, some Critick of Authority shou'd be set before the door, to keep out a Crowd of little Poets, who press for Admission, and are not of Quality" (*Works,* 5:275). The quality to whom Dryden refers are not, of course, aristocrats, but dedicated, professional writers like himself; in a deft turn of metaphor, he substitutes talent for social rank and dismisses those "Holiday Authors [who] writ for Pleasure" (*Works,* 5:340)—a group including amateur poets of high birth—as inadequate to the task of composing heroic verse.

44. Tonson's many letters to Dryden, however, reveal a relationship based upon mutual respect. Tonson sent the poet gifts, mailed letters and packages to Dryden's sons, and, while bargaining for more verses per guinea, humbly appeals to Dryden's sense of fair play: "I had rather have your good will than any mans alive . . . whatever you are pleasd to doe" (*Letters,* 52).

45. In his dedication of the *Aeneid,* Dryden comments on his intent to please readers of the highest social rank, a task that entailed modifying the language of the translation:

> I will not give the Reasons, why I Writ not always in the proper terms of Navigation, Land-Service, or in the Cant of any Profes-

sion. I will only say, that *Virgil* has avoided those proprieties, because he Writ not to Mariners, Souldiers, Astronomers, Gardners, Peasants, &c. but to all in general, and in particular to Men and Ladies of the first Quality: who have been better Bred than to be too nicely knowing in the Terms. (*Works,* 5:337)

46. Although writers of both genders invoked this metaphor of the poet as lover, Delariviere Manley, in her "Ode, on the Death of John Dryden," illustrates how such a trope prohibits women poets from claiming the muse's assistance with and validation of their work: "My weaker Voice [Melpomene] would not hear./Amongst the mighty Men She's busi'd now,/They, They, I find, best Charm *Immortal* Females too." *Luctus Britannici or the Tears of the British Muses; for the Death of John Dryden, Esq.* (London, 1700), 30.

47. Charles Brome, *To the Memory of Mr. Dryden* (London, 1700), 9.

48. Samuel Garth, preface to *Ovid's Metamorphoses in Fifteen Books. Translated by the most Eminent Hands* (1717), in *Critical Heritage,* 261. In a letter to Tonson, Luke Milbourne bestowed similar praise upon Dryden: "undecayed by age," the poet composes verses "Still smooth, as when, adorn'd with youthful pride,/For thy dear sake the blushing virgins dyed" (*Prose Works,* 1.1:316).

49. As quoted in J. G. Lockhart, *Memoirs of the Life of Sir Walter Scott,* 5 vols. (1839; reprint, New York: Houghton, Mifflin, 1902), 1:456-57.

50. Cedric D. Reverand, *Dryden's Final Poetic Mode: The Fables* (Philadelphia: University of Pennsylvania Press, 1988), 129.

51. Bevil Higgons, in "To Mr. Dryden on his Translation of Persius," provides an instance of such panegyric, praising almost the same kind of poetic instruction that Timotheus so dangerously performs in the Ode:

> Thy knowing Muse all sorts of Men does teach,
> Philosophers instructs to live, Divines to preach,
> States-men to govern, Generals to fight,
> At once Mankind you profit and delight.

Examen Poeticum: Being the Third Part of Miscellany Poems . . . by the Most Eminent Hands (London, 1693), 252.

Chapter Three

1. Mary Wollstonecraft, *A Vindication of the Rights of Woman* (New York: Knopf, 1992), 60.

2. Vicesimus Knox, *Essays Moral and Literary,* 2 vols. (London, 1782), 2:186.

3. Richard Savage, Article I, *A Collection of Pieces in Verse and Prose, which have been publish'd on Occasion of the* Dunciad (London, 1732), 4.

4. Anonymous, *The Poet finish'd in Prose. Being a Dialogue Concerning Mr. Pope and his Writings* (London, 1735), 17-18.

5. Claudia N. Thomas, *Alexander Pope and His Eighteenth-Century Women Readers* (Carbondale: Southern Illinois University Press, 1994), 13. Steve Clark traces remarks made over the past two centuries about Pope's feminine characteristics in "'Let Blood and Body bear the fault': Pope and Misogyny," in *Pope: New Contexts*, ed. David Fairer (London: Harvester, 1990), 81-101; and Carolyn D. Williams's *Pope, Homer, and Manliness: Some Aspects of Eighteenth-Century Classical Learning* (London: Routledge, 1993) examines charges that Pope's effeminacy perverted his translation of Homer.

6. Colley Cibber, *A Letter from Mr. Cibber, to Mr. Pope* (London, 1742), 49.

7. Thomas Bentley, for instance, remarked that he had "more Pleasure in reading or transcribing some of [Pope's] Writings, than in hearing *Farinelli*." See *A Letter to Mr. Pope, Occasion'd by 'Sober Advice from Horace'* (London, 1735), 10. Studies detailing the various prejudices against castrati include John Rosselli's *Singers of Italian Opera: The History of a Profession* (Cambridge: Cambridge University Press, 1992); James P. Carson's "Commodification and the Figure of the Castrato in Smollett's *Humphrey Clinker*," *The Eighteenth Century: Theory and Interpretation* 33 (1992): 24-46; and Todd Gilman's "The Italian (Castrato) in London," in *The Work of Opera: Genre, Nationhood, and Sexual Difference*, ed. Richard Dellamora and Daniel Fischlin (New York: Columbia University Press, 1997), 49-70.

8. Anonymous, *A Compleat Collection of all the Verses, Essays, Letters and Advertisements, which Have been occasioned by the Publication of Three Volumes of Miscellanies, by Pope and Company* (London, 1728), 27.

9. Giles Jacob, *The Mirrour: or, Letters Satyrical, Panegyrical, Serious and Humorous, on the Present Times* (London, 1733), 7.

10. Walter Harte, *An Epistle to Mr. Pope, On Reading his Translations of the* Iliad *and* Odyssy *of Homer* (London, 1731), 11; Bezaleel Morrice, *Three Satires. Most Humbly Inscribed and Recommended to that* Little *Gentleman, of Great Vanity, who has just published, A Fourth volume of Homer* (London, 1719), 8.

11. Joseph Warton, *An Essay on the Genius and Writings of Pope*, 2 vols. (New York: Garland, 1970), 2:481.

12. William Cowper, *Table Talk*, *The Complete Poetical Works of William Cowper*, ed. H. S. Milford (London: Henry Frowde, 1905), 652-55.

13. David B. Morris, "Pope and the Arts of Pleasure," in *The Enduring Legacy: Alexander Pope Tercentenary Essays*, ed. G. S. Rousseau and Pat Rogers (Cambridge: Cambridge University Press, 1988), 104-05.

14. Leopold Damrosch, *The Imaginative World of Alexander Pope* (Berkeley: University of California Press, 1987), 5. Thomas Woodman also discusses Pope's alienation from official culture in "'Wanting nothing but the Laurel': Pope and the Idea of the Laureate Poet," in *Pope: New Contexts*, 45-58.

15. Alexander Pope, preface to the *Works of Alexander Pope, The Poems of Alexan-*

der Pope, ed. John Butt (New Haven: Yale University Press, 1963), xxv. All references to Pope's poems are to Butt's edition.

16. Alexander Pope, *The Correspondence of Alexander Pope*, ed. George Sherburn, 5 vols. (Oxford: Clarendon Press, 1965), 1:109-10.

17. Laura Brown, *Ends of Empire: Women and Ideology in Early Eighteenth-Century English Literature* (Ithaca: Cornell University Press, 1993), 130.

18. Kristina Straub, *Sexual Suspects: Eighteenth-Century Players and Sexual Ideology* (Princeton: Princeton University Press, 1992), 70.

19. Robert Halsband offers an account of the escalating tensions between Pope and Hervey in *Lord Hervey: Eighteenth-Century Courtier* (Oxford: Oxford University Press, 1974), 141-44.

20. As quoted in Halsband, *Lord Hervey*, 142.

21. John, Lord Hervey, *An Epistle from a Nobleman to a Doctor of Divinity* (London, 1733), 7. References to this poem are cited by page number.

22. John, Lord Hervey, to Stephen Fox (1731), as quoted in *Lord Hervey and His Friends, 1726-38,* ed. Giles Stephen Holland Fox-Strangways, earl of Ilchester (London: John Murray, 1950), 83-84.

23. John, Lord Hervey, *A Letter to Mr. Cibber* (London, 1742), 20.

24. See Halsband, *Lord Hervey,* 37; 144.

25. Maynard Mack offers several reasons for the *Letter's* remaining in manuscript form: "One explanation attributes its suppression to a request from Walpole; another, tentatively, to a possible desire of the Queen, 'apprehensive that it might make her counsellor insignificant in the public esteem'; a third, to prudential considerations on the poet's part. Pope being the man he was, we ought probably to add to this list considerations of artistic effect." *Alexander Pope: A Life* (New York: Norton, 1986), 609.

26. Alexander Pope, *Letter to a Noble Lord, On occasion of some Libels written and propagated at Court* (1733), *The Prose Works of Alexander Pope, Volume II, 1725-1744,* ed. Rosemary Cowler (Hamden, CT: Archon Books, 1986), 2:443.

27. Jean Baudrillard, *For a Critique of the Political Economy of the Sign,* trans. Charles Levin (St. Louis: Telos Press, 1981), 32.

28. Baudrillard, *Critique,* 32. Baudrillard examines the shift in values that occurs as capitalist production and a consumer market gain complete dominance over residual systems of creating wealth (like estate ownership): "One must wonder whether social salvation by consumption, whether prodigality and sumptuous expenditure (formerly the appendage of chiefs and notables) is not today *conceded* to the lower and middle classes. For this selective criterion has long ago given way as the foundation of power to the criteria of productive responsibility, and economic and political decision" (*Critique,* 61-62).

29. Adam Smith, *The Theory of Moral Sentiments,* ed. D. D. Raphael and A. L. Macfie (Oxford: Clarendon Press, 1976), 54. For an account of Smith's conflicting attitudes toward commerce and masculinity, see Stewart Justman's

The Autonomous Male of Adam Smith (Norman: University of Oklahoma Press, 1993).

30. Smith, *Theory,* 55.

31. Helen Deutsch analyzes Pope's rhetorical transformation of his disability into cultural power in *Resemblance & Disgrace: Alexander Pope and the Deformation of Culture* (Cambridge, MA: Harvard University Press, 1996).

32. Anonymous, *Tit for Tat. To which is annex'd, An Epistle from a Nobleman To A Doctor of Divinity* (London, 1734), 6.

33. As quoted in Halsband, *Lord Hervey,* 109-11. Halsband notes that this attack took "the form of a letter, dated 20 January [1731] and signed Caleb D'Anvers (the *nom de plume* of the *Craftsman's* writer)" (109); the pamphlet's title was *A Proper Reply to a Late Scurrilous Libel, Intitled Sedition and Defamation Display'd.*

34. To an extent that is both remarkable and disturbing, scholarly assessments of Hervey have echoed Pope's assumptions about the effect of sexual "deviance" on a writer's moral and literary capacity. In an early essay comparing Pope and Hervey, Camille Paglia attributes Hervey's "selfish individualism" and "false wit" to his homosexuality, calling him "a creature of surfaces who does not, or cannot, enter deeply into emotional experience" ("Lord Hervey and Pope," *Eighteenth-Century Studies* 6 [1973]: 364). Although more moderate in assessing Hervey's character, James Dubro also links Hervey's "homosexual personality" to his "superficial and fashionably bitchy variety of gay wit"—a style that contrasted with Pope's insistence on "moralizing" his verse ("The Third Sex: Lord Hervey and His Coterie," *Eighteenth- Century Life* 2 [1975]: 91). Finally, Maynard Mack casts suspicion on a group of men, including Hervey, who seem bound together by sodomy as well as "scoundrelism": "[Hervey] was one of Walpole's young men and it is well known that Walpole made a point of debauching the political morals of his boys" *(Alexander Pope: A Life,* 648). It seems clear that, in the words of Carole Fabricant, Pope succeeded brilliantly in "establishing the categories that have been so influential in shaping our cultural perceptions" of his adversaries ("Pope's Moral, Political, and Cultural Combat," *The Eighteenth Century: Theory and Interpretation* 29 [1988]: 180). For a more even- handed account of Hervey's cultural significance, see Jill Campbell, "Politics and Sexuality in Portraits of John, Lord Hervey," *Word and Image* 6 (1990): 281-97.

35. Lady Mary Wortley Montagu and John, Lord Hervey, *Verses Address'd to the Imitator of the First Satire of the Second Book of Horace. By a Lady* (London, 1733), 5. References to this poem are cited by page number.

36. Clark, "'Let Blood and Body bear the fault': Pope and Misogyny," in *Pope: New Contexts,* 88.

37. Pope's strategy here did not preserve him entirely from attack: in *Sawney and Colley, A Poetical Dialogue* (London, 1742), an anonymous critic compares Cibber's much-noted—and, he implies, much more normal—promiscuity

to Pope's overwrought esteem for his mother: "[Pope] is perpetually TRUM-
PETTING forth his *filial Piety* to his *Mama,* and the many Virtues and Excel-
lencies of that good old Lady, whilst at the same Time he runs riot on all
the rest of her Sex, for which . . . *High Treason,* against the *Fair,* no apter
Punishment, we deem, could be inflicted, than that he should have his
Bumkin scourged to the Bone, by a Committee of MATRONS chosen for
that Purpose" (11, n.).

38. W. H. Dilworth, *The Life of Alexander Pope* (London, 1759), 122.
39. Ian Donaldson, "Concealing and Revealing: Pope's 'Epistle to Dr Arbuth-
    not,'" *Yearbook of English Studies* 18 (1988): 189.
40. G. Douglas Atkins, *Quests of Difference: Reading Pope's Poems* (Lexington:
    University Press of Kentucky, 1986), 136; 137.
41. According to Marlon B. Ross in *The Contours of Masculine Desire: Romanti-
    cism and the Rise of Women's Poetry* (New York: Oxford University Press,
    1989), "the Augustans are threatened by the feminizing implications of the
    all-male clique and attempt to repress those implications by reaffirming the
    conventional productivity of the patrilineal relationship (67). Jill Campbell
    agrees that Pope depicts his own domestic life and private pleasures to
    emphasize his distance from the eroticized bonds of Hervey's homosocial
    network ("Politics and Sexuality in Portraits of John, Lord Hervey," 285).
    Yet Pope himself proudly announced his close ties to Bolingbroke, the earl
    of Oxford, Arbuthnot, Swift, and others, and was instrumental in publish-
    ing the works of his own literary coterie, the Scriblerus Club. What aroused
    Pope's suspicions was not the existence of such affective relationships, but
    rather the unmanly subordination and dependency fostered by the eco-
    nomics of patronage—a system that in his view perverted attachments
    among men.
42. Brean Hammond, *Pope* (Sussex: Harvester, 1986), 83.
43. Dustin Griffin, *Literary Patronage in England, 1650-1800* (Cambridge: Cam-
    bridge University Press, 1996), 124.
44. *The Prose Works of Alexander Pope, Volume I, 1711-1720,* ed. Norman Ault
    (Oxford: Basil Blackwell, 1936), 1:78.
45. Griffin, *Literary Patronage,* 129.
46. Hammond, *Pope,* 85.
47. Dustin Griffin, *Alexander Pope: The Poet in the Poems* (Princeton: Princeton
    University Press, 1978), 173.
48. Bruce R. Smith, *Homosexual Desire in Shakespeare's England: A Cultural Poet-
    ics* (Chicago: University of Chicago Press, 1991), 194. Michael McKeon
    locates a rejection of these eroticized relations in the eighteenth century,
    when the "criterion of difference superintends sexual identity as such,"
    rather than the criteria of birth and rank. See "Historicizing Patriarchy:
    The Emergence of Gender Difference in England, 1660-1760," *Eighteenth-
    Century Studies* 28 (1995): 309.
49. Smith, *Homosexual Desire,* 194.

50. As quoted in G. S. Rousseau, "The Pursuit of Homosexuality in the Eighteenth Century: 'Utterly Confused Category' and/or Rich Repository?," in *'Tis Nature's Fault: Unauthorized Sexuality during the Enlightenment*, ed. Robert P. Maccubbin (Cambridge: Cambridge University Press, 1985), 135.

51. Edward Coke, *The Third Part of the Institutes of the Laws of England* (Buffalo: William S. Hein, 1986), 59.

52. Horace Walpole, *A Catalogue of the Royal and Noble Authors of England, Scotland, and Ireland, enlarged and continued to the present time by Thomas Park*, 5 vols. (London, 1806), 4:251.

53. Cameron McFarlane, *The Sodomite in Fiction and Satire, 1660-1750* (New York: Columbia University Press, 1997), 39.

54. McFarlane, *The Sodomite in Fiction and Satire*, 33-34. Campbell argues that Pope's portrayal of Hervey as Sporus and allusion to Milton "imply that Hervey's sexuality represents a threat to the normative domestic units of the heterosexual couple and of the family" ("Politics and Sexuality in Portraits of John, Lord Hervey," 285).

55. Shawn Lisa Maurer, *Proposing Men: Dialectics of Gender and Class in the Eighteenth-Century English Periodical* (Stanford: Stanford University Press, 1998), 26. Maurer claims that middle-class men of this period reconstituted patriarchal structures of previous centuries by making the household rather than the state the "sphere of action and thus of virtue" (25). Yet as "Arbuthnot" suggests, Pope's status within this new configuration of masculine power is problematic at best, since performance within the public sphere is essential for the male poet's claims to authority.

56. Ripley Hotch, "The Dilemma of an Obedient Son: Pope's 'Epistle to Arbuthnot,'" in *Pope: Recent Essays by Several Hands*, ed. Maynard Mack and James A. Winn (Hamden, CT: Archon Books, 1980), 428-43.

57. Most readings of the *Dunciad* have focused on the dunces', rather than the aristocrats', threats to culture. For instance, Dennis Todd's "The 'Blunted Arms' of Dulness: The Problem of Power in the *Dunciad*" (*Studies in Philology* 79 [1982]: 177-204) concludes that Pope, in the last version of the poem, portrays the dunces as powerful because of their impotence, triviality, and childishness, while Brean Hammond argues that the "*Dunciad*'s values enshrine the interests of a highly-educated aristocratic elite" (*Pope*, 130). Yet the poem's repeated attacks on the authority of that elite reveal Pope's critical distance from the ideology of the upper classes.

58. Catherine Ingrassia provides an account of Pope's response to opera as a feminized genre in *Authorship, Commerce, and Gender in Early Eighteenth-Century England: A Culture of Paper Credit* (Cambridge: Cambridge University Press, 1998), 57. McFarlane notes that opera's associations with luxury, effeminacy, and ultimately sodomy arise from anxieties about the preservation of English national purity: "Italian opera is coded as sodomitical because it is a conspicuous site at which foreign culture is seen to penetrate the social body of England" (*The Sodomite in Fiction and Satire*, 32-33).

59. Carolyn D. Williams notes that although Pope believed that a classical education, including Homer and Virgil, was "the most effective way to teach manliness," he was aware that patterns of effeminate behavior lay within the "fabric of the epic itself" ("Breaking Decorums: Belinda, Bays and Epic Effeminacy," in *Pope: New Contexts*, 60). Aristocratic youths, then, may learn effeminate conduct from the very institutions that supposedly guard against it.

60. Straub observes that "Pope's focus on the schoolboy as the abject product of a perverse political and sexual hierarchy foregrounds the failure of masculine sexuality and authority . . . [while he] places that failure 'outside' the poet as the product of a corrupt political and social order" (*Sexual Suspects*, 80). As a bourgeois outsider to aristocratic institutions like the public school, Pope could claim that he remained untainted by their perversions.

61. Owen Ruffhead, *Life of Alexander Pope*, 2 vols. (Dublin, 1769), 2:132.

62. Samuel Johnson, *Lives of the English Poets*, 3 vols. (1905; reprint, New York: Octagon, 1967), 3:199.

Chapter Four

1. Archibald Campbell, *The Sale of Authors, a Dialogue, in Imitation of Lucian's Sale of Philosophers*, in the *Correspondence of Thomas Gray*, ed. Paget Toynbee and Leonard Whibley, 3 vols. (Oxford: Clarendon Press, 1935), 3:1217-18.

2. These descriptions of Gray are given in a letter of the Reverend John Sharpe, Fellow of Corpus Christi College, Cambridge, to the Reverend John Denne (12 March 1756). See John Nichols, *Illustrations of the Literary History of the Eighteenth Century*, 8 vols. (1831; reprint, New York: AMS Press, 1966), 6:805.

3. Walpole to Mason, 17 April 1774, *Horace Walpole's Correspondence*, ed. W. S. Lewis, 48 vols. (New Haven: Yale University Press, 1937-83), 28:152.

4. Samuel Johnson, *Lives of the English Poets*, ed. George Birkbeck Hill, 3 vols. (1905; reprint, New York: Octagon, 1967), 3:434.

5. Oliver Goldsmith, *An Enquiry into the Present State of Polite Learning in Europe, Collected Works of Oliver Goldsmith*, ed. Arthur Friedman, 5 vols. (Oxford: Clarendon Press, 1966), 1:315.

6. For detailed accounts of cultural anxieties regarding conspicuous consumption, see *Consumption and the World of Goods*, ed. John Brewer and Roy Porter (London: Routledge, 1993); and *The Consumption of Culture, 1600-1800: Image, Object, Text*, ed. Ann Bermingham and John Brewer (London: Routledge, 1995).

7. Suvir Kaul, *Thomas Gray and Literary Authority: A Study in Ideology and Poetics* (Stanford: Stanford University Press, 1992), 67.

8. The rhetorical power of this ideal is investigated in John Barrell's *English Literature in History 1730-80: An Equal, Wide Survey* (New York: St. Martin's Press, 1983) and in J. G. A. Pocock's *The Machiavellian Moment: Florentine*

Political Thought and the Atlantic Republican Tradition (Princeton: Princeton University Press, 1975). Pocock's *Virtue, Commerce and History: Essays on Political Thought and History, Chiefly in the Eighteenth Century* (Cambridge: Cambridge University Press, 1985) expands on this theme.

9. James Boswell, *The Life of Samuel Johnson*, ed. George Birkbeck Hill, rev. L. F. Powell, 6 vols. (Oxford: Clarendon Press, 1934-50), 1:419.

10. Malcolm Hicks, "Gray Among the Victorians," in *Thomas Gray: Contemporary Essays*, ed. W. B. Hutchings and William Ruddick (Liverpool: Liverpool University Press, 1993), 263.

11. Johnson, *Lives*, 3:430-31. Johnson emphasizes the poet's lack of maturity and manliness throughout his "Life of Gray": when censuring the mythology in Gray's "Progress of Poesy," for instance, he remarks that "Criticism disdains to chase a schoolboy to his common-places" (3:436).

12. Percival Stockdale, *An Inquiry into the Nature, and Genuine Laws of Poetry* (London, 1778), 98.

13. William Mason, *The Poems of Mr. Gray, to which are prefixed Memoirs of his Life and Writings* (York, 1775), 434. Quotations from this edition are identified by section, since the *Poems* and *Memoirs* are paginated separately.

14. Like some of Gray's contemporaries, a number of recent scholars also attribute his reluctance to publish, refusal of the laureateship, and much-noted obscurity (especially in his later poems) either to his psychological makeup or to a typically "pre-Romantic" alienation from his age, a conventional self-characterization of the poet as "a sensitive fugitive from his society" (John Sitter, *Literary Loneliness in Mid-Eighteenth-Century England* [Ithaca: Cornell University Press, 1982], 12). Among those who charge Gray with antiprofessionalism are J. W. Saunders (*The Profession of English Letters* [London: Routledge and Kegan Paul, 1964], 158); Donald M. Foerster ("Thomas Gray," in *The Age of Johnson: Essays Presented to Chauncey Brewster Tinker*, ed. Frederick W. Hilles [1941; reprint, New Haven: Yale University Press, 1964], 217); and W. Powell Jones (*Thomas Gray, Scholar: The True Tragedy of an Eighteenth-Century Gentleman* [Cambridge, MA: Harvard University Press, 1937], 146). Robert L. Snyder argues that Gray could not perform well in the "painfully alien culture" surrounding him (136), but does not explain why this culture was so inhospitable for the poet ("The Epistolary Melancholy of Thomas Gray," *Biography* 2 [1979]: 125-40). Wallace Jackson, by contrast, states that Gray's "failure" to realize his talent fully is "utterly and completely personal" rather than culturally produced ("Thomas Gray and the Dedicatory Muse," *ELH* 54 [1987]: 277). Finally, Robert F. Gleckner's *Gray Agonistes: Thomas Gray and Masculine Friendship* (Baltimore: Johns Hopkins University Press, 1997) analyzes Gray's verse as "poetic autobiography" inflected with "intrapsychic scripts" detailing the poet's relations with both Milton (his greatest influence) and Richard West (his most intimate friend). While not discounting the importance of psychobiographical readings of Gray, Kaul's *Thomas Gray and Literary Authority* and William Levine's

"'Beyond the Limits of a Vulgar Fate': The Renegotiation of Public and Private Concerns in the Careers of Gray and Other Mid-Eighteenth Century Poets" (*Studies in Eighteenth-Century Culture* 24 [1995]: 223-42) usefully emphasize the social determinants of the poetic subjectivity portrayed in Gray's verse.

15. Jean Baudrillard, *The Mirror of Production,* trans. Mark Poster (St. Louis: Telos Press, 1975), 19-20; 31.

16. Gray to Wharton, June 1758, *Corresp.*, 2:571. In criticizing Gray's inability to write on demand, Johnson endorsed the prevailing idea that production for sale is the goal of writers. Two of his most famous maxims—"No man but a blockhead ever wrote, except for money" and "a man may write at any time, if he will set himself *doggedly* to it"—advocate this concept. See Boswell, *Life,* 3:19 and 5:40.

17. Lewis Hyde observes that the "gift labor" that writers feel they perform "requires a kind of emotional or spiritual commitment that precludes its own marketing" (*The Gift: Imagination and the Erotic Life of Property* [New York: Vintage, 1979], 107).

18. These sensitive and perceptive accounts of Gray's homoerotic attachments include Jean Hagstrum's "Gray's Sensibility" (in *Fearful Joy: Papers from the Thomas Gray Bicentenary Conference at Carleton University,* ed. James Downey and Ben Jones [Montreal: McGill-Queen's University Press, 1974], 6-19); William H. Epstein, "Assumed Identities: Gray's Correspondence and the 'Intelligence Communities' of Eighteenth-Century Studies" (*The Eighteenth Century: Theory and Interpretation* 32 [1991]: 274-88); Raymond Bentman, "Thomas Gray and the Poetry of 'Hopeless Love'" (*Journal of the History of Sexuality*) 3 [1992]: 203-22); George E. Haggerty, *Men in Love: Masculinity and Sexuality in the Eighteenth Century* (New York: Columbia University Press, 1999); and Gleckner's *Gray Agonistes.*

19. Gleckner, *Gray Agonistes,* 17.

20. Kaul, *Thomas Gray and Literary Authority,* 12.

21. William Wordsworth, preface to *Lyrical Ballads* (1850), *The Prose Works of William Wordsworth,* ed. W. J. B. Owen and Jane Worthington Smyser, 3 vols. (Oxford: Clarendon Press, 1974), 1:131. As Roger Lonsdale notes in his edition of Gray, defenders of the "Sonnet" included Coleridge and Gerard Manley Hopkins (*The Poems of Gray, Collins, and Goldsmith* [London: Longman, 1969], 64). I am indebted to Lonsdale's bibliographical work throughout this chapter.

22. Epstein, "Assumed Identities," 279.

23. Wayne Koestenbaum argues that "men who collaborate engage in a metaphorical sexual intercourse, and . . . the text they balance between them is alternately the child of their sexual union, and a shared woman." *Double Talk: The Erotics of Male Literary Collaboration* (New York: Routledge, 1989), 3. Gray, however, stops short of suggesting that he and Walpole are the

seminal source of each other's verses, implying instead that they act as surrogate fathers for the poems.

24. Lonsdale, *The Poems of Gray, Collins, and Goldsmith*, 65.

25. Peter J. Manning, "Wordsworth and Gray's Sonnet on the Death of West," *SEL* 22 (1982): 517.

26. Hélène Cixous, "Castration or Decapitation?," trans. Annette Kuhn, *Signs* 7 (1981): 48. Koestenbaum elaborates on Cixous's separation of the erotic from the economic: "A writer turns to a partner not from a practical assessment of advantages, but from a superstitious hope, a longing for replenishment and union that invites baroquely sexual interpretation" (*Double Talk*, 4).

27. Paul Oppenheimer, *The Birth of the Modern Mind: Self, Consciousness, and the Invention of the Sonnet* (New York: Oxford University Press, 1989), 184. See also Joel Fineman, *Shakespeare's Perjured Eye: The Invention of Poetic Subjectivity in the Sonnets* (Berkeley: University of California Press, 1986).

28. "De Principii's Cogitand," Book II, 332. All references to Gray's poems are to Lonsdale's edition.

29. Gleckner, *Gray Agonistes*, 122.

30. Haggerty, *Men in Love*, 125.

31. Haggerty, *Men in Love*, 126.

32. Kaul, *Thomas Gray and Literary Authority*, 112.

33. In *Before Novels: The Cultural Contexts of Eighteenth-Century English Fiction* (New York: Norton, 1990), J. Paul Hunter presents an extensive overview of scholarship on literacy, concluding that "after a literacy boom in the first three quarters of the seventeenth century, few new readers (in terms of percentages) were added to the literacy rolls," with a very moderate rate of increase throughout the eighteenth century: "Readers of novels in, say, 1750, may well have been 'new' readers in the sense that they came from groups who, in 1600, had little or no access to print, but most of them were, by the time of Richardson, the Fieldings, and Lennox, at least third-generation readers, many of them sixth- or seventh" (67). The work of Lawrence Stone ("Literacy and Education in England 1640-1900," *Past and Present* 42 [1969]: 69-139) and David Cressy (*Literacy and the Social Order: Reading and Writing in Tudor and Stuart England* [Cambridge: Cambridge University Press, 1980]) supports this conclusion, while Cressy's "Literacy in Context: Meaning and Measurement in Early Modern England" (in *Consumption and the World of Goods*, ed. John Brewer and Roy Porter [London: Routledge, 1993], 305-19) recommends a cautious approach to studies of literacy, arguing that the high value that modern society places upon reading and writing was not necessarily shared by early modern populations: "The cultural and economic changes of the eighteenth century seem not to have been accompanied by an overall surge in basic literacy. In practice, the importance of literacy varied with social, cultural and historical circumstances, and some of those circumstances could restrain literacy as well

as advance it" (309). Richard Altick suggests that while the relatively small number of copies printed in an edition (seldom more than 4,000 for novels and at the most 2,000 for nonfiction) implies a limited readership, the high cost of books in relation to wages depressed sales: "Down to 1774 [with the determination against perpetual copyright], the prosperity of the pirates is the best evidence we have that the demand for books was greater than the supply provided by the regular booksellers." *The English Common Reader: A Social History of the Mass Reading Public, 1800-1900* (Chicago: University of Chicago Press, 1957), 52. Gray was not alone in fearing an expansion of the reading audience. In the 1750s and 1760s, attempts to regulate the preferences of unlearned readers—the thereby reestablish aristocratic standards of taste—found expression in the pages of reviews like the *Monthly* (established in 1749) and the *Critical* (established in 1756), yet this exertion of institutionalized control over consumer preferences met with little success. See Frank Donoghue, *The Fame Machine: Book Reviewing and Eighteenth-Century Literary Careers* (Stanford: Stanford University Press, 1996), 16-55.

34. James Steele's "Thomas Gray and the Season for Triumph" (in *Fearful Joy,* 198-240) describes Gray's class and family background in detail: among Gray's friends and associates were Horace Walpole, son of the former minister; Richard West, son of the chancellor of Ireland; William Mason, chaplain to the king and private secretary to a secretary of state; Lord John Cavendish, brother to the duke of Devonshire (who held the post of lord chamberlain); Richard Hurd, bishop of Lichfield and Coventry and bishop of Worcester; James Brown, vice-chancellor of Cambridge University; and Charles Victor de Bonstetten, son of the treasurer of Berne.

35. *London Chronicle,* 26 (27-29 July 1769): 103.

36. Gray shared his contemporaries' distrust of literature composed to attract patrons, such as Richard Bentley's *Patriotism, A Mock-Heroic* (1763): as he writes to Walpole, "I hope no body found out, how good some of it is. has he made his market by it?" (*Corresp.,* 2:835).

37. Lonsdale, *The Poems of Gray, Collins, and Goldsmith,* 266.

38. See Sitter's *Literary Loneliness,* especially the chapter on "The Flight from History in Mid-Century Poetry," 77-103; and Wallace Jackson and Paul Yoder, "Wordsworth Reimagines Thomas Gray: Notes on Begetting a Kindred Spirit," *Criticism* 31 (1989): 291.

39. Henry Weinfield, *The Poet Without a Name: Gray's* Elegy *and the Problem of History* (Carbondale: Southern Illinois University Press, 1991), 94-95.

40. Charles Churchill, "The Author" (1763), *The Poetical Works of Charles Churchill,* ed. Douglas Grant (Oxford: Clarendon Press, 1956), 87-88, 91. All references to Churchill's poems are to this edition. Robert Lloyd, "To George Colman, Esq. A Familiar Epistle," *Poems* (London, 1762), 106-07.

41. Thomas Cooke, *Some Observations on Taste, and on the Present State of Poetry in England* (London, 1749), 4; Aaron Hill, *Advice to the Poets* (London, 1731), ix.

42. Percival Stockdale, *The Poet* (London, 1773), 42. All references to this poem are cited by page number.

43. Barrell notes the writer's replacement of the gentleman as the possessor of a coherent, disinterested perspective on English society in his introduction to *English Literature in History,* 17-50.

44. According to Clifford Siskin, "the breakdown of the uniform human community inevitably entails the collapse of the elite literary community grafted upon it. . . . Without those natural bonds, even the most productive mid- and late eighteenth-century poets (Goldsmith, Gray, Collins, Cowper, etc.) read themselves as helpless. For *us* to read their bleak descriptions of poetry's present and future as evidence of personal failings—madness, lack of genius, inferiority complexes—is to indulge in ahistorical psychologizing" (*The Historicity of Romantic Discourse* [New York: Oxford University Press, 1988], 73). Contemporary attacks on Gray, however, reveal that the cultural conditions of writing for eighteenth-century poets included public debate regarding their psychological and sexual proclivities.

45. John Brown, *An Estimate of the Manners and Principles of the Times,* 2 vols. (London, 1758), 1:42-43. Brown's social analysis holds that "the ruling Character of the present Times is that of a vain, *luxurious,* and *selfish* EFFEMINACY" (1:67), and this cultural decline appears most obviously in the form of an encroaching androgyny: "The sexes have now little other apparent Distinction, beyond that of person and Dress: Their peculiar and characteristic Manners are confounded and lost: the one Sex having advanced into *Boldness,* as the other have sunk into *Effeminacy*" (1:51). John Sekora provides an extensive context for such views in *Luxury: The Concept in Western Thought, Eden to Smollett* (Baltimore: Johns Hopkins University Press, 1977).

46. Dustin Griffin carefully examines how alienation from audiences is thematized in Gray's verse, yet he dehistoricizes this problem by attributing it to the poet's emotional state. See "Gray's Audiences," *Essays in Criticism* 28 [1978]: 208-15).

47. Definitions of the features peculiar to odes seem a perennial concern for critics, but all concur that odes primarily represent their speaker's subjectivity. Northrup Frye argues that the "radical of presentation" for lyric poetry is marked by the poets' unawareness of their audience: "The lyric poet normally pretends to be talking to himself or to someone else: a spirit of nature, a Muse . . . a personal friend, a lover, a god, a personified abstraction, or a natural object. . . . The poet, so to speak, turns his back on his listeners, though he may speak for them, and though they may repeat some of his words after him" (*Anatomy of Criticism: Four Essays* [Princeton: Princeton University Press, 1957], 249-50). Similarly, Paul Fry maintains that writers' separation from their audience is a definitive component of odes, whose speakers want us to believe that their verses are pure vocal sound—implying their immediate presence to us—instead of signs for this sound, which implies their absence. Thus "the ode survives in our anthologies

because it is the most challenging proving ground for presentation" (*The Poet's Calling in the English Ode* [New Haven: Yale University Press, 1980], 3). While Anne Williams categorizes lyrics according to the different possible ratios between the implied poet and the speaker of the poem, she nevertheless defines the lyric as the expression of a particular subjectivity: "In a lyric we always sense the organizing consciousness as a kind of *logos* within the poem, a centripetal force which subordinates argument, narrative, or even other consciousness to itself" (*Prophetic Strain: The Greater Lyric in the Eighteenth Century* [Chicago: University of Chicago Press, 1984], 16). If critics are correct in stating that the very structure of odes attempts to resist the absence of author's originating voice, it should be added that in Gray's time, commercialized print made this absence an inescapable fact of literary production.

48. I have taken this phrase from M. H. Abrams, who uses "pragmatic" to describe an aesthetic theory that perceives art "chiefly as a means to an end, an instrument for getting something done, and tends to judge its value according to its success in achieving that aim" (*The Mirror and the Lamp: Romantic Theory and the Critical Tradition* [Oxford: Oxford University Press, 1953], 15).

49. Patricia Meyer Spacks, identifying the speaker in the ode with Gray, argues that the poem ultimately "discloses the genuine pathos of Gray's sense of himself" (*The Poetry of Vision: Five Eighteenth-Century Poets* [Cambridge, MA: Harvard University Press, 1967], 94). Fry claims that the "Ode on the Spring" is about Gray's "alienation from the weather," his ability to see, but not feel, the "force of nature" (*The Poet's Calling*, 66). Other scholars who interpret Gray's poems primarily in light of his psychology include Roger Martin (*Essai sur Thomas Gray* [Paris: Les Presses Universitaires de France, 1934]) and Jean H. Hagstrum ("Gray's Sensibility," in *Fearful Joy*, 6-19).

50. Jonathan Culler, *The Pursuit of Signs: Semiotics, Literature, Deconstruction* (Ithaca: Cornell University Press, 1981), 146; 148.

51. Culler, *The Pursuit of Signs*, 135.

52. Clark Sutherland Northup, *A Bibliography of Thomas Gray* (New Haven: Yale University Press, 1917), 74-76.

53. *Monthly Review* 4 (1751): 309.

54. Leo Braudy, *The Frenzy of Renown: Fame and Its History* (New York: Oxford University Press, 1986), 417. Descriptions of the sensibility peculiar to great writers were common in literary discourse of the time. In the middle decades of the century appeared a number of essays concerned with delineating the innate qualities of character responsible for individuals' artistic talent; these essays include Edward Young's *Conjectures on Original Composition* (London, 1759); William Duff's *Essay on Original Genius* (London, 1767); and Alexander Gerard's *An Essay on Genius* (London and Edinburgh, 1774).

55. Lonsdale, *The Poems of Gray, Collins, and Goldsmith*, 113. Gray apparently believed that the "Elegy"'s commercial success diminished his dignity. Braudy identifies this "antisocial" disdain for public praise as a stance com-

monly adopted by writers in the late eighteenth and early nineteenth centuries: "To be too clearly visible, to be too easily understandable, in short, to be containable by the great and growing public, was beginning to be a mark of shallowness and insignificance" (*The Frenzy of Renown,* 424).

56. John Guillory, *Cultural Capital: The Problem of Literary Canon Formation* (Chicago: University of Chicago Press, 1993), 120-21.

57. Thomas Gisborne, *An Enquiry into the Duties of the Female Sex* (London, 1797), 231.

58. Colin Campbell, *The Romantic Ethic and the Spirit of Modern Consumerism* (London: Basil Blackwell, 1987), 90. Somewhat similarly, Weinfield argues that the "Elegy" introduces the "problem of history" (the "thematic constellation of poverty, anonymity, alienation, and unfulfilled potential") into English verse, articulating a concern with deprivation that cannot be contained by pastoral conventions (*The Poet Without a Name,* xi).

59. The response of Richard ("Dicky") Lord Edgcumbe to Gray's recitation of the odes suggests the frustration that aristocratic readers felt over Gray's obscurity: "When Gray had got to the second stanza Mr. Edgcumbe leant toward Mr. Williams who sat near him and said, 'What is this? It seems to be English, but by G_d I don't understand a single word of it'" (*The Diaries of Sylvester Douglas, Lord Glenbervie,* ed. Francis Bickley, 2 vols. [London: Constable, 1928], 1:135). For a history of the public's response to the poems, see W. Powell Jones ("The Contemporary Reception of Gray's *Odes,*" *Modern Philology* 28 [1930]: 61-82), and Alastair Macdonald ("Gray and His Critics: Patterns of Response in the Eighteenth and Nineteenth Centuries," in *Fearful Joy,* 172-97).

60. After hearing his readers' complaints, though, Gray admitted he found the Intelligent "still fewer, than even I expected" (*Corresp.,* 2:518); he relented under pressure from friends and included extensive notes to the sister odes in the 1768 edition of his poems.

61. Spacks, *The Poetry of Vision,* 110.

62. Jean H. Hagstrum, *The Sister Arts: The Tradition of Literary Pictorialism and English Poetry from Dryden to Gray* (Chicago: University of Chicago Press, 1958), 302.

63. Reginald Harvey Griffith, "The Progress Pieces of the Eighteenth Century," *The Texas Review* 5 (1920): 218.

64. Sitter also observes the supernatural qualities of the Bard's speech, noting that he possesses "the kind of linguistic power which William Law had attributed to God: 'What he speaks he acts'" (*Literary Loneliness,* 97).

65. For a different account of how "The Bard" recuperates political authority for poets, see Anne Janowitz, *England's Ruins: Poetic Purpose and the National Landscape* (Cambridge, MA: Blackwell, 1990), 69-72. Kaul observes that in Gray's later translations from the Welsh (including "The Fatal Sisters," "The Descent of Odin," "The Triumphs of Owen," "The Death of Hoel," and two fragments—"Caradoc" and "Conan"), "the circuit of poetic desire is

profoundly male, and is arrived at (in part) by containing potentially threatening female voices" (*Thomas Gray and Literary Authority*, 244). Gray's explanatory note to the "Descent of Odin" shows his awareness of women's cultural power as prophets: "Women were looked upon by the Gothic nations as having a peculiar insight into futurity; and some there were that made profession of magic arts and divination. They travelled round the country, and were received in every house with great respect and honour. Such a woman bore the name of Volva Seidkona or Spakona" (Mason, *Poems*, 103).

66. Frank Lentricchia, "Lyric in the Culture of Capital," in *Subject to History: Ideology, Class, Gender*, ed. David Simpson (Ithaca: Cornell University Press, 1991), 208.

67. *London Magazine* 41 (1772): 140.

68. Purposely excluded from Mason's edition were "Tophet" (1749), "The Candidate" (1764), and "On Lord Holland's Seat near Margate, Kent" (1768). Bliss Carnochan notes Gray's "double life" as a lyric poet and satirist in "The Continuity of Eighteenth-Century Poetry: Gray, Cowper, Crabbe, and the Augustans," *Eighteenth-Century Life* 12 (1988): 119-27.

69. Lonsdale, *The Poetry of Gray, Collins, and Goldsmith*, 243-44.

70. John Wooll, *Memoirs of Joseph Warton* (London, 1806), quoted in Lonsdale, *The Poems of Gray, Collins, and Goldsmith*, 246. "The Candidate" was finally printed in its entirety in 1917.

71. As Thomas Lockwood observes, changes in the composition of the reading public strongly affected the form and content of satires in this period; the growing gap between readers and poets appears in "the gradual abandonment of epistolary and dialogue verse conventions" and in the satirist's awareness that a common ground of cultural, moral, and political values is lacking. See *Post-Augustan Satire* (Seattle: University of Washington Press, 1979), 161.

72. Richard Sheridan, "A Familiar Epistle to the Author of the Heroic Epistle to Sir William Chambers," in *The Plays and Poems of Richard Brinsley Sheridan*, ed. R. Crompton Rhodes, 3 vols. (Oxford: Basil Blackwell, 1928), 3:186.

73. An extended discussion of architecture's ethical significance appears in Paul Fussell's *Rhetorical World of Augustan Humanism: Ethics and Imagery from Swift to Burke* (Oxford: Clarendon Press, 1965).

74. Thomas James Mathias, ed., *The Works of Thomas Gray*, 2 vols. (London, 1814), 2:616.

75. *London Magazine* 44 (1775): 217.

76. *London Magazine* 44 (1775): 219.

77. *London Magazine* 44 (1775): 216; 217; 219.

Chapter Five

1. James Boswell, *The Life of Samuel Johnson,* ed. George Birkbeck Hill, rev. L. F. Powell, 6 vols. (Oxford: Clarendon Press, 1934-50), 3:137.
2. Samuel Johnson, *Lives of the English Poets,* ed. George Birkbeck Hill, 3 vols. (1905; reprint, New York: Octagon, 1967), 1:xxvi.
3. Robert Halsband, "The 'Penury of English Biography' before Samuel Johnson," in *Biography in the Eighteenth Century,* ed. J. D. Browning (New York: Garland, 1980), 123.
4. Lawrence Lipking, *Samuel Johnson: The Life of an Author* (Cambridge, MA: Harvard University Press, 1998), 259.
5. Thomas F. Bonnell, "Bookselling and Canon-Making: The Trade Rivalry over the English Poets, 1776-1783," *Studies in Eighteenth-Century Culture* 19 (1989): 65. Two additional essays by Bonnell also provide comprehensive and insightful accounts of the rival editions, and I am indebted to them throughout: see "John Bell's *Poets of Great Britain:* The 'Little Trifling Edition' Revisited," *Modern Philology* 85 (1987): 128-52, and "Patchwork and Piracy: John Bell's 'Connected System of Biography' and the Uses of Johnson's *Prefaces,*" *Studies in Bibliography* 48 (1995): 193-228.
6. Bonnell, "Bookselling," 55; 63.
7. Lipking, *Samuel Johnson,* 262; 263.
8. Martine Watson Brownley, "Johnson's *Lives of the English Poets* and Earlier Traditions of the Character Sketch in England," in *Johnson and His Age,* ed. James Engell, Harvard English Studies 12 (Cambridge, MA: Harvard University Press, 1984), 29-53.
9. Pat Rogers, "Johnson's *Lives of the Poets* and the Biographic Dictionaries," *Review of English Studies* 31 (1980): 156. Rogers observes that the importance of collective dictionaries to Johnson's project is apparent in the brevity of his last few prefaces: "This thinning-out of materials in the later sections of the work has two causes: the absence of single lives, and the omission of these recent poets from the biographic collections. That the first cause is not sufficient by itself is shown by the more confident treatment of figures such as Garth earlier on, where single lives were again lacking" (170).
10. William R. Keast, "Johnson and Cibber's *Lives of the Poets,* 1753," in *Restoration and Eighteenth-Century Literature: Essays in Honor of Alan Dugald McKillop,* ed. C. C. Camden (Chicago: University of Chicago Press, 1963), 89. Walter Raleigh describes the Cibber/Shiels collaboration in "Early Lives of the Poets," in *Six Essays on Johnson* (Oxford: Oxford University Press, 1910), 98-127; he concludes that Shiels wrote the entire text except for the lives of Aaron Hill, Eustace Budgell, and Mary Chandler, while Cibber revised the manuscript (124).
11. Samuel Johnson, *The Idler,* No. 85, *The Yale Edition of the Works of Samuel Johnson,* 16 vols. to date (New Haven: Yale University Press, 1958-), 2:265.

12. Lawrence Lipking, *The Ordering of the Arts in Eighteenth-Century-England* (Princeton: Princeton University Press, 1970), 427.

13. Keast, "Johnson and Cibber's *Lives,*" 98.

14. Isobel Grundy, "Samuel Johnson as Patron of Women," *The Age of Johnson* 1 (1987): 66. Overall, Grundy views Johnson as progressive in his treatment of writing women: "Right to the end of the century the general public's level of acceptance still fell far short of Johnson's recognition of women as a natural part of the broad, general scene in which writers struggle—mostly with regrettable lack of success—for fame or even bread" (62).

15. Judith Phillips Stanton, "Statistical Profile of Women Writing in English from 1660 to 1800," in *Eighteenth-Century Women and the Arts,* ed. Frederick M. Keener and Susan E. Lorsch (New York: Greenwood Press, 1988), 248.

16. Stanton, "Statistical Profile," 249-50.

17. See Robert Folkenflik, *Samuel Johnson, Biographer* (Ithaca: Cornell University Press, 1978); and James Battersby, "Life, Art, and the *Lives of the Poets,*" in *Domestick Privacies: Samuel Johnson and the Art of Biography,* ed. David Wheeler (Lexington: University Press of Kentucky, 1987), 26-56, for extended discussions of Johnson's interest in "private" life and literary biography.

18. Bonnell, "Bookselling," 57.

19. Judith Phillips Stanton, in "'This New-Found Path Attempting': Women Dramatists in England, 1660-1800," in *Curtain Calls: British and American Women and the Theater, 1660-1800,* ed. Mary Anne Schofield and Cecilia Macheski (Athens, Ohio: Ohio University Press, 1991), 325-54, provides extensive data on the popularity of female playwrights during those years, and finds that plays by Centlivre, Behn, and Elizabeth Inchbald (in that order) were most often staged.

20. The *English Short Title Catalogue* shows a sparse publication record for these poets, with few (if any) reprints of their collected or individual verses and plays.

21. A few exceptions to this are evident. While not directly addressing the issue of women's absence from the *Lives,* Dianne Dugaw's "Dangerous Sissy: Gendered 'Lives,' John Gay and the Literary Canon," *Philological Quarterly* 75 (1996): 339-60, argues that Johnson's prefaces "articulated a moral ideal of autonomous, forceful and prevailing manliness" (346), and in doing so, helped provide the gendered vocabulary that later commentators used to evaluate the masculinity of their biographical subjects.

22. From a survey of texts printed in London, C. J. Mitchell concludes that "printing did not increase steadily during the century but almost everywhere suffered during the middle decades of the century a contraction so severe that the level of output achieved during the first third of the century was not regained, if at all, until near the end of the century" (318). "The Spread and Fluctuation of Eighteenth-Century Printing," *Studies on Voltaire and the Eighteenth Century* 230 (1985): 305-21. Ian Maxted notes a corresponding decline in the number of booksellers during the same

period; see *The London Book Trades, 1775-1800* (Folkestone, Kent: Dawson, 1977). Marcus Walsh, in "The Superfoetation of Literature: Attitudes to the Printed Book in the Eighteenth Century," *British Journal of Eighteenth-Century Studies* 15 (1992): 151-61, provides a discussion of how such data challenges current theories about print culture's creation of authorial anxiety, while Alvin Kernan insists upon the dramatic cultural and epistemological effects of "print logic" in *Printing Technology, Letters & Samuel Johnson* (Princeton: Princeton University Press, 1987).

23. Raymond Williams, *Marxism and Literature* (Oxford: Oxford University Press, 1977), 116.

24. Geoffrey Holmes, *Augustan England: Professions, State and Society, 1680-1730* (London: Allen & Unwin, 1982), 7-8.

25. Magali Sarfatti Larson, *The Rise of Professionalism: A Sociological Analysis* (Berkeley: University of California Press, 1977), 32.

26. According to James McLaverty, *The Poetical Register's* bias toward aristocrats, its generous praise of minor talents, its solicitation of biographies from the poets themselves, and its glaring errors (such as the inclusion of the nonexistent Joseph Gay) produced a version of the English poetic tradition that led Pope to feature Jacob prominently in the notes to the *Dunciad Variorum* (1729). See "Poetry and Giles Jacob's *Lives of the Poets:* The *Dunciad* as Alternative Literary History," *Modern Philology* 83 (1985): 22-32.

27. Robert Potter, *Inquiry into some passages in Dr. Johnson's* Lives of the Poets (1783), in *Johnson: The Critical Heritage*, ed. James T. Boulton (New York: Barnes and Noble, 1971), 297.

28. Archibald Campbell, *Lexiphanes* (London, 1767), xviii.

29. Hester Lynch Piozzi, *Anecdotes of the Late Samuel Johnson, LL.D., Johnsonian Miscellanies*, ed. George Birkbeck Hill, 2 vols. (Oxford: Clarendon Press, 1897), 1:199.

30. Paul Fussell, *Samuel Johnson and the Life of Writing* (New York: Harcourt Brace Jovanovich, 1971), 256.

31. Dustin Griffin's *Literary Patronage in England, 1650-1800* (Cambridge: Cambridge University Press, 1996), 220-45, discusses at length how Johnson negotiated the balance between social subordination and the proper exercise of literary authority.

32. Griffin, *Literary Patronage*, 175.

33. Michael McKeon, "Writer as Hero: Novelistic Prefigurations and the Emergence of Literary Biography," in *Contesting the Subject: Essays in the Practice of Postmodern Theory and Practice of Biography and Biographical Criticism*, ed. William H. Epstein (West Lafayette: Purdue University Press, 1991), 23. McKeon's description of the modern man of letters—"a fiction whose effect is to constitute 'the self' only in the act of disseminating it with the aid of a vast social network whose indispensability is expressly denied" (35)—fundamentally conflicts with Johnson's stress on the importance of readers in constructions of authorship.

34. For analyses of the reader's role in Johnson's criticism, see Clarence R. Tracy, "Johnson and the Common Reader," *Dalhousie Review* 57 (1977): 405-23; Leopold Damrosch, Jr., "Samuel Johnson and Reader-Response Criticism," *The Eighteenth Century: Theory and Interpretation* 21 (1980): 91-108; Kernan, *Printing Technology, Letters & Samuel Johnson*, 226-40; and Robert DeMaria, Jr., *Samuel Johnson and the Life of Reading* (Baltimore: Johns Hopkins University Press, 1997).

35. Williams, *Marxism and Literature*, 116.

36. Alexander Pope, *The Dunciad* (1743), *The Poems of Alexander Pope*, ed. John Butt (New Haven: Yale University Press, 1963), 1.178.

37. Ruth Perry, "George Ballard's Biographies of Learned Ladies," in *Biography in the Eighteenth Century*, ed. J. D. Browning (New York: Garland, 1980), 90.

38. Perry, "George Ballard's Biographies," 90.

39. Perry argues that Ballard deeply identified with the women whose lives he recorded, since "restrictions of class sensitized him to restrictions of gender" and thus "heightened his awareness of thwarted intelligence wherever he saw it" ("George Ballard's Biographies," 95).

40. According to Margaret Ezell, Ballard's "model suggests that authorship and education are upper- and middle-class activities, designed for the benefit of the writer and her immediate circle, not for a popular or commercial audience, and that, in fact, virtue and modesty are as important as literary success for women." *Writing Women's Literary History* (Baltimore: Johns Hopkins University Press, 1993), 87. Ezell's insights have been indispensable to my study of women's representation in literary biographies.

41. George Ballard, *Memoirs of Several Ladies of Great Britain* (1752), ed. Ruth Perry (Detroit: Wayne State University Press, 1985), 269.

42. Philips's disclaimer was originally enclosed in a letter to her friend and patron Sir Charles Cotterel (master of ceremonies at the court of Charles II), who later helped to publish an "authorized" volume of her verse. Philips requested Coterrel to circulate the disclaimer as a form of damage control: "You may, if you please, shew it to any body that suspects my ignorance and innocence of that false edition of my verses; and I believe it will make a greater impression on them, than if it were written in verse" (*General Dictionary*, 8:373n). For accounts of Philips's strategies in manipulating her public image, see Claudia A. Limbert, "Katherine Philips: Controlling a Life and Reputation," *South Atlantic Review* 56 (1991): 27-42; and Maureen A. Mulvihill, "A Feminist Link in the Old Boys' Network: The Cosseting of Katherine Philips," in *Curtain Calls*, 71-104.

43. Ezell, *Writing Women's Literary History*, 87.

44. Catherine Gallagher's *Nobody's Story: The Vanishing Acts of Women Writers in the Marketplace, 1670-1820* (Berkeley: University of California Press, 1994) examines at length the sexualized rhetoric of female authorship, especially in the initial chapter on Aphra Behn (1-48).

45. Keast, "Johnson and Cibber's *Lives*," 98.

46. The development of Thomas's public reputation is the subject of Ann McWhir's "Elizabeth Thomas and the Two Corinnas: Giving the Woman Writer a Bad Name," *ELH* 62 (1995): 105-19.

47. Laura Mandell's *Misogynous Economies: The Business of Literature in Eighteenth-Century Britain* (Lexington: University Press of Kentucky, 1999), argues that anthologies like Colman and Thornton's *Poems*, while ostensibly celebrating female poets, actually prohibit their inclusion in the canon by equating them with the perishable physical body, in opposition to the incorporeal, transcendent nature of male poets (107-28).

48. Ezell, *Writing Women's Literary History*, 91, 112. Ezell states that changes made in four subsequent editions of the anthology (featuring poems "characterized by decorous delicacy") "suggest the beginning of the formation of a more sharply defined notion of 'feminine' writing and its relationship to the male literary world" (112).

49. Griffin, *Literary Patronage*, 267-68.

50. John Duncombe, *The Feminiad: A Poem* (1754), Augustan Reprint Society 207 (Los Angeles: William Andrews Clark Memorial Library, 1981), 11-12. References to this poem are cited by page number. Published in 1774, Mary Scott's *The Female Advocate; A Poem Occasioned by Reading Mr. Duncombe's* Feminead [*sic*] even more strictly emphasizes the virtue, morality, and religion of female writers, perhaps to justify the benign nature of literary study for women. In doing so, it whitewashes the history of women poets, omitting all mention of "controversial" (and professional) writers like Behn, Manley, Centlivre, and Pilkington.

51. Rebecca Gould Gibson, "'My Want of Skill': Apologias of British Women Poets, 1660-1800," in *Eighteenth-Century Women and the Arts*, 80. In a verse preface to *Miscellany Poems on Several Occasions* (London, 1713), Anne Finch investigates the motives behind the apologia—a convention apparently already over-used early in the century:

> Our Vanity we more betray
> In asking what the World will say,
> Than if, in trivial Things like these,
> We wait on the Event with ease;
> Nor make long *Prefaces*, to show
> What Men are not concern'd to know

("Mercury and the Elephant. A Prefatory Fable," 34-39)

52. *Monthly Review* 6 (1752): 214.

53. *Monthly Review* 6 (1752): 214.

54. *Monthly Review* 5 (1751): 27.

55. *Monthly Review* 5 (1751): 27.

56. *Monthly Review* 13 (1755): 156.

57. *Monthly Review* 13 (1755): 156.

58. Although the text created no stir among critics and reviewers at the time of its publication, Perry notes that "all [subsequent] histories of women in England . . . have relied upon Ballard's book," Introduction, *Memoirs*, 12.

59. Cheryl Turner, *Living by the Pen: Women Writers in the Eighteenth Century* (London: Routledge, 1992), 56. For Turner, the "essential paradox" for female authors is that "the emergence of women's professional writing was at least partly dependent upon the confirmation of more reductive notions of women's abilities" (58).

60. *Gentleman's Magazine* 50 (1750): 423.

61. Allen T. Hazen describes Johnson's assistance to Williams in *Samuel Johnson's Prefaces and Dedications* (New Haven: Yale University Press, 1937), 214-15.

62. Hazen, *Samuel Johnson's Prefaces*, 215-16.

63. Roger Lonsdale, ed., *Eighteenth-Century Women Poets: An Oxford Anthology* (Oxford: Oxford University Press, 1989), 241; Hazen, *Samuel Johnson's Prefaces*, 215.

64. See the verse preface to Dorothy Dubois's *Poems on Several Occasions* (Dublin, 1764); Catherine Jemmat, in *Miscellanies, in Prose and Verse* (London, 1767), reveals that "it was quite a different motive to that of fame that first determined me to publish these trifles," and declares that only the encouragement of friends "perhaps more sanguine in my interest, than strictly scrutinous into the merits of the work" led her to join "the list of authors" (n.p.). Similarly, Mary Whateley's preface to *Original Poems on Several Occasions* (London, 1764) discounts her poetic genius ("there will not be much of Novelty found in them"[5]) to emphasize her verses' role in sustaining her relationships with benefactors: "If the Pieces addressed to particular Persons may transmit my friendship, Gratitude, and Regard . . . all my Hopes are fully gratified" (7). John Jones's preface to the blind Priscilla Pointon's *Poems on Several Occasions* (Birmingham, 1770) immediately informs readers that charity, not poetic talent, brought Pointon so many subscriptions ("with a heart over-flowing with gratitude she embraces this opportunity of returning her thanks to her numerous Benefactors [who] honour'd her with their names more from a principle of humanity than any exalted ideas they might have been induced to entertain of her poetical abilities" [v-vi]); the preface ends by stating that her poems are at best "*modest, meek, and instructive*" (ix).

65. Clara Reeve, *Original Poems on Several Occasions* (London, 1769), xi. The first poem in Reeve's collection, however, confirms the inferiority of women's intellect: "To My Friend Mrs.——, On Her Holding an Argument in Favour of the Natural Equality of Both the Sexes" allows that "[P]artial heav'n design'd,/To [men] the more capacious mind" (5), and notes the censure brought upon Reeve by her own unfeminine talent (11). Mary Latter, by contrast, displayed a bolder confidence in her right to address the public; the

epigraph to her *Miscellaneous Works, in Prose and Verse* (Reading, 1759) is an excerpt from Prior's "In Imitation of Anacreon" (1708):

> Let 'em censure, What care I?
> The Herd of Critics I defy:
> Let the Wretches know I write
> Regardless of their Grace or Spite.

66. Mary Savage, *Poems on Various Subjects and Occasions,* 2 vols. (London, 1777), 1:ii–iv.
67. *Critical Review* 44 (1777): 151.
68. *Critical Review* 44 (1777): 151–52.

Afterword

1. Writing of Johnson's posthumous reputation in the *Monthly Review*, Arthur Murphy observed that "many who would have trembled to have assaulted him when living, have mustered up resolution enough to treat him with a hearty kick *after he was dead,*" 77 (1787): 457. As quoted in *Johnson: The Critical Heritage,* ed. James T. Boulton (New York: Barnes and Noble, 1971), 32.
2. William Johnson Temple, *The Character of Dr. Johnson* (London, 1792), 1.
3. Robert Potter, *The Art of Criticism as exemplified in Dr. Johnson's Lives of the Most Eminent English Poets* (London, 1789), 191.
4. Richard Cumberland, *Memoirs,* 2 vols. (London, 1807), as quoted in *Johnson: The Critical Heritage,* 417. While aware that writing for booksellers imposed limits upon Johnson's "proper genius," Cumberland also declares that necessity alone induced him to write: "If fortune had turned him into a field of clover, he would have laid down and rolled in it. The mere manual labour of writing would not have allowed his lassitude and love of ease to have taken the pen out of the inkhorn, unless the cravings of hunger had reminded him that he must fill the sheet before he saw the table cloth" (416–17).
5. James Thomson Callender, *A Critical Review of the Works of Dr Samuel Johnson* (Edinburgh, 1783), n.p.
6. Thomas Carlyle, *Critical and Miscellaneous Essays,* 5 vols. (New York: AMS, 1969), 3:77.
7. Thomas Babington Macaulay, *The Works of Lord Macaulay,* 8 vols. (New York: Longmans, 1897), 5:522.
8. Interesting discussions of Victorian anxieties about masculinity in the industrial age are provided by Norma Clarke, "Strenuous Idleness: Thomas Carlyle and the Man of Letters as Hero," in *Manful Assertions: Masculinities in Britain since 1800,* ed. Michael Roper and John Tosh (London: Routledge, 1991), 25–43; James Eli Adams, *Dandies and Desert Saints: Styles of Victorian Masculinity* (Ithaca: Cornell University Press, 1995); David Rosen,

"The Volcano and the Cathedral: Muscular Christianity and the Origins of Primal Manliness," in *Muscular Christianity: Embodying the Victorian Age*, ed. Donald E. Hall (Cambridge: Cambridge University Press, 1994), 17-44; and Herbert Sussman, *Victorian Masculinities: Manhood and Masculine Poetics in Early Victorian Literature and Art* (Cambridge: Cambridge University Press, 1995).

9. Rosen, "The Volcano and the Cathedral," 21.
10. Adams, *Dandies and Desert Saints*, 7. As Adams points out, the labor of self-regulation that guaranteed the manliness of professional men was considered exclusive to their gender, on the grounds that women's "passionlessness" precluded their exercise of such discipline against distracting desires.
11. As quoted in Adams, *Dandies and Desert Saints*, 33.
12. George Birkbeck Hill, *Dr. Johnson: His Friends and His Critics* (London: Smith, Edler, 1878), 120; Leslie Stephen, *Samuel Johnson* (1878; reprint, London: Macmillan, 1919), 165; Sarah K. Boulton, "Dr. Samuel Johnson" (1885), in *Rare Early Essays on Samuel Johnson*, ed. Carmen Joseph Dello Buono (Darby, PA: Norwood, 1981), 100-03; George Dawson, "Dr. Samuel Johnson" (1886), in *Rare Early Essays*, 116.
13. Stephen, *Samuel Johnson*, 57.
14. Thomas Hitchcock, "Dr. Johnson and Mrs. Thrale" (1891), in *Rare Early Essays*, 132.
15. Hitchcock, "Dr. Johnson and Mrs. Thrale," 132.
16. Robin Gilmour discusses nineteenth-century responses to Chesterfield in *The Idea of the Gentleman in the Victorian Novel* (London: George Allen & Unwin, 1981), 17.

BIBLIOGRAPHY

Primary Sources

Anonymous. *A Compleat Collection of all the Verses, Essays, Letters and Advertisements, which Have been occasioned by the Publication of Three Volumes of Miscellanies, by Pope and Company*. London, 1728.

Anonymous. *The Poet finish'd in Prose. Being a Dialogue Concerning Mr. Pope and his Writings*. London, 1735.

Anonymous. *Sawney and Colley, A Poetical Dialogue*. London, 1742.

Anonymous. *Tit for Tat. To which is annex'd, An Epistle from a Nobleman To A Doctor of Divinity*. London, 1734.

Ballard, George. *Memoirs of Several Ladies of Great Britain*. Ed. Ruth Perry. Detroit: Wayne State University Press, 1985.

Behn, Aphra. *The Works of Aphra Behn*. Ed. Janet Todd. 6 vols. to date. Columbus: Ohio State University Press, 1992-.

Bentley, Thomas. *A Letter to Mr. Pope, Occasion'd by 'Sober Advice from Horace.'* London, 1735.

Biographia Britannica: or, the Lives of the Most Eminent Persons Who Have Flourished in Great Britain and Ireland. 7 vols. London, 1747-66.

Boswell, James. *The Life of Samuel Johnson*. Ed. George Birbeck Hill. Rev. L. F. Powell. 6 vols. Oxford: Clarendon Press, 1934-50.

Brome, Charles. *To the Memory of Mr. Dryden*. London, 1700.

Brown, John. *An Estimate of the Manners and Principles of the Times*. 2 vols. London, 1758.

Brown, Tom. *A Description of Mr. Dryden's Funeral*. London, 1700.

Callender, James Thomson, *A Critical Review of the Works of Dr Samuel Johnson*. Edinburgh, 1783.

Campbell, Archibald. *Lexiphanes*. London, 1767.

Carlyle, Thomas. *Critical and Miscellaneous Essays*. 5 vols. New York: AMS, 1969.

Churchill, Charles. *The Poetical Works of Charles Churchill.* Ed. Douglas Grant. Oxford: Clarendon Press, 1956.

Cibber, Colley. *A Letter from Mr. Cibber, to Mr. Pope.* London, 1742.

Cibber, Theophilus, and Robert Shiels. *The Lives of the Poets of Great Britain and Ireland.* 5 vols. London, 1753.

Coke, Edward. *The Third Part of the Institutes of the Laws of England.* Buffalo: William S. Hein, 1986.

Cooke, Thomas. *Some Observations on Taste, and on the Present State of Poetry in England.* London, 1749.

Cowper, William. *Table Talk.* In *The Complete Poetical Works of William Cowper.* Ed. H. S. Milford. London: Henry Frowde, 1905.

Cutts, John. *La Muse de Cavalier, or, An Apology for such Gentlemen, as make Poetry their Diversion, not their Business.* London, 1685.

Dilworth, W. H. *The Life of Alexander Pope.* London, 1759.

Douglas, Sylvester, Lord Glenbervie. *The Diaries of Sylvester Douglas, Lord Glenbervie.* Ed. Francis Bickley. 2 vols. London: Constable, 1928.

Dryden, John. *The Critical and Miscellaneous Prose Works of John Dryden.* Ed. Edmond Malone. 3 vols. London, 1800.

———. *The Letters of John Dryden.* Ed. Charles E. Ward. Durham: Duke University Press, 1942.

———. *The Poems and Fables of John Dryden.* Ed. James Kinsley. Oxford: Oxford University Press, 1962.

———. *The Works of John Dryden.* Ed. Edward N. Hooker, H. T. Swedenberg, et al. 20 vols. Berkeley: University of California Press, 1956-.

Dubois, Dorothy. *Poems on Several Occasions.* Dublin, 1764.

Duff, William. *Essay on Original Genius.* London, 1767.

Duncombe, John. *The Feminiad: A Poem.* Augustan Reprint Society 207. Los Angeles: William Andrews Clark Memorial Library, 1981.

Dunkin, William. *Select Poetical Works of the Late William Dunkin, D. D.* 2 vols. Dublin, 1769-70.

Dunton, John. *The Life and Errors of John Dunton, Late Citizen of London: Written by Himself in Solitude.* London, 1705.

Fielding, Henry. *The Complete Works of Henry Fielding.* Ed. William Ernest Henley. 16 vols. New York: Croscup and Sterling, 1902.

Finch, Anne. *Miscellany Poems on Several Occasions.* London, 1713.

General Dictionary, Historical and Critical. 10 vols. London, 1734-41.

Gerard, Alexander. *An Essay on Genius.* London and Edinburgh, 1774.

Gisborne, Thomas. *An Enquiry into the Duties of the Female Sex.* London, 1797.

Goldsmith, Oliver. *Collected Works of Oliver Goldsmith.* Ed. Arthur Friedman. 5 vols. Oxford: Clarendon Press, 1966.

Gray, Thomas. *Correspondence of Thomas Gray.* Ed. Paget Toynbee and Leonard Whibley. 3 vols. Oxford: Clarendon Press, 1935.

Harte, Walter. *An Epistle to Mr. Pope, on Reading his Translations of the* Iliad *and* Odyssy *of* Homer. London, 1731.

Hawkins, Sir John. *The Life of Samuel Johnson, LL.D.* London, 1787. Reprint. Johsoniana 20. New York: Garland, 1974.

Hervey, John, Lord. *An Epistle from a Nobleman to a Doctor of Divinity.* London, 1733.

———. *A Letter to Mr. Cibber.* London, 1742.

Hickeringhill, Edmund. *The Mushroom: or a Satyr Against Libelling Tories and Prelatical Tantivies.* London, 1682.

Higgons, Bevil. "To Mr. Dryden on his Translation of Persius." *Examen Poeticum: Being the Third Part of Miscellany Poems . . . by the Most Eminent Hands.* London, 1693.

Hill, Aaron. *Advice to the Poets.* London, 1731.

Horace. *Epistulae, Liber 2.* Ed. Niall Rudd. Cambridge: Cambridge University Press, 1989.

Jacob, Giles. *The Mirrour: or, Letters Satyrical, Panegyrical, Serious and Humorous, on the Present Times.* London, 1733.

———. *The Poetical Register.* 2 vols. London, 1719-20.

Jemmat, Catherine. *Miscellanies, in Prose and Verse.* London, 1767.

Johnson, Samuel. *Lives of the English Poets.* Ed. George Birkbeck Hill. 3 vols. 1905. Reprint. New York: Octagon, 1967.

———. *The Yale Edition of the Works of Samuel Johnson.* 16 vols. to date. New Haven: Yale University Press, 1958-.

Knox, Vicesimus. *Essays Moral and Literary.* 2 vols. London, 1782.

Latter, Mary. *Miscellaneous Works, in Prose and Verse.* Reading, 1759.

Lee, Nathaniel. *The Works of Nathaniel Lee.* Ed. Thomas B. Stroup and Arthur L. Cooke. 2 vols. New Brunswick, NJ: Scarecrow Press, 1954.

Lloyd, Robert. *Poems.* London, 1762.

Lockhart, J. G. *Memoirs of the Life of Sir Walter Scott.* 5 vols. 1839. Reprint. New York: Houghton, Mifflin, 1902.

Lonsdale, Roger, ed. *Eighteenth-Century Women Poets: An Oxford Anthology.* Oxford: Oxford University Press, 1989.

———, ed. *The Poems of Gray, Collins, and Goldsmith.* London: Longman, 1969.

Lord, George deForest, et al., eds. *Poems on Affairs of State: Augustan Satirical Verse, 1660-1714.* 7 vols. New Haven: Yale University Press, 1963-75.

Macaulay, Thomas Babington. *The Works of Lord Macaulay.* 8 vols. New York: Longmans, 1897.

Manley, Delariviere, ed. *The Nine Muses, or, Poems Written by Nine Several Ladies Upon the Death of the late Famous John Dryden, Esq.* London, 1700.

———. "Ode, on the Death of John Dryden." In *Luctus Britannici or the Tears of the British Muses; for the Death of John Dryden, Esq.* London, 1700.

Mason, William. *The Poems of Mr. Gray, to which are prefixed Memoirs of his Life and Writings.* York, 1775.

Mathias, Thomas James, ed. *The Works of Thomas Gray.* 2 vols. London, 1814.

Montagu, Lady Mary Wortley and John, Lord Hervey. *Verses Address'd to the Imitator of the First Satire of the Second Book of Horace. By a Lady.* London, 1733.

Morrice, Bezaleel. *Three Satires. Most Humbly Inscribed and Recommended to that Little Gentleman, of Great Vanity, who has just published, A Fourth Volume of Homer.* London, 1719.

Nichols, John. *Illustrations of the Literary History of the Eighteenth Century.* 8 vols. 1831. Reprint. New York: AMS Press, 1966.

Oldham, John. *The Poems of John Oldham.* Ed. Harold F. Brooks and Raman Selden. Oxford: Clarendon Press, 1987.

———. *The Works of Mr. John Oldham Together with his Remains.* 2 vols. London, 1722.

Parks, Stephen, ed. *The Literary Property Debate: Six Tracts 1764-1774.* New York: Garland, 1975.

Parsons , Robert. *A Sermon Preached at the Funeral of the Rt. Honorable John Earl of Rochester.* Oxford, 1680.

Pepys, Samuel. *The Diary of Samuel Pepys.* Ed. Robert Latham and William Matthews. 11 vols. Berkeley: University of California Press, 1976.

Piozzi, Hester Lynch. *Anecdotes of the Late Samuel Johnson, LL.D.* In *Johnsonian Miscellanies.* Ed. George Birkbeck Hill. 2 vols. Oxford: Clarendon Press, 1897.

Pointon, Priscilla. *Poems on Several Occasions.* Birmingham, 1770.

Pope, Alexander. *The Correspondence of Alexander Pope.* Ed. George Sherburn. 5 vols. Oxford: Clarendon Press, 1965.

———. *The Poems of Alexander Pope.* Ed. John Butt. New Haven: Yale University Press, 1963.

———. *The Prose Works of Alexander Pope, Volume I, 1711-1720.* Ed. Norman Ault. Oxford: Basil Blackwell, 1936.

———. *The Prose Works of Alexander Pope, Volume II, 1725-1744.* Ed. Rosemary Cowler. Hamden, CT: Archon Books, 1986.

Potter, Robert. *The Art of Criticism as exemplified in Dr. Johnson's Lives of the Most Eminent English Poets.* London, 1789.

Prior, James. *The Life of Oliver Goldsmith.* 2 vols. London, 1837.

Prior, Matthew. *The Literary Works of Matthew Prior.* Ed. H. Bunker Wright and Monroe K. Spears. 2 vols. 2nd ed. Oxford: Clarendon Press, 1971.

Ralph, James. *The Case of Authors by Profession or Trade.* 1758. Reprint. Gainesville, FL: Scholars' Facsimiles & Reprints, 1966.

Reeve, Clara. *Original Poems on Several Occasions.* London, 1769.

Ruffhead, Owen. *Life of Alexander Pope.* 2 vols. Dublin, 1769.

Rymer, Thomas. Introduction. *Poems, &c. On Several Occasions: with Valentinian, a Tragedy, Written by the Right Honourable John Late Earl of Rochester.* London, 1691.

Savage, Mary. *Poems on Various Subjects and Occasions.* 2 vols. London, 1777.

Savage, Richard. Article I. In *A Collection of Pieces in Verse and Prose, which have been publish'd on Occasion of the* Dunciad. London, 1732.

Scott, James. *The Perils of Poetry: An Epistle to a Friend.* London and Cambridge, 1766.

Scott, Mary. *The Female Advocate; A Poem Occasioned by Reading Mr. Duncombe's* Feminead. Augustan Reprint Society 224. Los Angeles: William Andrews Clark Memorial Library, 1984.

Scott, Sir Walter. *The Life of John Dryden.* Ed. Bernard Kreissman. Lincoln: University of Nebraska Press, 1963.

Shadwell, Thomas. *The Medal of John Bayes.* London, 1682.

Sheridan, Richard Brinsley. *The Plays and Poems of Richard Brinsley Sheridan.* Ed. R. Crompton Rhodes. 3 vols. Oxford: Basil Blackwell, 1928.

Smith, Adam. *An Inquiry into the Nature and Causes of the Wealth of Nations.* Ed. Edwin Cannan. 2 vols. Chicago: University of Chicago Press, 1976.

———. *The Theory of Moral Sentiments.* Ed. D. D. Raphael and A. L. Macfie. Oxford: Clarendon Press, 1976.

Spence, Joseph. *Anecdotes, Observations, and Characters of Books and Men.* Ed. J. M. Osborn. 2 vols. Oxford: Clarendon Press, 1966.

Stockdale, Percival. *An Inquiry into the Nature, and Genuine Laws of Poetry.* London, 1778.

———. *The Poet.* London, 1773.

Swift, Jonathan. *The Prose Works of Jonathan Swift.* Ed. Herbert Davis and Irvin Ehrenpreis. 14 vols. Oxford: Basil Blackwell, 1941-68.

Temple, William Johnson. *The Character of Dr. Johnson.* London, 1792.

Thompson, E. M., ed. *Correspondence of the Family of Hatton.* 2 vols. Westminster: Camden Society, 1878.

Thornton, Bonnell, and George Colman. *Poems by Eminent Ladies.* 2 vols. London, 1755.

Villiers, George, duke of Buckingham. *The Rehearsal.* Great Neck: Barron's Educational Series, 1960.

Walpole, Horace. *A Catalogue of the Royal and Noble Authors of England.* 2 vols. Strawberry Hill, 1758.

———. *A Catalogue of the Royal and Noble Authors of England, Scotland, and Ireland, enlarged and continued to the present time by Thomas Parke.* 5 vols. London, 1806.

———. *Horace Walpole's Correspondence.* Ed. W. S. Lewis. 48 vols. New Haven: Yale University Press, 1937-83.

Ward, Ned. *The London Spy.* London, 1698-1700.

Warton, Joseph. *An Essay on the Genius and Writings of Pope.* 2 vols. New York: Garland, 1970.

Whateley, Mary. *Original Poems on Several Occasions.* London, 1764.

Wilmot, John, earl of Rochester. *The Complete Poems of John Wilmot, Earl of Rochester.* Ed. David M. Vieth. New Haven: Yale University Press, 1968.

———. *The Letters of John Wilmot, Earl of Rochester.* Ed. Jeremy Treglown. Oxford: Basil Blackwell, 1980.

———. *The Poems of John Wilmot, Earl of Rochester.* Ed. Keith Walker. Oxford: Basil Blackwell, 1984.

———. *Rochester's Poems on Several Occasions.* Ed. James Thorpe. Princeton Studies in English 30. Princeton: Princeton University Press, 1950.

Wollstonecraft, Mary. *A Vindication of the Rights of Woman.* New York: Knopf, 1992.

Wordsworth, William. *The Prose Works of William Wordsworth.* Ed. W. J. B. Owen and Jane Worthington Smyser. 3 vols. Oxford: Clarendon Press, 1974.

Young, Edward. *Conjectures on Original Composition.* London, 1759.

Secondary Sources

Abrams, M. H. *The Mirror and the Lamp: Romantic Theory and the Critical Tradition.* Oxford: Oxford University Press, 1953.

Adams, James Eli. *Dandies and Desert Saints: Styles of Victorian Masculinity.* Ithaca: Cornell University Press, 1995.

———. "The Economics of Authorship: Imagination and Trade in Johnson's *Dryden.*" *SEL* 30 (1990): 467-86.

Altick, Richard. *The English Common Reader: A Social History of the Mass Reading Public, 1800-1900.* Chicago: University of Chicago Press, 1957.

Armstrong, Nancy and Leonard Tennenhouse. *The Imaginary Puritan: Literature, Intellectual Labor, and the Origins of Personal Life.* Berkeley: University of California Press, 1992.

Atkins, G. Douglas. *Quests of Difference: Reading Pope's Poems.* Lexington: University Press of Kentucky, 1986.

Bains, Paul. "From 'Nothing' to 'Silence': Rochester and Pope." In *Reading Rochester.* Ed. Edward Burns. Liverpool: Liverpool University Press, 1995. 137-65.

Barash, Carol. *English Women's Poetry, 1649-1714: Politics, Community, and Linguistic Authority.* Oxford: Oxford University Press, 1996.

Barker-Benfield, G. J. *The Culture of Sensibility: Sex and Society in Eighteenth-Century Britain.* Chicago: University of Chicago Press, 1992.

Barrell, John. *English Literature in History 1730-80: An Equal, Wide Survey.* New York: St. Martin's Press, 1983.

Battersby, James. "Life, Art, and the *Lives of the Poets.*" In *Domestick Privacies: Samuel Johnson and the Art of Biography.* Ed. David Wheeler. Lexington: University Press of Kentucky, 1987. 26-56.

Baudrillard, Jean. *For a Critique of the Political Economy of the Sign.* Trans. Charles Levin. St. Louis: Telos Press, 1981.

———. *The Mirror of Production.* Trans. Mark Poster. St. Louis: Telos Press, 1975.

Belanger, Terry. "Publishers and Writers in Eighteenth-Century England." In *Books and Their Readers in Eighteenth-Century England.* Ed. Isabel Rivers. New York: St. Martin's Press, 1982. 5-25.

Beljame, Alexander. *Men of Letters and the English Public in the Eighteenth Century.* Ed. Bonamy Dobrée. Trans. E. O. Lorimer. London: Routledge and Kegan Paul, 1964.

Bentman, Raymond. "Thomas Gray and the Poetry of 'Hopeless Love.'" *Journal of the History of Sexuality* 3 (1992): 203-22.

Bonnell, Thomas P. "Bookselling and Canon-Making: The Trade Rivalry over the English Poets, 1776-1783." *Studies in Eighteenth-Century Culture* 19 (1989): 53-69.

———. "John Bell's *Poets of Great Britain*: The 'Little Trifling Edition' Revisited." *Modern Philology* 85 (1987): 128-52.

———. "Patchwork and Piracy: John Bell's 'Connected System of Biography' and the Uses of Johnson's *Prefaces.*" *Studies in Bibliography* 48 (1995): 193-228.

Boulton, James T., ed. *Johnson: The Critical Heritage*. New York: Barnes and Noble, 1971.

Braudy, Leo. *The Frenzy of Renown: Fame and Its History*. New York: Oxford University Press, 1986.

Breitenberg, Mark. *Anxious Masculinity in Early Modern England*. Cambridge: Cambridge University Press, 1996.

Brewer, John. "'The most polite age and the most vicious': Attitudes towards Culture as a Commodity, 1660-1800." In *The Consumption of Culture 1660-1800: Image, Object, Text*. Ed. Ann Bermingham and John Brewer. London, Routledge, 1995. 341-61.

Brown, Laura. *Ends of Empire: Women and Ideology in Early Eighteenth-Century English Literature*. Ithaca: Cornell University Press, 1993.

Brownley, Martine Watson. "Johnson's *Lives of the English Poets* and Earlier Traditions of the Character Sketch in England." In *Johnson and His Age*. Ed. James Engell. Harvard English Studies 12. Cambridge, MA: Harvard University Press, 1984. 29-53.

Burns, Edward. "Rochester, Lady Betty and the Post Boy." In *Reading Rochester*. Ed. Edward Burns. Liverpool: Liverpool University Press, 1995. 66-83.

Campbell, Colin. *The Romantic Ethic and the Spirit of Modern Consumerism*. London: Basil Blackwell, 1987.

Campbell, Jill. *Natural Masques: Gender and Identity in Fielding's Plays and Novels*. Stanford: Stanford University Press, 1995.

———. "Politics and Sexuality in Portraits of John, Lord Hervey." *Word and Image* 6 (1990): 281-97.

Carnochan, Bliss. "The Continuity of Eighteenth-Century Poetry: Gray, Cowper, Crabbe, and the Augustans." *Eighteenth-Century Life* 12 (1988): 119-27.

Carson, James P. "Commodification and the Figure of the Castrato in Smollett's *Humphry Clinker*." *The Eighteenth Century: Theory and Interpretation* 33 (1992): 24-46.

Castle, Terry. "Lab'ring Bards: Birth Topoi and English Poetics 1660-1820." *Journal of English and Germanic Philology* 78 (1979): 193-208.

Chartier, Roger. "The 'Frustrated Intellectuals.'" *Cultural History: Between Practices and Representations*. Trans. Lydia G. Cochrane. Ithaca: Cornell University Press, 1988. 127-50.

Chernaik, Warren. *Sexual Freedom in Restoration Literature*. Cambridge: Cambridge University Press, 1995.

Cixous, Hélène. "Castration or Decapitation?." Trans. Annette Kuhn. *Signs* 7 (1981): 36-55.

Clark, J. C. D. *English Society, 1688-1832: Ideology, Social Structure and Political Practice during the Ancien Regime*. Cambridge: Cambridge University Press, 1985.

Clark, Steve. "'Let Blood and Body bear the fault': Pope and Misogyny." In *Pope: New Contexts*. Ed. David Fairer. London: Harvester, 1990. 81-101.

———. "'Something Genrous in Meer Lust'?: Rochester and Misogyny." In *Reading Rochester*. Ed. Edward Burns. Liverpool: Liverpool University Press, 1995. 21-41.

Clarke, Norma. "Strenuous Idleness: Thomas Carlyle and the Man of Letters as Hero." In *Manful Assertions: Masculinity in Britain since 1800.* Ed. Michael Roper and John Tosh. London: Routledge, 1991. 25-43.

Cohen, Michèle. *Fashioning Masculinity: National Identity and Language in the Eighteenth Century.* London: Routledge, 1996.

Collins, A. S. *Authorship in the Days of Johnson.* New York: E. P. Dutton, 1929.

Corse, Taylor. "Manliness and Misogyny in Dryden's *Aeneid.*" In *The Image of Manhood in Early Modern Literature: Viewing the Male.* Ed. Andrew P. Williams. Westport, CT: Greenwood Press, 1999. 73-94.

Crawford, Patricia. "Attitudes to Menstruation in Seventeenth-Century England." *Past and Present* 91 (1981): 47-73.

Cressy, David. *Literacy and the Social Order: Reading and Writing in Tudor and Stuart England.* Cambridge: Cambridge University Press, 1980.

————. "Literacy in Context: Meaning and Measurement in Early Modern England." In *Consumption and the World of Goods.* Ed. John Brewer and Roy Porter. London: Routledge, 1993. 305-19.

Culler, Jonathan. *The Pursuit of Signs: Semiotics, Literature, Deconstruction.* Ithaca: Cornell University Press, 1981.

Damrosch, Leopold, Jr. *The Imaginative World of Alexander Pope.* Berkeley: University of California Press, 1987.

————. "Samuel Johnson and Reader-Response Criticism." *The Eighteenth Century: Theory and Interpretation* 21 (1980): 91-108.

DeMaria, Robert, Jr. *Samuel Johnson and the Life of Reading.* Baltimore: Johns Hopkins University Press, 1997.

Dello Buono, Carmen Joseph, ed. *Rare Early Essays on Samuel Johnson.* Darby, PA: Norwood, 1981.

Dentith, Simon. "Negativity and Affirmation in Rochester's Lyric Poetry." In *Reading Rochester.* Ed. Edward Burns. Liverpool: Liverpool University Press, 1995. 84-97.

Deutsch, Helen. *Resemblance & Disgrace: Alexander Pope and the Deformation of Culture.* Cambridge, MA: Harvard University Press, 1996.

Donaldson, Ian. "Concealing and Revealing: Pope's 'Epistle to Dr. Arbuthnot.'" *Yearbook of English Studies* 18 (1988): 181-99.

Donoghue, Frank. *The Fame Machine: Book Reviewing and Eighteenth-Century Literary Careers.* Stanford: Stanford University Press, 1996.

Dubro, James. "The Third Sex: Lord Hervey and His Coterie." *Eighteenth-Century Life* 2 (1975): 89-95.

Dugaw, Dianne. "Dangerous Sissy: Gendered 'Lives,' John Gay and the Literary Canon." *Philological Quarterly* 75 (1996): 339-60.

Eisenstein, Elizabeth. *The Printing Press as an Agent of Change: Communications and Cultural Transformations in Early-Modern Europe.* 2 vols. Cambridge: Cambridge University Press, 1979.

Epstein, William H. "Assumed Identities: Gray's Correspondence and the 'Intelligence Communities' of Eighteenth-Century Studies." *The Eighteenth Century: Theory and Interpretation* 32 (1991): 274-88.

Ezell, Margaret J. M. *The Patriarch's Wife: Literary Evidence and the History of the Family.* Chapel Hill: University of North Carolina Press, 1987.

―――. *Writing Women's Literary History.* Baltimore: Johns Hopkins University Press, 1993.

Fabricant, Carole. "Pope's Moral, Political, and Cultural Combat." *The Eighteenth Century: Theory and Interpretation* 29 (1988): 165-87.

―――. "Rochester's World of Imperfect Enjoyment." *Journal of English and Germanic Philology* 73 (1974): 338-50.

Farley-Hills, David, ed. *Rochester: The Critical Heritage.* New York: Barnes and Noble, 1972.

Feather, John. *A History of British Publishing.* London: Crooms Helm, 1988.

Ferguson, Moira. *Eighteenth-Century Women Poets: Nation, Class, and Gender.* Albany: State University of New York Press, 1995.

Fineman, Joel. *Shakespeare's Perjured Eye: The Invention of Poetic Subjectivity in the Sonnets.* Berkeley: University of California Press, 1986.

Fletcher, Anthony. *Gender, Sex and Subordination in England 1500-1800.* New Haven: Yale University Press, 1995.

Foerster, Donald M. "Thomas Gray." In *The Age of Johnson: Essays Presented to Chauncey Bewster Tinker.* Ed. Frederick W. Hilles. 1941. Reprint. New Haven: Yale University Press, 1964. 207-26.

Folkenflik, Robert. *Samuel Johnson, Biographer.* Ithaca: Cornell University Press, 1978.

Fox-Strangways, Giles Stephen Holland, earl of Ilchester, ed. *Lord Hervey and His Friends, 1726-38.* London: John Murray, 1950.

Fry, Paul. *The Poet's Calling in the English Ode.* New Haven: Yale University Press, 1980.

Frye, Northrop. *Anatomy of Criticism: Four Essays.* Princeton: Princeton University Press, 1957.

Fussell, Paul. *Rhetorical World of Augustan Humanism: Ethics and Imagery from Swift to Burke.* Oxford: Clarendon Press, 1965.

―――. *Samuel Johnson and the Life of Writing.* New York: Harcourt Brace Jovanovich, 1971.

Gallagher, Catherine. *Nobody's Story: The Vanishing Acts of Women Writers in the Marketplace, 1670-1820.* Berkeley: University of California Press, 1994.

George, M. Dorothy. *Hogarth to Cruikshank: Social Change in Graphic Satire.* New York: Viking, 1967.

Gibson, Rebecca Gould. "'My Want of Skill': Apologias of British Women Poets, 1660-1800." In *Eighteenth-Century Women and the Arts.* Ed. Frederick M. Keener and Susan E. Lorsch. New York: Greenwood Press, 1988. 79-86.

Gill, James. "The Fragmented Self in Three of Rochester's Poems." *Modern Language Quarterly* 48 (1988): 19-37.

Gilman, Todd. "The Italian (Castrato) in London." In *The Work of Opera: Genre, Nationhood, and Sexual Difference.* Ed. Richard Dellamora and Daniel Fischlin. New York: Columbia University Press, 1997. 49-70.

Gilmour, Robin. *The Idea of the Gentleman in the Victorian Novel.* London: Allen & Unwin, 1981.

Ginger, John. *The Notable Man: The Life and Times of Oliver Goldsmith.* London: Hamish Hamilton, 1977.

Gleckner, Robert. *Thomas Gray and Masculine Friendship.* Baltimore: Johns Hopkins University Press, 1997.

Golden, Morris. "Goldsmith's Reputation in His Day." *Papers on Language and Literature* 16 (1980): 213-38.

Griffin, Dustin. *Alexander Pope: The Poet in the Poems.* Princeton: Princeton University Press, 1978.

———. "Dryden's 'Oldham' and the Perils of Writing." *Modern Language Quarterly* 37 (1976): 133-50.

———. "Gray's Audiences." *Essays in Criticism* 28 (1978): 208-15.

———. *Literary Patronage in England, 1650-1800.* Cambridge: Cambridge University Press, 1996.

———. "Rochester and the 'Holiday Writers.'" In *Rochester and Court Poetry.* Papers presented at a Clark Library Seminar, 11 May 1985. Los Angeles: William Andrews Clark Memorial Library, 1988. 35-66.

Griffith, Reginald Harvey. "The Progress Pieces of the Eighteenth Century." *The Texas Review* 5 (1920): 218-33.

Grundy, Isobel. "Samuel Johnson as Patron of Women." *The Age of Johnson* 1 (1987): 59-77.

———., and Susan Wiseman, eds. *Women Writing History: 1640-1740.* Athens, GA: University of Georgia Press, 1992.

Guillory, John. *Cultural Capital: The Problem of Literary Canon Formation.* Chicago: University of Chicago Press, 1993.

Haggerty, George E. *Men in Love: Masculinity and Sexuality in the Eighteenth Century.* New York: Columbia University Press, 1999.

Hagstrum, Jean H. "Gray's Sensibility." In *Fearful Joy: Papers from the Thomas Gray Bicentenary Conference at Carleton University.* Ed. James Downey and Ben Jones. Montreal: McGill-Queen's University Press, 1974. 6-19.

———. *The Sister Arts: The Tradition of Literary Pictorialism and English Poetry from Dryden to Gray.* Chicago: University of Chicago Press, 1958.

Halsband, Robert. *Lord Hervey: Eighteenth-Century Courtier.* Oxford: Oxford University Press, 1974.

———. "The 'Penury of English Biography' before Samuel Johnson." In *Biography in the Eighteenth Century.* Ed. J. D. Browning. New York: Garland, 1980. 112-27.

Hammond, Brean S. "'An Allusion to Horace,' Jonson's Ghost, and the Second

Poets' War." In *Reading Rochester*. Ed. Edward Burns. Liverpool: Liverpool University Press, 1995. 165-86.

———. *Pope*. Sussex: Harvester, 1986.

———. *Professional Imaginative Writing in England, 1670-1740*. Oxford: Clarendon Press, 1997.

Hazen, Allen T. *Samuel Johnson's Prefaces and Dedications*. New Haven: Yale University Press, 1937.

Helgerson, Richard. *The Elizabethan Prodigals*. Berkeley: University of California Press, 1976.

———. *Self-Crowned Laureates: Spenser, Jonson, Milton and the Literary System*. Berkeley: University of California Press, 1983.

Hicks, Malcolm. "Gray Among the Victorians." In *Thomas Gray: Contemporary Essays*. Ed. W. B. Hutchings and William Ruddick. Liverpool: Liverpool University Press, 1993. 248-69.

Hill, George Birkbeck. *Dr. Johnson: His Friends and His Critics*. London: Smith, Edler, 1878.

Hobby, Elaine. *Virtue of Necessity: English Women's Writing 1649-88*. London: Virago, 1988.

Holmes, Geoffrey. *Augustan England: Professions, State and Society, 1680-1730*. London: Allen & Unwin, 1982.

Hotch, Ripley. "The Dilemma of an Obedient Son: Pope's 'Epistle to Arbuthnot.'" In *Pope: Recent Essays by Several Hands*. Ed. Maynard Mack and James A. Winn. Hamden, CT: Archon Books, 1980. 428-43.

Howe, Elizabeth. *The First English Actresses: Women and Drama 1660-1700*. Cambridge: Cambridge University Press, 1992.

Hunter, J. Paul. *Before Novels: The Cultural Contexts of Eighteenth-Century English Fiction*. New York: Norton, 1990.

Hyde, Lewis. *The Gift: Imagination and the Erotic Life of Property*. New York: Vintage, 1979.

Ingrassia, Catherine. *Authorship, Commerce, and Gender in Early Eighteenth-Century England: A Culture of Paper Credit*. Cambridge: Cambridge University Press, 1998.

Jackson, Wallace. "Thomas Gray and the Dedicatory Muse." *ELH* 54 (1987): 277-98.

Jackson, Wallace and Paul Yoder. "Wordsworth Reimagines Thomas Gray: Notes on Begetting a Kindred Spirit." *Criticism* 31 (1989): 287-300.

Janowitz, Anne. *England's Ruins: Poetic Purpose and the National Landscape*. Cambridge, MA: Blackwell, 1990.

Jones, W. Powell. "The Contemporary Reception of Gray's *Odes*." *Modern Philology* 28 (1930): 61-82.

———. *Thomas Gray, Scholar: The True Tragedy of an Eighteenth-Century Gentleman*. Cambridge, MA: Harvard University Press, 1937.

Justman, Stewart. *The Autonomous Male of Adam Smith*. Norman: University of Oklahoma Press, 1993.

Kaul, Suvir. *Thomas Gray and Literary Authority: A Study in Ideology and Poetics*. Stanford: Stanford University Press, 1992.

Keast, William R. "Johnson and Cibber's *Lives of the Poets*, 1753." In *Restoration and Eighteenth-Century Literature: Essays in Honor of Alan Dugald McKillop*. Ed. C. C. Camden. Chicago: University of Chicago Press, 1963. 89-101.

Kernan, Alvin. *Printing Technology, Letters & Samuel Johnson*. Princeton: Princeton University Press, 1987.

Kershaw, Baz. "Framing the Audience for Theatre." In *The Authority of the Consumer*. Ed. Russell Keat, Nigel Whiteley, and Nicholas Abercrombie. London: Routledge, 1994. 166-86.

Kinsley, James and Helen Kinsley, eds. *Dryden: The Critical Heritage*. New York: Barnes and Noble, 1971.

Koestenbaum, Wayne. *Double Talk: The Erotics of Male Literary Collaboration*. New York: Routledge, 1989.

Kramer, David. *The Imperial Dryden: The Poetics of Appropriation in Seventeenth-Century England*. Athens, GA: University of Georgia Press, 1994.

Landry, Donna. *The Muses of Resistance: Laboring-Class Women's Poetry in Britain, 1739- 1796*. Cambridge: Cambridge University Press, 1990.

Larson, Magali Sarfatti. *The Rise of Professionalism: A Sociological Analysis*. Berkeley: University of California Press, 1977.

Lentricchia, Frank. "Lyric in the Culture of Capital." In *Subject to History: Ideology, Class, Gender*. Ed. David Simpson. Ithaca: Cornell University Press, 1991. 191-216.

Levine, Laura. *Men in Women's Clothing: Anti-Theatricality and Effeminization, 1579-1642*. Cambridge: Cambridge University Press, 1994.

Levine, William. "'Beyond the Limits of a Vulgar Fate': The Renegotiation of Public and Private Concerns in the Careers of Gray and Other Mid-Eighteenth Century Poets." *Studies in Eighteenth-Century Culture* 24 (1995): 223-42.

Limbert, Claudia A. "Katherine Philips: Controlling a Life and Reputation." *South Atlantic Review* 56 (1991): 27-42.

Lipking, Lawrence. *The Life of the Poet: Beginning and Ending Poetic Careers*. Chicago: University of Chicago Press, 1981.

———. *The Ordering of the Arts in Eighteenth-Century England*. Princeton: Princeton University Press, 1970.

———. *Samuel Johnson: The Life of an Author*. Cambridge, MA: Harvard University Press, 1998.

Lockwood, Thomas. *Post-Augustan Satire*. Seattle: University of Washington Press, 1979.

Love, Harold. "But Did Rochester *Really* Write *Sodom*?" *Publications of the Bibliographical Society of America* 3 (1993): 319-36.

———. *Scribal Publication in Seventeenth-Century England*. Oxford: Clarendon Press, 1993.

———. "Shadwell, Rochester and the Crisis of Amateurism." *Restoration: Studies in English Literary Culture, 1660-1700* 20 (1996): 119-34.

———. "Who Were the Restoration Audience?" *The Yearbook of English Studies* 10 (1980): 21-44.

Macdonald, Alastair. "Gray and His Critics: Patterns of Response in the Eighteenth and Nineteenth Centuries." In *Fearful Joy: Papers from the Thomas Gray Bicentenary Conference at Carleton University*. Ed. James Downey and Ben Jones. Montreal: McGill-Queen's University Press, 1974. 172-97.

Mack, Maynard. *Alexander Pope: A Life*. New York: Norton, 1985.

Mandell, Laura. *Misogynous Economies: The Business of Literature in Eighteenth-Century Britain*. Lexington: University Press of Kentucky, 1999.

Manning, Peter J. "Wordsworth and Gray's Sonnet on the Death of West." *SEL* 22 (1982): 505- 18.

Marotti, Arthur F. *Manuscript, Print, and the English Renaissance Lyric*. Ithaca: Cornell University Press, 1995.

Martin, Roger. *Essai sur Thomas Gray*. Paris: Les Presses Universitaires de France, 1934.

Maxted, Ian. *The London Book Trades, 1775-1800*. Folkestone, Kent: Dawson, 1977.

Maurer, Shawn Lisa. *Proposing Men: Dialectics of Gender and Class in the Eighteenth-Century English Periodical*. Stanford: Stanford University Press, 1998.

McFarlane, Cameron. *The Sodomite in Fiction and Satire, 1660-1750*. New York: Columbia University Press, 1997.

McGhee, Jim. "Obscene Libel and the Language of 'The Imperfect Enjoyment.'" In *Reading Rochester*. Ed. Edward Burns. Liverpool: Liverpool University Press, 1995. 42-65.

McKenzie, D. F. *The London Book Trade in the Later Seventeenth Century*. Sandars Lectures Typescript. Cambridge University, 1976.

McKeon, Michael. "Historicizing Patriarchy: The Emergence of Gender Difference in England, 1660-1760." *Eighteenth-Century Studies* 28 (1995): 295-322.

———. *The Origins of the English Novel, 1600-1740*. Baltimore: Johns Hopkins University Press, 1987.

———. "Writer as Hero: Novelistic Prefigurations and the Emergence of Literary Biography." In *Contesting the Subject: Essays in the Practice of Postmodern Theory and Practice of Biography and Biographical Criticism*. Ed. William H. Epstein. West Lafayette: Purdue University Press, 1991. 17-41.

McLaverty, James. "Poetry and Giles Jacob's *Lives of the Poets*: The *Dunciad* as Alternative Literary History." *Modern Philology* 83 (1985): 22-32.

McWhir, Ann. "Elizabeth Thomas and the Two Corinnas: Giving the Woman Writer a Bad Name." *ELH* 62 (1995): 105-19.

Mitchell, C. J. "The Spread and Fluctuation of Eighteenth-Century Printing." *Studies on Voltaire and the Eighteenth Century* 230 (1985): 305-21.

Morris, David B. "Pope and the Arts of Pleasure." In *The Enduring Legacy: Alexander Pope Tercentenary Essays*. Ed. G. S. Rousseau and Pat Rogers. Cambridge: Cambridge University Press, 1988. 95-117.

Mosse, George L. *The Image of Man: The Creation of Modern Masculinity*. Oxford: Oxford University Press, 1996.

Mulvihill, Maureen A. "A Feminist Link in the Old Boys' Network: The Cosseting of Katherine Philips." In *Curtain Calls: British and American Women and the Theater, 1660-1800*. Ed. Mary Anne Schofield and Cecilia Macheski. Athens, OH: Ohio University Press, 1991. 71-104.

Northup, Clark Sutherland. *A Bibliography of Thomas Gray*. New Haven: Yale University Press, 1917.

Ong, Walter J. *Orality and Literacy: The Technologizing of the Word*. New York: Methuen, 1982.

Oppenheimer, Paul. *The Birth of the Modern Mind: Self, Consciousness, and the Invention of the Sonnet*. New York: Oxford University Press, 1989.

Paglia, Camille A. "Lord Hervey and Pope." *Eighteenth-Century Studies* 6 (1973): 348-71.

Pask, Kevin. *The Emergence of the English Author: Scripting the Life of the Poet in Early Modern England*. Cambridge: Cambridge University Press, 1996.

Payne, Deborah C. "Reified Object or Emergent Professional? Retheorizing the Restoration Actress." In *Cultural Readings of Restoration and Eighteenth-Century English Theater*. Ed. J. Douglas Canfield and Deborah C. Payne. Athens, GA: University of Georgia Press, 1995. 13-38.

Pearson, Jacqueline. *The Prostituted Muse: Images of Women and Women Dramatists, 1642- 1737*. New York: Harvester Wheatsheaf, 1988.

Perry, Ruth. "George Ballard's Biographies of Learned Ladies." In *Biography in the Eighteenth Century*. Ed. J. D. Browning. New York: Garland, 1980. 81-111.

Peters, Julie Stone. *Congreve, the Drama, and the Printed Word*. Stanford: Stanford University Press, 1990.

Plant, Marjorie. *The English Book Trade: An Economic History of the Making and Sale of Books*. 1939. Reprint. London: George Allen & Unwin, 1965.

Pocock, J. G. A. *The Machiavellian Moment: Florentine Political Thought and the Atlantic Republican Tradition*. Princeton: Princeton University Press, 1975.

———. *Virtue, Commerce, and History: Essays on Political Thought and History, Chiefly in the Eighteenth Century*. Cambridge: Cambridge University Press, 1985.

Pollard, Graham. "The English Market for Printed Books." *Publishing History* 4 (1978): 7-48.

Porter, Peter. "The Professional Amateur." In *Spirit of Wit: Reconsiderations of Rochester*. Ed. Jeremy Treglown. Oxford: Basil Blackwell, 1982. 58-74.

Prinz, Johannes. *Rochesteriana: Being Some Anecdotes Concerning John Wilmot, Earl of Rochester*. Leipzig: privately printed, 1926.

Prior, Mary, ed. *Women in English Society 1500-1800*. London: Methuen, 1985.

Raleigh, Walter. "Early Lives of the Poets." *Six Essays on Johnson*. Oxford: Oxford University Press, 1910. 98-127.

Ransom, Harry. "The Rewards of Authorship in the Eighteenth Century." *University of Texas Studies in English* 18 (1938): 47-66.

Reverand, Cedric D. *Dryden's Final Poetic Mode: The Fables*. Philadelphia: University of Pennsylvania Press, 1988.

Robinson, Ken. "The Art of Violence in Rochester's Satire." In *English Satire and the Satiric Tradition*. Ed. Claude Rawson. Oxford: Basil Blackwell, 1984. 93-108.

Rogers, Pat. *Grub Street: Studies in a Subculture*. London: Methuen, 1972.

———. "Johnson's *Lives of the Poets* and the Biographic Dictionaries." *Review of English Studies* 31 (1980): 149-71.

Roper, Michael and John Tosh, eds. *Manful Assertions: Masculinities in Britain since 1800*. London: Routledge, 1991.

Rose, Mark. *Authors and Owners: The Invention of Copyright*. Cambridge, MA: Harvard University Press, 1993.

Rosen, David. "The Volcano and the Cathedral: Muscular Christianity and the Origins of Primal Manliness." In *Muscular Christianity: Embodying the Victorian Age*. Ed. Donald E. Hall. Cambridge: Cambridge University Press, 1994. 17-44.

Rosenthal, Laura J. *Playwrights and Plagiarists in Early Modern England*. Ithaca: Cornell University Press, 1996.

Ross, Marlon B. *The Contours of Masculine Desire: Romanticism and the Rise of Women's Poetry*. Oxford: Oxford University Press, 1989.

Rosselli, John. *Singers of Italian Opera: The History of a Profession*. Cambridge: Cambridge University Press, 1992.

Rousseau, G. S., ed. *Goldsmith: The Critical Heritage*. London: Routledge and Kegan Paul, 1974.

———. "The Pursuit of Homosexuality in the Eighteenth Century: 'Utterly Confused Category' and/or Rich Repository?" In *'Tis Nature's Fault: Unauthorized Sexuality during the Enlightenment*. Ed. Robert P. Maccubbin. Cambridge: Cambridge University Press, 1985. 132-68.

Runge, Laura. *Gender and Language in British Literary Criticism*. Cambridge: Cambridge University Press, 1997.

Saunders, David. *Authorship and Copyright*. London: Routledge, 1992.

Saunders, David and Ian Hunter. "Lessons from the 'Literatory': How to Historicize Authorship." *Critical Inquiry* 17 (1991): 479-509.

Saunders, J. W. *The Profession of English Letters*. London: Routledge and Kegan Paul, 1964.

Sedgwick, Eve Kosofsky. *Between Men: English Literature and Male Homosocial Desire*. New York: Columbia University Press, 1985.

Sekora, John. *Luxury: The Concept in Western Thought, Eden to Smollett*. Baltimore: Johns Hopkins University Press, 1977.

Selden, Raman. "Oldham, Pope, and Restoration Satire." In *English Satire and the Satiric Tradition*. Ed. Claude Rawson. Oxford: Basil Blackwell, 1984. 109-26.

———. "Rochester and Oldham: 'High Rants in Profaneness.'" In *Reading Rochester*. Ed. Edward Burns. Liverpool: Liverpool University Press, 1995. 187-206.

Siskin, Clifford. *The Historicity of Romantic Discourse*. New York: Oxford University Press, 1988.

———. *The Work of Writing: Literature and Social Change in Britain, 1700-1830*. Baltimore: Johns Hopkins University Press, 1998.

Sitter, John. *Literary Loneliness in Mid-Eighteenth-Century England.* Ithaca: Cornell University Press, 1982.

Smith, Bruce R. *Homosexual Desire in Shakespeare's England: A Cultural Poetics.* Chicago: University of Chicago Press, 1991.

Snyder, Robert L. "The Epistolary Melancholy of Thomas Gray." *Biography* 2 (1979): 125-40.

Spacks, Patricia Meyer. *The Poetry of Vision: Five Eighteenth-Century Poets.* Cambridge, MA: Harvard University Press, 1967.

Spencer, Jane. *The Rise of the Woman Novelist: From Aphra Behn to Jane Austen.* Oxford: Basil Blackwell, 1986.

Spender, Dale. *Mothers of the Novel: 100 Good Women Writers before Jane Austen.* New York: Pandora, 1986.

Stallybrass, Peter and Allon White. *The Politics and Poetics of Transgression.* Ithaca: Cornell University Press, 1986.

Stanton, Judith Phillips. "Statistical Profile of Women Writing in English from 1660 to 1800." In *Eighteenth-Century Women and the Arts.* Ed. Frederick M. Keener and Susan E. Lorsch. New York: Greenwood Press, 1988. 247-54.

———. "'This New-Found Path Attempting': Women Dramatists in England, 1660-1800." In *Curtain Calls: British and American Women and the Theater, 1660-1800.* Ed. Mary Anne Schofield and Cecilia Macheski. Athens, OH: Ohio University Press, 1991. 325- 54.

Steele, James. "Thomas Gray and the Season for Triumph." In *Fearful Joy: Papers from the Thomas Gray Bicentenary Conference at Carleton University.* Ed. James Downey and Ben Jones. Montreal: McGill-Queen's University Press, 1974. 198-240.

Stephen, Leslie. *Samuel Johnson.* 1878. Reprint. London: Macmillan, 1919.

Stone, Lawrence. *The Crisis of the Aristocracy 1558-1641.* Oxford: Clarendon Press, 1965.

———. "Literacy and Education in England 1640-1900." *Past and Present* 42 (1969): 69-139.

———., and Jeanne C. Fawtier Stone. *An Open Elite? England 1540-1880.* Oxford: Clarendon Press, 1984.

Straub, Kristina. *Sexual Suspects: Eighteenth-Century Players and Sexual Ideology.* Princeton: Princeton University Press, 1992.

Sussman, Herbert. *Victorian Masculinities: Manhood and Masculine Poetics in Early Victorian Literature and Art.* Cambridge: Cambridge University Press, 1995.

Tenger, Zeynep and Paul Trolander. "Genius versus Capital: Eighteenth-Century Theories of Genius and Adam Smith's *Wealth of Nations.*" *Modern Language Quarterly* 55 (1994): 169-89.

Thomas, Claudia. *Alexander Pope and His Eighteenth-Century Women Readers.* Carbondale: Southern Illinois University Press, 1994.

Thompson, James. *Models of Value: Eighteenth-Century Political Economy and the Novel.* Durham: Duke University Press, 1996.

Thormahlen, Marianne. *Rochester: The Poems in Context.* Cambridge: Cambridge University Press, 1993.

Todd, Dennis. "The 'Blunted Arms' of Dulness: The Problem of Power in the *Dunciad*." *Studies in Philology* 79 (1982): 177-204.

Todd, Janet. *The Sign of Angellica: Women, Writing and Fiction, 1660-1800*. New York: Columbia University Press, 1989.

Tracy, Clarence R. "Johnson and the Common Reader." *Dalhousie Review* 57 (1977): 405-23.

Trumbach, Randolph. "The Birth of the Queen: Sodomy and the Emergence of Gender Equality in Modern Culture, 1660-1750." In *Hidden from History: Reclaiming the Gay and Lesbian Past*. Ed. Martin Bauml Duberman, Martha Vicinus, and George Chauncey, Jr. New York: New American Library, 1989. 129-40.

————. "Sodomy Transformed: Aristocratic Libertinage, Public Reputation and the Gender Revolution of the 18th Century." *Journal of Homosexuality* 19 (1990): 105-24.

Turner, Cheryl. *Living by the Pen: Women Writers in the Eighteenth Century*. London: Routledge, 1992.

Vieth, David M. *Attribution in Restoration Poetry: A Study of Rochester's Poems of 1680*. New Haven: Yale University Press, 1963.

Wall, Wendy. *The Imprint of Gender: Authorship and Publication in the English Renaissance*. Ithaca: Cornell University Press, 1993.

Walsh, Marcus. "The Superfoetation of Literature: Attitudes to the Printed Book in the Eighteenth Century." *British Journal of Eighteenth-Century Studies* 15 (1992): 151-61.

Weber, Harold. "'Drudging in Fair Aurelia's Womb': Constructing Homosexual Economies in Rochester's Poetry." *The Eighteenth Century: Theory and Interpretation* 33 (1992): 99-117.

Weinbrot, Harold D. "The 'Allusion to Horace': Rochester's Imitative Mode." In *John Wilmot, Earl of Rochester: Critical Essays*. Ed. David Vieth. New York: Garland, 1988. 315-40.

Weinfield, Henry. *The Poet Without a Name: Gray's Elegy and the Problem of History*. Carbondale: Southern Illinois University Press, 1991.

White, Eric Walter. *A History of English Opera*. London: Faber and Faber, 1983.

Wilcox, Helen. "Gender and Artfulness in Rochester's 'Song of a Young Lady to her Ancient Lover.'" In *Reading Rochester*. Ed. Edward Burns. Liverpool: Liverpool University Press, 1995. 6-20.

————, ed. *Women and Literature in Britain, 1500-1700*. Cambridge: Cambridge University Press, 1996.

Wilcoxson, Reba. "Rochester's Sexual Politics." *Studies in Eighteenth-Century Culture* 8 (1979): 137-49. Reprinted in *John Wilmot, Earl of Rochester: Critical Essays*. Ed. David M. Vieth. New York: Garland, 1988. 113-26.

Williams, Anne. *Prophetic Strain: The Greater Lyric in the Eighteenth Century*. Chicago: University of Chicago Press, 1984.

Williams, Carolyn D. "Breaking Decorums: Belinda, Bays and Epic Effeminacy." In *Pope: New Contexts*. Ed. David Fairer. London: Harvester, 1990. 59-79.

————. *Pope, Homer, and Manliness: Some Aspects of Eighteenth-Century Classical Learning.* London: Routledge, 1993.

Williams, Raymond. *Marxism and Literature.* Oxford: Oxford University Press, 1977.

Wilson, John Harold. *The Court Wits of the Restoration: An Introduction.* Princeton: Princeton University Press, 1948.

Winn, James Anderson. *John Dryden and His World.* New Haven: Yale University Press, 1987.

Wintle, Sarah. "Libertinism and Sexual Politics." In *Spirit of Wit: Reconsiderations of Rochester.* Ed. Jeremy Treglown. Oxford: Basil Blackwell, , 1982. 133-65.

Woodman, Thomas. "'Wanting nothing but the Laurel': Pope and the Idea of the Laureate Poet." In *Pope: New Contexts.* Ed. David Fairer. London: Harvester, 1990. 45-58.

Woodmansee, Martha. *The Author, Art, and the Market: Rereading the History of Aesthetics.* New York: Columbia University Press, 1994.

————. "The Genius and the Copyright: Economic and Legal Conditions of the Emergence of the 'Author.'" *Eighteenth-Century Studies* 17 (1984): 425-48.

Woods, Samuel H. "The Goldsmith 'Problem.'" *Studies in Burke and His Time* 19 (1978): 47-60.

Ziggerell, James. *John Oldham.* Twayne's English Authors Series 372. Boston: Twayne, 1983.

INDEX

AEE-3061

Printed in the United States
935400001B